THE ASSOCIATION FOR SCOTTISH LITERARY STUDIES
NUMBER THIRTY-SEVEN

SCOTTISH PEOPLE'S THEATRE

PLAYS BY GLASGOW UNITY WRITERS

✳

THE ASSOCIATION FOR SCOTTISH LITERARY STUDIES

The Association for Scottish Literary Studies aims to promote the study, teaching and writing of Scottish literature, and to further the study of the languages of Scotland.

To these ends, the ASLS publishes works of Scottish literature (of which this volume is an example); literary criticism and in-depth reviews of Scottish books in *Scottish Studies Review*; short articles, features and news in *ScotLit*; and scholarly studies of language in *Scottish Language*. It also publishes *New Writing Scotland*, an annual anthology of new poetry, drama and short fiction, in Scots, English and Gaelic. ASLS has also prepared a range of teaching materials covering Scottish language and literature for use in schools.

All the above publications are available as a single 'package', in return for an annual subscription. Enquiries should be sent to:

ASLS, Department of Scottish Literature, 7 University Gardens, University of Glasgow, Glasgow G12 8QH. Telephone/fax +44(0)141 330 5309 or visit our website at **www.asls.org.uk**

A list of Annual Volumes published by ASLS can be found at the end of this book.

THE ASSOCIATION FOR SCOTTISH LITERARY STUDIES

SCOTTISH PEOPLE'S THEATRE

PLAYS BY GLASGOW UNITY WRITERS

Edited by

BILL FINDLAY

Introduction by

RANDALL STEVENSON

GLASGOW

2008

*

First published in Great Britain, 2008
by The Association for Scottish Literary Studies
Department of Scottish Literature
University of Glasgow
7 University Gardens
Glasgow G12 8QH

www.asls.org.uk

Hardback
ISBN: 978 0 948877 78 0

Paperback
ISBN: 978 0 948877 79 7

A catalogue record for this book
is available from the British Library.

The Association for Scottish Literary Studies acknowledges
support from the Scottish Arts Council towards
the publication of this book.

Typeset by AFS Image Setters Ltd, Glasgow
Printed and bound by Bell & Bain Ltd, Glasgow

For Hannah and Martha, Bill's wee lasses

CONTENTS

PREFACE

Bill Findlay had still to finish work on this anthology of Glasgow Unity drama when he died, after a short illness, in May 2005, at the age of 57. After his death Jessica Burns, his widow, asked me if I might be able to complete the anthology, as Bill had wanted, when he realised he was too ill to finish it himself. It had long been his intention to make available again plays written in Scots which were either unpublished or had been out of print for many years.

He had made his choice of plays, preferring Ena Lamont Stewart's *Men Should Weep* in its previously unpublished first version, and including a play from the 1950s, *All in Good Faith*, by Roddy McMillan, who had begun his career as one of Unity's outstanding performers. Along with Unity's celebrated achievements in the late 1940s – Robert McLeish's *The Gorbals Story*, George Munro's *Gold in his Boots*, and Benedick Scott's *The Lambs of God* – his choice allows Unity's work to be read together, for the first time, and seen fully in the context of its period and influence. One aspect of all these plays that appealed to Bill was the use of Scots far removed from the pantomime, music-hall and comedy of the contemporary stage, and capable instead of conveying genuine and universal emotions.

Bill had also finished preparing the playtexts published here. These are based on original typescripts in the Mitchell Library, Glasgow, and in the Scottish Theatre Archive in Glasgow University Library, and in the collection of scripts originally submitted to the Lord Chamberlain, for official approval for public performance, and now held in the British Library. Bill's daughter, Martha Findlay, assisted in textual preparation, painstakingly retyping *Men Should Weep* as the quality of type and numerous deletions made this frequently revised play impossible to scan. All the texts reproduce their originals as closely as possible: minor changes have been made in correcting obvious errors, and in eliminating some of the innumerable inverted commas, no longer as necessary as they seemed in the 1940s in representing the particularities of Scots speech.

Bill had not finished the anthology's Introduction, which has been pieced together from material he had assembled – lectures, essays, and articles describing Glasgow Unity's work. He had likewise barely begun the volume's glossary. This was completed through the meticulous, generous labour of Chris Robinson of Scottish Language Dictionaries.

Many other people have helped in completing the volume for publication. Permission to reproduce *Men Should Weep* was granted by Alan Brodie Representation Ltd, and I'm grateful to Roddy McMillan's family – to Stuart Calder, Sine and Norma McMillan in particular – for allowing the reproduction of *All in Good Faith*. In other cases, every effort has been made to trace copyright holders. For advice and support, I'm grateful to

John Binnie, Jessica Burns, Sarah Carpenter, John Corbett, Cairns Craig, Christopher Deans, Duncan Jones, Linda Mackenney, Colin Mortimer and the staff of Special Collections in Glasgow University Library. Also to Anna Stevenson, gem for reading throughout, to Abbie Garrington, for diligent and determined research, and to the Association for Scottish Literary Studies.

Bill hoped that the volume would introduce a new generation of readers to a key phase of Scottish theatre. I hope it will also strengthen memories of Bill himself, and of all he achieved for Scottish drama and its history.

Randall Stevenson
University of Edinburgh
April 2006

INTRODUCTION:
Glasgow Unity Theatre

Glasgow Unity grew into the most celebrated and influential of mid-twentieth-century Scottish theatre companies, successfully developing the theatrical styles and political commitments of amateur groups working in Glasgow in the later 1930s. Unity's foundation in the winter of 1940 resulted largely from recent wartime pressures on these groups. Short of resources, and of members, regularly called away to the armed forces, five of them decided to work together, following the examples of London Unity Theatre, established in 1937, and of the wider Unity Theatre movement of the time. The groups involved were the Glasgow Corporation Transport Players, the Jewish Institute Players, the Glasgow Workers' Theatre Group, the Clarion Players and the Glasgow Players, formerly the Scottish Labour College Players. Each had left-wing leanings. The Scottish Labour College, for example, had been founded in 1915 by the Red Clydeside leader John MacLean. Each also had differing traditions and specialisms – ones which contributed variously to the new Glasgow Unity company, and were for a time distinctly maintained within its work. For its first production, in January 1941, Unity simply adopted the Jewish Institute Players' version of the left-wing US dramatist Clifford Odets's *Awake and Sing*, directed by the Players' founder and leading playwright, Avrom Greenbaum.

Strong influences within the new Unity company also came from the Glasgow Workers' Theatre Group, founded in 1937. Its members included Robert Mitchell, a trade unionist and electrician who became Unity's first full-time director, in 1945. Like Mitchell, several Workers' Theatre Group members had belonged earlier to another politicised amateur company, the Clarion Players, a broadly socialist group committed to relatively conventional versions of George Bernard Shaw, Henrik Ibsen and Eugene O'Neill. Huge audiences for the Workers' Theatre Group's first production – of Odets's strike play *Waiting for Lefty* – helped raise money for the Republican cause in Spain, and the company went on to develop innovative combinations of working-class entertainment, political agit-prop, declamatory poetry, and documentary-style staging. These tactics were comprehensively deployed in *U.A.B. Scotland*, its final production as an independent group, in March 1940. Harry Trott's play used the 'living newspaper' style, developed during the 1930s, to attack contemporary social and economic deprivation, and in particular the work of the Unemployment Assistance Board – 'the dole', 'the Burroo', or 'the Panel', often similarly targeted by plays included in the present volume.

The legacies of the Glasgow Workers' Theatre Group ensured that forms of 1930s experimental political theatre remained an influence on Unity's early work, alongside longer-established styles favoured by others among its constituent companies. An innovative element was particularly evident in the work of Unity's 'Outside Group', which took short revues and sketches to hospitals, factory canteens, rallies, and trade union meetings. Glasgow Unity's work during the war years, however, was usually more conventional theatrically, and often more moderate in its political aims. These were summed up in the motto from the Russian dramatist Maxim Gorki which was reproduced in the company's programmes and on the cover of *Scots Theatre*, the magazine it published after the war: 'the theatre is the school of the people – it makes them think and it makes them feel'. Earlier, in 1943, Unity likewise defined itself as

> a group of Glasgow workers, interested in the theatre, who intend to put on Real Plays for the entertainment and education of our fellow workers. Our main purpose is to build a People's Theatre in Glasgow. All our activities are centred to this aim, for we believe that Glasgow has great need for a Real Theatre, where life can be presented and interpreted without prejudice or without being biased by the controlling interests which have so far strangled the professional theatre.[1]

For a time, these ambitions were pursued – as they had been by some of the amateur groups named above, such as the Clarion Players – through conventionally staged plays, drawn from the international repertoire and chosen for their more or less strong elements of social or political commentary. Along with Soviet drama – *An Optimistic Tragedy*, by Vsevolod Vishnevsky, staged in 1942 – Unity continued in this way to produce several plays by Clifford Odets. With a production of *Juno and the Paycock* in 1942, it also began what was to be a sustained, influential association with the Dublin tenement realism of Sean O'Casey, described by Robert Mitchell as 'the great playwright [who] comes nearest to serving the needs of Unity Theatre'.[2]

Another development, influential for the company's later work, was initiated towards the end of the previous year with the production of *Major Operation* by the shipyard worker and novelist James Barke, also Unity's first Chairman. This production and later Barke plays such as *The Night of the Big Blitz* (1944) were only moderately successful. Yet by depicting the everyday lives of ordinary Glaswegians, staged with insight and humour, each production encouraged the company's commitment to Scottish writing, and to a 'People's Theatre' staging not only the international repertoire, but also plays reflecting the experience of a local audience. Unity's Souvenir Brochure in 1947 confirmed this dual commitment, explaining that 'aims for the immediate future are simple: – to present side by side with the best works of international literature as many new and virile Scottish plays as we can find'. A year or so earlier, in

September 1946, Robert Mitchell had already emphasised a need for 'plays which hold their position in world literature but also plays which reflect the life and times of the world and country we live in'.

Outlining in the same article the 'Foundations of a Scots Theatre Tradition', Mitchell also noted the extent to which 'the Scottish public is now demanding Scottish plays', adding that 'we pray for the time when a Scotsman will emulate the great Irishman [Sean O'Casey] and produce such plays of the people'.[3] Mitchell was instrumental in ensuring that these demands were met, and his own prayers answered. Immediately after the war, he directed, often having commissioned, Unity's major successes: Ena Lamont Stewart's *Starched Aprons* (1945) and *Men Should Weep* (1947), Robert McLeish's *The Gorbals Story* (1946), George Munro's *Gold in his Boots* (1947) and Benedick Scott's *The Lambs of God* (1948). The idiom of such 'plays of the people' was in many ways already established, even before the war was quite over, by Mitchell's adaptation and direction of Maxim Gorki's *The Lower Depths* in April 1945. Successful enough to transfer to London Unity Theatre, and later to Edinburgh, the production strongly appealed to its first Glasgow audiences through its grimly familiar urban setting, but also its use of what Mitchell described as a 'Scottish idiom and rhythm – plus an artistic policy to develop it'. Unity's *Lower Depths* was one of the first productions in Scottish theatre to make international material simultaneously local, and Mitchell's Glasgow-accented production consolidated a key component of the company's post-war appeal. Harnessing the particularities of Scots speech and manner – specifically, of the Glasgow working-class idiom familiar to its audiences – contributed crucially to the success of Unity's subsequent productions, including all the plays reproduced in this volume. Each confirms the view of the Scottish stage the playwright Robert McLellan offered in Unity's Souvenir Brochure: that 'Scots . . . is the language best suited to our voices and temperament. It must be so, for it was moulded by these'.[4]

Other factors contributed to Unity's success at the end of the war. Encouraged by the reception of *Starched Aprons*, as well as *The Lower Depths*, Unity transformed itself into a professional theatre company early in 1946. This transformation was never complete. An amateur section of the company, or a 'part-time' one, as it preferred to be designated, continued to work under the direction of Donald McBean, formerly of the Glasgow Corporation Transport Players. It often shared performers with the professional company, maintaining Unity's 'group ideal' and policy of 'no stars – only co-workers co-operating . . . as a collective'.[5] It had several successes of its own, including the first production of *Men Should Weep* in 1947. The move towards professional or 'full-time' status nevertheless crucially benefited a number of Unity performers, and the company's work generally. For several key company members, theatre had previously been only an evening or holiday sequel to days working in mines, shipyards, factories, or steel mills, or as shop assistants, typists or hairdressers. The London transfer of *The Lower Depths*, for example, had been made possible only by performers giving up their Glasgow Fair Fortnight holiday to make the trip, in July 1945. By allowing fuller, practised development of the speech, manner and stage rhythms Mitchell mentions, professional status raised performance standards and consolidated a coherent identity and artistic policy for the company as a whole.

Much as internal restructuring contributed to Unity's success in the later 1940s, this was probably owed still more to external political events – in particular, to contemporary hopes for the radical restructuring of post-war Britain as a whole. Though Glasgow Unity was originally a creation of the Second World War, its greatest successes were a consequence of the peace, and of the atmosphere following victory in the war against fascism and the landslide Labour victory in the General Election in 1945. The election of a reforming Labour government, committed to creating the Welfare State, contributed in the years that followed to an unusual combination of dejection and optimism. Pressing awareness of enormous social problems – ones often lasting since the depression of the 1930s, and exacerbated by the war – mixed with a sense of new opportunities for problem-solving and with genuine hopes for the creation of a better, fairer world. As Mrs Mutrie observes in *The Gorbals Story*, even while people were still finding that they 'canna get a place tae sleep', 'talk about a new world' somehow seemed to continue (Act II).

Unusual and historically specific, these mixed feelings may have been experienced especially sharply in Glasgow. A city cursed since the Industrial Revolution by exceptional economic and social problems, Glasgow was also a city partly redeemed by a resulting sense of community in adversity, and by a radical politics projecting utopian vision beyond present distress. Such feelings at any rate strongly colour each of the 1940s Glasgow Unity plays included in this volume, and continue to haunt Roddy McMillan's *All in Good Faith* (1954). In each, unrelenting emphasis on urban poverty, unemployment and despair often allows dejection to predominate. Yet the very bleakness of the picture – as in Gorki's *The Lower Depths* – may be implicitly enabling, challenging audiences with the urgent need for reform, and encouraging their will for change. Most of the plays do also hint at opportunities for escape to a better life, sometimes suggested through artist-figures, such as Johnny in *The Gorbals Story*, who may be partly representative of their authors. *The Gorbals Story* is also, of course, often entirely explicit in its politics and in its will for change. As Unity realised, Robert McLeish's sustained attack on the contemporary housing crisis was topical enough to allow a new directness of contact between theatre and city, using the stage quite literally as a political platform. The audience for the first Glasgow performance was partly made up of squatters, ensconced as guests in the circle, while the Lord Provost, Sir Hector McNeill, and other city dignitaries sat uneasily beneath them in the stalls. Immediately before the play began, the squatters' spokesman, Peter Colin Blair MacIntyre, delivered a fiery address from the stage, 'terrin' intae the Corporation', one audience member recalled.[6]

Of all the plays in the present volume, only Ena Lamont Stewart's *Men Should Weep* – published here for the first time in its original 1947 version – seems devoid of much hope for improvement or escape, political or personal. Perhaps, intriguingly, this was simply because political awareness in the 1940s, even in the newly optimistic period after the war, still had so little to offer some of the problems the play depicts, ones rooted in gender relations as well as social deprivation. Revising the play thirty years or so later, at a time when freer roles for women seemed within reach, Ena Lamont Stewart could offer a hopefulness the 1947 version mostly lacks. When it was staged again in 1982, and in all subsequent productions, *Men Should Weep* allowed Maggie to survive, with her family mostly intact, and likely to be saved from poverty by her daughter's earnings, regardless of how these have been acquired.

Even in its original version, of course, there is an inherent affirmation in the sustained resilience, love and ingenuity with which Maggie confronts her circumstances – virtues displayed, more or less, by female characters in all these plays, as in O'Casey's, and, occasionally at least, by the men, too. Such virtues were often much supported by the nature and style of the plays themselves. Audiences challenged by the depths of misery depicted on stage were also empowered, or at the very least entertained, by the wit even of the most long-suffering characters, by the laughter they shared with them, and by the imaginative vitalities inherent in their Glaswegian speech. A community of language and experience, and a sense of the possibility of laughing off adversity, regularly flowed out in this way from stage to audience. Warmth and humour, even in depicting the bleakest of circumstances, was at least as much a factor in Unity's successes as any more direct 'message', political or otherwise, that could be taken from them. *The Gorbals Story*, in particular, owed its appeal more to its gallus Glasgow patter, and to its determination – like one of its characters – to 'laff alla time, laff alla time', than to its criticism of the post-war housing crisis, however topical.

This appeal as entertainment secured immediate popularity and financial success. *The Gorbals Story* earned £4,000 in box office at the Queen's Theatre, Glasgow, in the late summer of 1946. Its five-week first run would have been greatly extended had Unity not promised the theatre to another left-wing company committed to working in Glasgow at the time, Ewan McColl and Joan Littlewood's Theatre Workshop. Instead, Unity went on tour around Scotland, ensuring that *The Gorbals Story* was seen by more than a hundred thousand people in its first six months alone. The scale of this success quickly vindicated Unity's move towards 'new and virile Scots plays', allowing Mitchell to develop further work by Ena Lamont Stewart, and by George Munro and Benedick Scott. *The Gorbals Story* also long supported Unity's shaky finances, earning £100,000 in its first three years. Further extensive tours followed in 1947 and 1948, in Scotland and England, along with a six-week season at the Garrick Theatre in the West End of London early in 1948. Other London seasons followed, along with a film of the play in 1950.

Yet there were signs by then that the success of *The Gorbals Story* might have been a mixed blessing. Almost entirely dependent on box-office income, Unity was forced to rely too heavily on its most reliable money-spinner, sometimes to the exclusion of working in Scotland, of new writing, or even of other plays altogether: by 1950, the company was staging almost nothing else. Numerous performances of *The Gorbals Story* – six hundred, by 1949 – also ran a risk of weariness and repetitiveness among the performers, some of whom were eventually lured away from Unity by more remunerative professional contracts on offer elsewhere. Financial constraints involved the further danger of ignoring the play's political pointedness and range of mood in favour of exploiting only its comedy and entertainment. This was a regular complaint among reviewers of later productions: the *Glasgow Herald*, for example, suggested of a 1948 production that 'the play as it is could be entitled "Fun in the Gorbals"'.[7]

Much of this might have been avoided. Unity's rapid success after the war coincided with the foundation of the Arts Council – another product of the new mood of social reform and democratisation of the late 1940s. Some financial support was acquired from this source in May 1946, but it was withdrawn little more than a year later, and further requests refused, ostensibly on the grounds of what the Scottish playwright James Bridie described as Unity's 'scatter-brained finances'.[8] There may have been other, more political motives. An ex-Chairman of the Arts Council's Scottish Committee, Bridie was also Chairman of Glasgow's Citizens Theatre – a rival company, competing for theatre spaces, resources and audiences, and scarcely sharing Unity's ambitions for a 'People's Theatre'. Unity's left-wing commitments may also have deterred the establishment, Bridie included: the television playwright Edward Boyd recalled encountering in later years bizarre dreads of Unity's supposed Communism. At any rate, bereft of Arts Council funding, mired in increasing financial difficulties, and encumbered by the lack of a permanent base for its productions, Glasgow Unity ceased work in 1951.

Its demise could be seen as an unmitigated disaster for theatre in Scotland, or at least as a setback whose effects lasted for twenty years or more. Unity's collapse was exacerbated by Theatre Workshop's departure from Glasgow to Stratford East, London, and by the death of Bridie – little though he had favoured Unity's work – around the same time. By comparison with the 1940s, and with what followed in later decades, the

1950s and much of the 1960s were leaner times for Scottish drama, competing increasingly with television as well as the cinema, and dispirited, in its political phases, by a succession of Tory governments after 1951. When things did improve in the 1970s, it sometimes seemed as if it was only through learning Glasgow Unity's lessons all over again. Playwrights such as Bill Bryden, Tom McGrath, and John Byrne once again developed the language and humour of the West of Scotland for the stage, along with sharp depictions of impoverished working-class life, and sometimes of resultant political radicalism. This kind of radicalism also extended powerfully through John McGrath's work in Scotland with 7:84 Theatre Company, starting with the hugely popular *The Cheviot, the Stag and the Black, Black Oil* in 1972. In some ways, 7:84's work was closer to the idiom of the Glasgow Workers' Theatre Group's agit-prop revues and sketches in the late 1930s than to the rounded socialist realism Unity developed in the next decade. Yet McGrath's commitment to immediate political issues, and to the working experience of audience members, seemed familiar to anyone who remembered Unity's work. Summing up his tactics in 1980, in *A Good Night Out: Popular Theatre, Audience, Class and Form*, McGrath might have been quoting one of Unity's credos when he talked of 'an emergent mode of theatre . . . which speaks the language of working class entertainment and tries to develop that language to make critical, progressive theatre primarily for popular audiences'.[9]

Such similarities between the 1940s and the 1970s are less fortuitous than they appear, and might even allow Unity's demise in 1951 to be understood as a disaster more mitigated than it sometimes seemed. Looking back from the 1970s, Edward Boyd remarked

> It seems to me now that Unity was a *seminal* Phenomenon, years ahead of its time . . . Unity was more than just a theatre. It was an explosion, a release of energies and aspirations that had been repressed by wartime exigencies, and, stretching far beyond that, by the incredible deprivation, physical and spiritual, of the West of Scotland.[10]

As he suggests, some of Unity's work *was* years ahead, anticipating developments which became central to late-twentieth-century British theatre generally. In recording in 1947 'a mood of red-hot revolt against cocktail time, glamorous gowns, and under-worked, about-to-be-deceived husbands', Ena Lamont Stewart was a decade or so ahead of the angry, kitchen-sink school of drama and cinema which emerged in England only in the mid-1950s.[11] Her own plays, and Unity's generally, were among the first in the twentieth century to allow large audiences, from outwith the middle classes, to witness on stage contemporary lives close to their own – the kind of 'Real life. Real People' and 'Real Theatre' Ena Lamont Stewart and Unity demanded.

In quite specific ways, too, Unity's influence long outlasted its brief years of success in the late 1940s, its 'explosion' setting off movements – directly and indirectly – which could hardly have been anticipated in 1951. The company might even be credited, for example, with founding the Edinburgh Festival Fringe. Determined that Scottish theatre should be represented at the first Edinburgh Festival, in 1947, Unity decided to perform some of its own work unofficially – the only company to do so that year. Along with Robert McLellan's *Torwatletie*, Robert Mitchell's adaptation of *The Lower Depths* was staged at the Little Theatre in the Pleasance. Both productions were received with acclaim, despite the hostility of the Arts Council and the Edinburgh Festival Society – though perhaps partly because of resulting publicity, focused around a vociferous defence of the company from Hugh MacDiarmid, soon to be its Honorary President.

Unity's legacy was more directly in evidence in the later work of the many performers and other theatre workers it had helped to train, or otherwise strongly influenced. Edward Boyd himself was one of these, hard-worded television dramas such as *The View from Daniel Pike* extending into another medium, and towards a much wider audience, some of the tactics which shaped Unity plays. In television drama, as well as on the stage, former Unity performers made up a kind of roll-call of later stars, including Stanley Baxter, Andrew Duncan, Andrew Keir, and Russell Hunter, who played Johnnie in *The Gorbals Story* and Tommy in *Gold in his Boots*. In his later career, Roddy McMillan extended not only the idiom of Unity performers – he had played Hector in *The Gorbals Story* and Claverley in *Gold in his Boots* – but also of its playwrights, as the inclusion of his *All in Good Faith* in this volume helps to show. Like *Gold in his Boots*, McMillan's play highlighted the difficulties of escaping an impoverished, claustrophobic background, even when money is acquired: the bleakness of its vision contributed to hostile criticism when it was first produced at the Citizens in 1954. Deterred by its reception, McMillan wrote nothing further for the stage for nearly twenty years, until conditions once again seemed propitious for new Scottish material, at the Royal Lyceum Theatre in Edinburgh, with Bill Bryden as one of the directors, in the early 1970s. Portraying the vicious rigours of factory work, McMillan's second play, *The Bevellers* (1973), extended some of Unity's idiom into the early 1970s, contributing influentially to the revival of Scottish theatre at the time.

This idiom was also extended towards the 1970s, though less in-fluentially, by the plays of George Munro. Almost alone among authors who began work with Unity, Munro continued to write for the theatre, and to develop strongly as a playwright, after the company itself ceased to operate. Later plays such as *Mark but this Flea*, produced posthumously by Glasgow University in 1970, and *Gay Landscape* (1958), continued to explore the oppressive urban environments, further sullied by the drunkenness or violence of their inhabitants, first examined in *Gold in his Boots*. Munro's own upbringing in the Plymouth Brethren made him an acute commentator on religious bigotry and intolerance, examined in all these plays, and a career as a journalist and sports reporter may have contributed to his detailed, persuasive portrayals of destructiveness, dirt, and despair in West of Scotland city life. Munro's work, the now misleadingly named *Gay Landscape* in particular, is among the best of Scottish theatre's mid-century achievements, though one which has seldom been fully appreciated.

Benedick Scott's *The Lambs of God* (later renamed *This Walking Shadow*) has likewise lacked later appreciation. Though successful enough to be toured to London and Oxford, the first production in 1948 may scarcely have done justice to a play genuinely some years ahead of its time. One of the first works of Scottish literature to look in any detail at homosexuality, *The Lambs of God* is also distinguished by the dreamlike or nightmarish quality of its many nocturnal scenes. This occasionally lyrical, even expressionist aspect did not adjust easily with Unity's generally realist performance style, and may have been less successfully represented by the first production's actors than by its imaginatively designed set. Published for the first time in this volume, *The Lambs of God* benefited from a revival by the newly formed Clyde Unity Theatre in 1986, at a time of generally more relaxed expectations – social, sexual, and theatrical. Inspired by Glasgow Unity's example, the new company extended its predecessor's ambition to reach audiences who might not regularly attend the theatre, choosing *The Lambs of God* as its first production.

Of all the Unity playwrights, Ena Lamont Stewart gained most through later revival and changed social conventions. Towards the end of the century, *Men Should Weep* came to be considered a classic of Scottish theatre, and of feminist drama. The version revised in the 1970s was regularly staged in new productions, and widely studied in schools and universities. Its new appeal may partly have resulted from a happier ending, but it was also owed to a social climate much changed since the 1940s, and much more adjusted, in the last decades of the century, to the interests of *Men Should Weep*. When first staged – perhaps, once again, 'years ahead of its time' – some audiences were uneasy with what seemed unrelenting criticism of male behaviour, and ill-prepared for the subtler vision the play offers of the damage inflicted, throughout society, by inflexible conventions and gender roles. But later appreciation of *Men Should Weep* was also owed to a specific 1980s theatrical event, one which reawakened interest in Glasgow Unity's work as a whole: 7:84 Theatre Company's 'Clydebuilt' season of Scottish Popular Theatre, staged at venues throughout Scotland in 1982.

Giles Havergal's production of *Men Should Weep* was a particular highlight, re-emphasising the play's huge verbal powers and excruciating conflicts by edging away from realism towards expressionist modes of staging – ones which might also have been appropriate for *The Lambs of God*. As its lead performer recalled, 7:84's production entirely rejuvenated Ena Lamont Stewart's reputation: by its end, 'every national paper had acclaimed her from the *Wall Street Journal* to the *Aberdeen Evening Express*'.[12] Along with *Men Should* Weep, 7:84 staged *Gold in his Boots* and *U.A.B. Scotland*, as well as plays by Ewan McColl and by the Fife miner Joe Corrie. These revivals and rediscoveries had many important consequences for Scottish theatre. One of these was the season's contribution to the Scottish Theatre Archive, set up in Glasgow University Library by 7:84's researcher, Linda Mackenney, and a repository for the documentary and script material she unearthed in helping to prepare the 'Clydebuilt' season. Since 1982, the expanding Archive collection has offered many opportunities for research into the history of Scottish drama, as well as, crucially, preserving from possible loss a set of original theatre scripts – ones used in preparing the texts of several of the plays in this volume.[13]

The most direct, immediate effect of the 'Clydebuilt' season, however, was in consolidating a sense of history not only for researchers, but for audiences and theatre companies themselves. The season was originally conceived partly in response to regular recollection by 7:84's audiences of earlier work resembling the company's own. In one way, 'Clydebuilt' was a further reminder, for these older audiences – or a discovery, for younger ones – of what McGrath described as the labour movement's 'strong cultural side'; a 'long, rich and neglected tradition' of working-class struggle in Scotland.[14] But the season was also an act of discovery for 7:84 itself, and for the like-minded companies which continued its work after McGrath's directorship, in its turn, succumbed to Arts Council allegations of 'scatter-brained' finance in the later 1980s. For 7:84 and other theatre practitioners, 'Clydebuilt' offered an enabling cultural genealogy: a rediscovery of forebears and traditions which also offered fuller understanding of present practices and priorities.

Comparisons of present and past, of the 1980s and the 1940s, suggested that companies such as Glasgow Unity and 7:84 might in different ways have developed strengths perhaps perennial in Scottish theatre, and intermittently in evidence throughout its history. That opening night of *The Gorbals Story* – with the Lord Provost and his Corporation enduring a squatter's speech as well as the politicised play which followed – might well recall James V's nobles and bishops, four centuries earlier, encountering criticism of their treatment of ordinary people in an early version of *Ane Satyre of the Thrie Estaitis*. It might likewise recall, in later years, McGrath's carefully researching local issues before performances of *The Cheviot, the Stag and the Black, Black Oil* and ensuring that, if appropriate, views of these were delivered directly from stage to audience. In these instances and many others, Scottish theatre has long thrived on the directness and immediacy of its political commentary, and, concurrently, on the shared outlook and experience of stage and spectator. An early review of *The Gorbals Story* described it as 'democratic drama . . . of the Glasgow people, for the Glasgow people, by one of the Glasgow people'. The first editorial in *Scots Theatre* likewise explained that Glasgow Unity's 'actors, playwrights and technicians have been drawn from the ranks of ordinary working people, whose background and everyday life is identical with the masses who form its audiences'.[15] Identities of this kind would obviously be a convenient component for any democratic drama, world-wide. But as the drama in this volume illustrates, they have a particularly productive place in Scottish theatre, strengthened by communities of outlook, background, humour and, perhaps above all, language, especially in the Glasgow region. As explained earlier, Glasgow Unity's successes belonged very particularly to a historical period: to those dusty, shining days just after the Second World War. Their work may seem dated, in later years, as a result. Yet Unity's best plays – published together here for the first time – may also introduce audiences in the twenty-first century to the perennial potentials of Scottish theatre, as well as to the particular power with which these were realised in the middle of the twentieth.

Endnotes

[1] Note in the programme for Unity's production of Clifford Odets's *Golden Boy* (17–20 March 1943)

[2] Robert Mitchell, 'Foundations of a Scots Theatre Tradition', *Scots Theatre*, 1 (Sept. 1946), p.10

[3] *Souvenir Brochure: Glasgow Unity Theatre: International Arts Festival: Season Aug. – Sept. 1947*, p.2; Robert Mitchell, 'Foundations of a Scots Theatre Tradition' (note 2), pp.3, 10, 11

[4] Robert Mitchell, quoted by the anonymous author of 'Stands Scottish Drama Where It Did?', *Scots Theatre*, 3 (November 1946), p.5; *Souvenir Brochure* (note 3), p.4

[5] *Souvenir Brochure* (note 3), p.2

[6] 'D.C.', 'Three Glasgow First Nights', *Scots Theatre*, 2 (October 1946), p.10

[7] Robert McLeish, *The Gorbals Story*, ed. and intro. Linda Mackenney (Edinburgh: 7:84 Publications, 1985), p.109

[8] Quoted in Linda Mackenney, *The Activities of Popular Dramatists and Drama Groups in Scotland, 1900-1952* (Lewiston, NY: Queenstown, Ontario; Lampeter, UK: The Edwin Mellen Press, 2000), p.230

[9] John McGrath, *A Good Night Out – Popular Theatre: Audience Class and Form* (London: Methuen, 1981), p.100

[10] Edward Boyd, 'A Word on a Blackboard', *New Edinburgh Review*, 40 (Feb. 1970), p.33

[11] Quoted in Linda Mackenney, *The Activities of Popular Dramatists and Drama Groups in Scotland* (note 8), pp.157-8

[12] Elizabeth MacLennan, *The Moon Belongs to Everyone: Making Theatre with 7:84* (London: Methuen, 1990), p.104

[13] See Preface

[14] *Souvenir Programme: 7:84 Theatre Company Scotland: Clydebuilt: A Season of Scottish Popular Theatre from the '20s, '30s and '40s* (Edinburgh: 7:84 Publications, 1982), p.3
[15] Robert McLeish, *The Gorbals Story* (note 7), p.99; 'The Curtain Rises', *Scots Theatre*, 1 (Sept. 1946), p.9

THE GORBALS STORY

A PLAY IN FOUR ACTS

by

Robert McLeish

The Gorbals Story was first performed in an abridged version at Buchanan Castle, at the time a military hospital, on 1 August 1946, and then at the Little Theatre in the Pleasance, Edinburgh, for a short season later in the month. It opened at the Queen's Theatre, Glasgow, on 2 September with the following cast:

Occupants of the Ground Floor Flat

PEGGIE, *a woman of uncertain occupation* . . . . Betty Henderson
HECTOR, *a Highland baker* . . . . Roddy McMillan
JOHNNIE MARTIN, *a newsboy* . . . . Russell Hunter
WULLIE MUTRIE . . . . Howard Connell
JEAN MUTRIE, *his wife* . . . . Marjorie Thomson
AHMED, *an Indian pedlar* . . . . Heinz Leyser
MAGDALENE, *a cinema cleaner* . . . . Maisie Hill

Occupants of the Upstairs Flat

MRS GILMOUR, *the landlady* . . . . Sybil Thomson
PETER REILLY, *an Irish labourer* . . . . Jack Hislop
MRS REILLY, *his wife* . . . . Bertha Cooper
NORA REILLY, *their daughter* . . . . Mary Walton
FRANCIS POTTER . . . . Norman Thomson

A couple in search of rooms: ALEC CAMERON . . . . Archie Jack
MAGGIE, *his wife* . . . . Julia Wallace

Another couple in search of rooms: MAN . . . . Reg Allan
WOMAN . . . . Sybil Thomson

Directed by . . . . Robert Mitchell
Décor . . . . Tom Macdonald
Assistant Producer . . . . Howard Connell
Stage Director . . . . Ian Dalgleish

1

Stage Manager . . . . Jack Hislop
Costume Mistress . . . . Julia Wallace
Properties . . . . Sybil Thomson
Production Manager . . . . Leon Schuster

THE SCENE

The scene is the communal kitchen of an eight-apartment house in the Gorbals district of Glasgow. On the prompt side, a section of the landing is seen with stairs leading to the upper floors. Outside Magdalene's door stands a pram in the way. Beside the outside door stands a bicycle also in the way.

The scene is the same throughout, but in Acts II and III the curtains are closed, in Act I the window and curtains are open, in Act IV the window is closed and curtains open.

Act I Friday, 12.00 noon

Act II Friday, 7.00 p.m.

Act III Friday, 10.30 p.m.

Act IV Saturday, 6.00 p.m.

ACT I

On the fanfare introduction of 'I belong to Glasgow', the curtain goes up to reveal the tenement drop cloth. As the second chorus starts, the house lights fade and the lighting goes slowly down to nothing, in the midst of this chorus, the backing flies revealing the set lit from behind. At the end of the third chorus, on the cue 'Glasgow' the cloth flies and the lights fade in as the overture ends. MRS MUTRIE, with sweeping brush, is seen off in room with MR MUTRIE. HECTOR at sink.

MRS MUTRIE Can you no' lift your feet, Wullie?

MR MUTRIE My God, woman, can you no' sit doon?

MRS MUTRIE It's aw right for you. I've got tae get on wae ma work. We're no' aw on the Panel.

(She closes door. Enter PEGGIE.)

PEGGIE Ach, this is daft – a hale pot o' soup all tae yoursel. The last time Ah made a pot o' soup maist o' it went doon the mickey.

HECTOR Aye! It's the sad thing.

PEGGIE *(Startled)* Oh, you're there, Hector. I didna notice ye.

HECTOR Sometimes I talk to myself too, Peggie.

PEGGIE *(A little embarrassed)* I've got a good reason, Hector. Two good reasons, in fact. I like to talk to a sensible body, and I like to hear a sensible body talking.

HECTOR Talking! Ha, Ha! that just about covers everything, eh, Peggie? Sometimes I talk to myself but never for very long – I bore myself to death.

PEGGIE You know, Hector, it's a wonder tae me, livin a' these years in Glasgow an' never losin your brogue.

HECTOR People smile. After twenty years in Glasgow I still see them smile when they hear the lilt of the Islands in a man's tongue – you can see them sendin searching looks into your face an' them all ready to laugh because you're a Highland man.

PEGGIE I wouldna say that, Hector.

HECTOR It's a fact, Peggie. It's only when a man comes to live in a place like this with people packed in on top of one another like herrings that they realise that a Highland man is just like themselves.

MRS MUTRIE *(Enters with cup)* Is there a wee drap hot water?

HECTOR Ay, there's some in the kettle here, Jean.

MRS MUTRIE Thanks, Hector.

HECTOR Back home in the Islands, Peggie, it's a better life. It's a hard life though.

PEGGIE It's a hard fight, Hector.

MRS MUTRIE That man o' mine is a lazy old midden. He wouldna stir his stumps and me wi a sair leg tae.

HECTOR Aye, as you say, Peggie, it's a hard fight. You have to fight the sea if you want to go with the drifters and you've got to fight the land if you want to make things grow. That's what puts the lilt in a man's tongue, that he can live and get the better of all the things that would hold a man down.

PEGGIE Well, that's one way of looking at it.

HECTOR Aye, and it's the same here too, Peggie – nothing can keep a man down forever, no matter how hard or powerful it is.

PEGGIE You've never been on the Means Test, Hector.

HECTOR Means Test or no'. Someday everybody will come into their own and all the politicians and the people who would tell us black was white will be swept to the one side like so much rubbish, and all the things they do that would stop a man from following his star, will be named as a crime. Back home in Mull, I've seen people with sore hearts at a bad catch or a bad harvest, but never so that they would despair. No, they would bend their backs and work harder.

PEGGIE The less they get the harder they have to work. That sounds awful familiar – just like Glesca.

MRS REILLY *(Enters)* Hurry up, Peter, your chips'll get cauld.

MR REILLY Hullo, Peggie.

(They exit upstairs)

HECTOR Sometimes I wish I had gone back – but I wouldn't be much use on the land now – I've forgotten the trade, Peggie.

PEGGIE Aye, you're kinda like a farmer's boy, Hector. Ach, farmin's a hard life. I wance got the chance to go to Canada when I was a lassie. Yon idea, miles and miles o' long grass, and no' a tram caur in sight, naw, no' me.

HECTOR A man could get on in Canada. A man could get on in Scotland, too – if things were put to rights. Handin over our country to people who let the bracken strangle it, so that it's only fit for sheep to live on. When you get on the train to come to Glasgow, your eye grows weary looking at the miles and miles of good land lying fallow, and it's so easy to pretend it's lyin fat an' sleepy under a heavy crop. And when you come into the Gorbals, the people are walking about with a hungry look in their hearts, so you want to rush up to them and say – look up there, up there, there's acres and acres all lyin useless.

PEGGIE Its no' acres we want in Glesca, Hector – it's bakers, just like yoursel.

HECTOR I'm boring you, Peggie?

PEGGIE *(Putting turnip in soup)* Don't be daft, Hector. I once listened tae one o' thae Scottish Nationalist fellas – he had on a kilt and was fair gaun his dinger about Scotland – terrify ye, listenin tae him. Staunin up there like

Wallace, fair bashin it oot o' him. My, it was a lovely kilt he had on – it must have cost a lot o' money.

HECTOR *(Coming down from sink)* Aye, people are tired of Guy Fawksin – the longer they live the bigger the scunner they get. You know you can't educate people by telling them they're damn fools.

PEGGIE Ach, Scotland doesna mean much tae Glesca folk, Hector – yon pictures they print on boxes o' shortbread – big blue hills and coos that need a haircut.

HECTOR You're a comic, Peggie.

(MRS REILLY enters and puts knickers on pulley)

PEGGY *(Re-enters from her room with plate)* I see by the papers that somebody says there should be about ten million folk in Scotland. Is that a lot?

HECTOR *(Smiling)* Aye, it's wan or two!

PEGGIE Well, I hope they don't bring them intae the Gorbals – I think there must be about ten million weans up this close. That stair's terrible. It's nae sooner done than it's needin done aw ower again.

(MAN from upstairs passes MRS REILLY on the stair)

HECTOR Aye. There's a lot of strangers about here off and on.

PEGGIE Ye'd think the Government would dae something about these people – trailin about lookin for rooms. I think it must have been the blitz that caused it.

HECTOR It was bad before the blitz – it was bad before the war even.

PEGGIE It's a funny thing tae me – a' thae sodgers that come here during the war. They didnae need to go about looking for rooms.

HECTOR That was different, Peggie.

PEGGIE Was it? – the people's war, and only the sodgers can get hooses.

HECTOR *(Prepares to wash his face. Smiles.)* Ye know, Peggie, there's always something fresh about a woman's logic.

PEGGIE That's owld-fashioned patter, Hector – men just talk about logic. They condemn honest folk tae live three or four in a room and they gie a burglar a room tae himsel. Aye, ye can laugh. But you mark my words, Hector. Women chained themsels onto lamp-posts tae get the vote. One o' these days a woman will chain herself onto an empty house.

HECTOR *(Smiling)* And where would they find that?

PEGGIE Oh, they'll find them all right. Same as they found the huts.

(Enter JOHNNIE. He is carrying a drawing and pencil and is talking crossly to someone off.)

JOHNNIE All right! All right! Stop yer natterin.

PEGGIE Hello, Johnnie.

JOHNNIE Hello.

PEGGIE What's biting you?

JOHNNIE I was sitting through at the front room, drawin – there's mair light there – but these damn weans.

PEGGIE Do they worry ye?

JOHNNIE Aye, a wish they squatters had ta'en them all away wi them.

CHILD'S VOICE (Off) Haw, Maw!

HECTOR They're after you again.

CHILD (Off) Haw, Maw!

JOHNNIE Ach, them! If I let that worry me I'd have mair worries than Joe Stalin.

PEGGIE It would be good if the people got stayin where they are.

JOHNNIE In a Nissen Hut?

HECTOR It's a gey draughty place to be puttin your head down and the winter not very far off.

CHILD (Off) Haw, Maw!

HECTOR It doesn't seem to have made much difference to the weans – there's more than ever.

CHILD (Off) Haw, Maw!

(HECTOR looks out the window)

HECTOR Aye, it's a wonder tae me they don't get killed runnin about the streets an' climbin the dykes. Weans livin in the city don't get a chance. They never see the green fields, and when the sun shines, it only makes the middens smell worse.

JOHNNIE Hector, if you're brought up in a place like this, they're right on your top before you're even out your cradle. They whip the dummy tit oot yer mooth and land ye a slap on the kisser.

CHILD (Growing desperate) Haw, Maw!

HECTOR Who the devil's that?

PEGGIE (Goes over to the window. HECTOR lets her by.) It's that wee boy up the stair. (Raises window. Shouts.) Your maw's sleepin.

CHILD I want a piece 'n jelly.

PEGGIE Wait there. (She goes to dresser and returns to table with bread and jam) My God, cherubs! (She spreads a slice of bread from an open jam jar)

JOHNNIE My maw used tae say that a' weans should be born about seventy and work back the way.

HECTOR Aye, there's a lot in what you say, Johnnie.

PEGGIE I should roll this up in a hankie. (Puts her hand in her overall pocket) I'll put a penny in it.

HECTOR You'll be havin the whole battalion shouting.

PEGGIE Weans! (Goes to window, leans over, throws parcel) Catch! Wullie, son! Blaw your nose in the paper. (She comes in) It would make you greet to look at them.

JOHNNIE Ach, you're daft, Peggie! If you let everything you see mean something to you – ye might as well take a flyer aff the Jamaica Bridge.

HECTOR You're quite right, Johnnie – it's the happy man that never takes anything to heart – till he's too auld to be hurt by it.

PEGGIE (*Resuming her grating*) You were out late last night.

JOHNNIE Me! I had a swell night – went to the pictures.

PEGGIE Yersel?

JOHNNIE (*He looks up slowly and smiles*) Is this me gettin put in the witness-box?

PEGGIE I heard you talkin, when ye came in.

HECTOR Johnnie, when a woman asks a leadin question – the answer is either yes or no. If the answer is yes, then you say no – because she'll believe the opposite, anyway.

JOHNNIE Eh! (*He is blank*) Is that Hielan talk? Hector, I think you must be goin daft. (*HECTOR laughs, turns to sink*) Heh, Hector, put your heid under the tap.

PEGGIE The owld yin was kickin up hell aboot somebody leavin greasy papers in the hearth. It attracts rats.

JOHNNIE It was me – I had chips. I'm all for leaving them something to eat out here – if I don't they're liable tae come intae my room and get one of my toes.

PEGGIE (*Horrified*) Johnnie!

JOHNNIE Aye, many a wan in the Gorbals has slept wi a rat in the bed.

HECTOR (*His face covered with soap*) Eh?

JOHNNIE No' *you*, Hector. No' you.

HECTOR I once knew an owld woman, that used tae take the cat to bed with her on a winter night when she would have no coal. She took it there for a heat.

JOHNNIE Huh! (*Smiles*)

PEGGIE That wee man that used tae stay in the back room – he used to go round to the steamie when the coal was scarce. Ach, I've been promising myself some soup for weeks. There's nothing like a good plate of soup to put a heat in you. (*To JOHNNIE*) Do *you* like soup?

JOHNNIE (*Without looking up*) Naw.

PEGGIE You can have some of this if you want it. I'll never eat a hale pot of soup.

JOHNNIE Ach, soup – I'd rather have a fish supper anytime.

PEGGIE Twelve o'clock in the day and you . . .

JOHNNIE (*He looks up and is ashamed of his answer*) I'm sorry. Sure I'll take a plate of soup. I was . . . (*He jabs at his drawing, lost for the correct words*) I was trying to copy this cartoon.

PEGGIE (*Looks at it*) You're a clever boy, Johnnie. My, it's that like it. (*To HECTOR*) Did you see this one of Johnnie's?

HECTOR (*Picks up the towel*) I liked the one of Donald Duck. (*He moves *over and studies it)* Och aye. *(He shows his approval of it)* It's a gift – you should be an artist and not a paper boy is – why don't you draw Peggie?

JOHNNIE Ach, I'm no' very good at faces – but I can draw them better than I used to. *(He is warm inside)* I wish I could be a cartoonist like Low, but you've got to know a' about Politics – an' I listen to a' yon owld blokes that chow the fat o'er at the green on a Sunday night and there's an awful lot o' politics.

PEGGIE *(Lifting carrot on saucer)* You'll be an artist someday. *(Gives him the stump of the carrot)* Never you mind about Politics.

HECTOR It's a pity you can't get a job somewhere drawing.

PEGGIE Would *you* like some soup, Hector?

HECTOR *(Smilingly shocked)* Soup at bedtime? *(Shakes his head)*

PEGGIE Can you no' get on the day shift wi that job o' yours?

(Door opens. Enter MR MUTRIE.)

MR MUTRIE *(Over his shoulder)* Aw! Away and bite your grandfather . . . *(Sees the others)* How is it, Hector, that when a woman sees a man enjoying himself she's got to get busy?

(Enter MRS MUTRIE)

HECTOR Joys of married life, eh, Wullie?

MRS MUTRIE *(Carrying firewood and hatchet)* Suit yoursel – if you don't break the sticks you don't get the fire lit.

PEGGIE I've got some sticks broken in my room.

MRS MUTRIE Naw – I wouldna encourage him. Come on now, Wullie.

MR MUTRIE If I don't fill up my coupons it'll be too late. *(He sits in armchair)*

JOHNNIE All right, I'll break them for you.

MRS MUTRIE *(Hands him wood and hatchet)* You're a toff! *(To PEGGIE)* The Doctor signed him off the Panel last night – tellt him he was suffering fae Chronic Inertia – imagine him coming hame and saying a thing like that.

(Exit JOHNNIE smiling)

MR MUTRIE Well, I thought it was a disease.

MRS MUTRIE By God, it's no' half. *(Sniffs)* Rare smell!

PEGGIE I'm just making a wee drop soup.

MRS MUTRIE It smells good.

PEGGIE I've got a wee bit flank mutton – I like soup made wi a wee bit mutton – it sends your stomach to sleep.

MRS MUTRIE Flank mutton! I like it. You know, Peggie, I got some spare ribs the day. You know, it cost me one and ten pence for a cabbage you could put in your eye. *(To HECTOR)* Hello, Hector, are you still on the smalls?

HECTOR No rest for the wicked, Jean.

MRS MUTRIE You'll no' be so hard worked noo wi these lighter loaves. Huh! the brave new world – stealin the bread out the mouths of the poor.

HECTOR I didna think anybody noticed the difference.

MR MUTRIE Pay nae heed tae her, Hector – the hale o' Europe starving and she yelps about the two slice o' breid that she lights the fire wi in the morning.

MRS MUTRIE That's a lie – you never see me burnin breid – it's unlucky.

PEGGIE You're a right pair of cross-talk comedians.

MRS MUTRIE He's an auld slanderer – if you see his plate when he's finished – He never eats a crust – it's put years on me runnin doon tae the pigs' bin wi his leavings – You know this? He's that damned lazy, he'll no even chow his meat. *(They laugh)* Do you know what he said to me the other night? *(To WULLIE)* Will I tell them?

MR MUTRIE *(Beaming broadly)* Aye, tell them! Tell them!

MRS MUTRIE I was gien him his tea intae bed an' do ye know what he said to me?

HECTOR What did he say, Jean?

MRS MUTRIE He says to me – ye know, Jean, I once knew a man and his wife used to wash his face for him.

MR MUTRIE *(Grinning)* I was only kiddin the buff out ye.

MRS MUTRIE Ye'll no' get me to believe that!

(They laugh at his discomfort)

MR MUTRIE Ach away – You canna wash your ain face.

MRS MUTRIE *(To HECTOR)* Aye, ye can laugh! A could tell ye things aboot him that ye widna believe. Ye jist wouldna credit it.

MR MUTRIE Ye're a helluva blether, Jean – Does your tongue never get tired? These people are scunnered to death listening tae ye.

HECTOR Pay no heed tae him, Jean – he's a lucky man. Well, I'll need tae see to my beauty sleep. *(He moves to exit. To WULLIE)* See ye later, eh?

MR MUTRIE Aye, aye, sure!

JOHNNIE *(Off)* Is there anything tae pay for it?

VOICE *(Off)* Naw.

(Enter JOHNNIE with sticks broken and a telegram)

JOHNNIE Heh, Hector, your ear's full o' soap.

(Exit HECTOR)

Heh, Mrs Mutrie, here's a telegram for the old woman – maybe somebody's snuffed it.

(Hands over sticks)

MRS MUTRIE If you die in the Gorbals they send the polis tae tell you – you'd better take it intae her, Johnnie.

JOHNNIE *(Straightening his lapels and tidying his tie)* Watch me doin' a bit o' sookin in – Yes, Mrs Gilmour – No, Mrs Gilmour. Certainly, Mrs Gilmour. *(He bows and scrapes in a pansified manner, then suddenly glares at the telegram)* I'd love tae kick her teeth in. So I would – So I would. *(He exits)*

MRS MUTRIE Some people get a' the luck. You're a lazy owld midden lettin the boy break the sticks. You'll be in at the fire quick enough. *(To PEGGIE)* Where did Johnnie go?

PEGGIE Eh? Oh, you mean Ahmed. I thought you meant Johnnie. He went doon to the corner for fags.

MRS MUTRIE It's a pity for that poor sowl – somebody should take him intae a corner and shake the wits oot o' him.

MR MUTRIE You know, Jean should never have got married. She thinks the hale world's built roun about her.

PEGGIE *(Lights a cigarette end)* This is a man's world – women never get a fair crack o' the whip.

(Enter JOHNNIE and AHMED. AHMED is a tall, moderately well-dressed Indian pedlar, with a ready smile.)

AHMED *(Entering)* Is she in?

JOHNNIE Naw, she's no' back yet – here, that was a helluva lookin tie you left for me. If I went out wi that somebody'd do me.

MR MUTRIE Hello, Johnnie.

AHMED Hello. *(He smiles broadly because he means it)*

JOHNNIE What's a' the parcels?

AHMED Dinner! *(Putting one parcel on table)* Potatoes. *(Laying second parcel down)* Chile pepper. *(Next)* Flour for Chipatte. *(Last one)* Curry. *(Shakes his head)* No fish sipper. *(He laughs at his own joke)*

JOHNNIE God's truth, you darkeys take a bit of beating! A pennyworth o' totties and a half a crown's worth of pepper. *(He smiles, throws out his chest, smacks himself)* Heh listen, you – nothing wrong wi a good owld fish supper – that's what whacked the Nazis – fish suppers and tanner sausages – that right, Wullie?

MR MUTRIE Eh? Oh, how do you fancy Queen's Park the morrow?

JOHNNIE *(Raising one finger prophetically)* A win. *(AHMED is selecting a pot)* How many goes are you havin?

MR MUTRIE Half a crown.

(Enter MRS MUTRIE with basket and shawl)

MRS MUTRIE You'll get nae half-crown aff me.

MR MUTRIE God's truth! Aw, Jean! It's bound tae win sometime!

MRS MUTRIE I go about stannin in queues trying to save a penny and fill your belly and a' you think o' is your fitba coupons. *(She exits)*

JOHNNIE (*Sings*)
  I wish I was single, again, again,
  I wish I was single, again.
  For when I was single,
  My pockets did jingle,
  I wish I was . . .
MR MUTRIE What the hell's so funny?
PEGGIE (*Laughing*) Ach, never mind, Wullie – I'll lend you it.
MR MUTRIE Naw, Peggie, it wouldna be the same!
AHMED A hard job. Mooching a living – nobody want to give money – nobody waste money – no?
MR MUTRIE Ach! You bloody heathens don't know how tae live – give me the man that can take a chance – jist like yoursel – faint heart never won fair lady!

(AHMED is resentful at this)

AHMED You think because my skin is black I no good enough?
JOHNNIE Keep the heid, keep the heid, Johnnie – He's no' talkin about you and Magdalene. He means that, if you don't try, you don't do good. (*AHMED is angry*) Like me, Johnnie, see. (*Picks up his drawing*) See, I draw picture! But if I don't draw it, well I don't draw it good. See!
AHMED (*Looking at drawing*) Good! (*Smiling*) Good!
JOHNNIE (*To PEGGIE*) Sit down, it's all right.
AHMED Sorry, Wullie. Ahmed no stupid!
MR MUTRIE Naw, you're no' stupid, Ahmed.
AHMED Glasgow white man's country. Indian must be like doormat – no' me. Me good fighter. (*He is at a loss*) You my *friends*, no' fight.
MR MUTRIE Aye, we're a' friends here.
PEGGIE Ahmed, I'll peel your totties for you.
AHMED No, missus! White girl peel tottie too thick.

(He demonstrates abandoned potato peeling)

MRS GILMOUR (*Off*) You shouldnae bother yersel, Mrs Mutrie.
MRS MUTRIE (*Off*) Oh it's nae bother. I've one all washed and ironed.

(Enter MRS GILMOUR. MRS GILMOUR is thin, ascetic-looking. She is holding a telegram. MRS GILMOUR is the landlady.)

MRS GILMOUR I'll go now. I'll get a bus. There are plenty of buses.
PEGGIE Is it your sister?
MRS GILMOUR Aye, I'll need to go to Falkirk.
MRS MUTRIE Everything will be a' right here. Sure it will.
MR MUTRIE What's up?
MRS GILMOUR She's no' well – she can't look after herself.
PEGGIE Poor soul! It's her legs again?

MRS GILMOUR I think so. I don't want any carry-on here. I might be back tonight. *(To AHMED)* Don't you be bringing up your country brothers here. *(He smiles)* Now, mind! I mean it! I'm no' goin to have the house full o' darkeys the minute my back's turned – even tho' you do sleep ten in a bed. *(She looks round them all and lastly at PEGGIE)* That goes for everybody!
JOHNNIE Well, how about that old plate of soup?
PEGGIE The carrot's just newly in. *(She smiles to cover her hurt)*
JOHNNIE Raw carrot's a'right. It helps you to see in the dark.

(MRS MUTRIE and MRS GILMOUR go into MRS MUTRIE's room)

MR MUTRIE Have you any fags?
JOHNNIE *(Whispers)* She's a bloomin old battle-axe. If I was her man I'd kick her teeth in!
AHMED *(Sitting on sink, shaving the potatoes)* Johnnie, today, a man say for hankie ten-penny. I say, 'No, meester, twelve-penny, like dis' *(holds up his ten fingers, smiles)* and some more. *(Holds up two fingers)* He say ten-penny. I say a'right. S'good ten-penny s'good. *(PEGGIE is lifting soup)* Missus, she say, Ahmed, six shilling for bed. Aw, naw! *(Shakes head)* Six shilling fo sleep. *(Nods his head)*

(PEGGIE gives JOHNNIE plate of soup)

JOHNNIE Don't you give us that patter, Johnnie – you'd sublet your shirt if you could get somebody else into it along wi you. How about taking that tripe aff the table – it stinks like hell! *(He smiles)* Pepper!
AHMED *(Goes over and removes parcels)* Indian food make you hot.
JOHNNIE There must be a helluva lot of married women in the Gorbals eatin that stuff!
MR MUTRIE *(To PEGGIE)* You got any fags, Peggie?

(PEGGIE lifts a cigarette from the mantelpiece and throws it to him silently. He catches it in his newspaper.)

JOHNNIE Blimey! Wullie, do you never get tired tappin?
MR MUTRIE Aye, it's demoralising ain't it?

(He lights it. Enter MRS GILMOUR and MRS MUTRIE.)

MRS GILMOUR I'll wash it before I gie ye it back. *(She is folding a nightdress)*
MR MUTRIE Jean!!!
MRS MUTRIE Never mind, Mrs Gilmour. I can sine it out in a few minutes. *(To WULLIE)* What's up wi you?
MR MUTRIE Jean, I've got my coupon.
MRS MUTRIE I tellt ye already, I'm . . . *(She softens, opens her purse and gives him a half-crown)* I'm dafter than you. But mind, I'll cast it up tae you.

JOHNNIE Och – for God's sake. Well, don't cast it up tae us a' – this week again!

MRS MUTRIE *(Disdainful wave of her hand)* Aw, you're just a fly paper-boy! But it'll no' get you anywhere here. *(To MRS GILMOUR)* Now, you don't need to worry, Mrs Gilmour. Everything'll be all right. Sure it will.

(Enter MRS REILLY. She is small, Irish and around fifty.)

MRS REILLY There you are, Mrs Gilmour. That man o' mine just got in. It's the God knows how he got past the pub! Ah but you'll be wantin your rent.

(She looks round and smiles. MRS GILMOUR counts money.)

MRS GILMOUR Thanks, Mrs Reilly, and thanks again, Mrs Mutrie.

MRS MUTRIE Ye're very welcome.

MRS REILLY Big family we've got the day, eh?

MRS MUTRIE Well, I'm going down to the post office.

JOHNNIE Hello, Mrs Reilly!

MRS REILLY *(She likes JOHNNIE – smiles)* Good luck to the gosson – every time I see you you're eatin. *(To AHMED)* Hello, Johnnie.

(Exit MR MUTRIE to room followed by MRS MUTRIE. MRS GILMOUR leaves room.)

AHMED Hello, Missus.

JOHNNIE Um! This is Irish broth, Mrs Reilly – the kind the angels eat.

MRS REILLY *(Smiles to PEGGIE)* Somebody knows the way to a man's heart is through his stomach. *(She laughs. PEGGIE is embarrassed.)*

PEGGIE You old fool – gien the boy a plate o' soup. What the hell are you talkin about?

JOHNNIE Keep the heid, Peggie.

MRS REILLY It's the bad mood ye're in the day surely.

PEGGIE Aye, I surely am! You and your blasted papish way of lookin at things.

AHMED You show missus picture – like you show me.

JOHNNIE It's no' just the same thing, Johnnie, it's . . .

MRS REILLY I'll no' stay here to be insulted. I'll go when I'm not wanted. *(She exits huffily)*

JOHNNIE What in God's name was up wi you?

PEGGIE *(She goes over, takes his chin in her hands)* Have you ever had a shave, Johnnie?

JOHNNIE *(Grins bashfully)* Sure, I shave once every fortnight whether I need to or no'. *(He rubs his chin and chaffs her)* Do you fancy the fellas wi the beards?

PEGGIE Sure, sure.

(Enter MAGDALENE. She is tall, thin and slightly gawky – she has no hat and is wearing a long, dark coat which is too long. She has a loaf and pound of margarine. She is around thirty years of age.)

JOHNNIE Oh, here's Juliet! *(He rises – puts empty plate on table)* Heh, Romeo's been greetin for you.

MAGDALENE Och! You're a helluva fella, Johnnie – every time I see you you're giving us the patter. Aw! My feet's just about killin me, these auld shoes are a' twisted. I think the woman that had them before me must have had a club foot. *(To AHMED)* Hello, Johnnie. I thought you were going to Larkhall – Did you get any stockins? Oh! Who had the soup?

PEGGIE I'm just going to have some.

MAGDALENE Oh! I'd love some – it's no' ladylike to say it – but my belly thinks my throat's cut. *(She throws the load on the table, lets the margarine fall from the crook of her arm and sits down)* You know, that's a helluva picture-house to clean out. I'm gonna object – the back row! – the things you find there – it's terrible!

PEGGIE Here, there's some soup. Now shut up.

JOHNNIE Well! *(Lifting his drawing)* When the whole of Glasgow know what the rest of the world's doing, I'll be back. *(Puts his hand under MAGDALENE's chin)* Be that time I'll have ma pockets bulging with gold and a chocolate biscuit for the lady with the big brown eyes.

MAGDALENE You're a helluva fella, Johnnie.

(Enter MR MUTRIE – he has on his cap, etc.)

MR MUTRIE I'll see you down the length o' the post office. Hello, Magdalene, *he* was lookin for you.

MAGDALENE He hasna opened his mouth since I came in.

MR MUTRIE Rare smell. *(Winks, smiles and exits)* Cheerio.

JOHNNIE You've got on yer bunnet helluva straight. Put it to wan side for God's sake.

PEGGIE Here, auld Gilmour's away to Falkirk.

MAGDALENE She's away – oh, good! We'll have a party.

PEGGIE Sh . . . *(Jerks her thumb at Mutrie's door)* She's got the stripes.

MAGDALENE Auch, *her*! Two halfs and you can put her tae bed for the night. Here, we might get another party – I seen that bloke Trotter doon the stairs.

PEGGIE Who?

MAGDALENE You know, the wee baldie man that lives in the back room in the top flat.

PEGGIE Oh, you mean Potter.

MAGDALENE I think *she's* just about due. I wouldna like to have a wean born in a room – would you?

PEGGIE She'll no' go intae the maternity.

MAGDALENE I know, she tellt me – she's a fearty.

(AHMED has brought pot of potatoes over to the fireplace – he is footering about)

PEGGIE You want the gas, Johnnie? I'll let you in. *(She lifts the pot)*
AHMED You put penny.
PEGGIE It's a'right, Johnnie – you can use the gas.

(AHMED takes out purse and opens it)

MAGDALENE Johnnie, you should ile that purse. Every time you open it the hinges squeal like an iron gate.
AHMED *(His smile dies – he returns penny, looks at her questioningly and shakes his head)* No penny, missus?
PEGGIE Want some soup, Johnnie?
AHMED No please – Indian soup. *(He knits with hands)*
PEGGIE I know, I know it's better.
AHMED Curry soup good. *(Smiles)* I give soup to Magdalene.
MAGDALENE Aye, so he did.
AHMED She say, 'Johnnie – bloody good!'

(They laugh at his attempt to imitate her. Doorbell rings once.)

MAGDALENE There's somebody at the door. Come on an' we'll no' open it.
PEGGIE It might be the postman.
MAGDALENE The postman always rings twice.

(Doorbell rings twice)

PEGGIE Away an' open it, g'on.
MAGDALENE Not me, it might be the Parish Inspector. The last time I let him in I nearly got my head in my hauns.

(Doorbell rings three times)

You go – if it's for me say I'm out.

(Bell rings loudly, four times)

PEGGIE God, they want in anyway – I'll go.

(Exits as bell keeps ringing)

MRS MUTRIE Is naebody goin tae answer that door?
MAGDALENE You're bothered wi your nose – well, Peggie's away.
MRS MUTRIE I'm never off my feet a' day. You know that fine. A never get a minute's peace.

(Exits. Bangs door.)

AHMED I got special for *you. (He dotes on her)*

MAGDALENE You know, Johnnie, you're no' bad lookin for a darkey – how is it you never get any stockings?

AHMED I got special for you. *(Smiles and puts his finger to his lips)*

MAGDALENE *(Hushed, expectantly as he draws nearer)* What did you get?

AHMED For you, long stockings. *(He puts his hand on his thigh to show the length)*

MAGDALENE Now, now, Johnnie – nane o' that – how much are they?

(AHMED puts his two arms on table and leans towards her. She is in her own earthy way embarrassed by his nearness.)

AHMED For you, I make good bargain.

MAGDALENE Did you, Johnnie?

AHMED Naw! – I no' make – I make *now.*

MAGDALENE Aw! *(She is master of the situation)* Well, you can just wear them yoursel, Johnnie.

AHMED Johnnie got money. *(Puts his hand on his breast)* Johnnie wants friends.

MAGDALENE You'll get plenty of friends here if you've got the money. *(Smiling)*

AHMED *(Stands up and looks at her a moment)* Johnnie want friends – *your* friends. *(He puts his hand near the floor and raises it by steps and stairs)* This friend and this friend, and this friend – good!

(He is embarrassed at the expression of amazement of her face. She rises, comes to him and looks earnestly into his face.)

MAGDALENE *(Quietly)* D'ye mean – you, you want to marry me? Me?

AHMED *(Nods, smiles nervously)* Ahmed no' stupid?

MAGDALENE *(Throws her arms around his neck)* Naw! You're no' stupid, Johnnie. You're the wisest man in the whole world – so ye are!

(She is flushed and in her unexpected ecstasy is almost pretty)

AHMED Good! *(Smiles)* Good! *(Nods)* Good! *(Kisses her)*

(Enter PEGGIE. She is alarmed and is assisting a young woman into the kitchen. She is followed by a young man carrying a battered suitcase and a small bundle of clothes.)

PEGGIE You'll be all right in a minute – sit down here.

ALEC *(To MAGDALENE)* Are you the wummin? The landlady?

(PEGGIE gets a drink for MAGGIE. Enter MRS MUTRIE.)

MAGDALENE Naw! She is.

MRS MUTRIE What's adae? *(To ALEC)* What are *you* wantin?

ALEC My wife's no' well, missus – she took a wake turn at the door – we're looking for a room – we've been lookin a' day. We were tellt tae come to you – we wouldna be any bother; we would sleep anywhere.

(He looks at MAGGIE)

MRS MUTRIE Well, you see . . .
ALEC We'd sleep on the flair, missus.
MRS MUTRIE The landlady's no' in – she's . . .
ALEC Oh!
PEGGIE You can sit here for a wee while if you like.
ALEC Do you think we could maybe get a place here? We've tramped all over the town.
MAGDALENE Aye! It's a helluva job – isn't it?
MAGGIE *(Weakly)* Thanks.
PEGGIE Feelin better now?

(MAGGIE nods, drops her gaze)

MRS MUTRIE Maybe you would like to lie down somewhere?
MAGDALENE If you like, missus, you can lie down on my bed.
ALEC She'll be a'right. *(To MAGGIE)* Feeling better?
MAGDALENE *(Brushing aside his argument)* Awch – let her lie down – it's no puttin me about. A wee cup o' tea'll put her on her feet.
PEGGIE I'll make a wee cup.
MRS MUTRIE Are ye – expectin?
MAGGIE No – I'm . . . *(She starts to weep)*
ALEC *(Goes over to her, puts his arm around her)* There, noo! Maggie . . . you've no' to be greetin. Come on, noo. *(He looks at the others, says quietly)* She'll be a'right.
MAGDALENE Take her intae my room. *(Helps her)* You can lie down for an hour or two.

(ALEC looks lost)

MAGDALENE You can bring your case, if you like.
MRS MUTRIE Mrs Gilmour's no' gonny be very pleased when she hears about them.
MAGDALENE *(Glaring at her)* Aye! but we'll *no'* tell her. Sure we'll no'.

(AHMED lifts lid of potato pot – goes over to dresser, brings salt, salts the spuds)

PEGGIE They're just a couple of weans; imagine married and livin in rooms.
MRS MUTRIE An' what's wrang wi that?
PEGGIE For them it's bad – you've got to be able to fight to live in rooms.

(Enter NORA astonished looking – carrying three cups, saucers, plates, etc.)

NORA Who's that?

PEGGIE They were lookin for a room – the lassie fainted at the door.

NORA What's wrong with her?

PEGGIE If you're walkin about lookin for a place to live – that's enough to make anybody take a weak turn.

NORA *(At sink washing cups etc.)* She's nice. *(To AHMED)* What are you *laughing* at, Johnnie?

AHMED Good! *(Taps head)* In *here*, good!

MRS MUTRIE They canna stay here! Mrs Gilmour'll maybe think . . .

PEGGIE Aw! Mrs Gilmour's no' such a monster.

NORA Maybe they can get our room – we're goin to a new house.

PEGGIE A *new house*?

NORA Aye, we got a postcard this morning.

PEGGIE My! It must be wonderful!

MRS MUTRIE How is it that some people can get a house?

NORA Maybe you're no' saying your prayers at night, Mrs Mutrie.

PEGGIE *(Smiles)* That's about right, hen. It has something tae dae wi the supernatural.

(Exit MRS MUTRIE)

MRS MUTRIE *(As she exits)* Flamin papes!

NORA *(Grins mischievously, shrugs her shoulders to PEGGIE, and points to retreating figure of MRS MUTRIE, saying loudly)* Billy or a Dan?

(PEGGIE smiles, lifts cigarette. AHMED is trying spuds with a fork.)

PEGGIE Gie them a chance, Johnnie – what are you laughing at?

NORA He would make a good advertisement for Maclean's toothpaste.

AHMED Magdalene. *(Puts his finger on his chest, smiles)* Friends good.

PEGGIE Hangin up your hat wi her, Johnnie?

NORA That's a right wicked look he's got in his eye. *(He grins)*

AHMED Good! *(Nods)*

NORA I'm saying that you're a right rascal, Johnnie.

AHMED *(He is still nodding and saying –)* Good!

(PEGGIE laughs)

NORA I'm saying that I wouldna like to trust you very far – that right, Johnnie?

AHMED *(Nods smiling)* Good! Friends! *(He grabs pot as it begins to boil)*

(Enter MAGDALENE)

MAGDALENE *(She is looking depressed)* Poor soul! She lost her wean – fell down the stair . . . fortnight ago.

PEGGIE Maybe she can stay. Nora says they will be moving. *(MAGDALENE looks at NORA)* They're gettin a new hoose.

NORA Well! We got a postcard. My ma's gone up the day to see about it.

MAGDALENE A new hoose? I wish I could get a new house, but I don't suppose I ever will. *(AHMED is smiling to her, she catches his eye – she smiles)* They don't gie houses to people wi names like crossword puzzles, but I don't care.

PEGGIE What's go'n on?

(MAGDALENE grins shyly)

NORA Ha, Ha! *(Laughs – points her finger to AHMED)*

AHMED Good!

MAGDALENE *(Goes over – stands beside him, takes his hand)* Johnnie an' me . . . we're gonna get married.

PEGGIE Married! Oh, Meg! *(Runs over and puts her arms round MAGDALENE's neck)*

AHMED *(Very pleased with himself)* Good! Good!

NORA *(Goes over and shakes his hand)* Johnnie! Congratulations.

(Doorbell sounds loudly)

AHMED *(Suddenly understanding the handshake)* A Happy New Year! A Happy New Year!

(They all laugh)

MAGDALENE *(To PEGGIE)* You'll be ma best maid?

(Doorbell rings again. MRS MUTRIE puts her head round the door.)

PEGGIE Aye! I'll be delighted. It'll be marvellous.

(Doorbell is still ringing)

MRS MUTRIE *(Angrily)* Is naebody gonny answer the door?

(She slams the door)

NORA I'll get it! Wait till my ma hears about this.

(Enter POTTER in his shirt sleeves)

Was it you at the door?

POTTER *(He is small, bald and very agitated)* Naw! I hope you don't mind me comin in. My wife's no' well – she, she asked me to get Meg Flynn – is she in?

(Exit NORA)

19

MAGDALENE That's me, mister.

POTTER She's bad. She's no' near due yet but . . . she asked me to get you.

MAGDALENE I don't know, mister . . . I've . . . well, you've got to know what to dae.

POTTER Aw, the doctor will be coming.

PEGGIE I'll come wi you.

MAGDALENE Well all right then.

(She exits upstairs)

POTTER *(Puts his hand to his head)* I wish it was a' bye wi.

PEGGIE Sit down. No, don't worry. She'll be all right.

(Enter ALEC)

ALEC Have you got a match, missus?

PEGGIE *(Lifts packet of cigarettes and matches – hands them to POTTER)* Here! *(To ALEC and POTTER)* Have a smoke. No, don't worry. She'll be all right.

POTTER Thanks.

(PEGGIE exits)

ALEC A light, Mac.

(POTTER sits at table, gets light from ALEC. AHMED has gone to fireplace to steam his potatoes.)

POTTER Aye, God has gae poor taste that comes visiting these rat holes.

ALEC What's up, Mac?

POTTER It's the wife. She's havin a kid.

ALEC I wish my wife had had one.

(AHMED is at the doorsteps and smiles. They look at him.)

AHMED *(He grins broadly)* Ah! Good! Good! Good!

(He goes through the steps and stairs routine and gives them the thumbs-up sign, signifying that he thinks that kids are the greatest thing in the world, as of course they are. He exits grinning and the two men sit a little bit uncomfortably. They are both in the presence of strangers. ALEC lights a match and gives POTTER a light. POTTER takes a draw and exhales the smoke, and then becomes immersed in his cares. ALEC does likewise. A thought strikes him and he turns slowly to POTTER.)

ALEC Do you know anywhere I could get a room, mister?

(POTTER looks up wearily at the question and shakes his head slowly, as the curtain closes)

POTTER Naw.

(Part chorus of 'My Ain Wee Hoose')

CURTAIN

END OF ACT I

ACT II

About seven o'clock the same evening. The curtains are closed, but the set is pretty much the same except that the cooking utensils appear to be in a greater state of disarray. There is a fire burning in the grate. Through the window the purple tint of twilight fills the sky. MRS MUTRIE is sitting knitting in the armchair. NORA is sitting on a small stool before the fire. MRS MUTRIE is talking. The gas-light is only half turned on.

MRS MUTRIE An' then my father bought a villa in Ibrox. Oh it was lovely. It had upstairs and downstairs and the outlook was grand. We could see the railway away in the distance . . . just where the Rangers have their park noo. We had a happy life – my two sisters Vi' and Maggie and me. But then a big sweetie work opened in Ibrox – Mutrie was the name and my father had an awful job. When Wullie came after me . . . I can aye mind my father sayin a Mutrie's came to ruin my business and a Mutrie's comin tae ruin my daughter. Of course, Wullie was nothin tae the sweetie-folk. It was a coincidence. *(She stops knitting and lies back)* Aye, they were happy days – things were quiet and restful just like the noo. My father used tae take doon his fiddle on a Sunday night. Vi' was the singer – she used to sing alto in the choir – it was divine. *(She is lost in her memories and the potency of her dreams has affected NORA, who is now watching her attentively)* We had two pictures of Edinburgh wi green plush frames and we had jinglin glass which hung at the door an' made music when the wind blew.
NORA I seen them at the Barras.
MRS MUTRIE And we had a statue o' Auld Hawkie who used tae staun at the Trongate wi a penny in his haun cryin oot 'Cover that – Cover that'. *(She laughs and looks at NORA)* What am I tellin a lassie a' this fur?
NORA I like it . . . *(Pause)*
MRS MUTRIE Aye, we had an awful happy life in my young days.
NORA What like was your house? *(Pause)*
MRS MUTRIE Everything in it was our ain. My father never owed a penny while we were there. *(Pause)* Vi' never was strong. She was a good lassie, Vi'. The night she died she never complained. She sat up in bed an' smiled at us, just as she always did. My father was heartbroken – he ran awa' for the doctor at twelve o'clock at night – through a' the rain. She died before he got back. Aye, she was a good lassie, Vi'. *(She wipes her nose in her apron)* Ach! But what am I telling a young lassie all this for?
NORA What happened tae your sister Maggie?
MRS MUTRIE Maggie was steerin – she got married tae a master baker. After Vi' died, my father lost heart. He sellt the house and we moved tae the south side. Maggie – she was the lady – she wouldna stay there. I *had* tae stay, there was naebody to look after him.

(Enter HECTOR who has just risen from bed. He takes towel to sink.)

HECTOR It's nice and quiet in the dark, eh?

MRS MUTRIE Hello, Hector. *(To NORA)* Screw up the gas, hen. *(To HECTOR)* You'll need the light to shave.

HECTOR No! Night off.

NORA *(Turning up the gas)* I think you've got a girl-friend up your sleeve somewhere you're no' lettin on.

HECTOR *(He smiles, turns down his shirt neck)* I'm waitin till you grow up.

MRS MUTRIE Aye, Nora will make a grand wife.

NORA *(She notices he is slightly embarrassed)* Not me – I'm goin to be an old maid.

HECTOR It's good when you can be what you want to be.

MRS MUTRIE Never be an auld maid, Nora – your troubles are twice as bad 'cause they're a' your ain. Ach! But you're too bonny tae be an auld maid. You're only nineteen. *(NORA nods)* You have plenty of time – plenty of time.

(Enter MR MUTRIE with two fish suppers)

MR MUTRIE Jean! *(She looks round)* Any tea? *(He holds up the suppers)*

MRS MUTRIE There's some in the teapot in front o' the fire.

MR MUTRIE I . . . I got ye a fish supper.

MRS MUTRIE Aw, Wullie, you shouldna have bothered. Where did you get the money?

MR MUTRIE *(With mock disdain)* Now, now! Ask no questions, and ye'll be tellt nae lies.

HECTOR *(In the middle of washing his face)* Been robbing the bank, Wullie, eh?

MR MUTRIE Hello, Hector. You'll be about the night? *(MRS MUTRIE has risen – she takes fish suppers and exits)*

HECTOR *(Finishes washing, starts to dry his face)* Aye!

MR MUTRIE I'll buy you a beer for a change. *(He smiles as he exits)*

HECTOR *(To NORA)* Not going to the pictures tonight, eh?

NORA Don't know yet.

HECTOR No money?

NORA Naw! I . . . it's no' that.

HECTOR *(Puts his hand in his pocket and offers her half a crown)* Here, take yoursel out.

NORA *(Blushing)* No! I . . . couldn't take it.

HECTOR *(Smiling)* Don't be daft. *(He forces it on her)* That's right.

NORA Please! No! I couldn't!

HECTOR You're just a wee lassie. If I was twenty years younger I'd *take* ye out tae the pictures myself.

NORA Thanks, Hector . . . My da was angry the last time you gave me money.

HECTOR You tell him to come to me, he doesna know how lucky he is. *(He makes to leave, stops at the door)* You're a nice wee lassie, I like you.

(NORA sits, looks at the half crown in her open palm, closes her hand on it and looks into the fire. Enter MRS MUTRIE with some chips on a plate.)

MRS MUTRIE Here's some chips for you – we've got too many.

NORA You've got enough now?

MRS MUTRIE Aye, take them!

NORA *(Taking chips)* Thanks.

MRS MUTRIE That's an awful man o' mine – he's away intae bed tae get his tea – ye'd think he was an invalid. The attention some folk need – I tell you, it'll be a sad day for him the day I die.

(MRS MUTRIE exits. NORA sits eating her chips. Enter JOHNNIE quietly.)

JOHNNIE Gie's a chip.

(NORA looks up startled – smiles and offers him the plate. He comes slowly over and takes a chip. He sits on the armchair, holds up the chip, opens his mouth wide, moves the chip as though he was going to ram it into his mouth, stops when it looks inevitable that he will swallow his hand as well. He nibbles the chip daintily; she laughs happily; he grins at her.)

JOHNNIE *(Putting the chip into his mouth)* I like them Kosher. It takes the Yidds to make a good fish supper. *(He throws the last three papers on the floor)* There's the profit on a dozen – I had a good day – I sold fourteen quire the day. *(He looks at her, quietly, thinking)*

NORA Going to Barrowland?

JOHNNIE The dancin? Oh naw! The old plates o' meat'll no' let me. *(He wags his foot)*

NORA Magdalene and Johnnie are gettin married.

JOHNNIE *(Nods his head)* Aye, imagine! They'll get wee darkey weans – there's one thing anyway, I wouldna marry a darkey – would you?

(They both discuss this quite gravely)

NORA Well, it depends.

JOHNNIE Depends on what? *(He is incredulous)*

NORA Well it depends – you know – when two people get married it's because they like each other.

JOHNNIE No' always. Look at the film stars in Hollywood!

NORA Well they like each . . .

24

JOHNNIE Naw they don't – they only like themselves.

NORA Och, you're just wantin tae argue. *(Offers him more chips)*

JOHNNIE Naw I'm no'.

NORA I'd like tae get married – it would be nice.

JOHNNIE I'm gonny be an artist like Low! You know I'd . . . like tae paint you.

NORA *(Wide-eyed)* Wi nae claes on?

JOHNNIE Naw I don't mean *that* way.

(NORA laughs)

NORA Mrs Mutrie told my ma you're just a fly paper boy.

JOHNNIE Sometimes Mrs Mutrie is only an owld eejit.

NORA How would you paint me, Johnnie? Like a ballet dancer? *(She rises and poses with her hand in a ballet pose)*

JOHNNIE Come here, Nora. Sit down. *(He draws her on his knee – she lies back in the chair)*

NORA *How* would you paint me?

JOHNNIE Well, I don't know. It's all inside me – just how I feel about you; sometimes, when I'm goin for my papers, I think, every paper I sell I make a faurdin. Every time I think about you, Nora, I feel richer – but it's no' faurdins – some day if I sellt enough papers I'd be well off . . . an' . . .

NORA Ach, Johnnie, you're daft.

JOHNNIE I wish I had a house o' my ain, an' you . . .

NORA Do you like me, Johnnie? *(She lays down her plate)*

JOHNNIE You're no' bad for a Shamrock. Though mind ye I could get ten tarts that don't think I'm daft.

NORA *(Opening her hand, showing half crown)* I don't need anybody – I can go mysel.

JOHNNIE *(Throwing his eyes to heaven)* God, the wean's rich!

NORA *(Laughs)* Aye, it's my *money* you're after?

JOHNNIE *(Bending over and kissing her)* Nora, I'm gonna weary you all the days of your life till you're an owld wummin wi a yella face.

NORA *(Smiles, puts her head back and closes her eyes)* Are you, Johnnie?

JOHNNIE I'm going to weary you telling you how much I love you.

NORA I love you, Johnnie.

(They kiss again)

JOHNNIE Some day we'll have a wee house o' wur ain – an' we can go out rambles on a Sunday – I don't mean wi the Ramblin Club – just wur two sells!

NORA We'll no' stay in a tenement – eh no! I'd like a wee hoose wi grass at the front and flowers.

JOHNNIE *(Hopelessly)* Maybe we'll get that.

NORA Look at me, Johnnie.

JOHNNIE Och, I'd live in a tent if I had you, Nora. How can we no' get married? – Magdalene and Johnnie can dae it.

NORA Well, ask me right. *(She is impatient)* Johnnie! *(Pleading)* Ask me nice – like you did last night, last night.

(Pause)

JOHNNIE *(He moves close to her, looks down at her young, happy face. Smiles.)* Well, somewhere maybe faur away maybe up the next street there's a wee house – and there's a wee grate wi red tiles at the back an' the steel's are shinin like a new shillin; an' there's a brass rod in the grate; an' there's pictures on the wall; an' a big clock that plays music every hour.

(Pause)

NORA *(Prompting)* Aye?

JOHNNIE An' the table has a red cloth on it an' there's a canary in a cage whistlin; an' the kettle's on the bile; an' a big orange cat on the fender purrin into the fire – an' you're sittin there smiling because you're happy, because you know that I love you more than anything else in the world. Will you mairry me, Nora?

NORA *(She is radiant and looks at him tenderly before she puts her arms around his neck)* I love you, Johnnie.

(They kiss as MRS REILLY enters. She is astonished for a moment and then very angry.)

MRS REILLY Nora Reilly! *(NORA is up in a flash)* You shameless bitch! You brazen tinker! Sittin there on his knee! You should be ashamed of yourself.

NORA It's all right, Ma.

MRS REILLY All right, is it?

JOHNNIE It was my fault she . . . she . . .

MRS REILLY Gaun, you dirty blackguard; puttin your hauns on the lassie. *(She shoves him angrily)*

NORA But, Ma . . .

MRS REILLY Don't Ma me. *(She spits on the floor)* It's bringin disgrace on us you'd be. Get up there, get up there.

(She slaps NORA's face hard. NORA runs off.)

JOHNNIE Gaun, ya old swine. Lay her alane.

MRS REILLY As for you . . . *(She moves forward threateningly)*

JOHNNIE *(Affects a boxing stance)* Just you keep your distance or I'll do you. Nora an' me's gettin married and you'll no' get hittin her then.

MRS REILLY *You're* marryin my Nora? My God! You. *(She spits the words out)* You're daft!

JOHNNIE Ach, away ye go an' bile your heid! *(He turns his back on her, makes to sit down)*
MRS REILLY By God, you'll hear more about this!

(Enter MR REILLY)

MR REILLY *(He is big and tough looking)* Who hit her?
JOHNNIE *(On his feet)* She did!
MR REILLY Why did you hit her?
MRS REILLY She was sittin on his knee.

(Enter MRS MUTRIE)

MR REILLY *(Looks angrily at JOHNNIE)* What were you doin wa' her?

(He grabs JOHNNIE's two lapels in his one hand, draws back his fist)

MRS REILLY *(Alarmed)* Aw, don't hit him, Peter!
JOHNNIE *(Stands like a frightened lamb)* I wasna daen anything.
MR REILLY *(Drawing back his ham of a fist)* By God! For nithin at a' I'd bash your brains in. *(He almost does)*
JOHNNIE Nora's said she'd marry me.
MR REILLY *(So dumbfounded that he lets go his hold of JOHNNIE and roars)* What? . . . Nora? . . . You?
JOHNNIE *(Recovering)* Aye, sure!
MR REILLY *(He straightens his lapels)* By God! I'm goin to kill ye, boy – if you've been touchin my lassie.
MRS REILLY That'll dae now, Peter. Don't hit him Peter. You know what happened the last time. Ye'll get ten years . . . *(She natters on)*
MR REILLY Shut your big mouth! Shut your big mouth! *(Pointing)* Get her in here! *(Roars)* Get her in here! *(He shoves her roughly. Exit MRS REILLY.)*
MRS MUTRIE What's up, Peter? What is it?
MR REILLY This lousy leprechaun an' my lassie. *(Puts his fist under JOHNNIE's nose – JOHNNIE's confidence has ebbed again)* I'm tellin ye, I'll tear the tripes out ye!

(Enter NORA pushed by MRS REILLY. MR REILLY turns to her.)

MR REILLY What's going on between you? Answer me?
NORA *(Sullenly)* Nothing.
MR REILLY Answer me! What were youse doin?
NORA We weren't doin anything.
MR REILLY Do you want to marry this leprechaun? . . . God keep my hans offa ye! Will ye *answer* me?

(NORA starts to cry)

JOHNNIE Lay her alone.

MR REILLY By God, that's the last straw! *(He grabs JOHNNIE)*

NORA Oh, Da! Da! leave him! – You'll only get the jail.

MR REILLY He said you wanted tae marry him – do you?

NORA *(Terrified, embarrassed and humiliated, she shakes her head)* Naw! Oh naw!

(She runs off. Exit MRS REILLY at her back.)

MR REILLY So, you want to be an artist do ye? You'd do better writin fairy tales! *(He flings him roughly aside and into the chair, goes to the door, stops and glares at him)* Eejit!

(He exits)

MRS MUTRIE *(She is completely at a loss; she throws an embarrassed side glance as she picks up paper off floor, puts it on the table)* I'll – I'll just take this *Times*, Johnnie.

(She exits to her room. JOHNNIE sits for a long time without moving. He is completely defeated. His world has tumbled about his ears. He rises slowly, goes over to the sink, takes a drink of water and looks up at the sky, turns, picks the two papers off the floor, lays them on the table, looks at the fire, and slowly sits down in the chair at table. POTTER enters. He is drunk and comes in talking to himself.)

POTTER An' he says to me, 'Are you a Glaswegian?' So I says to him, 'Of course I'm a Glaswegian – born and brought up on the bonnie banks o' the Clyde', an' I says 'a man is just as auld as his arteries' – so I did! Aye, the aulder the fiddle the sweeter the tune. *(Sees JOHNNIE)* Oh! Hello, have *you* got any weans, eh? Oh, you don't want tae talk, eh? *(He staggers)* So you *won't* talk? Well, I've got five weans an' wan comin up in the hoist. Aye, five weans! *(He moves round the table)*

JOHNNIE Away ye go home tae your bed.

POTTER Hame tae my bed? If you seen the carry on that's goin on in my bed just noo – och, it's terrible! I couldna get a mantle anywhere. There's no much light aff a couple of candles but she'll do it – a great wee wumman. *(He is groping through his waistcoat pocket)* Do you know my wife? Ah! you'd like her. Just the night she says to me: 'Francie' – that's my name – 'Francie, you take the weans doon tae Granny Duffy's: it'll save you the bother of lookin efter them.' It's no' many women would have thought o' that, is it? Aye, a great wee woman! – but wait tae Ah tell ye aboot wee Tosh – he's three year auld. He wouldna go, flung his bunnet up in the air – broke the mantle he did. *(Sighs)* I tell ye, a family's a brake on a man.

JOHNNIE *(Looks at him and feels sorry for him against his will)* Well, why did ye no' stay sober, ya miserable owld swine?

(He pulls his cap on and exits)

POTTER Ye don't need tae take it like that – *(He stumbles and sits down in the armchair. He looks around)* Not a soul in sight . . . ! Everybody's away an' left me – I wish I had got a mantle: it's an awful job havin a wean in the dark . . . It's an awful job anyway! Maybe, maybe I could . . .

(He staggers into chair. Enter ALEC carrying a small aluminium pan and a packet of tea. MAGGIE is at the back and they both enter with the air of trespassers.)

ALEC Where's the wumman?
POTTER I got five weans . . . nearly six.
MAGGIE He's drunk.

(They look at each other like lost children)

ALEC *(Points to MUTRIES' door; moves over and knocks timidly)* Is there anybody there?
MRS MUTRIE Who's there?
ALEC *(Licks his lips)* It's . . . It's me!
MRS MUTRIE What are ye wantin?
ALEC *(Looks at MAGGIE in distress)* We . . . We would . . . would it be a'right if we make a wee cup o' tea, missus?
MRS MUTRIE *(Opens the door. She has a paper under her arm and her spectacles on)* What's adae wi ye?
ALEC Would it be a' right if we made a wee cup o' tea?
MRS MUTRIE Aye, on ye go! *(Sees POTTER)* My God! Mrs Gilmour's gonna have a fit if she comes back and finds the house full o' strangers.
MAGGIE We're just gaun, missus: it was good o' ye tae let us stay.
ALEC Sit down, I'll no' be long. *(MAGGIE sits at table)* There's nothin like a wee cup o' tea tae cheer ye up. *(MAGGIE makes no response but sits as though her spirit was crushed)* We'll get a place – soon as we get out – wait till you see!
MRS MUTRIE That lassie's no' well.
ALEC She'll be a'right.
MRS MUTRIE *(Sitting down at the table. POTTER snores)* D'you belong to Glesca?
MAGGIE *(Shakes her head)* No.
MRS MUTRIE It's an awful job trying tae get a place.
ALEC *(Quickly changing the subject)* Maggie comes fae Kilmarnock.
MRS MUTRIE That's where the honest men an' bonnie lassies come fae.

(MAGGIE smiles)

Is your Maw livin?
MAGGIE Aye!
MRS MUTRIE Can she no' put you up?
MAGGIE Aye!

(Uncomfortable pause)

ALEC We couldna agree.

MRS MUTRIE You young folks gettin married without a house – my, you're no' feart.

MAGGIE It was my fault. I didn't want tae wait ony longer.

MRS MUTRIE Are ye long married?

MAGGIE Six months.

MRS MUTRIE How many places have ye been?

MAGGIE We stayed wi my mither for two months – an' three ither places.

ALEC *You* don't know where we could get a place?

MRS MUTRIE Naw! Everybody's the same.

ALEC We could sleep on the flair.

MRS MUTRIE A' this talk about a new world an' people canna get a place tae sleep.

ALEC Everybody's daen their best. I wish *we* had wan o' thae prefabricated houses: even if the wa's *were* damp.

MRS MUTRIE Aye! A man an' a woman never know what marriage is till they get a house o' their ain – an' then it's lovely. You try hard, son.

ALEC I put ma name down for a house a year before we got married.

(Enter PEGGIE)

MRS MUTRIE *(Rising)* Is she no' by yet, Peggie?

PEGGIE Naw!

MRS MUTRIE Is she bad?

PEGGIE Aye! *(She is depressed; goes over to the sink: sits on the draining board)*

MRS MUTRIE *(Looks at POTTER asleep)* Well he's no' worryin.

PEGGIE Och, we had tae put him out – he's drunk.

MRS MUTRIE Is Magdalene still up there?

PEGGIE *(Nods)* Aye, she's still there. The doctor's there, tae. *(Puts her hand across her forehead)* Poor people havin weans is the saddest thing in the world.

(MAGGIE drops her gaze. Enter HECTOR – he looks around them all shyly.)

HECTOR *(To MRS MUTRIE)* Wullie?

MRS MUTRIE He's in bed, Hector. He lay down tae eat his fish supper and fell asleep. Away and waken him – can ye no' drink your ain money?

HECTOR *(Smiling)* Wullie has a lot of qualities you don't suspect.

MRS MUTRIE Aye! but he's got a lot o' qualities that I dae suspect. Nae honest man ever had a drouth like his.

HECTOR Ach, you're hard on him. *(He stops at door)* What's wrong, Peggie?

PEGGIE *(Smiles bravely)* Ach! Wife up the stair's havin a wean.
HECTOR *(Smiles, shakes his head)* Tch! Tch! wives and weans. Ready, Wullie?
MR MUTRIE Aye! Aye! I'm gettin up.

(He enters MUTRIE's room)

PEGGIE *(To MAGGIE)* You feelin better?
MAGGIE I'm a'right, noo – I just felt that I couldna last out any longer. I'm sorry I gave you a fright at the door.
PEGGIE You'll be all right when you get fixed up. I'm away for an aspirin.

(She exits to her room)

MR MUTRIE *(Sticking his head round door)* Heh, you never darned my socks.
MRS MUTRIE You'll get your black socks under the cushion – I'll darn it after. Here, put my specs on the mantelpiece.

(He comes out: he is dressed in his shirt and long drawers and is wearing one sock. He takes spectacles.)

MRS MUTRIE My God! Can ye no' put on your claes?
MR MUTRIE Awch! Give us them.

(He grabs specs and runs off. PEGGIE enters with aspirin – goes to sink for a drink.)

MRS MUTRIE Peggie, you just missed Wullie in his heavy drawers. *(She laughs)* It's worth gaun a mile tae see.
PEGGIE *(Takes drink)* Grandpaw in his gatchens!

(Enter HECTOR)

HECTOR *(He is finishing speaking to MR MUTRIE)* All right . . . I'll wait. *(To PEGGIE)* That's queer stuff to be drinkin on a Friday night.
PEGGIE I was takin an aspirin.

(Enter AHMED with teapot and cup)

AHMED *(Smiles)* Tea-water.
PEGGIE *(Making an effort to be cheerful)* Here's the groom. Did you know Johnnie's gettin married to Magdalene? *(She puts her arm round his waist)* Johnnie's all right, eh?

(He giggles and moves quickly away)

AHMED Johnnie tickle.
PEGGIE Easy tickled – easy courted. Magdalene's gonny have a lot of fun. *(She smiles indulgently on him)*
AHMED Good fun – laugh alla time – laugh alla time.

PEGGIE Good fun – laugh alla time.

(Enter MAGDALENE completely dejected. Everyone wheels round and looks at her – she walks over to the wall behind the door, turns her face towards the wall.)

Magdalene, what's up?

(MRS MUTRIE rises)

MAGDALENE She's died!

(Pause. ALEC sits on chair beside MAGGIE and puts his arms round her – faintly in the distance an accordion is playing 'Phil the Fluter's Ball'.)

MRS MUTRIE *(Quietly)* We'll need tae tell him. *(Points to POTTER)*
MR MUTRIE *(Coming out of his room)* What the hell's everybody so quiet for? *(He is awed at everybody's expression)*
MAGDALENE *(Goes over, shakes POTTER)* Francie – Francie – wake up! . . . wake up!
POTTER Wazza marrer? – Awch! *(Grunts, shakes himself and snores)*
MAGDALENE Wake up! Come on. Wake up!
POTTER Eh? Eh? *(He looks up drunkenly at her – studies her and runs his hand over his head)* What's up?
MAGDALENE Francie, are you listening?
POTTER *(He is stone sober in a flash)* The wean?
MAGDALENE It's your wife, mister – she's . . . *(She starts to cry)* . . . she's died.

(He looks round at them and as his eyes catch each they turn their backs on him slowly. He is stunned, rises slowly and says . . .)

POTTER My poor wee Nellie . . . I . . . I couldna get a mantle anywhere.

(He moves slowly off as the curtain falls. Chorus of 'My Ain Wee Hoose'.)

CURTAIN

END OF ACT II

ACT III

It is the same evening around ten-thirty. PEGGIE is just finished drying the cooking utensils and lays the dishcloth on the table as she stands them in a row on their accustomed places on the dresser. MRS MUTRIE is sitting on the armchair knitting. MAGDALENE sits quietly on the stool.

PEGGIE It's just the same wi a' the young folks that get married without a hoose – they get kicked about frae pillar tae post till they become hard inside an' when that happens – they just give in. That poor lassie never was away frae her mother in her life. She's hurt noo – hurt bad. Why are people no' kinder tae young folk? When you're young the good things are ten times nicer: a' the bad things seem ten times worse than they are. After you've been kicked aboot a' your life ye get an aul age pension. Why do they no' gie a pension tae the young people – that would keep them frae stealin and whorin and cheatin.

MRS MUTRIE Money's no' aye the cause when you're young!

PEGGIE *(She has replaced the pots, etc. – she lifts dishcloth and hangs it at the fire)* Naw! but life could be good.

MRS MUTRIE Life is good, Peggie – it's just livin like this that makes things seem bad. Isn't that right, Magdalene?

MAGDALENE *(She has been dreaming)* Eh? Aw! don't ask me – I think it's smashin.

PEGGIE You've got bells ringin in your ears.

MRS MUTRIE Where will ye be thinkin o' stayin, Magdalene?

MAGDALENE I don't know. Auld Gilmour will likely put us oot – but I don't care.

MRS MUTRIE It's a pity that you couldna get a hoose. I mind when you used tae pick your district and spend a hale day lookin at empty hooses. Every street had a dozen 'To Let' boards out. Aye, the factors were gey civil people in thae days!

MAGDALENE *(PEGGIE gives her a cigarette)* Thanks.

(They light cigarettes)

MRS MUTRIE My! in my young days it was an awful thing for a woman to smoke.

MAGDALENE It's an awful thing for a woman tae smoke noo – the price of them. Did you never try a puff yoursel?

PEGGIE Don't be tempting her, Meg.

MRS MUTRIE *(Laughing)* Get thee behind me, Satan. I used to have other bad habits, but no' that wan.

PEGGIE That used tae be a great sayin o' my mother's – Get thee behind me, Satan – she was always sayin it.

MRS MUTRIE I've never heard you talk of your mother before. *(PEGGIE sits)*

PEGGIE *(Smiling)* Did you think I didnae have a mother?

MRS MUTRIE Naw! Just I never heard ye speak about her.

PEGGIE *(Absently)* I didnae really.

MAGDALENE You don't look like an invention tae me, hen.

PEGGIE She was always drunk. *(She blows out a cloud of smoke absently, takes another quick puff and speaks slowly)* Sometimes I used tae wish I could strangle her. We had nae furniture – she sellt it a' for drink. We had a table just – wi nae drawers in it: she burnt them. She used to sit there wi her hair doon her back drinkin oot o' an old cracked cup. My brother an' me were just weans – but I can mind it. We used to sit in the bed frightened to say a word, an' she used tae fill up her cup, and every time she would drink, she would say: 'Get thee behind me, Satan!' *(Pause)* Some people should be wiped off the face o' God's earth – an' ma mother was wan o' them. I used tae watch a woman's wean – I got wan an' sixpence a week – an' she could spent it on wan drink.

MRS MUTRIE It's a terrible thing, drink. *(Hurriedly)* I mean when you canny watch it.

PEGGIE That wean used tae drag the life oot me. I was only eleven – I forgot how to play. *(Shakes her head sadly)* Och, well! I got owre it!

MAGDALENE It hasnae made ye bitter, anyway.

MRS MUTRIE When ye look back on a time ye aye just mind the pleasant times. And the bad times – ye just say Ach, well! I weathered the storm – that's what makes life worth livin.

PEGGIE Peter and Johnnie had an argument the night.

MAGDALENE Peter's an old windbag. He'd encourage you tae dae a thing – and then laugh in your face when you try your best.

MRS MUTRIE Ach well! There's no' much wrang wi a good honest windbag. Maybe you've got nae sense o' humour.

MAGDALENE Who, me? Mary Magdalene gettin married tae a darkey. *(They both laugh)* I could kill mysel laughin.

MRS MUTRIE You're an awful lassie, hen. *(She is trying . to stop laughing)*

MAGDALENE *(Smiling)* My hubby! Oh, gosh! *(She starts to laugh)*

PEGGIE I hope Gilmour lets you stay on.

MRS MUTRIE Sure she will – she'll shift you baith intae the wan room.

MAGDALENE I hope.

MRS MUTRIE This man has ma hert roasted. *(She is changing the needles over on her knitting)* When I think o' the time I've spent just sittin knittin socks for him – if it was a' added thegither, I must have been knittin ten years for him.

MAGDALENE I'd let him go in his bare feet.

MRS MUTRIE He'll no wear anything on his feet but hand-knit.

MAGDALENE You should get owre tae the Jolly Market – get him a pair for a penny.

MRS MUTRIE Penny socks! – on Wullie Mutrie! By God! if he ever heard about them he'd never go to work again. Every time I bring him in a shirt he's no' happy unless I tell him I bought it in Sauchiehall Street.

PEGGIE Sometimes I'm glad I missed a' this – humourin a man – it's a job!

MRS MUTRIE It starts aff as a job but it soon becomes second nature to ye. Wullie Mutrie's no a bad sowl – I could get worse. *(Scratches her chin)* Maybe! You know what they say: marriage is a lottery – for every win there's a hunner blanks – an' you never know what you're gettin.

MAGDALENE A hunner tae wan on – even the bookies havena got the brass face tae offer odds like that.

PEGGIE You'll be a'right, Mag. Johnnie's a nice fella – he'll be good tae you.

MAGDALENE Aye, he'd better be!

PEGGIE I wonder how that couple got on.

MAGDALENE What way did you no' let them stay – I could have slept wi you the night.

PEGGIE I asked them to stay, but I think they were feart – they went away just after Potter left. It's a pity for that wee sowl – I wonder what he'll dae.

MRS MUTRIE And all these weans tae.

PEGGIE What a big family to be left wae.

MAGDALENE At least he's got a place. Them two poor sowls walkin about – Friday night's a helluva night tae go lookin for a room.

(Enter PETER REILLY. He is carrying a shirt in his fist. He is rather shame-faced looking.)

MR REILLY Hello! H'm. Did – er – any of youse see the boy?

PEGGIE Who? – Johnnie?

MR REILLY Aye! I was thinkin he might be in.

MRS MUTRIE *(Sits up straight, looks at him)* He went out just after you were here. He hasna come back since.

MR REILLY I was . . . wantin tae speak tae him . . . I thought he might be in. *(To MAGDALENE)* I was hearin about you. *(Smiles, goes over and offers his hand)* Givin us all a big surprise, eh? *(They shake hands)*

MAGDALENE Och, well! You can only fight off your admirers for so long.

MR REILLY What was it now? *(He is thinking)* I hope you'll be happy, Magdalene. I know ye will. You have the same name as my owld mother – God rest her!

MAGDALENE Thanks, Peter.

PEGGIE I think you kissed the Blarney Stone.

MR REILLY Naw! I never did, Peggie – but I often wish I had. A man can get on easy in the world if he can talk somebody else intae his way o' thinkin. What about yoursel, Peggie? Are you not thinkin of takin a man?

PEGGIE *(Laughing)* Aye, I think about it, Peter – but that doesna help much!

MRS MUTRIE What are you daein wi the shirt?

MR REILLY I was wantin tae see the boy.

PEGGIE He should be in shortly. He sometimes goes dancin on a Friday. Were ye wantin something?

MR REILLY *(He looks at the shirt and scratches his head trying to explain)* I . . . ye see . . . well, I was lookin out me clean shirt an' I come across this wan an' it's too wee for me, an' I thought he might like to have it!

PEGGIE If you leave it for him . . .

MR REILLY Maybe you wouldn't mention it was me.

PEGGIE Why not?

MR REILLY Him an' me had the fur flyin – he towl me he was as good a man as I was.

PEGGIE *(Puzzled)* Johnnie?

MR REILLY Aye! He just looked at me in the eye when I was going to murder him – Aye! it's the eejit I am when I lose me temper. *(He looks around them)*

PEGGIE Johnnie's a good boy. He's never had a chance.

MR REILLY I'll jist leave it here. *(Puts shirt on top of the dresser)*

(Sounds of MR MUTRIE singing)

This'll be the boys – I'm away.

(He exits)

PEGGIE Ah'm away tae ma bed.

(She exits to her room)

MRS MUTRIE Listen to that galoot roarin his heid off.

MR MUTRIE *(Enters supported by HECTOR, who also is drunk, singing)*
I'm only a common old working chap,
As anyone here can see,
But when I get a couple o' drinks on a Saturday
Glasgow belangs tae me.

MRS MUTRIE *(She has risen)* Put him intae the room – intae bed wi them.

MR MUTRIE *(Pushes them off and stands in his drunken dignity)* Hector, when a man's teetotal he thinks that everybody's his boss. Well *(Slaps his chest)* I'm ma ain boss: I'm not gaun tae bed.

(HECTOR steadies him)

HECTOR Mrs Mutrie says you've t' go t' bed. *(Licks his lips and talks gravely)* Mrs Mutrie's a wise woman. Now, Wullie, you're drunk.

MR MUTRIE A man is never drunk when he can say *(Licks his lips)* Disestablishmentarianism. You canna say it, Hector. *(Laughs)* Disestablishmentarianism.

(MRS MUTRIE has brought a chair from the room)

HECTOR I can say bett'r'n that: I can say Anti-disestablishmentarianism – 's more words 'n you – A.N.T.Y. – *four* words.

MRS MUTRIE Sit doon an' make less noise.

HECTOR Wullie! You must sit down: the good lady says you must sit down: you're only makin a spectacle o' yoursel. *(HECTOR is smiling paternally)*

MR MUTRIE *(Going over)* Magdalene, allow me to congratulate you.

(HECTOR comes over, looks down at her and grins. MR MUTRIE holds out his hand.)

MRS MUTRIE Allow me tae congratulate *you.*

MR MUTRIE Pay no attention to her – she wants you to say 'How?', then she insults *me.*

(MAGDALENE takes his hand)

MAGDALENE You've been beltin the grape in a big way the night, eh?

MR MUTRIE You're ma pin-up girl. If I could get this yin intae her widden overcoat I would marry you masel. *(He hugs her)*

MAGDALENE Wullie!

MRS MUTRIE *(Laughing)* God! Is that him burying me already? *(He turns and looks at her)* You're a selfish owld rascal.

(HECTOR is wandering around looking for a place to sit)

MR MUTRIE Ah ha, a present for the lovely daughter of the Candy King. *(He struggles to remove a bottle from his hip pocket)*

MRS MUTRIE My feyther was a wholesale confectioner. *(Raising her voice)* – Stop calling him the Candy King!

MR MUTRIE *(Producing a half bottle of wine. Dramatically:)*
    Come fill me with the rosy wine.
    An' call a toast; a toast divine.
(He hands it to her) A present from the land of General Franco. *(He points to bottle)* 'S still killin the workin' class. How are ye, hen?

MRS MUTRIE *(To MAGDALENE)* Get glasses. *(To HECTOR)* Pull in the chair.

(HECTOR lifts chair near fire. He sits. MR MUTRIE draws in other chair. MAGDALENE brings glasses from dresser.)

MR MUTRIE Bring in the dark gentleman you're going to marry. *(To*

HECTOR) What's wrong with you, my baker friend? You're very quiet – or are you always so quiet in the presence of feminine pulchritude?

MRS MUTRIE *(Smelling the bottle)* By God, that's a good word, Wullie!

MR MUTRIE Hector is a sad man, a sad, sad man. He's never slept with a woman.

MAGDALENE Hey, blue nose, keep the party clean.

MR MUTRIE I apologise. *(He hiccoughs)*

HECTOR 'Pology accepted, Wullie – but I know – don't mean a thing. When's right way you jus' lie with your arm around her. Sh' puts her head on y' shoulder. *(They are all attention)* An' the moonlight steams in through the window so y' can see each other's eyes shinin in the dark. An' all the frozen dreams in here *(He taps forehead)* get thawed jus' like ice in summer time, an' it's good and you lie an' talk, you talk *all* night, an' it's good, an' waken in the mornin her head's still there *(Puts hand on collarbone)* an' all day you feel it still there an' when you get auld . . . that's the only way – other ways *(Shakes head)* – dirty!

> *(He sits suddenly. MAGDALENE smiles, pours out drinks.)*

MRS MUTRIE Hector, I'm quite convinced, you're drunk. No offence, of course, but you're drunk.

HECTOR S'alright. If I didn't think you was drunk I'd think you was jealous. – Sing, Wullie!

MR MUTRIE Oh aye. Ah'll gie ye a song. What will I sing?

MAGDALENE *(Handing them glasses)* Here! there's a drink!

MRS MUTRIE You shouldna have gien them so much.

MR MUTRIE We'll drink a toast. *(Holds up his glass, looks round)* A toast to Magdalene – to the blushing bride!

MAGDALENE Do you *think* I should blush?

HECTOR Blush? Here's to your big brown eyes.

> *(They drink)*

HECTOR A song, Wullie!

MR MUTRIE I'll give you a song. *(Stands up – staggers – sits again)* What'll I sing? Well, be quiet.

MRS MUTRIE There's naebody saying a word.

> *(MAGDALENE is whispering to MR MUTRIE)*

MR MUTRIE *(To MAGDALENE)* Hey there, gie's a bit o' order.

> *(She sits up, smiles. MRS MUTRIE lifts bottle, slips it down beside her chair.)*

MRS MUTRIE C'mon, Wullie, let's get it over wi.

> *(He stands up, clears his throat, licks his lips, sings 'The Bonnie Banks*

of Loch Lomand'. When he gets to the line 'Where me an' my true love', he realises that they have all joined in: he rises to give it extra volume. He staggers, clutches the chair, sings a couple of words and falls heavily. They laugh. He drowsily sings the last line lying flat.)

MRS MUTRIE *(Grabs him and hauls him into the room)* Intae bed wi ye. *(MAGDALENE is smiling)* Come on intae bed.

(He is all out; she wrestles him through the door. HECTOR sits for a moment, stands up, starts to sing; buttons up his overcoat.)

HECTOR By yon bonnie banks an' by yon bonnie braes,
　　　　Where the sun shines bright . . .
MAGDALENE Where are you gaun?
HECTOR *(Slowly)* For a long, long walk.
MAGDALENE It's bedtime – it's quarter tae eleven. *(She taps her forehead)* Are you sure it's no' wan o' them frozen dreams? *(She smiles)*
HECTOR Icicles! big cauld icicles. *(Stops at door)* I'll thaw them.

(He exits)

MAGDALENE *(Looks after him, shakes her head, smiles)* Daft beggar.
MR MUTRIE *(From room)* Lea' me alane – I kin take aff ma ain troosers! *Don't now*! I'm tellin ye – I'll punch ye right in the nose.

(Enter MRS MUTRIE)

MRS MUTRIE That's an awful man o' mine. I think I'll just go into bed. *(Goes over and lifts bottle)* It's no' faur aff eleven. Goodnight!

(She exits)

MAGDALENE Goodnight, Jean.

(She lifts glasses, takes them to sink, rinses them and replaces them in the drawer. Walks over to the fireplace, takes ring out of the pocket in her overall, puts it on, smiles, kisses it, looks at it.)

MRS MUTRIE Will I help you in?
MR MUTRIE *(Loudly)* Naw! I can manage myself.

(MAGDALENE looks round quickly – covers her ring, looks at the door – she is keeping her engagement ring a secret. She looks at it again, smiles and takes it off: puts it back in her pocket, replaces her handkerchief on top of it – runs her hand through her hair, stretches up to screw out the gas. Enter JOHNNIE slightly drunk.)

JOHNNIE Hey, you! Horse face! Leave that light on.

(She does so)

MAGDALENE Johnnie!

JOHNNIE Well, what about it? I can take a drink if I feel like it.

MAGDALENE (*Smiles*) Did they gie ye it in a sookin bottle?

JOHNNIE You trying tae be funny, eh? (*He is trying hard to smoke and he suddenly starts to cough*) What the hell are you laughing at?

MR MUTRIE (*From his room*) I'm a better singer than you are, so there.

(*JOHNNIE turns, surveys the door*)

MAGDALENE Go in to bed, Johnnie.

JOHNNIE I can look after masel'.

MAGDALENE What's up wi you?

JOHNNIE (*Sitting on armchair*) There's nothin up wi me.

MAGDALENE Well . . . You'll be a'right?

JOHNNIE Sure I'll be all right – I can fight anybody in this building.

(*MAGDALENE looks at him for a moment*)

MAGDALENE The wife up the stair died the night.

JOHNNIE (*Pause*) Well, that's good! I hope that everybody up this stair dies before the mornin.

MAGDALENE (*Her anger has been slowly rising*) Och you . . . Watch ye don't fa' in the fire . . .

(*She exits*)

MR MUTRIE My God, wummin! Can ye no' heat your feet before you come intae bed?

(*Pause – the gas starts to go down*)

JOHNNIE (*Shouting drunkenly*) Heh, a penny for the gas! Heh, a penny for the gas!

(*MAGDALENE looks in. Exits. Pause. Gas goes up again. JOHNNIE looks up at the light.*)

And the Lord said: 'Let there be light', an' then somebody put a penny in the gas!

(*He takes off his cap and throws it away – looks at the fire. Pause.*)

I'll do the bastard up in style! (*There is another pause*)

MR MUTRIE (*Singing*) For ye'll tak the high road . . . (*Etc.*)

(*JOHNNIE lifts the poker, flings it violently at the MUTRIES' door*)

JOHNNIE Shut your big mouth, Mutrie! People bawlin their heads off frae mornin to night.

(*He runs his hands through his hair; he is obviously thinking of NORA.*

He is sorry for himself, and there is a pause as he composes his thoughts. Enter PEGGIE dressed in her night attire.)

PEGGIE Johnnie!

(He lets his head sink back in the chair: answers softly)

JOHNNIE What?

PEGGIE What's wrong? *(She moves over to him)* You were shoutin.

JOHNNIE I'm drunk, Peggie.

PEGGIE Naw! You're no'. What made you go on the bash? Did some o' the boys dare you?

JOHNNIE Naw! I just took the notion.

PEGGIE It's a' right noo an' again at the new year – but . . .

JOHNNIE You think I'm jist a wee boy, daen't ye? I'm no' – I'm a man – I'll be twenty next month!

PEGGIE *(Lifts poker over to fire. He is watching her.)* Are ye cauld? *(She pokes the fire)* You should go tae bed. Peter was looking for ye.

JOHNNIE Was he? Well, Peter can have a go any time he fancies one! Personally I'm goin to do him – I'm gonny give him the business.

(He puts his hand inside his jacket, takes out razor, opens it, staggers across stage. She sees it.)

PEGGIE *Johnnie*!

JOHNNIE *(Viciously)* Aye! I'm gonny do him!

PEGGIE He was sorry: he left you this shirt. *(She gets it)*

JOHNNIE You givin us the patter? *(Examines shirt, throws it away)* An old rag!

(She picks it up)

PEGGIE Johnnie, give me that razor!

JOHNNIE Ye can come and get it, well.

(She approaches, cautiously takes it. She puts razor on mantelpiece. He sits down, catches her round the waist, pulls her onto his knee in the chair.)

PEGGIE Och, cut it out, Johnnie!

JOHNNIE Can I no' talk tae ye?

PEGGIE You don't need tae wrestle me onto the chair.

MR MUTRIE *(From room)* Well, get *ower* a bit! You'll have me through the wa' in a minute!

PEGGIE He's drunk.

JOHNNIE So am I. Did you no' get a drink? *(She goes to move)* Sit still!

PEGGIE Don't be daft, Johnnie! What would anybody think if they saw us like this?

JOHNNIE *Us!* A lovely wee word that, isn't it? *Us.* You an' me.

PEGGIE Mrs Gilmour might come back.

JOHNNIE Tae hell wi Mrs Gilmour – tae hell wi them a' – I don't like Mrs Gilmour's way o' talkin tae you.

PEGGIE *(Softly)* Dae ye no', Johnnie?

JOHNNIE Sometimes I'd like tae spit right in her eye just tae show her that she's no' such a big noise.

PEGGIE It's just her way. Now let me up, Johnnie!

JOHNNIE Sit still. *(He bends her back till her head rests on the crook of his arm)* You were peeved the night.

PEGGIE Was I?

JOHNNIE When the Irisher spoke about the soup – mind?

PEGGIE Oh! Her?

JOHNNIE It wasna so daft. But I like you, Peggie, even if you don't gimme soup.

PEGGIE You're a nice boy, Johnnie. Let me up!

JOHNNIE Just make up your mind tae sit here – cause you're no' gettin up.

PEGGIE *(Smiles, puts her head back)* You're a silly wee boy. If I just was to open my mouth and let oot wan scream – the kitchen would be full o' people in two jiffies.

JOHNNIE You wouldna dae that.

PEGGIE If you didna let me up I might.

(He eases back – she looks up at him and moves to rise – he puts his two arms round her and kisses her – puts her back into her original position)

JOHNNIE There's something nice about you, Peggie. *(He puts hand on her waist)* You've got nae claes on.

PEGGIE Aye, it's a habit o' mine! – I aye take ma claes aff before I go to bed. What's up wi you the night?

JOHNNIE Reilly, he's an owld bully.

PEGGIE He didna really mean it.

(Pause)

JOHNNIE You know, Peggie, I'd marry you, only in another twenty-one years you'll be sixty and I'll just be forty.

PEGGIE I could be your mammy. *(Smiles)*

JOHNNIE I wish you were, Peggie. I'd be good tae you. *(She puts her hand to the back of his head)* You're nice.

PEGGIE If I was your mammy you wouldna have me sittin on your knee.

JOHNNIE Maybe I would. *(Kisses her again)*

PEGGIE They're no' nice to you here, Johnnie.

JOHNNIE You're nice an' that's a' I'm carin aboot. You know sometimes

I wish that I could get away tae the country – like it is at the Berries. Sometimes I wonder why I don't go – you don't need a lot of money to live in the country. Don't you no?

PEGGIE That's what I'd like tae.

MR MUTRIE *(Shouting)* Well, take your big ear away – I've got tae breathe somewhere.

PEGGIE Let me go, Johnnie. Somebody'll see us. Here's somebody comin.

(He holds her tighter)

JOHNNIE Let them come.

PEGGIE Johnnie.

(Pause)

JOHNNIE How could you and me no' go away tae the country?

PEGGIE We'll go tomorrow. Now let me go.

JOHNNIE Do you like me, Peggie?

PEGGIE Aye, I like ye, Johnnie – I wouldna let anybody hurt you – you're such a wee boy.

(She raises her head, kisses him. She smiles at him, he bends her back and kisses her. She puts her arms round his neck and holds him tightly. He withdraws his face – his hair is disarranged – he is breathing heavily. She is suddenly alarmed and struggles to free herself.)

MR MUTRIE *(Singing)* The sun shines bright on Loch Lomond . . .

(PEGGIE runs to her room)

And me and my true love will never meet again,
On the bonnie, bonnie banks o' Loch Lomond.

(JOHNNIE sits as she has left him – his hair still disarranged. Pause. He rises unsteadily, screws out light.)

For me and my true love will never meet again . . .

(JOHNNIE moves over to PEGGIE's door. Exits – door shuts – lighting fades out. Slow curtain.)

CURTAIN

END OF ACT III

ACT IV

It is Saturday evening shortly after six. MR MUTRIE is sitting with his hands stuffed into his pockets and his legs stuck out in front of him. He has on his cap and muffler and is disconsolate because he is broke and cannot melt MRS MUTRIE's resolve. As the curtain rises, he is scowling and a pause ensues before MRS MUTRIE comes out with a loaf and bread-knife to cut it on the kitchen table.

MRS MUTRIE You're needin tae fix the leg o' that table in there, it coggles every time you touch it. *(She cuts the bread)* Ye're a helluva selfish man, Wullie – I've had nae pay aff ye fur a fortnight and ye sit there wi a petted lip on ye for beer.

MR MUTRIE Aw, shut your mouth! Buy yoursel a chapel if you want tae preach.

MRS MUTRIE It's a'right for you – you go out an' in and don't care about anythin. It's me that gets aw the worry, goin standin in lines.

MR MUTRIE What the hell are you cuttin a' the bread fur? *(She stops and looks at him, then continues cutting: she now has four slices cut)* Bread and margarine, again!

MRS MUTRIE If ye were hauf a man ye'd gie yoursel a shake – we'll be livin for the rest o' our lives in a room.

MR MUTRIE *(Embarrassed)* Awch! We'll get a hoose!

MRS MUTRIE Before ye can get a hoose you've got tae have a month's rent a' in wan bit.

(She exits)

MR MUTRIE Look, Jean. Just a coupla bob!

(Pause. He rises and goes to the window and looks out. Then he starts to go through his pockets slowly – finds nothing – returns and sits on his armchair and lies back.)

God's truth! Saturday night!

(Pause. Enter MRS MUTRIE.)

MRS MUTRIE I've got a wee bit cheese there, Wullie, would you like it?

MR MUTRIE Aye.

MRS MUTRIE *(Sadly)* I havena got it, Wullie. *(She goes over to him)*

MR MUTRIE *(Pause)* I'll pay you it back.

MRS MUTRIE What wi?

MR MUTRIE Och, never mind it! – you ask too many questions. *(Huffily)* You're like the coo that gies the can o' milk then kicks it owre wi its fut.

MRS MUTRIE Ah, ye crabbit owl midden! – you'll no' get the shillin for your cheek. *(She moves to the exit, stops)* A body wouldna know *how* to take *you*.

(She exits. MR MUTRIE sits moodily while she is gone. She enters.)

MR MUTRIE What could you buy wi a shillin, anyway?

MRS MUTRIE By God! I'd like tae buy you something wi a shillin – but I'd need tae sign for it at the chemists – sittin there like Gilbert the Filbert.

MR MUTRIE You're poisonin me quick enough, woman – I . . . *(He stops and looks at her, drops his gaze)* Ach! – Never mind the money, Jean – I'll be back at my work next week.

(She comes over and sits beside him)

MRS MUTRIE I wish we could get away oot o' here. That war and that bombin and things – we didna know we were well aff in our wee hoose!

MR MUTRIE Neither we did.

MRS MUTRIE I fell asleep on the chair there this afternoon – I'm getting gey done, Wullie – I dreamt I was back in our young days – just like it used to be.

MR MUTRIE Must have been the cabbage an' ribs – it aye makes *you* dream!

MRS MUTRIE You ate mair than me.

MR MUTRIE You know, Jean, I wish I had a lot o' money – I'd buy you something all to yoursel.

MRS MUTRIE Would you, Wullie? *(Smiles)* What would you buy me?

MR MUTRIE I don't know – did you no' dream I was buyin you something?

MRS MUTRIE *(Smiling)* Naw! I dreamt that you an' me were walkin alang a long road – and you took my hand just like yon day we were at Rothesay – an' we were lookin for somethin awful bad, I can mind we were in an awful state – and it was away at the end of this road – but the mair we walked, the further away it was. And then we met an auld man wi a red coat, an' he tellt us – 'You'll never get tae the end o' the road if ye dawner' he says. 'Ye'll need tae run' he says. 'Ye'll need tae run till you think your heart's gonny burst'. He says 'You're young – you can do it easy when people are young: they can dae anything – they can even change the hale world.'

MR MUTRIE That was daft.

MRS MUTRIE You werena listenin tae him – you just kept lookin at me – I kept tellin ye tae look at him – he was like your faither – an' he kept sayin – 'Run while you're young!'

MR MUTRIE Did you run?

MRS MUTRIE *(Sadly)* Naw! I woke up then an' I was an owld woman again.

MR MUTRIE What was it that was at the end of the road?

MRS MUTRIE I don't know – I canny remember.

MR MUTRIE Was it a big tree?

MRS MUTRIE Naw, it was happiness.

MR MUTRIE *(Smiling)* Oh, what about that bob?

(He lies back on the chair, looks all round the apartment)

MRS MUTRIE I'll need tae watch and keep something – I promised tae put a shillin tae a wreath for Mrs Potter.

(She gives him the shilling. He is immediately a man of some importance. He rises.)

MR MUTRIE You know, Jean, these houses are fine big places – an' yet they're slums. Even the new houses are slums! It must be the people, Jean! The papers used tae crack baurs about them keepin the coal in the bath – an' the women gaun about wi their shawls.

MRS MUTRIE It takes a brave woman tae be different fae her neighbours. Many a woman happed a big family in the wan shawl. The slums arena' the mark o' the people – it's poverty that makes the slums. *(She exits, stops)* I wish tae God I had a bath the noo – wi a bag o' coal in it!

(Enter AHMED and MAGDALENE. MAGDALENE is dressed 'in the height of fashion' – the 'Paraffin ile' as Johnnie might call it. It is a new outfit. She is flushed and happy and just a wee bit embarrassed at her unaccustomed, but wonderful, appearance. AHMED is like a dog with two tails. He is radiating waves of good humour.)

AHMED *(He is talking as he enters)* Good fun! Good fun! Laff alla time, laff alla time!

MAGDALENE *(To WULLIE, shyly)* Hello, Wullie!

(MR MUTRIE sits up: his jaw drops in amazement)

MR MUTRIE Magdalene! *(He smiles. He looks at her feet and back to her face)* Well! I'll be damned!

MRS MUTRIE Ye're lovely, Magdalene. Oh, my, ye suit it that well, tae! My!

AHMED Get married, haw, haw!

MRS MUTRIE Did ye get everything fixed up?

MAGDALENE Aye. *(She smiles)* A week'n Friday.

MRS MUTRIE My, whit a difference it makes! Would ye like a cup o' tea?

MAGDALENE Naw. We got our tea high class. *(She sits down and takes off her gloves)* We went to Woolworth's. Did I show ye my ring?

(They look)

AHMED *(To MAGDALENE)* Johnnie no' got in dumplin.

MAGDALENE I was kiddin him that he got it in a dumplin.

MR MUTRIE That's a beauty – you'd get a few bob on that in the pawn.

MAGDALENE Johnnie bought me the costume tae.
MRS MUTRIE *(Slapping him on the back)* Good for you, Johnnie.
AHMED Good for Johnnie. Laff alla time; laff alla time. Good!

(He is almost giggling. PEGGIE enters: she is sad looking. She stops when she sees MAGDALENE. MAGDALENE surveys her with a prim smile, as much as to say 'Well, don't you think I'm beautiful?' PEGGIE's eyes open wide, her gaze softens and her arms go round MAGDALENE's shoulders – smiles and kisses her.)

PEGGIE My wee Meg! It's lovely. *(MAGDALENE stands up and PEGGIE hugs her, holds her at arm's length, then smiles and says sadly)* Oh, Meg! I wish I was you! My God, the stars are out the night.
MAGDALENE D'you like it?
PEGGIE *(She turns to AHMED)* You're a lucky man, Johnnie.
MRS MUTRIE He's a nice fella.
AHMED Johnnie make party nex' Friday. Good! Laff alla time.
MR MUTRIE Sure we'll have a party. *(To MAGDALENE)* I'd like to buy ye a present, hen; but ye know I've been on the Panel – maybe next week.
PEGGIE Next week?
MAGDALENE *(She nods – flushes)* Aye! Week'n Friday.
PEGGIE You should take it aff now – save it.
MRS MUTRIE Aye, keep it good – it's lovely.
MAGDALENE I'm chuckin my job – I can get a better job noo I'm dressed.
MR MUTRIE Is that the teapot bilin?
MRS MUTRIE Oh!

(She exits quickly)

MAGDALENE *(To AHMED)* Sit down, Johnnie. I'm goin to change my claes.
AHMED Keep on! Nice!
MAGDALENE *(Hesitates)* I'll put it on again. *(To PEGGIE)* We're goin tae Brigton the night tae see my auntie.
PEGGIE Oh, she'll be surprised.
MAGDALENE She'll no half!

(She smiles at AHMED. Exits.)

PEGGIE Feelin good, Johnnie? *(She smiles)*
MR MUTRIE Aye! It's a rare feelin – the world would be a helluva lot of fun if it lasted.

(Claps AHMED's shoulder as he passes. Exits. PEGGIE sits down – AHMED moves round and sits on the table swinging his legs.)

AHMED Peggie no' get married? *(Smiles)*

PEGGIE Maybe I will, Johnnie, if I can get a man. *(She smiles)*

AHMED Get Indian man! *Good!* White man lazy bastid. *(She laughs)*

PEGGIE Aye, ye're right there. Some o' them are lazy so and so's.

AHMED *(Comes off table as he hears outside door opening)* Johnnie come – I fix.

(PEGGIE puts her hand across her forehead. JOHNNIE does not appear. Pause.)

AHMED No Johnnie! Udder people. *(Flicks speck of dust from his leg)* Good! *(Smiles)*

PEGGIE You'll like being a married man, Johnnie?

AHMED Good – get married – worried for rent, mooch a living! *(Demonstrates with his hand to his eyes, tears flowing)* Udder times: s'good!

PEGGIE Aye, you're right there, Johnnie – life's an up an' doon affair. I suppose we wouldna recognise the good if we didna have the bad. *(He does not understand)* You know. *(Holds up her right hand)* Good! *(Holds up her left hand)* Bad! *(Puts her two hands together)* Good! *(She smiles. He nods.)*

AHMED *(Face straightens)* In India, Bombay . . . *(He goes through the same motions)* Good! Bad! Bad! *(Enter NORA)* Hello, Nora! *(Quietly smiling)*

NORA *(She isn't very sure of herself as she thinks the others might know of the previous night's scene with JOHNNIE and her father)* Hello, Johnnie!

PEGGIE Hello, Nora! Haven't seen you all day.

NORA I was readin.

AHMED No' go to Palace? Lovely picture – laff alla time, last night. *(Smiles)* Laff alla time.

NORA *(To PEGGIE)* That's 'Murder at Miami' he's talking about.

PEGGIE It's good to be able to laugh at everything – sometimes I wish I could laugh at everything.

NORA What's up?

PEGGIE Ach! If I was a drinkin woman, I'd go on the spree – there's nothin worse than being fed up without a good reason.

NORA *(Sitting down)* We didna get the new hoose – my ma has to go back on Tuesday. This is a terrible place to live. *(She looks around)* I bet you if these wa's could speak, they'd tell a queer story. *(PEGGIE looks at her, thinking of the previous night)* A story of the Gorbals!

PEGGIE Ach! things are pretty much the same nae matter where you live – The Gorbals Story – The Springburn Story – The Maryhill Story – Poor people never have enough nae matter where they live!

(Enter MAGDALENE. She is wearing a cross-over overall over her skirt. AHMED rises when she enters, smiles.)

MAGDALENE Hello, hen. D'ye like my ring? *(Shows her ring)*

NORA *(Looks at it wide-eyed, looks up at MAGDALENE)* An engagement ring! *(She swallows a plunker and sighs)* Gosh, it's lovely!

MAGDALENE *(Laughing)* I'll gie you a wee shot o' it when *he* turns his back.

PEGGIE You an' me seem to be on the same shelf, hen, eh?

NORA I don't know.

PEGGIE The only ring I'll ever get'll be wi a ha'penny sooker. What about the tea?

(Enter JOHNNIE – he has some coloured Sports Finals *folded under his arm and a fag end in his mouth. His hands are buried in his trouser pockets.)*

MAGDALENE Johnnie an' me had wur tea up the toon.

PEGGIE *(With mock emphasis)* Oh! Lady Muck! Did ye no' bring us hame a cake in your bag?

(She sees JOHNNIE and is quiet)

JOHNNIE *(To MAGDALENE)* Hello! You've got your face washed!

MAGDALENE You an' me arena' speakin, Johnnie Martin.

JOHNNIE What's up now?

MAGDALENE Ye canny talk tae me like that an' get away wi it.

JOHNNIE *(Taking papers from beneath his arm and slamming them on the dresser)* You're nuts! I was only kiddin!

MAGDALENE Fine way tae kid, that! Bitin the nose aff me!

JOHNNIE Aw! Nark it, nark it, ye daft beggar!

MAGDALENE Well, ye might at least apologise!

JOHNNIE *(To AHMED, as he sits down on the sink)* Hey, Johnnie – You're tart's daft! *(To her)* What have I to apologise for?

MAGDALENE You called me horse face!

JOHNNIE *(Amazed)* Me?

MAGDALENE Aye, you! You were drunk.

(NORA turns round and looks at him)

AHMED *(Smiles to JOHNNIE)* Alla time, plenty money – white man drunk – lazy bastid!

JOHNNIE Hey you. Hey. You never changed that tie for me – you'll have me goin about like Mick O'Casey.

AHMED Nice tie – plenty sell – eighteen penny.

JOHNNIE You mean eighteen-a-penny!

AHMED *(Smiles and nods)* Aye! eighteen penny.

MAGDALENE You're changin the subject.

JOHNNIE Awright, I apologise – If I could mind o' saying it, I could apologise better.

MAGDALENE *(Looks at him suspecting a leg-pull)* That's a' right, Johnnie. *(She smiles)* You wance tellt me I looked like the second favourite for the Derby, but that was jist in fun.

JOHNNIE *(To NORA and PEGGIE)* How about a fish supper, you two? *(He is uneasy)*

NORA I had my tea.

> *(PEGGIE does not look at him)*

JOHNNIE *(To PEGGIE)* I . . . I'm sorry to you tae, Peggie.

MAGDALENE What did you call her? *(Smiles)*

JOHNNIE *(To PEGGIE)* Come on! What dae ye say – fish supper?

PEGGIE No, thanks – I've got something to fry.

JOHNNIE Aw, Hell!

PEGGIE *(Looks round at him and sees he is miserable and ill-at-ease)* I'll be makin tea in a wee while.

JOHNNIE *(Looks at her, then looks at NORA)* Aye, sure. Are you for a fag? *(Goes over and gives PEGGIE a cigarette)* I . . . you went out early this morning. *(PEGGIE looks at him and holds out her cigarette for a light. He lights a match and lights it for her. Smiles and realises he hasn't offered cigarettes to the others.)* Huh! *(Smiles)* Fag, Mag?

MAGDALENE I've got fags in my bag.

JOHNNIE Take wan! *(She does)*

MAGDALENE Thanks!

> *(Enter MR MUTRIE. He is searching his waistcoat pockets.)*

JOHNNIE *(To AHMED)* Fag, Johnnie?

> *(AHMED smiles and takes one. MR MUTRIE looks hungrily at the packet – his fingers are now at rest.)*

JOHNNIE I suppose you'll want one, tae?

MR MUTRIE *(Taking cigarette)* Did you have a good day, the day?

JOHNNIE A helluva lot you care! When are you gonny start buying a paper on a Saturday – then I might have a good day.

MR MUTRIE Everything comes to he who waits.

> *(MAGDALENE has lit a match – they all light up)*

JOHNNIE I brought ye the paper – that's the last. Next Saturday ye buy it!

MR MUTRIE You're just like a' the rest o' the capitalists! *(Sits down beside NORA)* You're helluva quiet, hen.

NORA It's him.

50

JOHNNIE Oh, the Queen's won! Mind I tellt ye?

MR MUTRIE *(Without enthusiasm)* Did they?

AHMED *(Smiling)* A lady fair – like Johnnie picture.

MR MUTRIE *(Puzzled)* What?

AHMED You do bad – you do good.

MR MUTRIE *(Does not understand)* Sure! Sure! You're a helluva blether, Johnnie.

PEGGIE *(To NORA)* Lost your tongue, tonight?

NORA Naw! *(Smiles)*

JOHNNIE Are ye no' gonny see your coupon?

MR MUTRIE *(Blowing a cloud of smoke)* I like a smoke after I have a tightner – coupon? *(Looks at the papers on the dresser)* Aye, I'll get it! *(Rises, exits to room)*

PEGGIE *(To NORA)* What's up, hen?

NORA Ach! Days and days and days – every wan's the same – I wish my da was a gaffer or something!

(MAGDALENE starts to cough)

MAGDALENE Johnnie! *(Affected pathos)* Johnnie, where did ye get these fags?

JOHNNIE If so many people didna tap me, I could afford tae smoke 'Lucky Strike'. I smoke them in *bed*. *(He laughs)* I'm the only man in the building that's got nervous bugs.

MAGDALENE *(Looks at cigarette)* They must have a smoker's cough, too.

(Enter MR MUTRIE with his coupon, followed by MRS MUTRIE. She has two cups and saucers.)

MRS MUTRIE Nae wonder, well! – throwin money up in the air.

MR MUTRIE *(Turning on her)* For God's sake, shut up, wummin! A' you need is a lilt an' you go on like a barrel organ.

(MR MUTRIE lifts the paper. Enter HECTOR in shirt sleeves with towel, etc.)

Hello, Hector! I'm jist staunin up for my rights.

JOHNNIE Sit down.

PEGGIE Hey, Wullie. Do I still get that fur coat, Wullie?

MR MUTRIE No' this week; but, the first time I win the prize . . . I'll . . .

JOHNNIE *(Smiling)* Ah bet you don't. You'll wait till you win it the second time.

MAGDALENE *(Prim smile to HECTOR)* It would be kinda late when you got in this morning, Mr McCallum?

HECTOR *(To MRS MUTRIE)* After you, Jean. What you sayin, Meg?

MAGDALENE I said it would be late when you got in this morning.

HECTOR *(Rubs his nose and smiles)* The spies have been busy.

MRS MUTRIE *(She has rinsed the cups, she stands back)* There y'are, Hector!

HECTOR *(To MAGDALENE)* You couldn't have been sleepin very sound, eh?

JOHNNIE Were you darnin, hen, sittin up knittin wee white things?

MAGDALENE You're a helluva fella, Johnnie.

HECTOR What's up wi the wean?

JOHNNIE What's up wi you, Nora?

NORA *(Looks up at him)* You didny talk tae *me*!

(JOHNNIE smiles)

JOHNNIE I thought . . . *(He catches PEGGIE's eye and falters)* I thought – maybe you were in the huff.

HECTOR By God! that watter's cauld!

PEGGIE That's the beauty o' the new hooses – hot watter in the well – and a bath in the hoose.

MRS MUTRIE There used tae be hot water in this house tae – but they say the biler got burst about ten years ago – these used tae be mansions.

JOHNNIE Well, the bugs don't wear collars and ties noo, anyway.

MR MUTRIE Bugs! – I drapped two in the fire last night: nearly blew the back out the grate!

NORA Well, we've got nae bugs in our room. My da plastered a' the holes and painted the flair wi creosote.

MRS MUTRIE Aye! *(She smiles)* They're chummy wee hooses. If you don't need Keating's Powder – you need Rodine!

(They laugh at her joke)

PEGGIE Aye, a fixed bayonet would be a gey handy thing, tae.

(She looks at JOHNNIE and blows out a puff of smoke. He is very uncomfortable.)

HECTOR *(Drying his neck)* What's this, Wullie?

MR MUTRIE Fitba' coupon.

JOHNNIE *(Covering his embarrassment)* How are ye gettin on wi it?

NORA Johnnie! *(He looks round)* I was . . . askin my da if I could get tae the dancin the night.

JOHNNIE *(Looks coldly at her. Embarrassed, he talks out the side of his mouth.)* What'd he say?

NORA He said I couldna go mysel.

(JOHNNIE looks at her, turns abruptly towards MR MUTRIE)

MAGDALENE Here, could we no . . . *(Looks round and smiles)* Could we no' a' go – well, I mean I'd go – so would Johnnie. *(AHMED smiles)* Dancin, Johnnie?

AHMED Good! Silk stockins for dancin, good!

MAGDALENE That's right. What the lasses buy the stockings for. How about you, Peggie?

PEGGIE *(Smiling)* My dancin's ten years oot o' date – you swing and jive an' things. Naw, no' me.

MAGDALENE What do you say, Johnnie? That would be a foursome!

JOHNNIE I don't know. What would your auld man say if *I* went wi ye?

NORA *(Smiles)* He might be angry.

JOHNNIE Right! I'll take ye: but mind, I'm gaun tae *dance*.

MAGDALENE What aboot you, Hector? Can you no' dance?

HECTOR Yon business, nowadays! – Yon's no' dancin!

JOHNNIE What do you call dancin? *(He pirouettes daintily in old-fashioned waltz style)* Yon cairry on! Ye haud your partner away oot as faur as you can. Nuts tae yon! I like to get chummy.

HECTOR Does it no' embarrass ye, cuddlin intae them in public?

JOHNNIE Not at all, Hector. Ye jist keep talkin – bumming your chat intae their ear.

(He grabs MAGDALENE and demonstrates a dance, talks in a sort of strangled voice)

Ye just give them the patter like this –

MRS MUTRIE That's no' decent!

(He glares at her. She smiles at his fooling.)

JOHNNIE Are ye workin? *(MAGDALENE laughs)* Stop laughin. *(They continue)* You're a smashin dancer. Is that your pal wi the green frock? Right wee neb – she's no' like you – you're class. Is anybody seein ye hame? Oh, ye come from Scotstoun – that's a peety – I've got an awful early rise in the mornin. *(He breaks apart and says to HECTOR)* See! What about you, Wullie? D'you no' fancy gaun to the jiggin? *(MR MUTRIE does not answer)* Wullie!

MRS MUTRIE *(Puzzled)* What's up wi you, Wullie?

MR MUTRIE *(Turns slowly to her – looks back at the table slowly, and speaks softly)* Ma coupon!

HECTOR How did you make oot this week, Wullie?

MR MUTRIE *(Slowly – slightly stunned)* Ma coupon – every one right!

JOHNNIE What! *(Dives at paper and compares them)*

MAGDALENE Let us see it!

MRS MUTRIE *(Anxiously)* What is it, Wullie?

(He looks at her sadly)

JOHNNIE XX-81! By God! His coupon's up!

HECTOR Aye! You've got it!

NORA What is it?

JOHNNIE His coupon's up! Hey, Wullie! *(Excited)* Your coupon's up! My God, look at him!

MRS MUTRIE Oh, Wullie! We can get a hoose noo!

HECTOR Aye! Ye can get a hoose if ye've got money.

MR MUTRIE I didna – I didna post the coupon.

MRS MUTRIE *(Sadly)* What was that, Wullie?

MR MUTRIE I didna post the coupon. *(He runs his hands through his hair)* I bought you a fish supper wi the money.

MRS MUTRIE *(Sits down, puts the two cups and saucers on her lap as though they had become too heavy to hold)* A fish supper! *(She looks at him and smiles sadly)* Ach poor Wullie! Ye tried that hard tae.

HECTOR Never mind, Wullie – I've got a bob or two. We'll have a good drink.

PEGGIE Never mind, Wullie – ye done it once so ye can dae it again.

JOHNNIE God Blimey! Would that no' scunner ye? *(AHMED laughs)* What the hell are you laughin at?

(MR REILLY enters downstairs and stumbles over ash-can)

MR REILLY Who the Hell left that ash-can there?

MRS REILLY *(Coming downstairs)* Ah did.

MR REILLY My God, woman, isn't there a big enough midden down the stairs for it?

MRS REILLY Be God, there's a bigger midden up here and ah'm nut mentioning any names.

(She lifts the can and exits downstairs)

(Enter MR REILLY)

MR REILLY Ah, there ye are. Nora! Your ma an' me's gaun roon tae the pictures. Are ye comin?

HECTOR Pictures? *(Raises one eyebrow)*

AHMED Lovely picture! Laff alla time!

MR REILLY *(Looks all round and sees WULLIE)* What's adae wi *ye,* Wullie?

HECTOR He marked up his coupon all correct and didna post it.

(MR REILLY laughs)

MR REILLY 'Clare to God, did ever ye hear the likes o' it? Never luk at the results if ye don't post it! It's terrible bad luck. Are you comin, Nora?

NORA Er – Magdalene and Ahmed are goin to the dancin.

MR REILLY *(Goes forward to JOHNNIE and offers his hand)* I wouldn't

be half a man if I couldn't be admittin I was wrong. *(JOHNNIE looks at him)* Wull ye not give us a shake o' your han'?
NORA *(She whispers)* G'wan, Johnnie.
JOHNNIE Well – *(Takes hand)* I'll consider it. *(He smiles)* I'll shake hauns while I'm considerin.
MR REILLY That wummin in there gets me intae a state beefin out her like an air raid syreen.
NORA Johnnie's gaun to the dancin, too.
MR REILLY Ye'll luk after her, now – mind them chair gangs an' things.
MRS REILLY *(Off stage)* Are ye comin, Peter? There'll be a queue.
MR REILLY Sure I'm comin. I hope there is a queue – gives you a grand excuse t'nip in fur a pint. *(Raising his voice)* Aye! I'm comin. So long! *(As he exits)* Watch yersel, hen.
MR MUTRIE The first time I don't post it, it comes off.
PEGGIE Ach, well, you'll maybe get it next week.
HECTOR What was the prize last week?
MR MUTRIE *(Quietly)* Nine hunner an' sixty-three quid *(Rises)* sixteen shillins.

(He exits)

MRS MUTRIE Ach! It'll come again. Life wouldna be worth livin if you couldna believe in the impossible. It would have been nice – we could have been rich a' wur days. I think I'll go in an' make him another wee cup o' tea.

(She exits)

PEGGIE Poor sowl!
NORA Imagine winnin nine hunner an' sixty-three quid!
HECTOR Ah, well! *(Smiles)* It's aye something to even get near it. I'll gie ye a shout, Wullie.

(Exits)

MAGDALENE Well, I don't know what I put on an overall for – I've got nae work tae dae. *(To AHMED)* We'll go to my auntie's the morra night. *(His face straightens)*
PEGGIE Take him tonight. Let him meet your auntie.

(MAGDALENE looks at her, then at JOHNNIE and NORA – a look of understanding crosses her face)

MAGDALENE Aw! We'll go tonight, Johnnie, eh? Good fun!
AHMED Good fun! Laff alla time! Laff alla time!
MAGDALENE That's right – laff alla time.
AHMED Good! Good!

(Doorbell jangles)

PEGGIE That's your faither back again – it must have come on to rain. *(She makes to rise)*
AHMED No go! Johnnie go!

(He smiles – exits)

JOHNNIE He's come back for his goloshes.
NORA Well, he's got rheumatism in his ankles – why should he no' wear goloshes?
JOHNNIE *(Laughs)* Elastic-sided boots.
MAGDALENE You're a helluva fella, Johnnie. D'ye never get fed up kiddin?
PEGGIE Aye, but he can't take it!

(Enter AHMED, backing in – he is followed by a couple in search of a room)

AHMED No' can tell, missus – come in ben hoose.
PEGGIE What is it, Johnnie? *(To WOMAN)* Who are you lookin for, missus?
WOMAN Mrs Gilmour. *(Apologetically)* We were tellt tae see her.
PEGGIE She's no' in.
WOMAN It was about a room.

(Enter MRS MUTRIE)

MRS MUTRIE *(She is carrying empty sugar bowl)* Peggie, hen, lend me a wee drap sugar. I havena got a grain. What is it? *(Not unkindly)* What is it, missus?
WOMAN We've been looking since twelve o'clock the day.
PEGGIE They're lookin for a room.

(JOHNNIE has sat down beside NORA and is whispering in her ear)

MAN My wife's no' well, missus. We're lookin for a room – we've been lookin a' day. We were tellt tae try here. We wouldna be any bother, we could sleep anywhere.
MRS MUTRIE Well, ye see, it's like this. . . .
MAN We'd sleep on the flair, missus!

CURTAIN

MEN SHOULD WEEP

A PLAY IN THREE ACTS

by

Ena Lamont Stewart

Men Should Weep was first performed at the Troon Concert Hall early in Jaunary 1947, and then at the Athenaeum Theatre, Glasgow, starting on the 30th, with the following cast:

MAGGIE MORRISON . . . . Bertha Cooper
JOHN MORRISON, *her husband* . . . . Charles Dinning
GRANNY, *his mother* . . . . Anna Welsh
Their children: ALEX . . . . Tom Scott
               JENNY. . . . . Shena Dalgleish
               EDIE. . . . . Kate Donaldson
               ERNEST . . . . Joe Robley
The voices of the younger Morrison children: MARINA
                                    CHRISTOPHER
LILY GIBB, *Maggie's sister* . . . . Maisie Hill
ISA, *Alex's wife* . . . . Lilian Paterson
Neighbours: MRS WILSON . . . . Alrae Edwards
            MRS HARRIS . . . . Elspeth Cameron
            MRS BONE . . . . Agnes Murray
LIZZIE MORRISON, *Granny's daughter-in-law* . . . . Elizabeth Gray
1st REMOVAL MAN . . . . Edward Boyd
2nd REMOVAL MAN . . . . Arnold Dunn

Directed by . . . . Robert Mitchell
Stage Director . . . . Ian Dalgleish
Stage Manager . . . . Alrae Edwards
Costume Mistress . . . . Julia Wallace
Property Mistress . . . . Hetty Van Dam
Lighting. . . . . James Dunbar
Production Manager . . . . Leon Schuster
Décor . . . . Elizabeth Low

ACT I

Scene 1

The scene is the same throughout – the kitchen of the Morrisons' three-apartment flat in the East End of Glasgow.

The action passes during a year in the 1930s.

There are two entrances, one right back, leading to the small lobby; one left, leading to the bedroom. There is a window right, with sink underneath, and flanking this the usual kitchen dresser. The dresser and a table, centre, are piled high with a miscellaneous collection of household and personal effects. Back centre there is an old-fashioned kitchen range, across which hangs a row of well-worn nappies. Left, there is a recess, bed, and above it, a cupboard. Any other touches can be left to the imagination of the Producer.

An evening in July.

When the curtain rises, MARINA and CHRISTOPHER, the owner of the nappies, are asleep in the bed. These children are heard, but are not seen. GRANNY is sitting, well wrapped up in old shawls and blankets drooling over the last of a 'black strippit ba''. All that can be seen of MAGGIE is her posterior, as she hangs out of the window.

MAGGIE *(At window)* Edie! Ernest! Wull yous two come in oot o' that when ye're tellt? If I've got tae cry on ye again, it'll be the worse for ye, I'm tellin ye. *(Shuts window)* Whit a life! *(She sinks down on chair and yawns widely)*

GRANNY *(Rocking herself)* Eh deary! Eh deary deary me! It's a sad sad life! *(She sings to herself in an old cracked voice)*

MAGGIE Oh Goad! I've you tae pit tae bed tae . . . here! Cut oot the music, Granny, I'm no fit for it the night. It's time you wis in yer bed. *(Bawling)* Time you wis in yer bed! Oh aye! Ye hear me a'right.

GRANNY No yet, Maggie. The nicht's ower lang when ye're aul' . . .

MAGGIE Oh I cannae be as aul as I feel then, for the nicht's a hell o' a sight tae short for me. Seems tae me I'm no sooner asleep than I've got tae get up again. It's a'right for you, singin tae yersel. If ye wis some use in the hoose it wouldnae be sae bad havin tae keep ye.

GRANNY That's right! Kest up whit ye're daein for me! *(Whining and rocking herself)* Oh! It's a terrible thing when ye're aul' and naebody wants ye. Naebody loves me! Oh, it's time I wisnae here!

MAGGIE You've said it. *(Giving another prolonged yawn)* It's time I wisnae here tae, I should be reddin up the place a bit afore Lily comes in. It's jist yin thing efter anither a' day, and when ye pit yer feet up for a bit at night, ye cannae sit at peace for thinkin o' a' the things that's waitin tae be din. Right enough, if a wumman did everything that ought tae be din in a hoose she'd go on a' day and a' night till she drapped doon deid.

GRANNY Eh? Whit's that, Maggie? Wha's drapped doon deid?

MAGGIE Oh no you, worse luck. You'll no drap. You'll jist sit it oot, like it wis a second roon' o' the pictures.

GRANNY Oh ye neednae worry, I'll be awa soon. Awa tae ma last hame. Mebbe afore the morn . . . I've had a kind o' presentiment . . .

MAGGIE Och I've heard o' they presentiments afore . . .

GRANNY Ma life's ebbin awa . . . ebbin awa.

MAGGIE Och it's been ebbin ever since I met ye, but the tide aye seems tae come in again.

GRANNY Oh aye! Ye can mak fun o' me . . .

MAGGIE Mak' fun o' ye? Goad no! Ye're no joke.

GRANNY I ken hoo it is, Maggie . . . I'm jist a useless aul' wumman, takin up space . . . mebbe I'd better go back tae Lizzie's the morn.

MAGGIE Ye're no due at Lizzie's till the end o' the month, and she'll no tak ye back a day afore ye're due.

GRANNY Oh I'll no bother ony o' ye . . . I'll jist awa tae the Poorshoose, and they can bury me frae there, it's you the disgrace'll fa' on, no me.

MAGGIE Whit disgrace? Yin hoose is as good as anither for gettin nailed doon. (GRANNY starts to cry, MAGGIE rises and goes over to her) Awa! Granny! Can ye no tak a wee joke? I didnae mean it! I wis only kiddin! . . . ye ken John and me wouldnae send ye tae the Poorshoose . . . och come on, stop greetin noo . . . I wis only takin a rise oot o' ye . . . (As GRANNY wails louder) Aw shut up, Granny! It's the only pleasure I've got makin a bit o' fun . . . Goad knows there's little enough tae mak fun aboot in this midden. (As GRANNY continues to wail on a higher note) Aw here! Can it I said. Ye'll waken the weans. (GRANNY continues tae wail and CHRISTOPHER joins in) There noo! Whit did I tell ye! And him toothin tae! Ma coanscience! Ye're worse than anither wean. (Goes across to bed) Aw ma wee lamb!

(Makes soothing noises to CHRISTOPHER. Enter EDIE. She is about eleven years old, tall, skinny, and adenoidal. She wears a miscellaneous collection of cast-off adult clothing, and her stockings are down about her ankles.)

EDIE Ba! Ba! Ernest won't cub id. I told hib to, but he won't.

MAGGIE Oh ye're in are ye? Ye deserve a good wallopin, but I havnae the energy. Gie's ower the sugar basin. (EDIE locates the sugar basin after a hunt on the table and dresser. MAGGIE dips the baby's dummy into it, and sticks it into his mouth, the wails cease abruptly. To GRANNY:) See whit ye did noo, ye aul' pest! I'm gonnae pit ye tae yer bed.

EDIE Ba! Ba! I'b hungry, Ba!

MAGGIE Oh stummicks! Stummicks! Am I no sick o' yous and yer stummicks. Cut yersel a bit breid, and there's jeely in the jar.

GRANNY It seems a lang while since I had onythin tae eat. There wouldnae be a wee drap o' tea left in the pot?

MAGGIE No there wouldnae! I squeezed it dry for ye the last time. But I'll tell ye whit I'll dae, I'll mak ye a wee cup and tak it ben tae ye when ye're in bed, eh?

GRANNY Wull ye? A nice hot cup? Wi' sugar? And condensed mulk? And a wee bit breid tae dook?

MAGGIE Aye, if ye let me pit ye tae yer bed noo? *(GRANNY struggles up)* That's the girl! Ups-a-daisy! Edie, pit the kettle on, and then come and help me wi' yer granny.

EDIE Oh, Ba! Bust I?

MAGGIE Nae arguin.

MARINA *(Shouting from bed)* Mammy! Can I have a piece?

MAGGIE Are you wakened noo? The lugs you weans have on ye. Whit way can ye no sleep peaceful? Edie, get Marina a bit breid and jeely. And if ye drap the jeely on the bed, Marina, I'll gie ye the daein ye should hae got fir spillin yer cocoa last night. It's comin tae it, when a mither's that tired she cannae wallop her ain weans . . . nae wunner the papers is fu' o' juvenile delinquency.

(MAGGIE and GRANNY go off, left. EDIE puts on the kettle, cuts and spreads bread for Marina and takes it to her.)

EDIE Here ye are, Marina, watch oot noo! Ma's been waterin the jam again.

(There is a ring and knock at the door. EDIE goes off right, and lets in LILY GIBB, MAGGIE's sister. Lily is in her thirties, a sharp-tongued, disillusioned spinster. She was, in her youth, 'let down' by a man, and her consequent bitterness towards the sex is in no way helped by the fact that she works in a third-rate licensed hotel.)

EDIE *(As they enter)* She's just puttin Graddy tae bed. Sit doon, Auntie Lily.

LILY Ben ye go then, and tell her I'm here. *(Shouting)* Hullo, Maggie! I'm no offerin tae help wi Granny, I havnae brought ma ody-colong.

MARINA Hullo, Auntie Lily.

LILY *(Going over to bed)* Are you no sleepin yet? Whit are ye eatin? Breid and jam at this time o' night! Are ye no ashamed o' yersel? And ye're a' jammy . . . wait till I wipe yer fingers. *(She has a long hunt for a towel, the end of which she dips in water and wipes MARINA's hands)* There noo! You go off tae sleep.

(She stands in the middle of the room and surveys the muddle. She sighs, takes off her coat and ties the towel round her waist, then she rolls up her sleeves and wonders where to start. Off stage BERTIE who sleeps with ERNEST in the parlour starts to cough. It is a T.B. cough, and continues intermittently throughout the action of this scene. She takes from her shopping bag a tin of baked beans and a bottle of cough mixture and looks for a corner to lay them down, then she hunts for a teaspoon which she looks at distastefully, washes, and shakes dry.)

LILY *(At door)* Bertie dear! I'm comin ben tae see ye. I'm comin wi somethin nice tae stop yer nasty cough . . . *(Goes off with bottle and spoon)*

(MARINA starts to sing)

MARINA Have ye ever seen a dream . . . walkin?
      Well I did.
      Did ye ever seen a dream . . . talkin?
      Well I did.
      An' a Heaven in yer airms sayin?
      I love ye . . . I do
      And the dream that wis walkin
      And the dream that wis talkin . . .

(Enter MAGGIE like a tornado. She swoops down on the singer and extinguishes the song, then goes off again to the bedroom. There can be off-stage noises from Granny as she is undressed, at the wish of the Producer. After a moment MARINA begins a subdued continuation of the song, she goes on until LILY returns with bottle and spoon.)

MARINA Auntie Lily. I'm wantin a drink.
LILY Ye're no gettin one.
MARINA Auntie Lily. I'm wantin a drink.
LILY Go tae sleep.
MARINA Auntie Lily. I'm wantin a drink o' wat . . . ter! *(LILY gives her a cup of water. Enter EDIE. She goes across to window and shouts out)*
EDIE Ernest! Ernest! Ye've tae come in at once. Ma's gonnae wallop the daylights oot o' ye . . . Auntie Lily, Ernest won'd cub id. I came id when Ma shouted, but Ernest won't.
LILY Fancy that! Aren't you a wee clever? Pull up yer stockings. Hev ye nae suspenders?
EDIE Suspenders? Do.
LILY Well hev ye nae garters?
EDIE Do, Auntie Lily.
LILY Well, hev ye nae elastic in yer breeks?
EDIE I've nae breeks.

(Enter MAGGIE)

LILY Maggie, has she no got a pair o' knickers tae her name?

MAGGIE She had an old pair o' her granny's cut doon, but they're wore oot noo. But ye ken that kirk at the corner o' Sawmull Street, they're hae'in a jumble sale on Saturday. I wis thinkin I might go doon and see whit I could get . . . if I've ony money left. I'm owin the grocer for last week.

LILY When I see you I'm right glad I stayed single. *(CHRISTOPHER starts to cry again)*

MAGGIE He's teethin. *(They both go across to bed)*

LILY He cannae aye be teethin, he's aye greetin when I come.

(MAGGIE brings out the dummy again and dips it in the sugar basin)

Ye shouldnae gie him that, Maggie, it's no good for him, it'll gie him worms.

MAGGIE Ach, worms yer granny!

LILY Ye're wastin him, so ye are. As if it wisnae bad enough lettin him walk too soon and giein him bowly legs . . .

MAGGIE Cri'icisin. All you can do is cri'icise. It's easy enough tae come here cri'icisin. It's a pity ye dinnae hae ony weans o' yer ain tae bring up, ye'd find it isnae as easy as it looks. Old maids are aye awfu' good at giein advice.

LILY I hope you don't think I'm jealous o' you because you managed tae get the haud o' a man. Look at ye! Dae ye never rin a comb through yer hair?

MAGGIE Oh shut up wi yer cri'icisin. Edie, rin you aff tae bed.

(EDIE, who has been listening to her elders with interest, grinning and scratching her head, pulls up her stockings)

LILY Has she got something?

MAGGIE Wis she scratchin? Edie, wis you scratchin? Come here! *(She seizes her roughly and examines her head with more vigour than mercy, then heaves a sigh of relief and thrusts her away)* That's one thing I wull not have in this hoose.

EDIE Mary Harris has got theb, so she has. Teacher says it.

MAGGIE Mary Harris! And her up this very close! Jist you wait till I get the haud o' that lazy mother o' hers, I'll gie her a piece o' ma mind. Listen you tae me, Edie, there's tae be nae mair hob-nobbin wi Mary Harris, till she's got her heid cleaned. We've no very much this side o' respectability, but there's aye soap and water.

LILY Tae look at her ye wouldnae think it.

EDIE I wis oot playin so I wis.

MAGGIE Nae back chat. Get oot the soap and flannel and dae yer neck the night, in case the teacher taks it intae her impident heid tae look the morn.

EDIE I haven't finished learding by Psalm, Ba.

MAGGIE Well ye should dae yer lessons afore ye go oot playin. *(EDIE searches the dresser, table, etc.)*

EDIE Ba! Ba! I can't fide the soap and fladdol, Ba.

MAGGIE *(Joining in the hunt)* Noo whaur did I see it last? . . . I did the wean afore he went oot ta-tas . . .

LILY How you ever find onythin in this hoose beats me.

MAGGIE It beats me tae, sometimes. Edie! Bend ower the sink and let me scart some of this dirt aff ye.

LILY D'ye no tak aff her claes tae wash her neck?

MAGGIE It's no Saturday!

LILY Onyway she's old enough tae dae it hersel. The wey you rin efter they weans is the limit. Nae wunner ye look hauf-deid.

MAGGIE I canny help ma looks ony mair than you can.

LILY The difference is, I try. Hev ye looked in the glass since ye got up this mornin?

MAGGIE I havnae time tae look in nae mirrors. And neither would you if ye'd a hoose and a man and weans tae see tae.

LILY Yin o' they days your lovin Johnny's gonnae tak a keek at whit he marriet and it's gonnae be ta ta Maggie.

MAGGIE I'm sorry for ye, Lily. Right enough I am.

LILY Sorry for me? Sorry for me! Whit a hell o' a cheek ye've got.

MAGGIE Mind yer bad languidge. There's an innocent child here.

LILY Innocent! Lookin for a needle in a haystack's naethin tae lookin for innocence in this locality.

MAGGIE *(Finishing off EDIE)* Comb yer hair noo, Edie . . . I wonder whaur it is? . . . I saw Christopher wi it this morn . . . *(They both look for comb, but fail to find it. MAGGIE clears the sideboard by stuffing things into the cupboard and closing the door.)*

EDIE Ba! Ba! I cannae fide it. Auntie Lily, could you lend me yours? *(Lily starts to look in her bag, then thinks better of it)*

LILY I didnae bring it wi me the night.

EDIE I've gote dae bugs, Auntie Lily.

LILY Jist the same, I didnae bring wi me.

EDIE Auntie Lily, would you hear be by Psalm?

LILY Onythin for a quiet life . . . Och sit doon, Maggie, I'll gie ye a haun when the kids is aff tae bed . . . sit doon, ye look that tired.

MAGGIE If I sit doon I'll no be able tae rize again. *(She sits and puts her feet up)*

EDIE *(With hands behind her back, in a sing-song voice)*
    'That bad hath perfect blessedness
    That walketh dot asdray
    Id council of ungodly ben
    Dor stands id siddors way.'

LILY Perfect blessedness!

EDIE 'Dor sittith id the scorners chair
　　But placoth his delight
　　Upod God's law and beditates
　　Od his law day and dight.'
LILY He'll no get much sleep at that rate.
EDIE I'b dot very sure of the last verse . . . Oh yes!
　　'And all he doth shall prosper well,
　　The wicked are dot so . . .'

(She sticks here, and repeats ad. lib., hopping from foot to foot)

LILY Oh are they no? It strikes me the mair wicked ye are, the mair ye prosper . . . *(Prompting)* 'But like they are . . .
EDIE Oh yes! I rebebor!
　　'But like they are udto the chaff
　　Which wids drive to ad fro. Abed.'
LILY Amen yersel. Noo scram, wull ye?
MAGGIE Aye, Edie, get aff tae yer bed afore yer faither comes in frae the library.
LILY Oh is that whaur he is?

(EDIE goes to door, takes down key to outside lavatory and goes out, still reciting her Psalm)

MAGGIE Whaur else would he be? He disnae go tae the pubs noo.
LILY Oh aye! I forgot he wis T.T. noo.
MAGGIE Ye ken fine he's T.T., but ye canny resist a dig at him. He hasnae been inside a pub since Marina wis born.
LILY That's whit he tells you, onyway.
MAGGIE My! The tongue you hev on ye, Lily. I've never heard ye say a good word for a man yet.
LILY I've never found yin that deserved it.
MAGGIE There's aye good as well as bad.
LILY Listen! You're no needin tae tell me onythin aboot men. I work in a pub don't I? They're a' rotten, the hale jing-bang o' them, and the yins that look the saftest are the rottenest o' the lot when they get hauf a chance.
MAGGIE It's a pity, Lily, that ye'd sich a disappointment when ye wis young, ye micht hae been sae happy wi a nice man and a few weans.

(LILY holds out her sleeve and laughs up it)

LILY Dae you think you're happy? In this muck heap?
MAGGIE Ye canny help it when there's kids in the hoose. I'm sure I work ma fingers tae the bone tryin tae keep it clean.
LILY If it wis me I'd gie it up as hopeless. Nae hot water, nae place tae dry

the weans' claes, nae room for the lot o' ye . . . and worst o' a' . . . nae money. If John would gie hissel a shake and get hissel a decent job . . .

MAGGIE You shut up and leave John alane! He's daein the best he can.

LILY No much o' a best. One kid after another . . . hauf the time oot o' a job, and the rest o' the time no earnin enough tae keep ye in breid and marge. It's jist as weel hauf yer weans didnae live.

MAGGIE Whit can ye expect onyway . . .

LILY Ye can expect whit ye get when ye marry a man that's aye on the dole.

MAGGIE Ye're aye pickin on John! I'll no hae ye rinnin him doon!

LILY Keep yer wig on. Ye're that touchy ye'd think ye wis jist new marriet. If it wisnae that I don't believe in love, I'd say ye still loved him. Goad help ye!

MAGGIE Love's a funny word tae use when ye've been marriet twenty-five year, but . . . I dae love John! And he loves me!

LILY Ye should get yer foties took and send them tae the Sunday papers and say 'Twenty-five year marriet in the slums and I still love ma husband. Is this a record?'

MAGGIE I'm sorry for ye, Lily. Ye're a right soor old maid.

LILY We're quits then. I couldnae be ony sorrier for masel than I am for you.

MAGGIE Scrubbin flairs and washin dishes a' day, and servin they dirty hulkin brutes o' men wi drinks at night.

LILY Livin in a slum and slavin efter a useless man and his greetin weans wi nae enough money tae feed them, let alane pit claes on their backs.

MAGGIE I'm workin for ma ain, no cleanin efter ootsiders.

LILY I'm peyed for ma work.

MAGGIE So am I. Mebbe no in money, but a lovin kuss maks up for a lot.

LILY A lovin kuss!

MAGGIE The trouble wi you, Lily, is yer mind's twistit. Ye cannae think onythin but ill o' folk. I'd raither be deid than be as bitter as you.

LILY I've got nae delusions left. You hev. You're fu' o' delusions. Ye think yer man's wonderfu' and yer weans is a' angels. Look at Jenny . . .

MAGGIE There's naethin wrang wi Jenny.

LILY No yet onyway.

MAGGIE Ye wis like Jenny yersel once, and don't forget it. There wis naebody fonder o' dressin up and rinnin oot wi the lods than you were . . .

LILY I went oot respectable so I did! No wi a' the riff raff o' the toon, a' dressed up like a bloomin tart, wi peroxided hair . . .

MAGGIE You watch whit y're sayin.

LILY I'm only tryin tae tell ye tae keep an eye on her. I ken a hale lot mair aboot Jenny than you dae. I'm in the way o' hearin things, workin in a pub.

MAGGIE Whit things?

LILY Never mind. Jist you watch her. Yon Nessie Tait's a bad lot, and her and Jenny's thick as thieves.

MAGGIE Ye cannae blame Jenny for bein discontented, wi things the way they are . . . Granny in the bedroom . . . and Edie, snorin the way she does wi her tonsils. Jist the same . . . it hurts terrible tae hear her goin on, and sayin she'll leave hame . . . I'm sure it's no ma fault! I'm sure I've din ma best for every yin o' them. *(She begins to cry. LILY goes over to her and puts her arm round her.)*

LILY I know ye've done yer best, Maggie, ye've been wonderful. Ye've no had a life fit for a dug. If ye wis a cuddy, the prevention for cruelty people would hae done somethin aboot ye . . . workin awa wi yer insides a' wrang efter the twins, and in and oot o' bed hauf the night wi sick weans . . . but there's nae society for the prevention o' cruelty tae women. I jist wish I could dae mair for ye.

MAGGIE Ye dae plenty, Lily, it's good o' ye tae bother at a'.

LILY I dae whit I can, but it's nae much.

MAGGIE Oh aye but it is. There wis yon black puddin ye brung intae us on Wednesday, and yon bit gingerbreid on Sunday, forbye a' the cast-affs and odd bobs ye've gi'en me . . . I'll no forget ye, Lily.

LILY That's a' right, Maggie. I've brought ye a tin o' baked beans the night. They'll mebbe dae yer dinner the morn.

MAGGIE If they're no ett afore.

LILY There ye are! That's jist like ye! I bring ye somethin tae yer dinner and it's ett afore ma back's turned. It's aye a feast or a famine wi you. The fryin pan's never aff yer stove frae Friday night tae Monday mornin, and efter that it's breid and marge for the rest o' the week. Why dae ye no spread things oot a bit? It would be faur mair sensible.

MAGGIE There's no much fun in bein sensible.

LILY Oh well, they're your beans, dae whit ye like wi them . . . Hev ye been back tae the hospital yet wi Bertie?

MAGGIE No. I wis that tired, I just couldnae think tae get dressed and trail away up yonder.

LILY Did the doctor no say ye wis tae go away up for the X-rays result?

MAGGIE Aye. I'll tak him up next week.

LILY Aye, Maggie, ye've no tae pit it aff. He's nae weel, the wee soul. I brought a bottle for his cough.

MAGGIE Oh my! Ye shouldnae hev spent yer money, Lily.

LILY Oh I didnae buy it, I had it geid me.

MAGGIE Jist the same, it's awfu' good o' ye.

(Re-enter EDIE, right. She hangs up key on wall. ERNEST comes in behind her and gives her hair a prolonged tug.)

EDIE Ow! Let go by hair, you bean thing!

ERNEST Aw wee greetin face, aw wee greetin face!

MAGGIE *(Seizing him roughly and clouting his ear)* Did I no tell you you wis tae come in here hauf an oor ago? *(Clout)* Did I? *(Clout)* . . . D'ye hear? *(Clout) (ERNEST struggles out of her reach)* Come you here when I want tae hit ye. *(Clout)* There! *(With a final clout she pushes him away and brushes back her dishevelled hair)* Get you tae that sink there and wash yer face.

> *(ERNEST feebly soaps the flannel and washes a small area round his mouth and nose, then he draws the flannel gently across the back of his filthy hands and dries himself)*

LILY Some wash!

ERNEST Did ye bring us onythin tae eat the night, Auntie?

LILY Aye, but ye're no gettin it noo.

ERNEST Aw! Whit wis it? A pie?

LILY Never you mind.

ERNEST A black puddin?

LILY Never mind.

ERNEST A white puddin? . . . Wis it a kipper? Aw, g'on, tell us.

MAGGIE It's baked beans, for yer dinner the morn.

ERNEST Jings! Aw! Can we no get eatin them the night?

MAGGIE *(Licking her lips and looking out of the corner of her eye at LILY)* Certainly nutt!

ERNEST Aw! Can I hev a piece and jeely?

MAGGIE *(Sighing)* This loaf wis new at tea time! *(Cuts and spreads a slice. ERNEST takes it and climbs on the sink where he eats it wolfishly)*

ERNEST Ma! I can hear Mrs Bone's wireless. Ma! It's playin jazz. Oh great! . . . Ma, I wisht we'd a wireless . . . Ma, when will we get a wireless?

LILY When yer feyther becomes King o' England!

MAGGIE Some day we'll hae a wireless, son.

LILY Aye. And a grand pianny tae.

ERNEST When we get a wireless I'm gonnae listen tae a' the jazz bands. *(He seizes a spoon and starts to beat out a jazz rhythm on a tin tray and pot lid. Marina wakens up.)*

MARINA Mammy! I want a piece and jeely.

MAGGIE *(Giving ERNEST a clout in passing, she goes to the loaf)* There noo! Ye've wakened Marina . . . Jist a minute hen, Mammy's comin. *(Goes across to bed with bread)* There noo, eat it a' up and go bye byes again . . . Christopher's aye sleepin wi his mouth open. I hope he's no goin tae get tonsils like Edie.

LILY Ye'd better see aboot him when ye go tae the hospital wi Bertie.

MAGGIE Aye, so I will.

LILY Like enough ye'll no bother yersel.

MAGGIE Oh it's no that I don't bother, it's jist that it's sich a job tae get up there, and then ye've tae sit a' day, and the weans gets that crabbit . . . it's a day's work in itsel . . . The school doctor says Edie's tae get her tonsils oot.

LILY It didnae need the school doctor tae tell me that.

MAGGIE Right enough. If it's no yin o' them, it's anither.

ERNEST *(Still on sink)* Ma! Old Bone must be drunk again. I can hear them fightin!

(Noises from above indicate a brawl; they get louder throughout the next few speeches, and die out or are revived according to the whim of the Producer)

MAGGIE Is that no terrible! At it again!

LILY I cannae understaun a woman that lets her man knock her aboot.

MAGGIE Whit else can she dae if she's got weans? Ye cannae jist lift yer weans and walk oot o' yer hoose! If ye've got weans ye've got tae pit up wi the fella that gied ye them.

LILY I see masel.

MAGGIE My! That wis a dunt! The plaster'll be doon in a minute.

LILY Wull I chap up tae them?

MAGGIE Aye, tak the brush and dunt the ceilin. No that it'll dae ony good, they'll never hear it . . . she'll be too busy dodgin . . . My! Did ye hear that! I bet ye she'll hae a black eye the morn. *(LILY mounts a chair and knocks up to the combatants with the sweeping brush)* But mind ye, that's yin thing I admire aboot Mrs Bone, she never lets on. Efter Hogmanay she'd a black eye, and dae ye ken whit she said? She said she'd walked intae the lavvy door in the night. *(She gives ERNEST a clout, bringing him sharply off the sink)* Get aff tae yer bed and don't sit there listenin tae yer elders. *(ERNEST goes off, right)* My! Boys is an awfu' proablem.

LILY I see ye're skelpin Ernest aboot plenty. I hope it does some good. Mebbe that's whit's wrang wi Alex, ye dinnae skelp him enough.

MAGGIE Alex wis aye that delicate.

LILY There's naethin delicate aboot him noo except the way he taks money aff ye. When did ye last see him?

MAGGIE Nae that lang ago.

LILY Well when ye dae . . . ach . . . never mind.

MAGGIE He's no owing ye onythin is he?

LILY If he is, it's naethin tae dae wi you. Did he no come roon' at the weekend?

MAGGIE No he didnae.

LILY The dirty dug! He can aye come runnin tae ye when he's wantin something, the rest o' the time ye can go tae the hot place for a' he cares . . . and wi his pockets fu' efter the dugs on Saturday. Did he no even come near ye wi a poke o' sweeties for the weans? Ach! They men!

MAGGIE Wha tell't ye he's won at the dugs?

LILY Isa wis boastin aboot it . . . he bought her yin o' they swagger coats aff his winnins.

MAGGIE He'd gie her the eyes oot o' his heid. Whit he sees in her I don't know . . . she's a bad lot yon.

LILY Aye, you try and tell him that. It seems tae me the mair a wumman cairries on wi other men, the mair her ain man thinks o' her. If ye sit at hame like an aul' has-been, washin oot the nappies and blackleadin yer grate, all the attention ye get's a bashin on a Saturday night.

MAGGIE I don't think Alex bashes Isa.

LILY Goad help her if he ever does stert, he'll no ken when tae stop. Ye mind the tempers he used tae get intae? Ye mind the day he flung the breid knife at me?

MAGGIE Och, Lily, I've enough tae keep me aff ma sleep at nights wioot you rakin up the past.

LILY Aw, Maggie, I'm sorry. I didnae mean tae upset ye . . . I wisnae thinkin . . .

MAGGIE It wis the day efter he threw the knife at you he got intae yon bother . . .

LILY Och, Maggie, forget it. I didnae mean tae remind ye . . .

MAGGIE I'm no likely tae forget . . . The polis . . . and the court . . . and yon Probation Officer . . .

LILY There's naebody but you remembers.

MAGGIE Mrs Harris remembers a'right. The nights I've lain in ma bed prayin she'd flit oot o' here, but like a lot o' ither prayers they wisnae answered. Every time her and Alex comes face tae face I can see her remembering.

LILY He wis only a wee lad then.

MAGGIE Sometimes I think he's no much mair than a lad yet.

(Enter JOHN, with books from the library under his arm. He is a big good-looking man. He puts down his books, goes to the sink and takes a drink of water.)

MAGGIE Are ye dry, John? I wis jist thinkin o' puttin the kettle on.

JOHN No a bad idea.

LILY Well, I'll away hame. Whit aboot that ironin ye said ye'd tae dae? I'll stay and rin them ower if ye like.

MAGGIE Och, let them bide. I'm that tired it would kill me tae watch ye.

LILY It'll be steamie day again afore ye've got them ironed.

MAGGIE Well, I cannae help it.

JOHN Yous women! Ye've nae system.

LILY Oh I suppose if you wis a wumman ye'd hae everything jist perfect! The weans a' washed and pit tae bed at six, and everything a' spick and span . . . I can see ye! Naethin tae dae a' night but twiddle yer thumbs!

JOHN I'd hae a system . . . . . .

LILY and MAGGIE A system!

JOHN Keep yer hair on! Ony man kens ye can dae naething, wioot ye hev a system.

LILY And ony wumman kens that there's nae system that wis ever invented that disnae go a' tae hell when ye've a hoose fu' o' weans and a done aul' Granny tae look efter.

MAGGIE Never heed him, Lily. He often talks like this, but ye should see him trying tae mak the breakfast on a Sunday! Ye'd get yer kill. He can only dae the yin job at a time.

JOHN Well, it's no ma job! If it wis ma job . . .

LILY Ye'd hev a system. We heard ye . . . Well, I'll away noo, if ye're sure there's naethin I can dae.

MAGGIE Wait and hae a wee cup.

LILY Och no, I'll mak yin when I get hame and hae somethin tasty tae it.

JOHN (*Winking at MAGGIE*) Aye, that's right, Lily, jist you go hame and mak yersel something tasty, for ye neednae hint for onythin tasty here.

LILY (*Not seeing the wink*) I like that! Hint! The cheek o' ye! That's a' the thanks I get for bringin delacasies intae the hoose. It wis me that brung in yon black puddin ye ate tae yer tea last Wednesday, and the ginger-breid on Sunday forbye. And it wis me brocht in yon tin o' baked beans that's sittin up on your dresser this very minute, and you've the cheek tae tell me I'm hintin . . .

MAGGIE Och he disnae mean it, Lily, he wis only jokin.

LILY Jokin! If that's a sense o' humour, I'm glad I havnae got yin. You men mak me sick.

JOHN I'd like tae see ye get the chance o' a man tae mak ye sick. If yin jist crep' ontae yer horizon, ye'd be at him like a cock at a grosset.

LILY (*Putting on hat and coat*) I'll no stay here tae be insultit, so I'll no. Ye can keep the beans, Maggie, but it's the last ye'll get till ye learn some folks mainners. And ye can tell yon Alex o' yours that the next time he maks enough at the dugs tae get fleein drunk in the middle o' Argyle Street, he can pay me back yon tenshillingy note I lent him. (*She goes off*)

MAGGIE Och ye shouldnae say things like that tae Lily. Yin o' they days she'll tak the huff and no come back.

JOHN Nae wunner she cannae get a man!

(*They sit for a minute in silence, broken by a fit of coughing from BERTIE*)

JOHN Whit aboot Bertie's X-rays? Did ye tak him up tae the hospital?

MAGGIE No. I wis that tired . . .

JOHN Tired or no ye'll have tae find oot whit's wrang wi him. He's no weel.

MAGGIE Aye, it's easy for you tae talk. I'm jist fair wore oot so I am, wi the weans and the hoose and everything.

JOHN Ach don't stert on aboot yer troubles, as if they wernae mines tae. If I could only get a steady job, but they're payin aff again, Maggie.

MAGGIE Well, whatever happens, I'm no goin oot cleanin again. I'm din.

JOHN There's naebody askin ye tae go oot cleanin!

MAGGIE But if ye get the sack . . .

JOHN Who said I wis gettin the sack?

MAGGIE You said . . . . . .

JOHN I did nutt! Och I'm sorry, Maggie, but it's that discouragin . . . a man disnae ken whit tae dae for the best . . . there's nae jobs in the papers.

(There is a knock at the door)

MAGGIE You go. It'll be yin o' the neighbours wantin a len' somethin.

JOHN Come in. Come in.

(Enter MRS HARRIS and MRS WILSON)

MAGGIE I hope it's no marge, for I've nane.

MRS HARRIS I like that! Ye'd think we never came near ye except tae borry . . . we came up tae tell ye there's been an accident at your Alex's.

MAGGIE Whit? Whit's happened?

JOHN Has the polis got him again?

MRS HARRIS Aye, the polis is there, but they're no efter him.

JOHN It's a wunner.

MRS WILSON It's the street. Your Alex's street. The hooses has collapsed. The close next your Alex's has come doon. They've pit a' the folks oot o' it, and the polis is there pittin a rope roon the street and yon wee red lamps . . . it wis awful excitin. Me and Mrs Harris wis at the Star and here we sees a' this crowd o' folks, and here, that's whit it wis. Fancy it bein your Alex's street!

MRS HARRIS It's jist like an earthquake . . . like yon fillum . . . wi Clark Gable and Jeanette McDonald . . . there's a sink sittin oot in the open air . . .

MRS WILSON And ye can see right intae somebody's room, and the drawers and things is a' ower the place . . .

MAGGIE Did ye see Alex?

MRS WILSON No, we didnae see him.

MRS HARRIS Nor Isa neither.

MRS WILSON But they said there wis nae deaths. Yin chap got his heid split open . . . but that wis a' the cas-u-al-ities as faur as we know.

MRS HARRIS Your Alex would be oot somewheres.

MAGGIE Wull ye go roon, John, and see?

MRS HARRIS Och, I wouldnae bother ma bunnet, Mr Morrison. The polis would hae come roon' for ye, if there had been onythin. Alex knows a' the polis hereabout.

JOHN Ye mean the polis a' know Alex.

MRS HARRIS Well, whichever way ye like tae pit it. It's a good job it wis only a sub-let. He'll hae nae furniture tae shift.

MAGGIE John, are you goin roon'? If you're no, I am.

JOHN Aye I'll go, but I ken fine I'll no see him this side o' midnight . . . they'll be oot at the dancin, and when they dae come hame, they'll be that pie-eyed they'll no care whether they've a hame or no.

MRS WILSON Aye, ye should go roon', Mr Morrison. It's worth seein. Whit a mess!

JOHN It's a bloomin nuisance, that's whit it is. Well we're no havin them here, Maggie, they can find another room.

MAGGIE They'll no can find anither room the night, John.

JOHN Well they can find it the morn. It'll gie the pair o' them somethin tae dae instead o' lyin in their beds. *(He goes off)*

MRS WILSON My! They men! They're right hard nuts!

MAGGIE That's jist talk . . . if onythin wis tae happen tae ony o' the weans, John would tak it jist as bad as me, if no worse. Men don't seem tae be able tae stand up tae things like us.

MRS HARRIS Jist the same, I can see his point. He's no wantin ony mair pit ontae ye efter whit the doctor said.

MRS WILSON Oh they doctors! 'Tak' it easy, and pit yer feet up, and hae a rest efter yer dinner' . . .

MRS HARRIS I hope ye're cairryin oot his instructions, Mrs Morrison.

MAGGIE Wi a housefu' o' weans' . . . whit a hope.

MRS WILSON Here! Did I tell ye? Mrs Thingummy doon the street that jist had the twins is tae hae an operation!

MAGGIE Ach! The doctor tell't me years ago I wis tae hae an operation. 'Right ye are' says I. 'Wull ye come in and look efter the hoose and the weans while I'm awa?' I'm still waitin on ma operations. Hauf the women in the street's needin operations.

MRS HARRIS Well I'm no needin one, but I'd let them open me up wi pleasure, if I could get a fortnight's rest efter it, wi a nice wee nurse bringin me ma breakfast on a tray and nae men comin in aside me, reekin like a distillery.

MRS WILSON Did yon pickcher the night no mak you awfu' thirsty, Mrs Harris? Yon time they wis a' sittin drinkin champagne, ma tongue wis fair hangin oot.

(MAGGIE gets up and puts on kettle)

MAGGIE I'll mak a wee cup, I promised yin tae Granny a while back.

(MRS WILSON and MRS HARRIS dig each other in the ribs)

MRS WILSON How is Granny keepin?

MAGGIE Jist the same.

MRS HARRIS Nae a word o' her kickin the bucket? . . . It's a trial for ye. Wait till she's bedridden though, it'll be worse.

MAGGIE That's right, look on the bright side.

MRS HARRIS When's she due at Lizzie's?

MAGGIE No till the end of the month.

MRS WILSON Whit'll ye dae if ye have tae pit up Alex and Isa?

MAGGIE Granny'll hev tae go tae Lizzie's.

MRS HARRIS She's a right skinflint yon. She'd screw the teeth oot o' yer heid if she could get onythin for them in the pawn . . . did Granny ever get back yon brooch she lost last time she wis at Lizzie's?

MAGGIE No.

MRS HARRIS H'm! I tell't ye! She'll never see it this side o' hell.

MRS WILSON Pair aul' Granny. It's pathetic, so it is, the way she comes wi yon aul' bed o' hers, and takes it wi her when she goes . . . right enough, old folks is an awfu' problem.

(MAGGIE pours tea and hands it round)

MRS HARRIS So is young folks.

MAGGIE So is weans. *(Goes off left, with cup of tea to GRANNY)*

MRS WILSON No tae mention husbands. The Bones wis at it again the night. He got overtime paid him.

MRS HARRIS Pair Mrs Bone! Oh here! *(Feeling in her pocket)* I forgot I'd a liquorice allsort here. *(Passes round bag. MAGGIE returns.)*

MRS WILSON Jenny no in the night?

MAGGIE No.

MRS WILSON I see she's got a new yin. I seen them courtin the other night.

MAGGIE She never says who she's wi. Girls gets kind o' difficult at that age.

(MRS WILSON exchanges glances)

MRS WILSON I see she's bacome a platinum blonde.

MAGGIE Aye. Her feyther's wild at her.

MRS HARRIS Somebody must hae tell't her that gentlemen prefers them. Wait till your Edie and my Mary gets started, Mrs Morrison.

MAGGIE Here! That jist reminds me! My Edie says the teacher says your Mary's got beasts in her heid.

MRS HARRIS *(Giving a long drawn screech of indignation)* Oh! The cheek! Beasts! Whit a thing tae say!

MAGGIE Can you deny it?

MRS HARRIS Oh! Wait till I get my hauns on yon teacher! Tae say sich a thing aboot ma wean! I'll hae the polis tae her, so I wull!

MAGGIE Can you deny that your Mary's got beasts in her heid?

MRS HARRIS I never heard sich cheek!

MAGGIE You look me in the eye, Mrs Harris, and tell me your Mary's got nae lice in her heid.

MRS HARRIS It's no fair, so it's no, tae accuse me . . .

MAGGIE See! Ye cannae dae it!

MRS HARRIS Ach well! Whit's an odd louse?

MAGGIE I'll tell ye whit an odd louse is. It's the mither o' a bad family that's no content tae play on hame grun' so jist you get somethin frae the chemist and get crackin or I'll get the Sanitary tae ye.

MRS HARRIS (*Rising with dignity*) Oh the Sanitary is it? If ye're for bringin in the Sanitary, there's a thing or two I could tell him aboot the dunny stairs no bein done when it's a certain party's turn.

(*They face each other belligerently. MRS WILSON rises apprehensively and plucks at MRS HARRIS's sleeve.*)

MRS WILSON Come on!

MAGGIE Are you insin-y-atin?

MRS HARRIS No I'm no insin-y-atin. I'm tellin ye.

MRS WILSON Come on!

MRS HARRIS I'm comin.

MAGGIE (*Shouting after them*) Mind, she's no playin wi ma Edie till she's cleaned.

MRS HARRIS Ye neednae fash yersel, I wouldnae let her!

CURTAIN

ACT I

Scene 2

Scene: The same, after midnight.

The stage is in darkness. MAGGIE is lying sleeping on a mattress on the floor, covered with a collection of old coats, blankets, etc.

Enter JOHN, ALEX, and ISA. They all carry a share of ALEX and ISA's belongings. ISA is dressed in a tawdry evening dress, both are slightly tipsy. MAGGIE sits up in bed as they enter.

JOHN Don't make such a bloomin row, ye'll waken the hale hoose.

ALEX *(Flinging down the suitcase noisily)* I'm no makin ony row . . . I'm no askin ony favours from naebody . . . I'm only askin a bit o' peace . . . nae place tae stey. Can I help it if ma bloody roof fa's in? . . . Whit's a' the ruddy fuss aboot? I didnae knock doon the hoose . . . did I? . . . Did I?

JOHN Shut yer row.

ALEX There ye are! Whit did I tell ye? That's the welcome I get . . . and nae hame o' ma ain . . . Is it ma fault I've nae hame? . . . Is it? . . . Is it? . . . I've got a wife an' I love her . . . I love ye, Isa . . . I love ye.

ISA Aw shut up, ye big pansy.

ALEX She disnae love me . . . when I want tae kiss her she . . . shoves me aff . . . like that. *(Makes drunken gesture and catches ISA in the stomach)*

ISA Ow! Ye drunken rotter!

MAGGIE John, pit him tae bed.

ALEX Aye that's right. Pit me tae bed.

JOHN Where's he tae lie?

MAGGIE Aside Bertie and Ernest. Isa, you'll need tae sleep on the sofie, I've pit through some blankets and things.

ISA Some sleep I'm gonnae get. *(Sits down and kicks off her high-heeled slippers)* Goad! Ma taes is tramped tae pulp . . . whit a rammy it wis the night!

JOHN Payin oot good money tae get battered aboot in yon crowd, I cannae understaun it.

ISA Wis you never young?

ALEX She shoves me aff . . . aye, she shoves me aff, but she disnae shove him aff . . . I seen ye! I seen ye the night. Jist wait. Jist you wait.

ISA Aw stow it. Ye're drunk. *(To JOHN)* That's whit aye happens when we've a night at the Pally. He mixes them, and I've got tae get somebody tae cairt him hame. Gie's a haun' wi him, he'll no waken noo till the afternoon.

JOHN *(To MAGGIE)* Is he gonnae lie aside Bertie stinkin o' stale beer?

MAGGIE Whit else can I dae?

JOHN Bertie's no weel . . . he can lie on the flair . . . whit I'd like tae dae is kick him oot intae the gutter.

ISA Whaur he belangs. Pit him oot on the landin.

(MAGGIE starts to cry)

MAGGIE It's terrible! I don't know whit tae dae wi him.

ISA I wish somebody would tak him oot an' lose him. I'm sick fed up wi him.

MAGGIE You havenae helped him ony.

ISA Ach he wis a rotten totty lang afore I wis saft enough tae get landed wi him. If ye ask me I've improved him. He'll dae whit I tell him . . . that's mair than you can say . . . I can twust him roon' ma wee finger. Come on, ye wee nyaff *(She takes him with a practised hand by the back of his collar, and jerks him off his chair)* Well! Are ye gonnae let me cairry him masel? Gie's a haun' for Pete's sake . . . I'm wantin ma bed.

(She and JOHN drag ALEX off, right)

Goodnight, sleep tight, see ye in the mornin.

(JOHN comes back, sits down and lights a fag)

JOHN Whit a son for a feyther tae be proud o' I used tae think, when he wis wee . . . it'd be rare tae hae his company when he grew up . . . I used tae think mebbe he'd be clever . . . mebbe go tae night school and learn a trade . . . and look whit I've got.

MAGGIE I'm sure I din ma best wi him . . . *(She begins to cry)*

JOHN I'm no blamin you, Maggie . . . it's no your fault. If I'm blamin onybody I'm blamin masel. A man's got nae right tae get married and bring kids intae the world, if he cannae provide for them.

MAGGIE I'm no sorry I married ye, John, ye ken that.

JOHN If I wis a woman, I'd hate the man that brought me tae this.

MAGGIE Jist so lang as you and me gets on a' right and you don't stert drinkin again . . .

JOHN I'll no dae that, Maggie . . . I've finished wi that. I caused ye enough trouble wi the drink . . . I swore I'd keep aff it when Marina wis born and you wis that bad, and I've kep' it . . . except for New Year, ye cannae count Hogmanay.

MAGGIE Sometimes ye wonder if it's worth it a' . . . the weans and the struggle it is tae keep them in claes, and bring them up decent . . . it's nae wunner folks disnae want weans noo.

JOHN Ye're no tryin tae tell me we're wantin a' we got? Oors wis a' invitet?

MAGGIE But once they're on the way, and ye've stopped sweerin aboot it, ye wouldnae be wioot them . . . it's as if they wis tied on tae ye . . . and they'll tug awa at ye till the day ye dee.

JOHN Aye. If it's no yin o' them worryin the wits oot o' ye it's anither . . . Bertie, cough, cough, coughin a' day and a' night, and Marina, that pinched and peaky, and Christopher, wi rickets.

MAGGIE It's no rickets!

JOHN Aye it is! Whit else is bowly legs but rickets? Models o' health and beauty, the hale lot o' them. It's a wunner they're living at a'.

MAGGIE Well, give over worryin the night. Come on tae bed.

JOHN Aye . . . Is there onythin tae eat in the hoose?

MAGGIE Oh help! If it's no yin stomach it's anither!

JOHN I'll get it masel.

MAGGIE No ye'll no.

JOHN Whit aboot they baked beans?

MAGGIE Whit aboot the morra?

JOHN Ach! Whit aboot the morra! *(He opens tin of beans, and puts them into a pan, goes to the stove and heats them, stirring and tasting)* Great tae hae the place tae oorsels. I think I'll tak tae stayin up at night, jist for the sake o' a bit o' peace.

MAGGIE I hope ye're no expectin me tae keep ye company . . . when it comes night, I'm mair dead than alive. I've cut some breid. Pit some o' they beans aside for the weans the morn.

(JOHN dishes out the beans)

JOHN If we jist had a nice bit Ayrshire bacon alang wi them.

MARINA Can I hev a bit Ayrshire bacon, Mammy?

MAGGIE Goad help us! Are you waken again? That wean wakens at the first mention o' grub. I'm beginnin tae wunner if she's got a worm. There's nae bacon, pet, would ye like a wee baked bean?

MARINA Aye. I'd like a wee baked bean.

JOHN Are ye sure it's a' right tae gi'e her baked beans in the middle o' the night?

MAGGIE Och aye! It'll nae dae her ony herm. *(Takes beans off her own plate and gives them to MARINA)*

JOHN Here! Hev some aff my plate.

MAGGIE Och I wisnae enjoyin them much onyway.

(There is a prolonged fit of coughing from BERTIE)

JOHN Maggie, ye'll need tae dae somethin aboot Bertie's cough.

MAGGIE I'm goin up tae the hospital wi him tomorrow.

JOHN Ye've been sayin that for the past week.

MAGGIE I got tired oot . . . and I'll hae tae bother Mrs Harris tae keep Granny and the weans . . . and I had words wi her the night.

JOHN Yous women! Whit wis it this time?

MAGGIE She said I didnae tak ma turn o' the dunny, and I said her Mary had somethin in her heid.

JOHN I've tellt ye and tellt ye! Can ye no keep yersel tae yersel?

MAGGIE No I cannae! It's only rich folks can afford tae keep theirselves tae theirselves . . . folks like us hev tae keep in wi oor neighbours, we've naebody else tae depend on . . . I'll mak up tae her the morn wi a wee taste cheese or somethin . . . hev you finished a' they beans?

JOHN There wisnae that much in them.

MAGGIE Can ye no be thankfu' for sma' mercies? D'ye want anither slice o' breid?

JOHN Whit aboot the weans' breakfast?

MAGGIE *(At loaf)* Yin for Ernie, yin for Edie, yin for Marina, yin for Bertie, if he'll eat it, a hauf each for Christopher and Granny's saps, aye, ye can hev anither.

JOHN Whit aboot yersel the morn?

MAGGIE Och, I'm no fussy aboot breakfast. I'll hae a roll after the weans is oot. Tak some jeely on yer breid.

JOHN Is this whit ye ca' jeely? Here! Hev you been waterin it again?

MAGGIE I've got tae, tae mak it spin oot, they weans would go through a jar a day.

JOHN Ye look jist dead beat, Maggie.

MAGGIE Aye. I'm gonnae lie doon.

JOHN Some day we'll hae a real bed, Maggie.

MAGGIE Yin on legs? Aff the flair? I havnae been on yin o' they since I wis in the Maternity wi Marina. Right enough, it wis lovely . . .

JOHN That'll dae ye . . . they beans is enough tae give me nightmares as it is.

MAGGIE *(In bed)* Hurry up. I'm lonely.

JOHN I'd better lock the door.

MAGGIE Och ye're no needin tae lock it.

JOHN *(Going towards door)* Jist in case somebody comes in and pinches yer jools.

MAGGIE John! Leave it! Jenny's no hame yet.

JOHN Jenny no hame! Is she oot at the dancin?

MAGGIE She didnae say. She disnae tell me naethin noo.

JOHN By Goad! She'll tell me somethin. I'm for nane o' this trapesin roon' the toon till a' oors.

(He goes across to window and opens it. A crowd of drunks are rolling homewards singing 'I'm alone because I love yew, love yew with all my heart' with mouth-organ accompaniment.)

JOHN Listen tae that! Goad knows whit sort o' scum's on the street at this time o' night. She's no gettin aff wi this.

MAGGIE Whit's the use? She pays nae attention when ye speak.

JOHN She'll pay some attention tae me. *(He looks out of window)* Nae sign o' her. Who'll she be wi?

MAGGIE She disnae bring hame her friends noo. Too posh I suppose . . . it wis an awful mistake her goin tae the Sauchiehall Street Branch, they should hae kep' her in Argyle Street. She'll no bring me hame naethin frae the shop . . . that feart the girls'll think onythin o' her gettin hame a few bashed tomaties . . . I miss them, it wis aye somethin tae mak a wee tasty bite.

JOHN Oh so she'll no bring hame bashed tomaties noo? I'll see aboot that! Wait till ma lady shows up the night.

MAGGIE Ye've no tae be rough wi her, John. Ye'll only drive her frae the hoose. She's aye threatenin tae leave hame.

JOHN Threatenin tae leave hame! She shairly wouldnae dae that!

MAGGIE Oh ye cannae blame her for bein fed up. It's no much o' a life.

JOHN Ye're right there . . . it's no much o' a life . . . D'ye think maybe I should go oot lookin for her?

MAGGIE Like as no she'll be wi Nessie Tait.

JOHN Nessie Tait! Yon painted Jezebel! She's naethin but a . . .

MAGGIE Noo! Ye've nae proof, John.

JOHN That's no the sort o' company for Jenny . . . sh! . . . whit wis that?

MAGGIE It's Bertie coughin again. I'd better awa through wi anither dose tae him.

JOHN I could hae swore I heard Jenny's laugh. By Goad! She'll be laughin on the ither side o' her face when I get her.

MAGGIE Oh, I'm that tired! I wisht Bertie's cough would stop. Every bloomin night I've got tae go through tae him. *(She starts to get up)*

JOHN Stay whaur ye are, I'll see tae Bertie.

MAGGIE The bottle's on the dresser, tak ben a spoon wi ye.

(JOHN goes out with spoon and bottle. There is a pause during which MAGGIE yawns loudly and repeatedly. Then JENNY's voice is heard faintly, then a man's voice, then their laughter, then silence. MAGGIE gets up and listens at the window.)

MAGGIE Jenny? Is that you Jenny?

(There is silence. MAGGIE scuttles back to bed, as JOHN returns with the spoon and bottle which he deposits. He then goes into the lobby, leaving the kitchen door open. Through it he can be seen listening at the outside door.)

MAGGIE Come on tae bed, John. Ye'll be that tired in the morning.

JOHN Jenny's doon there wi a fella.

MAGGIE Well if she's safe hame ye neednae worry . . . come tae bed.

JOHN I'll gie them anither minute, then I'm goin doon. *(He starts to put on his jacket)* It's a fine thing when a man has tae gae oot at this time in the mornin tae fetch his ain daughter.

MAGGIE I wouldnae gae doon, John, ye'll only vex her.

JOHN Vex her? I'll vex her a'right. And yon fella, he's no up tae much keepin a young lassie standin aboot the close at this time.

MAGGIE Ye could speak tae her in the mornin.

JOHN Whit's wrang wi ye, Maggie? Dae ye no kerr whit happens tae Jenny?

MAGGIE I'm no wantin her tae leave hame. I'm no wantin ony trouble atween the three o' us.

JOHN She's got tae be spoke tae.

(He goes out, leaving the door open. MAGGIE gets up quickly and stands at the kitchen door listening. Angry voices are heard off, then JOHN comes in holding JENNY by the arm. JENNY is about eighteen, an unnatural blonde, over made-up but good-looking in a bold way. Her lipstick is spread over her mouth and cheeks, her coat is open and her hair tousled.)

JENNY Leave me go! *(She shakes herself free of her father's hand and they stand glaring at each other. MAGGIE is sitting up in bed watching fearfully)* Makin a bloomin fool o' me!

JOHN Where wis ye till this time o' night?

JENNY Nane o' your bloomin business.

JOHN Don't you speak tae me like that. I asked ye where ye'd been.

JENNY And I tell't ye! Nane o' your damned interferin business!

MAGGIE Jenny! John!

(JOHN takes JENNY by the shoulders and shakes her)

JOHN Where wis ye? Answer me!

JENNY I wis at the pickchers.

JOHN The pickchers is oot at hauf past ten. Where wis ye efter?

JENNY Wi Nessie Tait and a coupla friends.

(He lets go and she flops into a chair glaring sullenly at him and rubbing her shoulders)

JOHN I don't approve o' yon Nessie Tait.

JENNY Whit a peety! I dae!

JOHN Ye impident little bitch. What I ought tae dae is tak ma belt tae ye.

JENNY Jist you try it!

JOHN The next time you come in here at this time o' the mornin wi yer paint spread a' ower yer face, I wull! Look at yersel. *(He drags her over to a mirror, then propels her, resisting, to the sink, where, holding her head under his arm, he scrubs off her make-up)*

JOHN There! And efter this, you'll let your hair grow tae the colour God meant it tae be, and leave it at that.

JENNY Maybe I wull and maybe I'll no. It jist depends.

JOHN I'm wantin nae mair sauce from you, Jenny. I'm speakin tae ye for yer ain good. Whit will the neighbours think? You comin hame at this time and staundin in the close wi a man.

JENNY Whit dae I care whit the neighbours think? And I suppose you never stood in a close yersel? Oh no! No likely!

(ERNEST enters, door right, and stands in the doorway, in his bare feet and wearing an old coat over tattered pyjamas, taking it all in)

JOHN I know ma ain sex, Jenny, and it's you I'm thinkin aboot.

JENNY Well ye can save yer breath. I ken hoo tae look efter masel, an' I'm no as green as I'm cabbage lookin . . . and talkin aboot cabbages . . . I'm leavin the shop.

JOHN Ye're whit?

JENNY You heard. I'm leavin. I'm goin intae a joolers . . . yon wis ma new boss I wis wi the night.

JOHN Whit joolers is this?

JENNY Ye'd like tae know, wouldn't ye?

JOHN *(Shaking her)* I would, and you're gonnae tell me.

JENNY Leave go! It's ma ain business, and I'm no tellin ye. I've had enough o' Ma waitin at the shop door for me every Friday, wi Christopher and Marina yellin the place doon, and Ma beggin for chipped apples and bashed tomaties, and disgracing me afore the hale shop.

MAGGIE I didnae mean tae aggravate ye, Jenny. It wis jist that I wis aye needin the money that sair . . .

JOHN The impidence o' ye! It's yer duty tae hand ower every penny ye earn tae the yin that's looked efter ye a' yer days.

JENNY Oh is that so? Well, ma duty's finished noo. From noo on, whit I earn is mines.

JOHN That's gratitude for ye! Hev ye no thought for a' the years yer mother and me's slaved for ye?

JENNY That wis yer job. I didnae ask tae be born.

MAGGIE Jenny!

JENNY Well! Neither I did! No intae this midden. The kitchen's never onythin else but a pig-sty. There's never onythin decent tae eat, and if there wis, ye'd hae nae appetite for it here. And sleepin wi a stinkin aul' wife and a wean that snores and snorts a' night. Owe you anythin? No fears. I don't owe you naethin.

JOHN Things'll no aye be like this, Jenny . . . I ken it's no the hame for you it ought tae be . . . but it's no oor fault . . . it's the way things are.

JENNY Ach! It's aye bad luck wi you. Every time ye lose yer job, it's bad luck.

JOHN Well so it is bad luck.

JENNY Some folks gets on and makes money, *(Looking contemptuously at her father)* ithers hasn't the brains. *(He is suddenly aware of her drink-laden breath)*

JOHN What have you been drinkin?

JENNY Water!

JOHN By Goad! If ever a girl asked for it! *(Shaking her)* What did you have tae drink?

JENNY I only had a couple gins.

JOHN *(Letting her go)* No content wi paintin yer face and dyin yer hair and stayin oot hauf the night, ye're drinkin gin! Right ye are, ma girl, cairry on! Ye'll land in the gutter, and when ye dae, ye neednae come tae me tae pick ye oot.

(EDIE appears, dressed in a torn nightgown. She stands listening, terrified.)

JENNY Don't worry! When I leave this rotten pig-sty I'll no come back. No even tae yer funeral. There's other things in life asides goin tae work in a rotten old fruit shop and handin ower a' yer wages. I'm gonnae get oot o' this and enjoy life. So ye'd better hang ontae yer job this time . . . if ye can!

(JOHN hits her across the face, EDIE screams with fright and runs across to her mother. JENNY and JOHN stand facing each other in frozen silence, broken by EDIE's sobs and her mother's condolences as EDIE gets her head underneath the bedclothes. MARINA wakens.)

MARINA Mammy! Is Daddy angry at Jenny?

MAGGIE No, pet, it's all right. You can go tae sleep.

(JENNY goes off, left, slamming the bedroom door. JOHN turns and sees ERNEST.)

JOHN Whit are you daen here? Get back tae yer bed! *(He assists him through the kitchen door with a kick then walks slowly to the window and looks out into the night)*

MAGGIE *(Timidly)* Come tae bed, John.

(JOHN does not answer. He lights a fag-end, and continues to stare out of the window as

THE CURTAIN FALLS

END OF ACT I

ACT II

Scene 1

Scene is the same. Afternoon, a week later.

The kitchen is fairly tidy. GRANNY's bed has been taken down, and it and the mattress are propped up against the wall, waiting for the men to remove it. GRANNY herself is sitting, dressed in her outdoor clothes, surrounded by bulging dilapidated shopping bags and an old straw basket, awaiting the arrival of LIZZIE.

GRANNY It's awfu' tae be aul' and be kicked aboot frae yin hoose tae the ither as if ye wis an aul' boot.

MRS HARRIS Cheer up, Granny, ye'll soon be deid.

GRANNY I wisht I wis! I wisht I wis!

MRS HARRIS Hev anither black strippit ba'. Whaur did ye pit them? *(Rummages through one of the bags and locates the sweets)* There ye are! *(To MRS BONE)* That'll keep her quiet for a wee while. Hoo's yer keeker the day? *(She examines MRS BONE mahogany-coloured eye)* It's no as bad as the last yin ye had. My! I never met onyone like you for bumpin intae things. Whit wis it this time?

MRS BONE The mangle . . . Mrs Morrison's shairly bein kep' a lang while at the hospital. I hope it's naething serious wi Bertie . . . that's an awful like cough he's got. Nicht efter nicht I hear him hechin awa . . . pair wee lad.

MRS HARRIS Chests is bad things . . . I mind when oor Wullie had the pewmony . . . I wis up a' day and a' nicht . . . no a wunk o' sleep did I get until efter he'd passed the crisis . . . and there wis his feyther, lyin, snorin his heid aff . . . fu' as a wulk! Never lifted haun' nor fit tae help me.

MRS BONE They men!

MRS HARRIS Aye, they men! But if their nebs is rinnin they think they're deein.

MRS BONE Well, I hope it's no pewmony wi Bertie, but I would nae be surprised at anythin, he's that delicate lookin.

GRANNY Eh dear! I'm deserted! Lizzie's no comin. It'll be the Poorshoose efter a' . . .

MRS BONE Lizzie'll be here in a minute, they'll no pit ye in the Poorshoose. *(To MRS HARRIS)* Pair aul' thing.

GRANNY I ken. I'm no that dottled that I dinnae ken I'm no wantit . . . I'm naethin but an aul' nuisance tae them.

MRS HARRIS Och awa! Ye're no an aul' nuisance at a' . . . I'm sure they'll a' miss ye somethin terrible when ye go.

GRANNY Na, na. They'll no miss me . . . but they'll miss ma pension tae buy a bit o' bacon on a Friday nicht. Maggie aye bought a bit bacon wi ma pension . . . no that I got ony o' it . . . I jist got the smell o' it and a bit dipped breid . . . a' very well sayin I'd naethin tae chew wi . . . wait till she's aul' hersel wi nae teeth.

MRS HARRIS It is terrible bad arrangement that . . . when ye loss yer teeth ye should loss yer appetite wi them, the yin's nae use wioot the ither.

GRANNY Tak a look oot the windy and see if ye see her, Mrs Harris.

MRS HARRIS *(Looking out)* Nae sign o' her. Don't worry yersel, she'll be here in a wee while . . . mebbe she's oot buyin something tasty for yer tea the night . . . a wee sausage mebbe . . . *(She digs MRS BONE in the ribs)* Aye! That's whit she'll be daein . . . she'll be oot buyin up Liptons.

MRS BONE Whit a hope!

(There is a peremptory knock at the door)

MRS HARRIS That'll be her, it's jist like the cheeky knock she'd hae. *(She goes to the door and brings in LIZZIE, a hard-faced harridan about fifty)*

MRS HARRIS *(Off)* Well, ye neednae be sae nippy! *(As they enter)* It's no ma fault if ye've been pit tae ony bother. She's been sittin here waitin on ye for a hale hauf oor, me and Mrs Bone be keepin her company.

LIZZIE *(To GRANNY)* Oh ye're dressed are ye? Thank Goad for that. Have ye got a' yer claes wi ye? And yer pension book?

GRANNY Aye, Lizzie, they're a' here.

LIZZIE Gie's a look at yer pension book. Hev they men no' been for the bed yet?

GRANNY Not yet.

(MRS BONE helps GRANNY to find her pension book)

LIZZIE Ye'v drawn this week's. Hev ye got the money?

GRANNY I gied it tae Maggie.

LIZZIE Well it's no Maggie's this week, it's mines. If ye're comin tae bide wi me, ye're no comin tae bide aff me.

GRANNY She got some things aff the grocer, and she wis needin a pair o' socks for Bertie goin up tae the hospital tae see the doctors.

LIZZIE Oh so Bertie gets new socks at ma expense, does he? And whit dae ye think you're gonnae live on for the next week? Air?

MRS HARRIS Ach, leave the pair aul' wife alane. Shairly ye can scrape up a bit breid for saps and an odd cup or two o' tea for a few days. It's no as if ye wis takin in a big hulkin brute o' a man tae feed.

LIZZIE I'm no takin in naebody tae feed. Folk that cannae pay for their meat'll find nae room in ma hoose.

MRS BONE That's terrible tae say tae yer poor husband's mother.

LIZZIE She's naethin tae me . . . naethin but a damned aul' nuisance. I've got tae earn every penny that comes intae ma hoose.

MRS HARRIS Aye, we ken that, and ye don't dae sae bad either. Buyin up aul' claes for a copper or two and selling them at sixpence a week and when the folks cannae pay, takin them back and selling them a' ower again.

MRS BONE Or she'll lend ye the money tae buy them ootright . . . at 50 percent interest.

MRS HARRIS Aye, she's got a right kind heart, she wouldnae see ye stuck, no if she could mak a good thing oot o' it onyway.

LIZZIE Ye're jealous! Because you havnae the brains tae mak a bit o' money yersels! But ye're no above tradin wi me. Whit aboot yon veloory hat ye bought aff me?

MRS HARRIS *(As if making a great effort to remember)* Veloory hat? Veloory hat? . . . Oh! Ye mean yon scabby aul' felt bunnet wi the moultin bird on tap? Oh aye! If yon wis veloory, I'm a Chinese dug.

LIZZIE It wis veloory! It belanged tae a lady in Kelvinside whaur I did a bit on a Saturday.

MRS HARRIS A bit whit? Pinchin?

LIZZIE Here! I could pit ye tae the polis for that.

MRS HARRIS No roon' aboot here ye couldn't. They a' ken ye.

GRANNY Oh I'm nae wantin tae leave here! I wisht I could jist bide wi Maggie till I dee.

LIZZIE Bide then, it'll no break ma heart.

GRANNY Alex and Isa cannae find a room.

LIZZIE It strikes me they havnae looked very hard.

MRS HARRIS Some folks is right selfish. You've naebody but yersel tae look efter, and ye'll no tak the pair aul' wife aff Maggie's haun's wioot a hale lot o' fuss. Strikes me she'd be better aff if she did go tae the Poorshoose.

GRANNY Oh no! Nae the Poorshoose.

MRS HARRIS Well ye'll be goin noo I suppose, she's a' ready.

LIZZIE Goin? Not me. I'm sittin right here till Maggie comes hame wi whit's left o' Granny's pension.

MRS BONE There'll no be much o' it left if I ken Mrs Morrison.

LIZZIE In that case I'll jist hae tae tak whit she bought. *(Goes across to cupboard and looks inside)*

MRS HARRIS *(Grabbing her and holding her back)* Here, you! Mrs Bone and me's in chairge o' this hoose, and ye'll keep yer dirty aul' neb oot o' the cupboards or we'll shout for the polis.

MRS BONE And ye're no wantin them up . . . not efter whit happened last Christmas . . . wis it ten days ye got for yon nice wee fraud ye did wi the Christmas Club Fund?

MRS HARRIS Aye. It wis right bad luck ye wis fun' oot, wisn't it?

(There is a ring at the door. Enter LILY.)

LILY Whaur's Maggie? Is she no back yet?

LIZZIE No yet, Lily. She's bein kep' a lang while at the hospital.

LILY And hev the men not been yet for the bed?

MRS HARRIS No yet. Ye ken whit they Hogg's men is. Aye like the coo's tail, and as much cheek when they dae show up.

GRANNY Eh dear dear! I'm gey wearied.

LIZZIE *You're* wearied! D'ye think ither folks isn't gey wearied o' you?

LILY I suppose you'll never be aul' yersel, Lizzie, an' need a bit lookin efter?

LIZZIE If I'm onythin like her, I'll stick ma heid in the gas oven lang afore I'm eighty.

MRS HARRIS If I wis you I'd dae it noo – nae poetry intended.

LIZZIE *(To LILY)* Whit are you dae'in here onyway? Hev they sacked ye at last?

LILY I'm servin the night. I can shairly get a bit o' the day tae masel . . . no that it's ony o' your business.

LIZZIE Funny tae me the way you can aye be bobbin in an' oot o' Maggie's. Ye must hev an awfu' nice boss. Or mebbe you're awfu' nice tae him, eh?

LILY *(Advancing threateningly)* Jist what dae you mean by that?

MRS BONE Tak no notice, Lily. Her tongue's that rotten it'll drap aff yin o' they days.

(There are sounds of girlish laughter on the stairs and ISA, JENNY and ALEX come in. The girls are arm in arm convulsed with laughter at some joke not shared by ALEX, who looks glum.)

ISA Oh Goad! The aul' yin's no awa yet.

JENNY I tell't ye we'd rin intae them, it taks a stick o' dennymite tae shunt Granny.

ISA Whaur's ma dear mither-in-law? Is she oot at the jiggin?

LILY Cut oot the impidence. She's at the hospital wi Bertie.

ISA Keep yer hair on, I jist thought she'd hev been here tae welcome me wi ootstretched airms.

LILY Ye'll get ma ootstretched airm in a minute and there'll be nae welcome aboot it.

ISA Keep yer hair on. Whit's the reason for a' the company? It's no a funeral is it?

LILY No yet.

JENNY *(To ISA)* D'ye see yon pair o' dried-up auld hags? D'ye ken whit they're efter? *(They shriek with laughter)*

ISA A coupla boyfriends.

JENNY They're efter a cup o' tea, it seems tae taste better in somebody else's hoose . . .

MRS HARRIS The impidence! And us lookin efter the aul' wife while you go traipsin roon' the toon.

JENNY It's nane o' your business whether I wis traipsin roon' the toon or sittin in the kirk . . . and the aul' yin's got plenty o' company noo, so ye can jist hop it.

ISA Aye. It's what ye might ca' a bit overcrowded here.

MRS BONE Well I'm sure I'm no wantin tae stay where I'm no wanted.

MRS HARRIS I've ma man's dinner to put on anyway.

JENNY Thank Goad this is the last I'll see o' you tea-tastin tabbies.

MRS HARRIS Dae ye tell me that noo?

JENNY Aye, I tell ye that. This little birdie's flyin awa frae the nest the day. Pit that in yer pipe and puff it oot tae the neighbours.

MRS BONE And whaur is the little birdie flyin tae, may I ask?

JENNY Ye can ask, but it disnae mean ye'll be tell't.

ISA High time ye wis flyin too, Jenny. Whit a nest!

LILY You wis glad enough tae fly tae it when yon midden ye wis in fell doon.

ISA Oh we jist came in tae help the aul' folk oot wi the rent. Ten shillings a week we're payin here, aren't we, Alex?

ALEX *(Looking surprised)* Aye. That's right.

LILY Ten shillings my eye. I can see you pairtin wi ten shillings a week.

ISA But I'm tellin ye! They cannae get on wioot us, can they, Alex? *(Gives him a kick in the shins)*

ALEX Aye. That's right enough.

LIZZIE Gettin ten shillings aff o' you and takin Granny's pension tae? Who says I'm no takin yon groceries?

LILY *(Grabbing her arm as she makes for the cupboard)* I says.

(There is a loud thump at the door. Enter two removal men.)

1st MAN Hiya, Granny! For the road again eh? My, the rare time you hae!

2nd MAN *(Grabbing bedstead)* Old iron, old iron, any any any old iron . . .

1st MAN *(Eyeing ISA and JENNY up and down and making 'the noise that makes horses and girls look round')* D'ye like blondes or brunettes, Joe?

2nd MAN Jist so lang's they're *(He illustrates 'curved')* I tak them ony way they come. Mind oot for ma taes!

1st MAN It's a wunner tae me this blisterin bed disnae walk doon the stairs and ontae the lorry itsel . . . I thought ye tell't us last time wis yer last trip, Granny? Did they gie ye a dose o' monkey gland here?

GRANNY Oh I'll no be botherin ye again. I'll no gang doon they stairs again wioot I'm carried in ma coffin. The Lord has beckoned me.

LIZZIE Well next time he beckons, just you go. But mind, I'm gie'in naethin towards yer funeral.

1st MAN Ach don't you worry, Granny, somebody'll bury ye, they'll no leave ye lyin aboot.

2nd MAN Come on. Get a move on. Here, we'll tak the bed doon first and come back for the mattress.

MRS HARRIS Well, I've ma man's dinner tae pit on.

(Exit men)

LIZZIE Well, are ye ready noo?

GRANNY Aye. I'm ready.

LIZZIE Come on then. But if ye think ye've heard the last o' the pension, ye can think again. I'll get it oot o' Maggie yet. I'm no sae saft as I look.

ISA Ye couldnae be ony safter.

LIZZIE If I wis you, Alex, I'd wallop that impident wife o' yours till she wis black and blue. It's the only thing that would learn her.

LILY For once I agree wi ye, Lizzie.

MRS BONE A good wallopin never did onybody ony harm when they needed it.

JENNY You should ken, you that's aye bumpin intae things efter yer man's been on the booze.

ISA Wallop me! He wouldnae dae that tae me! Would ye sweetheart?

(ALEX looks sheepish and hunts for a fag in his pockets. Enter the men.)

1st MAN Ups-a-daisy! *(To ALEX)* Here Mac, like tae gie's a haun'? That'll let Joe here tak doon the mattress.

(ALEX straightens up to comply, ISA pushes him aside)

ISA Here! Whit d'ye think ma husband is? A bloomin cairter?

1st MAN Ye don't mean tae tell me you're marriet tae *that*? *(Looks from one to the other and gives a long low whistle)* A good-lookin bit o' stuff like you?

2nd MAN Here! Are you thinkin o' stayin the night?

1st MAN It's an idea! *(He winks at ISA. The men go off with the bed-foot.)*

JENNY *(Not very pleased at the attention ISA has had)* Whit cheek those bloomin cairters has! I wouldnae waste ma breath on them.

MRS HARRIS Chance is a good thing. Well, I've ma man's dinner tae pit on.

ISA I seem tae have heard that somewhere before.

ALEX I could dae wi somethin tae eat masel.

ISA Could ye now? Just fancy that!

ALEX Whit aboot makin us some tea?

ISA Oh I couldnae dae that! This isnae ma hoose. I jist wait till I'm fed here.

LILY Oh ye dae, dae ye? Ye'll no last lang here at that rate. Maggie's got enough tae dae wioot lookin efter you. Hev ye nae word o' a room yet?

ISA I tellt ye! We're bidin tae help oot the old folks.

(Enter the men)

2nd MAN Cut it oot noo, we've anither job on. *(Seizes the mattress)*

1st MAN Sorry we cannae gie ye a lift in the cairt, Granny, but we're no allowed tae handle livestock.

LIZZIE We'll tak a penny on the tram, and if ye're no at the door in hauf an oor, I'll ken whaur tae look for ye.

1st MAN That's right, sweetheart, come right in and we'll let ye stand us a beer.

(Exuent the men, followed by GRANNY and LIZZIE. As they reach the door, MAGGIE enters wearily. Her hair is untidy and her face swollen with crying. She carries BERTIE's clothes in a bundle, and his boots, laces tied together, dangle from her finger.)

LILY *(Going to MAGGIE and taking her arm)* What is it, Maggie?

MAGGIE They've kep' him in.

(She breaks down and sobs. LILY takes her over to a chair and comforts her. The neighbours crowd around. LIZZIE and GRANNY stop in the doorway.)

GRANNY Maggie . . . Maggie . . . she says ye've tae gie back ma last week's pension.

MAGGIE Fancy them keepin him in . . . fancy them keepin him in . . . I never thought . . .

MRS HARRIS Is it the bronchitis, Mrs Morrison?

MAGGIE No. It's no bronchitis . . . it's T.B.

MRS BONE I kent it! I could hae tellt ye that . . . Whenever I heard him coughin I says tae masel it's T.B., as sure as I'm sittin here . . .

LILY Oh shut up . . . Don't cry, Maggie. It'll be a' for the best. They'll get him pit right in the hospital . . . they doctors kens everythin noo.

MRS HARRIS Puir wee felly! T.B.! My! That's bad.

MRS BONE Och awa. It's naethin at a'. They doctors is wonderfu wi lungs. They can tak them oot and pit them back in again wioot you knowin onythin aboot it.

JENNY Whit a lot o' rot . . . What kind o' nail varnish is that you've on, Isa?

ISA Coral. D'ye want a shot? *(Fishes in handbag and produces nail varnish. JENNY takes it and starts to paint her nails with care.)*

MRS HARRIS It's no' a lot o' rot! I kent a man that went tae hospital reg'lar tae hae his lings taken oot and blew up and pit back.

GRANNY Maggie, I'm awa. I'm awa tae Lizzie's and she says ye're tae gie back the pension ye cashed.

LILY Aw shut up aboot that bloomin pension! She's no gie'in it back, d'ye hear! Noo clear oot, Lizzie, and don't shut the door efter ye, Mrs Harris and Mrs Bone is just f . . .

MRS HARRIS Aye. I've ma man's dinner tae pit on.

MAGGIE He looked that wee and delicate in yon bed . . . and the doctors said he wis . . . said he wis . . . awa tae nothin . . . a little skellington, they said . . . *(She sobs again)*

LIZZIE Och pull yersel together, Maggie, he's no deid yet.

LILY Get oot! Go on, get oot, the lot o' ye. *(She rushes GRANNY and LIZZIE to the door, then holds it open for MRS BONE and MRS HARRIS)*

GRANNY *(At door)* I'm awa . . . Ye'll no' likely see me again.

LILY I wish we could count on that.

MRS HARRIS Well, I've ma . . .

JENNY and ISA . . . Man's dinner tae pit on.

MAGGIE Thanks for comin.

MRS HARRIS Oh that's a' right. Ye're welcome. *(Looking at JENNY and ISA)* In spite o' the insults.

MRS BONE We'll tak a wee look doon later, eh?

(They go off. ALEX goes across to his mother and feebly pats her back. She puts up her hand and holds his, and sobs again.)

MAGGIE I'm jist fit for naethin noo . . . Is the weans still oot playin? I'll need tae get them in and mak the tea . . .

LILY Sit doon, Maggie. I'll see tae the weans and the tea . . . when's John comin in?

MAGGIE I couldna say . . . he said he'd no be back for a while . . . How's ma Alex?

ALEX Fine, Ma . . . Ye havnae said hullo tae Isa.

MAGGIE *(Turning)* Are ye all right, Isa?

ISA *(Cockily)* Oh aye! I'm a' right. Sorry about Bertie.

JENNY Ye'll no have tae listen tae him coughin a' night noo.

MAGGIE *(Bursting into tears again)* Tae think that I ever grudged gettin up tae him.

JENNIE Oh cripes! Whit a hoose! Am I no glad tae be gettin oot o' this zoo!

MAGGIE Jenny, will ye no change yer mind noo?

JENNY Whit difference is there?

MAGGIE I wish ye'd stay. It's no natural for a girl tae want tae leave her hame . . .

JENNY It's natural tae this girl . . . I'm a' packed ready. I'm only waitin for Nessie tae get back, so I'll no go intae an empty hoose.

MAGGIE But ye'll come back and see us?

JENNY I'll see. *(Yawning)* I'm no makin ony rash promises. *(Goes off to bedroom. MAGGIE starts to cry again)*

MAGGIE I dinnae ken whit way tae bring weans intae the world at a' . . . slavin and worryin for them a' yer days . . . and naethin but heartbreak at the end o' it.

ALEX Aw come on, Ma, cheer up!

ISA Listen tae him! Mammy's big tumphy. G'on, ye big lump o' dough, awa oot and buy yersel a new dial, I'm seek lookin at that yin.

LILY Yin o' they days you'll get whit's comin tae ye, Alex's no sich a saftie as he looks.

(Enter JENNY in coat and hat, carrying battered suitcase)

ISA I'm glad tae hear it.

JENNY Well, I'm away. Cheerybye, everybody!

MAGGIE Ye're no goin like that?

JENNY Like what?

MAGGIE Wioot a kiss for me?

JENNY *(Opening door)* I'm no in the mood for kissin. *(When she opens door JOHN is standing in doorway. They look at each other)*

JOHN *(Quietly)* I thought you'd have gone.

JENNY *(Jauntily)* No, I'm just goin.

(He watches her go down the stairs, and comes slowly into the kitchen. He sees BERTIE's clothes on the table, picks up the little boots and dangles them.)

MAGGIE *(Beginning to cry)* They kep' him in, John.

JOHN I wis afraid o' that.

CURTAIN

ACT II

Scene 2

Scene: The same. Three months later.

ALEX and ISA are quarrelling in the bedroom. Their raised voices are first of all heard off, then ISA comes out in a soiled tawdry wrap with her hair about her shoulders.

ISA Aw shut up will ye . . . I'm sick o' yer jawin. *(Bangs bedroom door)*

ALEX *(Appearing at door in a half-dressed condition)* I'm tellin ye, Isa, I'll no staun' much mair o' it. I'm just tellin ye . . . that's a'.

ISA Aw can it. If ye think I'm goin on like this a' ma days ye can think again. You're no the only pebble on my beach, no by a lang chalk. If ye want tae keep me it's time ye wis makin a bit money again. I cannae live on air.

ALEX *(Placatingly)* We'll go tae the dugs the night, Isa, and mebbe I'll hae a bit o' luck.

ISA Aye, mebbe ye will and mebbe ye'll no.

ALEX Mind last time I won . . .

ISA Aye, and mind the last hauf dozen times ye lost . . . Whit did ye dae wi yon bag?

ALEX I flung it awa.

ISA Ye big fool! I'm needin a bag.

ALEX It's no safe, Isa . . . the polis . . .

ISA A coupla quid! A fat lot o' use that is tae us. Why the hell did ye no pick on a toff?

ALEX She looked like a toff . . . she'd on furs . . .

ISA Ach, rabbit likely. You're that dumb ye wouldnae ken the difference. I think I'll go wi ye next time.

ALEX It wouldnae be safe, ye've got tae be able tae rin.

ISA Aye. Rin! That's a' you're good for . . . rinnin. It's aboot time I wis daein the rinnin.

ALEX Isa! Ye're no tae talk like that.

ISA Ach! I'm sick o' ye! If I went wi Peter Robb I'd hae a fur coat, he proamised me . . . an' he's gettin a caur . . .

ALEX *(Hysterically)* Say that again an' I'll kill ye! I will! I'll kill ye! *(He takes her by the throat)*

ISA Stop it! Alex! Stop it! Ye're . . . chokin me.

ALEX *(Dropping her quickly)* Isa! Did I hurt ye? I didnae mean tae! . . . Isa! . . . I didnae mean tae hurt ye!

ISA Ye damned fool! Get oot! Get oot o' ma sight.

ALEX *(Abjectly)* Isa! I'm sorry, I jist see red when ye talk aboot Peter Robb

. . . I cannae see naethin but him and you together . . . and the way you wis last night . . . cairryin on wi him.

ISA Aye! Ye can use yer hauns a' right when it's a wumman ye're dealin wi, but if ye wis hauf a man, ye'd hev knocked his block aff last night.

ALEX He's bigger nor me . . . he'd hev hauf killed me.

ISA Fancy me mairryin a rat like you. The joke wis on me a' right that time.

ALEX Isa! I'll dae better by ye. I'll get ye a fur coat . . . I'll get ye onythin ye want, only don't leave me, Isa, I love ye! I dae, honest.

ISA Love! *(She laughs)* There's nae sich a thing. There's wantin tae sleep wi someone, or wantin someone tae pay for your clothes and feed ye, but there's nae love. No in this pairt o' the toon . . . don't kid yersel.

ALEX *(Trying to take her in his arms)* I love ye. I'm no fit for onythin when you're oot o' ma sight. I'm lost . . . and I get tae thinkin . . . and thinkin . . . and wonderin where ye are . . . and if . . .

ISA If I'm behavin masel? Well hauf the time I'm no.

ALEX Isa!

ISA Aw shut up! Ye're aye wantin tae slobber ower me. If ye wis onythin decent tae look at it wouldnae be sae bad, but ye're like somethin that's been left oot a' night in the rain . . . g'on, blow! Beat it! Get oot o' here afore I'm seek. I cannae staun' ye unless I'm canned. Get oot o' ma way noo, I'm gonnae get dressed and gae oot.

(She slams the bedroom door in his face. He stands looking at the closed door. Enter MAGGIE. She is dead beat. She carries her charing apron, rolled up, and a little dish of jelly. She clears a corner of the table for this and carefully lays it down, then she pulls up a chair and sinks into it.)

MAGGIE Whit is it, son?

ALEX Nothin! I'm a' right

MAGGIE Hev you an' Isa been at it again?

ALEX She's threatenin tae leave me.

MAGGIE Ye'd be better wioot her, she's nae use tae ye.

ALEX Don't you stert! I don't care whit you think! She's mines, and I'll no let ye speak aboot her, d'ye hear!

MAGGIE All right, all right . . . Look at they dishes still lyin there from the mornin . . . does naebody ever think o' me comin in tae this . . .

ALEX Aw shut up! Shut up! *(He suddenly sweeps everything off the table, then stands staring at the chaos on the floor)* I'm sorry, Ma! I didnae mean tae. I'll help ye clear it up.

MAGGIE *(On her knees clearing up)* Ye've broken the dish o' jelly Mrs Ferguson gied me tae tak up tae Bertie. I wis goin up the night wi it, tae gie it tae the nurse for his supper . . . he loves a wee bit jelly . . . well there's nae use greetin aboot it I suppose . . . are the weans a' right? *(Puts broken crockery, etc. in pail at sink)*

ALEX They've been oot a' day.

MAGGIE I tell't Isa tae mak a bit saps for them, dinner time.

ALEX She wisnae up.

MAGGIE It's no fair! Naebody lifts a haun' tae help me! I've tae go oot charin a' day, and then come home tae this. I wonder whit ye'd a' dae if I wis tae dee. Sometimes I think I'd be better aff deid. Whaur's yer feyther?

ALEX Havnae seen him.

MAGGIE I suppose you wis in yer bed tae a' mornin.

ALEX I wis tired.

MAGGIE I suppose ye wis too tired tae gae roon tae the Buroo wi yer feyther?

ALEX Whit's the use? There's nae jobs.

MAGGIE Nae work for the men. Aye plenty for the women. I'm that tired I could see the hale lot o' ye in hell. *(Taking out purse)* Would ye gae doon tae the chip shop and see if ye can get us a coupla pies and some chips for wur tea?

ALEX *(Trying to see what's in her purse)* Aye. A' right, Ma.

MAGGIE Get ninepence worth and anither loaf and a tin o' condensed. And see if ye can find Ernest and send him up and Edie tae, tae redd this place up a bit . . . I'm no fit tae dae naethin efter scrunnin a' day.

ALEX Ma, whit aboot a packet o' fags?

MAGGIE I've nae money for fags.

ALEX Jist ten Woodbines, Ma. I need them.

MAGGIE Ye're no needin them. Ye're jist wantin them, and ye'll hae tae dae a lot o' wantin afore ye're deid.

ALEX Aw shut up preachin, Ma! Ma nerves is a' tae Hell . . . I feel like cuttin ma throat.

MAGGIE Whit way is that tae talk?

ALEX There's nae use livin. Naebody cares a hang whit happens tae me.

MAGGIE Alex, ye ken that's no true. Dae ye think I don't care?

ALEX I wisht I could . . . but she's right . . . I havnae the guts.

MAGGIE Alex, whit is it, son?

ALEX She says she's goin wi Peter Robb . . . she says I'm nae use . . . Ma, I cannae staun' it if she goes wi him . . . I cannae staun' it!

MAGGIE I'll gie her a piece o' ma mind for gettin you intae this state. It's woke me up a bit tae find oot the way you two's been livin since ye came here. Ye're shakin, Alex. Hev ye had onythin tae eat the day?

ALEX I'd a cup o' tae.

MAGGIE I wisht we'd some spirits in the hoose! Whaur's Isa? Is she oot? *(ALEX points to the bedroom)* Isa! Isa! Alex, lie doon a minute ye're that white . . . *(She helps him over to the bed)*

ISA *(Coming out of bedroom)* What is it?

MAGGIE *(Pouring contents of purse on to table)* Alex's no weel. Rin doon quick and get a gill o' whisky.

ISA There's nae much in a gill.

MAGGIE Get a packet o' Woodbines tae . . . and you've tae leave aff tormentin him!

ISA Me? I'm no daein naethin!

MAGGIE Aye ye are! Threatenin tae leave him, when ye ken he's that daft aboot ye . . . Goad kens why, ye're a worthless slut if ever there wis yin.

ISA Keep yer insultin names tae yersel, ye dirty aul' bitch!

MAGGIE I'll learn ye tae ca' me a bitch!

(She slaps ISA's face. Enter JOHN in time to see the slap.)

JOHN Here! Whit's a' this?

ISA *(Crying)* She hit me! She's that rotten tae me . . .

JOHN Maggie! Whit dae ye think ye're daein?

MAGGIE Naethin she didnae deserve. She ca'd me a bitch.

JOHN Well ye're certainly actin like yin.

MAGGIE John!

JOHN Whit a hell o' a hoose tae come hame tae.

MAGGIE It's no ma fault! I've been oot cleanin a' day . . . and the hale lot o' ye's had naethin tae dae and ye couldnae even wash a dish for me. It's me that aye has tae dae twa jobs when you get the sack.

JOHN Aw shut up harpin on that string! It's no' ma fault. I've been oot a' day lookin for work.

MAGGIE I've seen yous men lookin for work! Haudin up the corner o' the Burroo, ca'in doon the Government and the Trade Unions and the Means Test and . . .

JOHN Shut yer row.

MAGGIE Ye might at least hev cleaned up a bit afore ye went oot.

JOHN I'm no turnin masel intae a bloomin skivvy . . . I'm a man, I've got tae keep ma self-respect. I don't mind dryin the dishes and keepin the weans noo and again, but tae hell wi this Jessie business every time I'm oot o' a job.

ISA Ye're quite right. A woman disnae respec' a man that's nae a man.

MAGGIE Some folks has funny ideas.

ISA Whit aboot this whisky?

JOHN Whit whisky?

ISA For Alex, he's no weel.

MAGGIE He's lyin doon.

JOHN If he's no weel it's mair likely because his system's poisoned wi the stuff a'ready. There's nae money goin oot o' this hoose on whisky. Alex, get oot o' that and show yer face.

MAGGIE I tell't ye he's no weel, John.

(JOHN goes across to the bed and drags ALEX out)

JOHN Get ootside and breathe some fresh air, at least whit passes for fresh air roon' here. Ye're gettin nae whisky. D'ye understaun?

MAGGIE Who earned that money? You or me?

(JOHN instantly drops ALEX and turns away. ALEX slinks out. There is a pause.)

ISA That's right. He's needin somebody tae tak him in haun'. *(Sits down and starts to cry)* He's beyond me. I can dae naethin wi him.
MAGGIE Oh will ye listen tae that!
JOHN Don't cry, Isa. He's no worth it.
MAGGIE It's her that's the worthless yin . . . if she'd leave him alane . . .
JOHN It's your fault, ye've spoiled him from the day he wis born.
MAGGIE John! That's no fair!
ISA Aye, he's spoilt. He's just like a great big baby. If he disnae get whit he wants, he greets. It maks ye that ashamet o' him.

(MAGGIE puts her hat and coat on)

JOHN Where are ye off tae?
MAGGIE Tae get somethin tae eat for the tea.

(ISA looks at her and starts to shriek with laughter; she laughs and laughs)

MAGGIE Whit's the joke?
ISA Yer hat! A fryin pan wioot a handle! I never seen sich a Pairris muddle. *(She shrieks again)*
JOHN Goad aye! I never looked at it afore! It's a stunner!

(He starts to laugh too. MAGGIE turns her back on them and wipes her eyes on her sleeve, then she faces them, half crying.)

MAGGIE If you could keep a job, mebbe ye could buy me a new hat once in ten years.

(Exit MAGGIE)

JOHN Keep a job!
ISA It's no fair o' her tae say that tae ye. It's no every woman's been as licky as she's been wi her man. If I'd had a feyther like you, mebbe I'd hae lived better but ma feyther wis never sober . . . he used tae knock me aboot . . .
JOHN I didnae ken that, Isa. Mebbe ye shouldnae be blamed . . .
ISA Oh I'm no sayin I shouldnae be blamed . . . I thought it would be great fun tae show a green lad a bit o' life, but Goad knows I didnae mean tae be stuck wi him for the rest o' ma life . . . if I could just hae looked intae the future and seen that he wis gonnae be sich a wash-oot, and that the baby wis gonnae die onyway . . . but whit's the use of talkin noo . . . there's nae future in this kind o' life.
JOHN Ye've mair chance o' seein a decent future than I hev. Ye're young.
ISA Aye. I wis just thinkin . . . it's right tough on you . . . if you wis single

you could gae aff tae Americky or Australia or somewhere and mak yer fortune.

JOHN Ma fortune!

ISA Aye, yer fortune! A great big handsome man like you . . . and wi an air aboot ye.

JOHN *(JOHN looks very pleased)* An air aboot me?

ISA Aye. As if ye wis somebody.

JOHN What? In these claes?

ISA There's some o' us can see whit's *un'er* the claes, if ye know whit I mean. Noo I can see you *(She half closes her eyes)* . . . I can see you dressed up in tails, like yin o' they posh waiter blokes at the Beresford. Wi your shoulders and yer height . . . ye'd look smashin. But whit's the use? You're pinned doon here wi Maggie and the weans.

JOHN *(Half-heartedly)* Ye're no tae say onythin against Maggie.

ISA Oh no! Maggie's a good sort. Kind o' ready wi her hands *(Feels her cheeks)*, but nae wunner wi a' they kids tae skelp aboot. Of course that's the only kind o' life Maggie would understaun' . . . bringin weans intae the world and wallopin them aboot. I can see you as yin o' they waiter fellies, but I'm blowed if I can see Maggie handin oot gin and T. She disnae dae naethin wi hersel . . . Even when she gaes oot wi you . . . I mean tae say . . . a man likes his woman tae deck hersel oot a bit. Am I no right?

JOHN Aye, that's true. But it's no very easy for Maggie. The children has aye come first wi her, and efter a few years ye begin tae forget whit ye used tae look like I suppose . . . I'm a bit o' a sight masel the noo?

ISA Well . . . Ye could dae wi a shave and a bit grease on yer hair.

JOHN Don't mention ma hair, Isa! It's fightin a losin battle. It's been retreatin for years.

ISA Still, I wouldnae say it wisnae quite distinguished-lookin. They wee bits o' grey above yer ears . . . like Clive Brook in the fillums . . . Noo that I come tae look at ye . . . ye're no unlike him!

JOHN Me! Like a fillum star! Ye're an awfu' lassie! . . . Alex'll mebbe hev some hair, eh?

ISA Aye, I believe he has.

JOHN I'll mebbe borry some sometime. So ye think I'd look a'right if I wis dressed?

ISA Ye'd look great. I wisht Alex had taken efter you.

JOHN I've kinda got intae a rut.

ISA A night oot would dae ye a lot o' good.

JOHN Och, I've given up thinkin o' that sort o' thing . . . when there's just the dole . . . it's no fair on Maggie.

ISA It'll no dae her ony herm you goin oot once in a while and enjoyin yoursel.

JOHN Jist the same . . .

ISA Ach, ye'll be an aul' man afore ye ken it, goin on like this.

JOHN I'm an aul' man noo . . . at least I feel it.

ISA Ye're just in the prime o' life.

JOHN I'll tell ye whit it is, Isa. When ye're responsible for a wife and a faimly and ye've nae steady job, ye get that anxious aboot them, ye stop thinkin o' yersel as a man . . . as the man ye used tae be when ye got merriet, and ye become jist . . . a feyther.

ISA That's no much fun, is it?

JOHN Are you tellin me? . . . Of course, there's no much fun in it for Maggie either.

ISA Och she disnae expect ony fun. She's no the type.

(Enter EDIE and ERNEST)

ERNEST Whaur's Ma?

JOHN Gettin messages . . . whit you should be daein for her. When I wis your age I'd hev got a good leatherin . . . you should be here when yer ma comes hame tae see whit she wants.

ERNEST Aw cripes! Ye cannae pit yer heid in the door but someone's jawin ye.

JOHN Cut it oot. Get on and redd this place up a bit.

ERNEST I dinnae ken whaur tae stert!

JOHN Neither dae I.

(EDIE starts to clear the table by the simple expedient of heaping things on to the dresser)

EDIE I'll set the table. Is the kettle on, Isa?

ISA Look and see. I'm nae wantin tea here. I'm goin oot tae mines.

EDIE *(In awstruck tones)* Goin oot tae yer tea! In a rest-ur-ant? By! Ye lucky dog! I wisht I wis grown up.

(ISA goes off to bedroom)

ERNEST She'll be meetin yon big fat toff she wis wi last night.

JOHN *(Giving him a cuff on the ear)* You keep yer trap shut.

(Enter MAGGIE. She puts down a loaf, a tin of milk, and a paper of chips.)

JOHN *(Sheepishly)* Ye wernae lang.

(MAGGIE does not answer. She is plainly 'at the end of her tether'. She moves about the kitchen making preparations for tea. Suddenly she sees ERNEST's boots, the toes of which are kicked to pieces, and what remains of her self-control gives way.)

MAGGIE Look at yer boots! *(She seizes him, shakes and hits him)* Ye've kicked the taes oot o' them again! I'll learn ye tae play fitba' . . . I'll learn ye tae kick the taes oot o' yer boots! *(She is crying hysterically and belabouring*

ERNEST) Where dae ye think I'll find anither pair for ye? . . . I cannae staun' any mair o' this . . . Oh I cannae staun' it!

(She collapses in a storm of weeping. EDIE puts down the bread she is cutting and joins in out of fear and sympathy. ERNEST shrinks against his father who puts his arm round his shoulders.)

JOHN It's all right, son, yer ma's just tired. She's been oot scrubbin a' day and she's wore oot. Women gets like that when they're tired. It's no that she disnae want ye tae play fitba', son . . . it's no that she disnae want ye tae enjoy yersel . . . it's just that . . . if ye kick the taes oot o' yer shoes, we'll hae tae find the money tae buy anither pair . . . that's whit it is . . . D'ye understand, son? It's no that's she's meanin tae be angry wi ye . . . it's just . . . the way things are . . .

CURTAIN

END OF ACT II

ACT III

Scene 1

Scene: The same. Christmas Eve.

The kitchen has been cleaned and tidied. The table is covered with a red cloth, and there are fresh curtains at the window. The dresser is clear for once. A new-looking wireless set has been added, covered with a lace doily, and topped with a vase of Woolworth's carnations. ERNEST has his ear glued to this, listening ecstatically to a jazz band, keeping time with a poker, and occasionally rising to 'jive' and emit the weird noises that emanate from a red hot rhythm fan. GRANNY is back again. She is sitting in the rocking chair, looking almost festive. The kitchen has been festooned with coloured streamers, and there is a microscopic Christmas tree, decorated with tinsel and little coloured candles.

MAGGIE enters, followed by JOHN. Both are laden with parcels. MAGGIE is wearing a bright red hat.

ERNEST Oh, Ma! Mair presents? Onythin fir me?

JOHN Whit would there be for you? Whit hev you done tae deserve onythin eh? *(Hands him a parcel)* Here! I didnae mean tae let you hev them till the morn, but I cannae help it. Open it. G'on, open it.

MAGGIE G'on, son. Open it. Let's see whit Santa's bought ye. *(ERNEST unties parcel)*

GRANNY Mair spending. Ye'd think ye'd come intae a fortune.

JOHN Listen, aul' yin! This is the first Christmas I've had a decent job for aboot ten year . . . and we'll maybe no be able tae say the same next year. We're hevin a splash. Money nae object . . . while it lasts . . . This Christmas is gonnae be somethin tae remember when Maggie and me's a coupla aul' toothless has-beens.

GRANNY Waste not. Want not. Ye'll rue the day . . . did ye get onythin for me?

MAGGIE You'll get your stockin the morn. D'ye like ma present frae John?

GRANNY Whit is it?

MAGGIE Can ye no see? Ma hat! *(Goes over to let GRANNY see it)*

GRANNY Fancy an aul' woman like you wi a red hat! Ye're nae wise.

JOHN It's a real tonic o' a hat, and it wis me that choosed it, and I'm a man o' taste.

MAGGIE Wait till Mrs Bone and Mrs Harris sees it.

(ERNEST has got his parcel open. He brings out a pair of football boots, and sits down, overcome.)

ERNEST Oh Ma! Oh Pa!

JOHN Well? Where's yer mainners? Whit dae ye say?

ERNEST *(With a lump in his throat)* Thank ye *awfu'* much. They're jist . . . *super!* *(He hugs them, then tears off his boots, and tries on the football boots, carefully arranging his holey socks over his toes. Then he walks around the kitchen in them, making imaginary tackles, sprints, and shooting imaginary goals. Every now and then he remembers the wireless and stops to 'jive'.)* Oh boy! This is the happiest day of my life. Fitba' boots and a wireless! Oh great!

MAGGIE *(Putting on kettle)* I think I'll chap Mrs Bone for a wee cup wi us. Her man'll be oot on the batter. *(She gets up on the chair and knocks the ceiling with brush. There is an answering thump. She goes to the window and leans out, shouting up.)* Comin doon? I've got the kettle on.

MRS BONE *(Screaming off)* Aye! I'll be right doon.

(MAGGIE gets out the cups, etc., still wearing her hat and admiring herself wherever she can see her reflection)

MAGGIE *(Singing)* God bless you merry gentlemen, let nothing you dismay . . .

JOHN *(Joining in)* Let nothing you dismay. Remember Christ our Sa-a-viour wis . . .

ERNEST *(Joining in)* . . . born on Christmas Day . . .

ERNEST This is the happiest day o' ma life!

(Enter MRS BONE and MRS HARRIS. MRS BONE has a large egg-shaped lump on her forehead.)

MRS BONE My! Whit swells we are! I chapped Mrs Harris in passin, seein the tea's bein made onyway.

MAGGIE Aye that wis right. We'll hae an Abernethy seein it's a special occasion. My coanscience! Whit a bump ye've got!

MRS BONE Och it's no much. Yer place is lookin a treat.

MRS HARRIS Whaur's the kids?

MAGGIE At the Mission. There's a treat. A present each and their tea, a' for sixpence. It's rare tae get them frae under yer feet.

MRS HARRIS Alex and Isa oot?

MAGGIE Aye.

MRS HARRIS Daein their Christmas shoppin, eh? *(There is a knock at the door)*

MAGGIE Ernie, go and see who that is, son. *(ERNEST lets in MRS WILSON)*

MRS WILSON *(With a shriek of simulated surprise)* Oh! A pairty!

MAGGIE *(MAGGIE rises for another cup)* Come in, Mrs Wilson. Ernie, pull up yon chair for Mrs Wilson . . . Mind yersel noo, Mrs Wilson, the back legs is broke.

MRS WILSON *(Seating herself gingerly)* I'll mind. Oh! Ye're a' decorated! My! Isn't that lovely. Ta! *(As MAGGIE hands her tea)* Who done it? *(Sucks up her tea with enjoyment)*

JOHN Me and the kids did the decorations.

ERNEST I done the big yins, didn't I, Pa? D'ye like ma fitba' boots? *(The women exclaim admiringly)*

MRS WILSON My! Rangers'll be signin ye!

ERNEST Rangers be damned. I'm Celtic.

MAGGIE Ernie, mind yer language in front o' the ladies.

ERNEST Aw g'on! I ken a hale lot mair. I ken . . . *(Counts on fingers)*

JOHN Mind it onyway. Y're too young tae be usin they words.

MRS BONE Whaur's yer sister Lily the night? Is she workin?

MAGGIE No she's aff. She's comin roon' later, she's workin a' day tomorrow.

MRS WILSON On Christmas Day! Whit a shame!

MAGGIE Och it makes nae difference tae Lily. She's nae carin.

MRS HARRIS She's a nice girl Lily. Funny the way she missed the boat. D'ye no think it's made her a bit soor-like?

MRS WILSON Considerin the number o' boats that sinks, she's as weel swimmin alang by hersel.

MAGGIE Well! I'm waitin.

MRS HARRIS Eh?

MAGGIE I'm waitin on ye sayin whit ye think o' ma new hat.

MRS BONE I've jist been sittin lookin at it. Is it yer ain?

MAGGIE Of course it's ma ain! It's John's Christmas tae me.

MRS BONE Is it no a wee thing wild for ye?

MAGGIE Naethin o' the sort. John likes me in it.

MRS HARRIS Some folks don't know when they're weel aff wi their men folks. I hope she appreciates ye, Mr Morrison.

MAGGIE I've always appreciated him. *(To GRANNY)* Here, Granny, here's a wee biscuit tae dip in yer tea.

MRS WILSON Aw! I never noticed ye sittin there, as quiet as a moose. Glad tae be back for Christmas, eh?

GRANNY Aye. I'm jist sittin here thinkin . . . it's the last time I'll hear the Christmas bells.

MRS WILSON Och awa! Ye'll see us a' in wur graves yet . . . I seen the men come wi Granny's bed the morn. My! Wis I mad! Big hob nails a' ower ma pipeclay . . . and the *impidence* o' them! Yon ugly big yin wi the navy blue chin, he says tae the wee yin, somethin aboot 'seein some rare views in this job', I just says says I, 'some back views is a hell o' a sight better than some front views, mentionin nae names'.

MRS HARRIS They've got tae be kep' in their places, they men.

JOHN *(Getting up)* Ye should hae threatened him wi yer man.

MRS WILSON Oh he wisnae up. He wis sleepin aff the night afore. Gettin intae trainin for Hogmanay.

MAGGIE *(To JOHN)* Whaur are you aff tae?

JOHN Oot.

MRS HARRIS Gettin intae trainin tae?

JOHN No me! It's nae worth it. I'm jist feelin a bit ootnumbered here. Four tae one's a bit thick. Cheerio, Mrs Wilson, see ye next year. *(He goes off)*

MRS HARRIS My! You're lucky, Mrs Morrison. There's no mony men can stay T.T. like that. Mine's aye makin proamises, but he cannae resist the smell o' a cork.

MAGGIE Well there's nae use pretendin I havnae had ma troubles in the past.

MRS HARRIS I'm no awfu' sure I'd like ma Boab tae go T.T. Of course, ma Boab's a regular Setterday nighter. Ye get intae the routine. I'm aye ready for onythin frae gettin a black eye tae puttin a corpse tae bed. If he wis tae go T.T. it would be like sittin on tap o' a volcany. I'd never ken when he wis gonnae erupt.

MAGGIE John's learnt his lesson. He kens I'd close the door on him if he sterted again.

MRS BONE Wull ye tell me hoo ye can close the door on a man? Mines would batter it doon.

MAGGIE Ye can close the doors o' yer heart on him, and once ye've din that tae yer man, batterin wull no get him in.

MRS WILSON My! Ye're that poetic, Mrs Morrison! The doors o' yer heart! I wonder hoo mony o' us has hearts left, let alane doors tae them.

(Enter LILY)

LILY Are ye haudin open hoose the night? Yer door wis open . . . Hullo, Mrs Wilson, hullo, Mrs Harris. My! Mrs Bone, whit's up wi yer forehead?

MRS BONE I fell doon the dunny stairs.

(ERNEST whistles 'And the band played believe it if ye like'. LILY puts some parcels down on the table and takes off her hat and coat.)

LILY That wis awfu'. Is this a pairty ye're hevin, Maggie?

MAGGIE We're no eatin nothin.

LILY I should hope no, tomorrow's Christmas. I think I'd better stay the night or ye'll hev the hale hoose ett afore the morn.

MAGGIE Whit's in they parcels, Lily?

LILY Oh jist a bit fruit cake, and a few sweeties for the kids' stockins. I bought ye a pair o' gloves. *(Gives MAGGIE parcel)*

MAGGIE Oh my! Aren't they lovely. *(Unwrapping a pair of yellow fabric gloves. MRS BONE and MRS HARRIS grab them and feel them, pass them to MRS WILSON, who holds them up to the light, and blows one up.)*

MRS BONE *(Under her breath to MRS HARRIS)* Sixpence each in Woolies.

LILY They wis nutt sixpence each in Woolworth's!

MRS HARRIS *(Glibly)* She'd hae been better wi a pair o' woollens . . . for winter, ye ken.

MAGGIE *(Putting on gloves)* Woollens isnae dress. These is posh. Thanks, Lily, I've somethin for you . . . ye'll get it later . . . it's a bit mair intimate than gloves.

MRS BONE A pair o' . . .

MAGGIE No it's no!

(Enter ALEX. He looks strained and nervous.)

ALEX Isa been in?

MAGGIE No, son.

ALEX Are ye sure?

MAGGIE I havnae seen her. You've been in a' efternoon, Ernie, hev you seen her?

ERNEST Nope. Ma, I think I'll awa oot and see some o' the chaps.

MAGGIE Right ye are . . . don't be late back or ye ken whit ye'll get. *(ERNEST starts for the door)* Ye're no goin oot in they boots?

ERNEST Sure I am! I'm no lettin these oot o' ma sight, no likely! *(He goes off)*

MAGGIE Is there onythin wrang, Alex?

(ALEX goes into the bedroom without answering)

MRS BONE Alex's no lookin weel, these days.

MRS WILSON Awfu' kind o' white and starey-like.

MRS HARRIS Alex wis aye a bit starey-like though, wisn't he?

LILY Naethin o' the sort! Starey-like yersel.

MRS BONE Maybe he's threatenin goitre? I kent a woman took the goitre . . .

(ALEX reappears)

MAGGIE Would ye like a cup o' tea, son?

ALEX No. Aye. I wull.

(MAGGIE starts to get up)

LILY Sit doon. I'll pour it. *(Gives ALEX tea)*

MAGGIE Whaur hev ye been a' day, Alex?

ALEX Oh jist roon' aboot.

MRS HARRIS He's no gien onythin away, are ye, Alex? *(She digs him in the ribs. He jumps nervously and spills his tea.)*

ALEX *(Shrilly)* Watch oot, ye old fool!
MAGGIE Alex!

(ALEX gets up. There is a pause.)

MRS WILSON Awful pretty the tree looks, doesn't it?
LILY It'll be prettier when the candles is lit. I'm lookin forward tae seein Christopher's face when he comes in. Bless his wee heart.
MRS BONE Yon's a lovely yin they hev in Bertie's ward at the hospital . . . nice he wis back frae the convalescent for Christmas . . . did that mean he'll be hame soon?
MAGGIE I wis hopin so, but the nurse said he wisnae ready yet, they're aye tryin new treatments. She said if he'd a room tae hissel at hame, and could get plenty o' fresh air . . . fancy thinkin ony wean has a room tae hissel hereaboots! No, he'll no be hame yet awhile. I doot it's a lang job.
MRS HARRIS Pair wee lad.
MAGGIE Ye havnae touched yer tea, Alex.
ALEX I'm no wantin it.
MAGGIE No wantin it efter it bein poured twice for ye?
ALEX All right, all right! I'll drink it if that'll shut ye up. Can ye no leave me alane? Ye'll drive me aff ma heid. Does yous women's tongues never staun still? Clatter clatter clatter, yap yap yap a' day . . . *(He goes off)*
MAGGIE I'm sure I dinnae ken whit's come ower him.
MRS BONE Aye. Whiles he's that quiet he cannae say boo tae a goose and whiles ye'd think he wis jist gettin ready tae knife ye.
MRS HARRIS He hasnae been drinkin has he?
MRS WILSON Sometimes it's difficult tae tell unless ye can get near enough tae get a smell at their breaths.
LILY They seem tae me tae act queer drunk or sober, and ye tell me I've missed masel no gettin a man.
MRS WILSON It's a peety there's no way o' gettin weans wioot a man tacked ontae them.
LILY Weans! They're supposed tae be poor man's riches. The way some o' them turns oot there's nae much riches aboot it.
MAGGIE I wisht ye hadnae said that, Lily. I've been tryin tae keep ma mind aff Jenny a' night. I've got a kind o' feelin aboot her.

(MRS BONE and MRS HARRIS exchange glances)

MRS BONE Well, me and Mrs Harris wisnae gonna say onythin, but we seen her last week.
MAGGIE How wis she? Whit did she look like? Wis she happy? *(They exchange glances again)* Did ye speak tae her? . . . Wis she alone, or . . .
MRS BONE Aye, she wis by hersel.
MAGGIE Where wis she? Whit wis she daen?
MRS HARRIS She wis jist walkin.

MAGGIE Did ye no speak tae her?

MRS BONE We didnae like.

LILY Oh forget her. People like Jenny can aye look efter themselves. I wouldnae waste ony sympathy on her. Ony sympathy I've got tae waste I waste on . . .

MRS HARRIS Yersel.

LILY No. On her. *(Pointing to MAGGIE)*

MAGGIE Well, ye can get ready tae waste a bit mair on me . . . I'm expectin again.

(The women let out screeches)

MRS HARRIS Ye're no?

MRS BONE Oh my! Is that no a dirty shame!

MRS WILSON Goad help ye!

LILY *(Getting up and going over to the window)* Ye're past praying for, Maggie. Ye ken whit the doctor said last time.

MAGGIE I ken . . . but ye cannae help these things . . . they jist happen.

LILY Well they've nae right to be allowed tae happen. Maggie!

MAGGIE Och it's all right, Lily. I'll get through it same as the ithers.

MRS HARRIS Whit *did* the doctor say?

MAGGIE Oh Ah cannae mind. Jist the usual haverins.

LILY He said she wis tae have nae mair, or he couldnae answer for the consequences. It's terrible, Maggie! And ye sit there as if nothin had happened.

MAGGIE Och well, ye've just got tae accept these things.

LILY And whit aboot the weans if anything wis tae happen to you?

MAGGIE Och naethin's gonnae happen tae me.

MRS BONES Whit does yer man say?

MAGGIE Oh Goad! I havnae tell't him yet. I'm feart! I'm no wantin tae spoil his Christmas.

LILY *(Viciously)* I'll tell him though! Jist wait! Maggie, ye'll come roon' tae the doctor's wi' me the night.

MAGGIE It's Christmas Eve!

LILY I don't care, ye'll come roon' wi' me the night.

MAGGIE Sit doon and be quiet. Ye'd think the world wis comin tae an end.

LILY Anither wean! Mair riches for the poor man!

(There is a thumping from upstairs. MRS BONE jumps as if she'd been shot and scurries to the door.)

MRS BONE That's ma man. See ye later. *(She goes off)*

MRS HARRIS Fancy that! I'd like to see my man thump doon for me. I'd thump him.

(There is a bang at the door. LILY goes, leaving the kitchen door open. Through it an irate voice is heard.)

VOICE Is ma woman there? Well tell her tae get the hell oot o' it . . . I'm wantin ma tea.

MRS HARRIS Well . . . I'll love ye and leave ye . . . I'll tak a wee look doon the morn tae wish ye a Merry Christmas.

MRS WILSON I'm comin tae – he's aboot due. *(They go off together)*

LILY Maggie!

MAGGIE Och stop worryin, Lily. I'll be all right . . . Fancy them seein Jenny! . . . The nights she's been in ma dreams! The times I've held oot ma airms tae her tae find she's no there efter a' . . . if she only come tae see me noo and again . . .

LILY She's no worth botherin aboot.

MAGGIE It's weel seen you never had a family, Lily. Once they've been laid in yer airms they're in yer heart tae the end o' yer days, and there's naething ye can dae aboot it. It taks a mother tae understand a mother . . . Oh drat it! There's Granny been asleep maist o' the efternoon, she'll be shoutin on me hauf the night noo, no sleepin . . . Lily? Whit aboot takin a wee rin up Sauchiehall Street tae see the shops? There's jist aboot time afore the weans comes in.

LILY Are ye sure y're no too tired?

MAGGIE No me. Besides, I'm wantin tae air ma new lid. *(She puts on her new hat and admires herself in the mirror then she pulls on her new gloves)* These are lovely, Lily. Ye're right good tae me. Ye didnae say ye liked ma hat.

LILY It's no bad.

MAGGIE No bad!

LILY Come on, if we're goin . . . ye're no wantin tae be oot lang, it's cold . . . Whit aboot Granny?

MAGGIE Aye. Isn't she an aul' pest! D'ye think we should pit her tae bed afore we gang?

LILY Aye. Gie her an asprin and a sweetie, that'll keep her quiet.

MAGGIE Come on, Granny. Bed time.

LILY *(Looking in bag)* I've an asprin here. *(They rouse GRANNY and take her, protesting, to the bedroom)*

GRANNY Whit? Why dae I need tae gang tae ma bed? I'm quite happy sleepin in ma chair.

MAGGIE Ye'll be mair comfortable in yer bed dear.

GRANNY Whit are ye up tae? Ye're goin oot! Ye're goin oot tae leave me!

MAGGIE No we're no! Whit gave ye that idea!

GRANNY It's Christmas Eve and I'm no goin tae ma bed . . . I'm no goin tae ma bed . . . it's no fair!

(They finally get her off. LILY crushes the aspirin, MAGGIE and

GRANNY can be heard, MAGGIE cajoling, GRANNY protesting, then MAGGIE emerges.)

MAGGIE Whew! I jist whipped aff her tap things and rolled her under . . . come on noo, Lily, I jist love tae see a' they posh shops . . . *(They go off)*

(The stage is empty for a few minutes. In the distance a Salvation Army band starts to play Christmas carols. The sound comes nearer throughout the scene until, at the end, the band is outside the house. After a moment, ISA walks in. She looks cautiously round the room, looks into the bedroom, then she goes in and shuts the door. There are sounds of drawers and boxes being opened and shut. Presently she emerges with a suitcase which she puts down. She then starts to make up her face quickly, glancing round from time to time. When she has finished, she picks up suitcase and goes to the door. When she opens it ALEX is standing on the threshold.)

ALEX *(Hysterically)* So ye're back are ye? Where wis ye last night?
ISA Oh did ye miss me?
ALEX Where wis ye? Isa! Where wis ye?
ISA Whit dis it maitter? I'm clearin oot. I'm leavin ye.
ALEX Were ye . . . wi him?
ISA Aye. We'd a rare time. He's got a caur noo, we wis oot at a nice wee pub in the country . . .
ALEX A car . . .
ISA Aye. I like caurs. And I like decent claes . . . whit I'm no likely tae get wi you. Noo if ye'll excuse me, I've a date.
ALEX Isa! . . . Isa!
ISA *(Looking up at him and arrested by his look)* Whit are ye lookin at me like that for?
ALEX I tellt ye I'd kill ye if ye did it. Ye thought I didnae hev the guts. Ye said I wisnae a man. But I'll show ye . . . *(He grabs her, she gets free and runs for the bedroom, she tries to hold the door against him, but he pulls her out)*
ISA Alex! . . . Alex, I didnae mean it. I'll stay wi ye. Honest I will. I love ye, Alex. I love ye. *(She throws her arms round his neck and presses herself against him, he gradually succumbs to her. They kiss.)*
ALEX Stay wi me, Isa . . . don't leave me. Stay wi me. Tell me ye never meant it . . . tell me ye love me. It's that lang since ye've kissed me . . . like that.
ISA I love ye, Alex.

(After another long kiss, he buries his face in her shoulder. She tries to think of a way of escaping his embrace after a moment.)

ISA A minute, Alex, ye're hurtin me. That's better. Hev ye got a fag?

ALEX Isa . . . Isa . . . I'm daft aboot ye.

(He gets out a packet of Woodbine and a match. As he is striking the match on the sole of his shoe, she puts out her foot and trips him up, then runs for the outside door. He catches her, the strains 'O Come All Ye Faithful' from the Salvation Army Band swell, as

THE CURTAIN FALLS

ACT III

Scene 2

Scene: The same. A summer evening seven months later.

The kitchen has reverted to its former untidy state. MAGGIE, in an obvious state of pregnancy, is sitting, and EDIE is holding a wet towel to her mother's forehead.

EDIE Is that better, Ma?

MAGGIE Aye, Edie. That's better. Jist gie me anither wee minute, then I'll get up and get on wi it.

EDIE Would ye no just go tae bed, Mammy? Auntie Lily will be here in a wee while.

MAGGIE It's no fair pittin it a' ontae yer Auntie Lily . . . she's her ain work through the day. Look and see if the weans is asleep yet.

> *(EDIE goes off right. MAGGIE holds the towel to her head and sighs. EDIE returns.)*

EDIE Marina's readin a coamic. Is that a' right?

MAGGIE Och I'm past carin if she's readin the encyclopaedia. Is Christopher a' right?

EDIE Aye. He's sleepin. I shut his mooth.

MAGGIE That's right. His tonsils'll need tae wait till I'm by.

EDIE I'm glad I had mines took out. Nae mair sore throats . . . Ma?

MAGGIE Aye?

EDIE Mrs Wilson wis asking me if Granny wis away tae the Poorshoose.

MAGGIE Whit did ye say?

EDIE I said I didnae ken.

MAGGIE Och the hale street kens she's awa . . . she kicked up enough row when they came for her . . . pair aul' thing.

EDIE My Auntie Lizzie's a mean thing. She'll go tae Hell when she dies.

MAGGIE There's plenty o' Hell here, wioot waitin tae dee.

EDIE Ma?

MAGGIE Whit is it noo?

EDIE People are always stoppin me and askin questions. Mrs Wilson wis askin me when Pa wis comin home . . . He hasnae gone away for good has he?

MAGGIE Yer pa'll be back . . . when he's ready tae come.

EDIE Gracie Brown's feyther left hame.

MAGGIE Don't you worry, Edie, Pa'll come back when he's got back his senses. I never thought I'd speak tae you like this aboot yer feyther, but ye may as well learn young. Ye've been brought up in the slums, and if ye marry ye'll marry in the slums, so ye may as well ken whit's in front o' ye.

EDIE Ma! Is it ever like it is in the fillums? Ye know . . . lovin a man?

MAGGIE I don't know, Edie. I'd like tae think it wis. Mebbe for some folks that are lucky enough never tae ken whit it is tae have poverty comin in at the door and drivin love oot the windy. Ye cannae be gentle and loving and kind when ye're worried oot o' yer wits for yer rent and yer food and yer claes, year in year out.

(Enter JOHN. He has obviously been on the batter, and remorse of conscience has set in. He is unsure of his reception.)

JOHN *(Putting his hand on EDIE's hair)* Hullo, Edie.

(EDIE dodges under his arm and runs out of the room)

MAGGIE Ye've got back hev ye?

JOHN Aye, I've got back. I'm sorry, Maggie . . . I didnae mean tae . . . it wis jist . . .

MAGGIE Och never mind. I'm tired o' a' that. If ye've naethin original tae say just shut up and leave me in peace . . . I've got a headache.

JOHN Can I haud the towel for ye?

MAGGIE No thank ye.

JOHN *(Beginning to get angry)* Oh I suppose I'm poison, am I? *(MAGGIE doesn't answer)* A man can only staun' so much.

MAGGIE But a woman's got tae stand anythin that comes alang.

JOHN It's the only way ye can forget. Ye feel ye can face folks when ye've a drink or two in ye.

MAGGIE Aye, forgettin's right. Ye forget that I'm sittin here waitin for ye tae come hame wi the dole tae get us somethin tae eat. I suppose it's a' gone again?

(She looks enquiringly at him. He avoids her eye and does not answer. MAGGIE starts to cry, after a minute JOHN goes over to her.)

JOHN Maggie! Maggie! I'll never dae it again . . . I swear it. I'll never dae it again . . . Maggie, I never meant tae dae this tae ye . . .

(MAGGIE gets up, still weeping, and makes her way towards the bedroom)

JOHN *(Following her)* I'll make it up tae ye . . . I'll never leave ye again, Maggie . . . I promise ye . . .

MAGGIE *(Entering bedroom)* I'm by carin whit ye dae.

(She closes bedroom door against him. He stands looking at it, then sits down and lights a fag end. Enter LILY.)

LILY Oh! So ye've condescended tae come back hev ye? Where's Maggie?

JOHN Lyin doon . . . she's got a headache.

LILY *(Looking at him contemptuously)* I'll say she's got a headache.

(She goes off to bedroom, returns after a moment and puts on kettle. In silence she gets out a couple of cups and saucers, milk, sugar, etc., and takes out a cake and some biscuits from her bag. JOHN watches her movements covertly. She leaves her purse lying on the table.)

JOHN I suppose there's nae use tryin tae explain.

LILY Nane at a'. Save yer stinkin breath. I'm no yer wife thank Goad.

JOHN It's the last time it'll happen, Lily. I deserve a good kick in the teeth.

LILY If I wis a man ye wouldnae need tae suggest it.

JOHN If I had a job I wouldnae hae sae much time tae think. It's no bein able tae stop thinkin that's drivin me crazy . . . if ever a man had a slice o' Hell dished oot tae him in the last year, I've had it. Naebody kent whit it meant tae me tae hev Jenny leave hame . . . Jenny wis ma girl . . .

LILY Jenny wis Maggie's girl tae . . . and Alex wis Maggie's lad. The trouble ye've gone through is naethin tae whit Maggie's had.

JOHN I've just gone tae pieces, Lily. I don't seem tae hae ony will power left.

LILY If ye could keep aff it for the last six years, ye can keep aff it again . . . it's great the way you men can do the disappearin act and no worry aboot whit's happenin at hame.

JOHN I kent you'd be roon' . . . It's no that I mean tae stay away . . .

LILY But ye just cannae find yer way hame tae yer responsibilities. Ye rotten selfish beast, tae let Maggie get like that again efter whit the doctor said. Maggie hasnae the strength tae staun' much mair.

JOHN Neither can I staun' much mair so stop jawin!

LILY If Maggie disnae get through this, ye'll be no better than yer son . . . only it's no the judge that'll gie ye life sentence, it'll be yer ain coanscience.

(JOHN gets up, picks up his cap and starts for the door)

LILY *(Catching his sleeve)* Jist a minute! I'm no finished wi ye. You'll stay sober . . . d'ye hear me? . . . You'll stay sober from noo till Maggie's by.

(MAGGIE calls off, LILY runs to her. JOHN waits twirling his cap till LILY returns.)

JOHN Is she all right?

LILY Aye she's all right. Nae thanks tae you. *(She busies herself with teacups, etc.)* And some folks thinks I missed masel no gettin married!

JOHN I'll mak it up tae her, Lily, when the baby's here . . . I'll look after it till she's well . . . and dae onythin I can . . .

LILY Aye. Ye're gonnae dae great things. Ye've some makin up tae dae, I'm tellin ye.

JOHN Well quit goin on at me! I've tell't ye I'm sorry!

LILY Sorry! If ye wis ma husband I'd mak ye sorry a' right.

JOHN Aw shut up! Shut up!

LILY Where d'ye think ye're goin noo? Oot on the batter again? (*Snatches his cap out of his hand*) Sit doon. And if ye want onythin tae eat ye can get it yersel, there's breid in the tin.

JOHN Your tongue would drive onyone oot on the batter.

LILY Drive! Ye need a lot o' drivin.

(*She goes off to the bedroom with the cups, etc. JOHN sits with his head in his hands, then rises and walk about the room, then takes off his jacket and rolls up his sleeves and starts to tidy room. After removing things from the table, he looks round helplessly for a place to deposit them, he continues to 'tidy' in a hopeless fashion, then abandons the attempt, and starts to sweep floor. He suddenly sees LILY's purse, handles it, and continues his sweeping. Covers the purse up with whatever is on the table, and gets on with the chores. LILY comes out, picks up the teapot, and goes towards bedroom, at the door she stops and looks round.*)*

LILY I wish ye could see yersel . . . ye're makin a rare mess. If I wis you I'd hae a system.

(*She goes off. JOHN goes across to table, quickly shakes out coins from LILY's purse, takes his cap and jacket and goes off. After a moment LILY puts her head round the bedroom door.*)

LILY (*Off*) Aye! He's gone oot. Thank Goad.

(*She comes out followed by MAGGIE, carrying cups, etc.*)

MAGGIE I wonder where he's off tae noo. Well, he cannae dae much, he's got nae money. My, Lily! Yon cup o' tea jist whet ma appetite. I havnae ett nothin a' day.

LILY Ye silly thing! Nae wunner ye've got a headache. Is there onythin I could cook ye? Hev ye an egg?

MAGGIE Och be yer age, Lily. There hasnae been an egg in the hoose since ye brocht some yersel.

LILY Ye'll need tae eat somethin, ye've two tae feed.

MAGGIE Aye. Mebbe three.

LILY Here! Nane o' that! Is one lot o' twins no enough for you?

MAGGIE I don't know whit I'd dae wioot ye, Lily. Ye'll no leave me, will ye? Ye'll bring doon yer claes soon won't ye? . . . There's Granny's bed ye can hev aside the weans in the parlour . . . if you're wi me, I'll no worry. I don't seem tae hae the strength I used tae. I get that tired.

LILY Nae wunner, when ye're no eatin.

MAGGIE Ye'll keep yer eye on Edie, and no let her start goin wi the boys and get like Jenny.

LILY *(At cupboard)* Stop haverin . . . There's no even a tin o' onythin.

MAGGIE Ye wouldnae like tae rin oot for some chips?

LILY They'll gie ye heartburn, Maggie.

MAGGIE I ken, but they're worth it.

LILY Right ye are then, if it's whit ye fancy, I'm needin a packet o' fags onyway. Keep that teapot hot and we'll hae anither cup wi them.

(She picks up her purse, opens it and draws in her breath. MAGGIE does not notice.)

MAGGIE It's a wunner Mrs Harris hasnae smelt the tea . . . she's got sich a nose for a fly cup.

(LILY puts her coat on in silent rage at her discovery. She knocks things off the table and bangs them in rage.)

LILY Blast and damn every bloomin man that wis ever born!

MAGGIE Whit is it noo, Lily?

LILY Naethin . . . I'm jist needin a fag. You sit still till I come back.

(LILY goes off. After a moment or two, EDIE comes in excitedly.)

EDIE Ma! Ma!

MAGGIE Whit's happened, Edie?

EDIE Oor Jenny's doon the stair!

MAGGIE Jenny!

EDIE She's wantin tae know if she can come up, she's been waitin at the close mooth, and she seen Auntie Lily gae oot . . .

MAGGIE Jenny! Gae doon and bring her in.

EDIE Ma, she says . . .

MAGGIE Quick, Edie, quick! Gae doon in case she goes away.

(EDIE runs out. MAGGIE stands at the door, waiting. EDIE and JENNY come in. JENNY is pale, haggard and drawn, her clothes are tawdry wrecks. She halts in the doorway.)

JENNY Hullo, Ma.

MAGGIE Hullo, Jenny.

(They look at each other, then MAGGIE takes JENNY in her arms)

JENNY I seen ye one day . . . comin frae the hospital . . . Ye didnae see me.

MAGGIE Jenny! Ye never let me pass ye!

JENNY I thought mebbe ye didnae want tae see me.

MAGGIE Jenny!

JENNY *(Looking round the room)* Ye've got new curtains . . . Has he got a job? . . . *(She moves rather unsteadily round the room, touching things)*

114

MAGGIE No. Jenny, tell me a' that's been happenin tae ye . . . ye've changed.

JENNY There's naethin tae tell. I lived wi him . . . ma boss . . . then he got somebody else and gied me the chuck . . . efter that . . . I just . . . *(She shrugs)* Are the kids in bed? *(She gestures towards bed)*

MAGGIE They're in the parlour bed noo. Oh Jenny! I cannae believe it's you. *(Wipes her eyes on her sleeve)*

JENNY When are ye due?

MAGGIE A coupla weeks.

JENNY Are ye keepin a' right?

MAGGIE Fine.

JENNY Where is he?

MAGGIE He went oot.

JENNY D'ye think he'd let me stay . . . mebbe a night or two . . . till I get a job?

MAGGIE This is yer hame, Jenny. There'll be naethin said tae ye. I suppose ye would see . . . aboot Alex?

JENNY Aye. I'd like tae hev come roon', Ma, but . . . I thought I'd mebbe be jist addin tae yer troubles. How's Bertie? Is he oot yet?

MAGGIE No yet.

JENNY Is he gettin better?

MAGGIE Oh aye, he's got rare pink cheeks. Ye're no lookin well yersel, Jenny.

JENNY Me? I'm a' right . . . Whit aboot Granny?

MAGGIE We'd tae pit her tae the Poorshoose. Lizzie wouldnae tak her, she wis gettin a bit queer . . .

JENNY Pair aul' Granny . . .

MAGGIE Will ye no sit doon, Jenny . . . ye're lookin awfu' white.

JENNY I couldnae . . . lie on the bed a wee while?

MAGGIE Aye, Jenny, of course . . . lie doon here, I'll cover ye up . . . would ye like a cup o' tea, there's yin in the pot no lang made, Lily and me's just had yin.

JENNY There wouldnae be a wee bit breid . . . ye could spare?

MAGGIE Oh Jenny! Are ye hungry! Why did ye no say . . .

(MAGGIE hurries to the loaf and cuts a slice. Enter LILY.)

LILY Are ye ready, they're hot. *(Puts chips on table and gets out salt, etc.)*

MAGGIE Lily!

LILY Whit is it, Maggie? Goad! Don't say ye've started!

MAGGIE No, I've no started . . . Jenny's come hame.

LILY *(When the news has sunk in)* Whit's brought *her* back? Whaur is she?

MAGGIE *(Pointing to bed)* She's lyin doon, she wis feelin faint.

LILY Faint! I'll gie her faint! Whit's she wantin tae come back for . . . tae land ye in mair trouble? Is she expectin? *(Goes across to bed)*

JENNY No. I'm no expectin!

LILY I suppose ye're broke then . . . I suppose ye've come hame tae see whit ye can scrounge. You wisnae comin back . . . No you! . . . You wisnae goin tae set fit inside the door, Miss High and . . . *(Pulls back the curtain and looks at JENNY, then turns away)* I'll heat up a bit milk and feed her some saps. She looks as if she hadnae ett for a week.

MAGGIE Oh Goad! I never thought! . . . Oh Lily!

LILY *(Preparing 'saps')* Sit doon, I'll attend tae her.

(The BONES start fighting; they fight throughout the next scene)

LILY *(Feeding JENNY)* That's enough noo . . . steady on . . . Ye'll get mair later on . . . lie doon noo.

JENNY I suppose ye're wonderin whit I've been daein?

LILY We're wonderin naethin. It's naebody's business but yer ain. Bygones is bygones in this hoose. Is that no right, Maggie?

MAGGIE That's quite right, Lily.

LILY Ye didnae get married did ye?

JENNY No.

LILY Well, the worst hasn't happened then.

(There is a knock at the door. LILY lets in MRS HARRIS.)

MRS HARRIS Is that no terrible up the stair? I cam' doon tae see if ye could lend us a wee drap tea for the breakfast, I've rin oot.

MAGGIE Aye, I can manage some. Will ye hae a chip?

MRS HARRIS *(With a screech of surprise)* Oh! Ye've chips! *(Draws in her chair)*

LILY The smell o' chips fair travels across the landin doesn't it?

MRS HARRIS Eh? Could I help masel tae a wee shake salt? . . . Ye havnae ony vinegair? . . . No matter . . . they'll dae as they are.

MAGGIE We've a surprise for ye . . . Jenny's hame.

MRS HARRIS *(Stopping with chip halfway to mouth)* Jenny hame! Is she in the family way?

JENNY I'm sorry tae disappoint ye, but I'm not.

MRS HARRIS *(Rising and going over to bed)* Well I declare! I'd hae passed ye on the street!

JENNY Ye did. But it wisnae because ye didnae recognise me.

(There is an extra loud thud from upstairs. MRS HARRIS runs to the window and shouts up.)

MRS HARRIS Are ye a' right, Mrs Bone?

MRS BONE Aye! *I'm* a' right.

(There is a ring at the door)

MRS HARRIS Will I go?
LILY If ye don't mind.

(MRS HARRIS goes to the door and lets out a screech, slams it shut and dashes back)

MRS HARRIS It's a polis! Oh I'm that feart o' polis! You go, Lily.
LILY *(Going to the door)* Ye silly ass! The polis cannae touch ye. *(Lily returns with paper, she goes slowly to the table and sits down reding the note)*
MAGGIE Whit is it, Lily?
LILY It's from the hospital . . . aboot Bertie.
MAGGIE Is he tae get hame, Lily? . . . Is he comin oot? . . . Whaur's ma glasses so's I can read it . . . Oh my! Lily, wouldn't it be rare tae hae the wee felly at hame again?

(She searches for her glasses. MRS HARRIS picks the paper out of LILY's hand, reads it and drops it with a screech.)

LILY Maggie dear . . . Bertie's no gettin hame . . . Bertie's . . . dead.
MAGGIE It's no true! It cannae be true! Bertie wis gettin on . . . they've made a mistake . . . they've got him mixed up wi somebody else . . .
LILY Maggie dear . . . Bertie wisnae gettin better.
MAGGIE I'm goin up tae the hospital. I'm goin up tae see. *(Goes to bedroom and emerges with red hat on, and coat on her arm)*
LILY Maggie, sit doon! If there's onybody goin oot, it's no you, you're no fit for that hill.
MAGGIE I'm goin, I tell ye . . .
LILY Well ye're no goin alane, I'm comin wi ye. Mrs Harris, can you stay till I come back?
JENNY I'm here, Lily.
LILY You lie still, Jenny. If the kids come in, would ye see they get tae bed, Ernie and Edie, I mean.
MRS HARRIS Aye, I'll see tae them, don't you worry.

(MAGGIE leans against the lintel of the door during above speeches, then straightens herself and goes out)

LILY Jist a minute, Maggie . . . I'm comin. Mrs Harris, is your man at hame the night?
MRS HARRIS Aye, he wis when I come ben here.
LILY Would ye rin over and ask him if he'd gae roon' the pubs and see if he can find Morrison?
MRS HARRIS Oh Goad, Lily, that's askin for it . . . but . . . right ye are, I'll tell him.

LILY Thanks. *(Goes off)*
JENNY It's awfu' good o' ye, Mrs Harris.
MRS HARRIS Aye, for a lot o' tea-tastin tabbies we don't dae sae bad when there's trouble.

CURTAIN

ACT III

Scene 3

Scene: The same. Late afternoon next day. The kitchen is tidy, some new-looking nappies hang across the range, and there should be several other indications that there is a new baby in the house.

On rise of the curtain ERNIE and EDIE are standing dressed for outdoors. LILY is fastening a black band to EDIE's sleeve. MRS BONE and MRS HARRIS are sitting at the table drinking tea. JENNY is moving about the kitchen, putting things away. There is a subdued air about all of them. MAGGIE's red hat is lying on the dresser.

LILY *(To ERNEST)* Did ye polish yer boots?
ERNIE Aye.
LILY *(To EDIE)* Whit did ye dae wi the handkie I lent ye?
EDIE In ma pocket.
LILY Wipe yer face then, Edie. *(EDIE does so. LILY puts her arms round her for a moment)* Get on then.
ERNIE Hoo lang hev we tae stay oot?
LILY *(Sighing)* As lang as ye can. Sit it roon twice if it's a good yin, and when ye come oot get yersels somethin at the Tallies. On ye go noo.

(ERNEST and EDIE go off)

MRS BONE It disnae seem right somehow, them goin tae the pictures.
LILY Whit's wrang wi it? It's better for them than hangin aboot here.

(LILY goes off right)

MRS HARRIS Right enough, Lily's wonderfu'.
JENNY I jist don't know whit I'd hae done wioot her.
MRS BONE Fancy her bein so good wi a baby! I never thought she ken't onythin aboot them.
JENNY It's the money I keep thinkin aboot. She payed for yon tin o' food and the bottle and teat and the shawl and things.
MRS BONE She's a right good sort.

(LILY comes back)

MRS HARRIS Is he still sleepin?
LILY Aye. It's gettin near his next feed.
MRS BONE The wee soul!
JENNY Dae ye think there's ony use . . . tryin again?
LILY *(Looking towards bedroom)* Ye can if ye like.

MRS HARRIS Terrible, isn't it?
MRS BONE It's no natural.
MRS HARRIS Hasnae ett nothin has he?
LILY No.
MRS HARRIS It's terrible.

(*JENNY takes a cup of tea and a plate of bread and goes across to bedroom. The attention of the others is focused on her movements. She opens the door to the bedroom and stands on the threshold.*)

JENNY Pa! Pa! . . . I've brought ye a cup o' tea . . . If I leave it doon will ye drink it? . . . Pa! . . . (*Pathetically*) Pa! (*She puts the tea in the bedroom and comes out*) He'll no answer.
MRS HARRIS Whit aboot a cup yersel? Ye look that white.

(*JENNY shakes her head*)

MRS BONE Ye cannae let him go on like this.
MRS HARRIS Right enough, ye're sorry for him, aren't ye?
LILY Sorry for him! I'm no sorry for him. I hope he's sufferin torments . . . I hope he suffers every minute o' the life that's left him . . .

(*There is a knock at the door. JENNY lets in MRS WILSON.*)

MRS WILSON Hev ye anither pair o' pants for Christopher? I've had tae wash oot the yins he'd on . . . (*LILY gets up and looks through the drawers*) Och never mind, if ye don't know where tae pit yer hands on them. (*LILY unearths a pair*) Aye, that's fine! (*Takes them*) Gosh! They're mair holy than godly, still, they'll dae . . . (*Nodding towards the bedroom*) Is he still wi her?
LILY Aye.
MRS WILSON It's awful, isn't it? Could ye no send roon' for the doctor, or get a minister?
JENNY He disnae seem tae hear ye when ye speak. Jist sits there lookin . . . and no seein . . . (*Goes across to bedroom*) Pa! Aw! Ye didnae tak yer tea . . . will ye no come ben tae the kitchen? . . . Pa! (*Comes back and sits at table*) He'll no gie ony sign he hears me! (*Drops her head on her arms over the table and sobs*)
LILY (*Going to bedroom*) John! Are you gonnae sit there a' night? . . . Ye're worryin the wits oot o' Jenny . . .
MRS HARRIS Maybe if somebody wis tae gie him a shock or somethin, they say that sometimes does it.
MRS BONE He'll end up in an asylum if he disnae watch oot.
LILY I'm no carin whaur he ends up . . . the dirty drunken rotter.
JENNY (*Sobbing*) Oh I don't know whit tae dae!
LILY Try tyin a bottle o' whisky tae his nose, then ye can lead him oot like a donkey wi a carrot.

MRS WILSON Well, I've left Marina and Christopher playin in the kitchen and I've a fire on. (*Gives JENNY a pat*) Cheer up, Jenny, it'll be a' right, you'll see. Knock me if ye want me through the night, Lily, I've had plenty o' experience wi babies. (*She goes off*)

MRS HARRIS Whit a cheek! Whit experience has she had that I havnae had! Ye're no needin tae knock her, Lily, ye can knock me . . . I can dae onythin that's needin done wi ony baby that wis ever born.

LILY Sh! Ye neednae shout.

MRS BONE I'm sure, Lily, ye've only tae chap on the ceilin tae me, and I'll come doon.

MRS HARRIS I've had mair experience than you.

MRS BONE That's no tae say ye ken mair than me.

LILY (*Wearily*) Oh shut up. I'll manage masel.

(*The baby starts to cry*)

MRS HARRIS That's him wakened!

MRS BONE The wee lamb!

JENNY He'll be wantin his feed.

LILY You see tae him, Jenny, and I'll mak it.

(*LILY gets out a tin of food, a spoon and a jug. Exuent MRS HARRIS, JENNY and MRS BONE. LILY starts to prepare baby's food. The baby continues to cry, his wails get louder, until the bedroom door opens and JOHN appears. He is haggard, unshaven and drawn. LILY looks up.*)

LILY Aye. That's yer son.

JOHN Lily! I cannae staun' it. I cannae staun' it! Can ye no dae onythin tae stop it . . .

LILY I'm gettin his feed, quick as I can.

(*JOHN sinks down on a chair and covers his face with his hands. The baby continues to cry. He is in such a position that he is not seen at first glance by MRS HARRIS when she enters.*)

MRS HARRIS Are ye no ready wi it yet?

LILY Jist aboot. (*Pours food into bottle*)

MRS HARRIS Wis the water boilin?

LILY No. It's jist aff the boil.

MRS HARRIS It should hev been boilin.

LILY Can you read?

MRS HARRIS Whit d'ye mean can I read?

LILY The directions is on the tin.

MRS HARRIS That's no the way tae pit on the teat. (*LILY gives her a withering glance*) Ye'll need tae test it, see if it's tae hot. (*Seizes bottle from LILY and puts it to her mouth. LILY grabs it back.*)

LILY Ye test it on the back o' yer hand!

MRS HARRIS D'ye think I didnae ken that?

LILY It disnae look as if ye ken't very much. *(Tries bottle on hand, snatches a nappie from the fireplace and goes off)*

MRS HARRIS They old maids!

(She sees MAGGIE's red hat. She picks it up and tries it on, then moves across to look in mirror. She suddenly sees JOHN and gives a squeal. JOHN looks up suddenly and sees the hat. He rises slowly to his feet, his eyes fixed on the hat. MRS HARRIS retreats.)

JOHN Y're wearin . . . her . . . hat!

(MRS HARRIS continues to retreat. He takes her by the shoulders and shakes her.)

JOHN Who . . . tell't . . . ye . . . ye . . . could . . . wear . . . her . . . hat?

(He tears it from her head. MRS HARRIS shrieks. JENNY runs in. She takes him by the arm and draws him away. MRS HARRIS runs from the room screaming for LILY and MRS BONE. JENNY leads her father to a chair. He sits, the hat screwed in his hands.)

JENNY Don't, Pa! . . . Don't! . . . I'll look efter ye noo . . . I'll stay wi you . . . we'll work thegether for the weans . . . Don't greet, Pa! It's no your fault – it's just the way things are!

FINAL CURTAIN

GOLD IN HIS BOOTS

A PLAY IN THREE ACTS

by

George Munro

Gold in his Boots was first performed at the Little Theatre in the Pleasance, Edinburgh, on 27th January 1947, with the following cast:

MR CRAIG .... Howard Connell
MRS CRAIG, *his wife* .... Marjorie Thomson
TOMMY CRAIG, *his son* .... Russell Hunter
RAB HUNTER, *a neighbour* .... Carl Williamson
KATE HUNTER, *his daughter* .... Betty McGregor
SARAH McCLARTY, *a neighbour* .... Betty Henderson
TOWSER GRAHAM, *a tousy centre-forward* .... Andrew Buggie
THE POUTER, *a trainer* .... Jack Hislop
SERGEANT .... Heinz Leyser
THE PROVOST .... James Sutherland
BOB McCOLL, *'CLAVERLEY', a reporter* .... Roddy McMillan
'SNATCHER' MacEWAN, *Manager of Drumont Rovers* James Sutherland
Fleet Street sports writers: MR SPALDING............ Howard Connell
                  MR McSPORRAN .... Andrew Buggie
Directors of Coaltown United: SIR JOSEPH PETTINGELL . Heinz Leyser
                  ALDERMAN RAMSHAWK.. Jack Hislop
DICK GRAVES, *Manager of Coaltown Rovers* .... Leslie Wright
TINY, *Trainer* .... Jack Stewart
'SAILOR' STOKES, *ex-Internationalist* .... James Sutherland
Assistant Trainers, Directors, etc. .... S. Kallin
                                    E. Whittington
                                    F. Purcell
COMISSIONAIRE.................................... E. Whittington
POLICE INSPECTOR .... Ian Dalgleish
Ambulance Men .... F. Purcell
                                    S. Kallin
Players: JOE, *Captain* .... Heinz Leyser
TAFFY .... Roy Hodges
PADDY... Howard Connell

123

David Gibson
Dennis McKenna
Jack Hislop
Peter Kramer
Andrew Buggie
Joseph Metzstein
Gordon Clark
Archie Jack

Directed by . . . . Robert Mitchell
Stage Director . . . . Ian Dalgleish
Stage Manager . . . . Archie Jack
Costume Mistress . . . . Julia Wallace
Property Mistress . . . . Sybil Thomson
Production Manager . . . . Leon Schuster
Lighting and Sound Effects . . . . James Dunbar
Décor . . . . Tom MacDonald

ACT I

Scene 1

Kitchen of CRAIGS' home in Clanmarnock, Lanarkshire. One o'clock, Saturday afternoon.

The kitchen is clean, scrupulously so. A coal fire, right, gives comfortable glow. The grate gleams where steel has been worried to silver sparkle, brass candlesticks are polished, the table is laid and nowhere is there evidence of the acute poverty that shadows the Craig household. At the back, centre, is the door; on the right, a window. On the wall, the 'hole in the wa'' bed used by MR and MRS CRAIG. On the left of the bed is a door leading into the only other room, occupied by TOMMY CRAIG. When the curtain rises, MR CRAIG is in bed, lying on his side; eyeing MRS CRAIG with calm benevolence as she busies herself about the grate, upon which are steaming pot and kettle. MRS CRAIG is arranging plates, cups and spoons at the table. MR CRAIG is a good-natured-looking little man in the middle fifties, who talks rather loudly in a broad, intelligible Lowland accent. His life is sunshine all the way, only clouded by unemployment and by his wife's evangelical zeal. His ambition is to see Scotland versus England in an international football match. MRS CRAIG is of an age with her husband, of medium height, pleasant features, distinguished by a quiet dignity born of long effort to preserve respect-ability. Her face, it is true, shows sign of mental and physical strain. When she permits herself the rare luxury of relaxation we see that the duties of wife and mother have almost exhausted bodily strength. But in eye and voice MRS CRAIG is young. In neither is there hint or bitter protest against years of labour, care and anxiety. Instead, there is strong witness to a character courageous, cheerful, indeed ennobled by inner faith and high purpose. Even when worried, exasperated or fearful, and her voice takes on a heightened sharpened note, we feel that there is no urge towards self-pity or a reaching for the martyr's halo.

MRS CRAIG Looking at you, John, a stranger'd think this was a hydropathic. One o'clock on Saturday morning and you still in bed.
CRAIG Hand me the *Chronicle*.

(MRS CRAIG picks up a morning newspaper from the table. She goes toward the bed. Hands it to CRAIG.)

MRS CRAIG Are ye memorising it?
CRAIG It's Claverley. He must be in the pay o' the Pope. *(Snarlingly satirical)* He just can't see Clanmarnock holding Troy Celtic, not even to a

draw. They're all alike these football writers; bletherskites. Look at McColl. There'll be times you wish ye had kilted your skirts and gaun skirling to McColl's tune, now he's the Solomon o' sports writers and I'm just a Means Test miner. To think o' McColl leaving the Raw to become a football reporter! When he lived here he couldn't tell a football from a melon. *(Explosively)* Damn it, he'll have free passes, too! The injustice of it all. I'm tellt he's not even married.

MRS CRAIG Bob McColl had aye a streak o' wisdom.

(Goes out into the bedroom)

CRAIG *(Rising up in bed)* Wisdom! Ah suppose that's a backhander at me? I'll bet every time McColl looks at a free pass and thinks o' you, he gets down on his knees and thanks God for me. If he was to come in that door now, on his way to the match, he'd look at me and say 'There am I but for the Grace of God and the Scottish Junior Cup Final'. Me, I'm lying here like something forgotten by the Scottish Mission to Lepers. The Scottish Junior Cup at stake and I'm in bed because I haven't got the entrance money. Bonnie Scotland, what I'm suffering for ye now. Dear God, will you listen to this *(Reads)*: 'Rangers lack punch in attack . . .' Lack punch! And Towser Graham's in the centre. I tell ye, Tommy, *(Raises his voice to the bedroom)* there's sabotage here. Creatin an inferiority complex, I'd say. Why, Towser, on his game, could beat Troy Celtic, the Dail, and St Alowishyus College single-handed. *(Wistfully)* Tommy, lad, ye'll no' have four-pence to spare? No; I forgot; I asked ye before. *(Reads)* 'Support your team and wear the colours.' *(Bitterly)* If gooseberries were three ha'pence a ton, I couldn't buy a hair o' one. *(Reads again)* 'It's safe to say all Clanmarnock will be there to see bully wee Rangers battle for the coveted trophy . . .' All Clanmarnock! *(Tears the paper in comic rage-frenzy)* That means: I'm dead and don't know it. Even the parish ghost'll see more o' the game than I will. Me! That's been a Rangers follower, man and boy, these fifty years. It's degradin, that's what it is. The first time Clanmarnock get into the Final, and my pockets are empty as a baby ear in the year o' the short corn, when growth was so stunted the sparrows got down on their knees to pick the corn. An' they blocked up all the spy holes in the palings. There's Christianity for ye. *(There is a discreet knock on the outer door)* Come in! Come in! Maybe ye'd like a butler to lead ye in. D'ye hear? Come in! *(HUNTER enters. A tall, solemn-looking man)* Oh it's you! Now my cup's fu'. Don't tell me ye've come to remind me there's a match on today?

HUNTER Where's the wife, John? *(He stands, hesitating)*

CRAIG Inbye. *(Pointing to the bedroom)* How?

HUNTER Stop the mournin. John Craig, there's a Samaritan on your doorstep! *(Steps back over the doorstep and we hear his urgent whisper)* Towser! Come in, Towser. John says you're as welcome as Insurance money after a wake.

(CRAIG hears the name 'Towser' and is at once alert. The door opens wide and TOWSER follows HUNTER into the kitchen. He lurches into the centre of the room, a whisky bottle perilously swinging from his jacket pocket. He is young, big, burly, bullet-headed, square-shouldered.)

CRAIG Paralysed! An hour before the kick-off.

TOWSER Keep your hair on, old-timer. I've had a dram; but I'm not paralysed.

(He drags the whisky bottle from his pocket, uncorks it, and lifts it to his lips)

CRAIG Another smell o' that stuff and he's out for good.

(TOWSER drinks a deep drink)

TOWSER *(Singing)* 'Wha wad be a traitor knave?
                              Wha sae base as be a slave?
                              Let him follow me!'

CRAIG *(Keening)* Man, Towser, there'll be glad hearts in the Vatican this day. Man, oh man, it'll be a walk-over for Troy Celtic. You're tight as an Orangeman's drum. Tanked! That's what ye are.

TOWSER *(Thrusting the bottle at CRAIG)* Tak' aff yer dram, auld hand. Have a dram wi Towser Graham, the tousy wee lad that's goin to make Troy Celtic goalkeeper look like a wan-legged wife trying to keep hens off a midden.

HUNTER No more for you, Towser. I judge ye've had enough. No! *(Hastily, seeing TOWSER give him a truculent face)* It's no' that ye're fu', Towser. Ha, ha! As Rabbie says: 'He wasna fu', he just had plenty.'

TOWSER *(Giving a little dance, sings boisterously)* 'Oh, we arena fu', we're nae that fu', there's aye a drappie in oor ee, The day may daw, the cock may craw, but aye we'll taste the barley bree . . .'

(MRS CRAIG appears in the doorway. Behind her, TOMMY. They look startled and afraid.)

CRAIG For God's sake, Towser, wheesht! The wife's in there. She's wi the boy.

TOWSER The boy? Oh, aye, the boy! Ma scholar crony? The sparrow that thinks he can whistle my lass to heel? Rob me when ah'm in possession, eh, Rab? But that's a tackle I can fix. Where is he? I'll tell him where he gets off wi Katie Hunter. Bring out the body, Rab.

HUNTER Some other time, Towser. *(Hurriedly)* Yes, yes, we ken all about you and Katie and Tommy Craig. But this is nae day for frivolous argy-bargyin. *(CRAIG sees MRS CRAIG and TOMMY and is making sheepish*

127

signal to RAB to be quiet) John! Towser's for taking us in as Players' Friends. We'll go in the Committee gate. How's that for a Samaritan turn?

TOWSER *(Suddenly belligerent)* Why should ah take in auld Lazarus? His whelp's trying to steal Katie from me.

MRS CRAIG Have you not a midden o' your own, Rab Hunter?

CRAIG Now the fat's in the fire.

HUNTER Ye're there, Meg? Aye, ye're there, ah see. Ye ken Towser? Towser Graham. A crony o' John's an' mine. He's leadin the Rangers' attack the day . . .

MRS CRAIG Lead him out o' my kitchen, Rab Hunter. As quick's you like.

(TOMMY comes right into the kitchen)

TOMMY What's the matter?

MRS CRAIG Go back to your books, Tommy, son. Mr Hunter's brought a stray dug into the kitchen.

TOWSER Dug? Me! That's the finish. I'll skite . . .

TOMMY You'll skite nothing.

HUNTER Come on, Towser. Man, ye shouldn't talk like that. They're a' fans here.

TOWSER I'll fan that nyaff wi ma bonnet. I'll make him think he's been hit wi a nelephant's knuckle duster.

(A bugle note is heard)

HUNTER Gosh! That's the Celtic. Ye've nae time for slaughter now. You've got to strip yet. Come on. A cold plunge and a rub-down and you'll be as right as rain.

TOWSER I've got time to belt the life oot o' any man thinks he can take Kate Hunter away from me.

HUNTER *(Humouring TOWSER)* Later.

TOMMY *(Thrusting past his mother)* Get out!

(MRS CRAIG grabs TOMMY. HUNTER flings his arms round TOWSER. MRS CRAIG manages to shove TOMMY back into the room, which she swiftly locks and then makes for the hob where a kettle is steaming. The kettle uplifted, she says:)

MRS CRAIG Out of here! Quick, before I jaw this water over ye.

(HUNTER succeeds in steering TOWSER through the door. On the doorstep, TOWSER wheels and bawls:)

TOWSER I'll be back!

MRS CRAIG *(To CRAIG)* Ye've got the choice friend, John Craig . . . *(Ostentatious dismissal of a distasteful interlude)* Come and have your dinner, Tommy!

(TOMMY enters from the bedroom. MRS CRAIG busies herself between the table and the fireplace.)

MRS CRAIG Did ye hear Kate's won another bursary or scholarship or something? They must be proud o' her at Glasgow University!

CRAIG I wish they'd gie Kate the university to keep. Judged by her prizes Kate must have won all. Even the key o' the university!

TOMMY I'm glad for Kate. She'll be a great lawyer.

CRAIG Lawyer! Kate?

TOMMY Yes. She's going in for Law and Politics.

CRAIG A lassie a lawyer? From the Raw!

MRS CRAIG Why not?

CRAIG She'll need a' her law to keep that auld father o' hers out of jail.

MRS CRAIG That'll do, John. Are ye rising?

CRAIG *(Sniffs and stares enquiringly)* It's no' broth, is it? If ah ever see kitchen again – a steak, a chop, a bit ham-and-haddie even – I'll think I've turned cannibal.

MRS CRAIG *(Protestingly, at breaking point)* One week's work in two years an' he expects to eat like Rab Ha' the Glasga' glutton.

TOMMY Maybe you'd like caviare and champagne.

CRAIG Ah'll take the soup.

MRS CRAIG Three grown-ups to feed on two weeks' wages in two years.

TOMMY Mother!

CRAIG Leave your mother alone. What sort of son are you? Four years left school and all you do is sit wi your head up the chimney reading books about engineering. A pity ye can't engineer yourself a job!

(The door opens: KATE HUNTER enters. She stands in the doorway, unseen by all except TOMMY. She has the figure of a ballet-dancer, good features, steady blue eyes, raven black hair. Her university muffler is flung loosely over her shoulders. She wears a Fraser tartan skirt, cut on the cross, and a tweed coat.)

MRS CRAIG I'm sorry. My nerves are on edge.

TOMMY Kate . . .

(Immediate mild hubbub)

MRS CRAIG If Tommy had won it, I couldn't be more pleased, Kate.

CRAIG It'll soon cost seven-an'-a-tanner to talk to ye, Katie, eh?

KATE For you a cut-rate, Mr Craig. My, I'm so excited.

(MRS CRAIG pats KATE fondly on the shoulder and for a moment they stand in quick, shy embrace. KATE talks without accent or mannerism.)

MRS CRAIG A plate o' broth, Kate!

CRAIG I was just saying, Katie, any mair soup an' I'll be ashamed to pass the plots.

MRS CRAIG Say grace, John.

(KATE seats herself in the chair offered by TOMMY)

CRAIG 'Lord, we thank Thee for Thy mercies. Bless and guide us, pardon all our sins, for Thy Son's sake, Amen.' *(Without break)* Man, I wish I'd the price o' the match.

KATE There's a free gate for The Unemployed.

CRAIG A free gate! Tommy, my trousers! *(Jumps up in bed, hands clutching the blankets' edge as though ready to fling them recklessly aside)*

MRS CRAIG My broth, John Craig!

CRAIG Broth! Talks about broth when there's a free gate! My trooers. My God, I weesh I was a nudist!

(KATE laughs)

TOMMY D'ye want your working trousers?

CRAIG I want *any* kind o' covering for my legs. The Scottish Junior Cup is at stake. Why a man should worry about . . .

TOMMY Here they are.

(Tosses a pair of trousers, braces flapping, onto the bed. MR CRAIG at once hauls the side curtain half across the bed, concealing him from view.)

MRS CRAIG My curtains!

CRAIG Towser Graham's in a bashing mood the day.

KATE I saw Towser bashing his way back into the Clanmarnock Arms a minute ago.

(The curtain comes flashing back again. MR CRAIG, one bare leg in the air, is searching wildly for a trouser leg. MRS CRAIG screams alarmed fear.)

CRAIG Ye're joking. Man, Katie, don't mock about sacred things. Towser in a rammy would mean Clanmarnock out o' the Cup.

KATE That would be tragedy. It seems the brains he should have in his head aren't in his feet even.

MRS CRAIG Shut the curtain, John Craig. Take that goatish look off your face. From what we've seen o' the great Towser, jail's the best place for him.

CRAIG If ye mean that wash-hoose story about him and Martha Haggarty – the . . .

MRS CRAIG John!

CRAIG *(Sadly)* Maybe Pouter was right? It's no' a centre-forward he should be, it's a stallion. *(Rising to slip his braces over his shoulders)* Man, this is a wae day for Clanmarnock.

(The door opens, THE POUTER bursts in. THE POUTER is fat, bald, besweatered. He is Clanmarnock Rangers' Trainer. He stares incredulously at TOMMY's soup and almost flings himself at the table.)

POUTER *(To MRS CRAIG)* Soup! Ten minutes before the kick-off! Are ye mad, missus? A wee bit steamed fish maybe, but soup . . .

(THE CRAIGS and KATE stand in alarm. MR CRAIG looks ready to leap out of bed, one brace over his shoulder, the other held wide and taut.)

MRS CRAIG My good broth. Take your hands off my son, you drunkard.

POUTER Drunkard! The Pouter? Me, that's bald trying to make boys believe embrocation's the only liquid should ever be bottled. Except, maybe, a taste o' olive oil . . .

CRAIG Tommy! *(As he yells, he flings his arms upwards and the braces snap)* Ma galluses . . .

(The door bursts open again. In comes RAB HUNTER. He drags with him TOWSER, now hopelessly drunk.)

TOWSER *(Sings)* 'Oh, Dolly's braes, an' Dolly's braes,
        an' Dolly's braes no more.
        The tune they played was "Kick the Pope",
        right over Dolly's braes.'
(Scattering dishes. Dancing into fighting position.) Bring out yer ten men, and your big fancy lodger; ah'll bate the lot. So? It's a double-cross! Ye'd play this sparrow? Instead of Towser?

HUNTER There, there, Towser. Stop the slaughter. *(HUNTER is fuddled)*

MRS CRAIG Tak' that foul smell out of my kitchen, Rab Hunter.

TOWSER Hey, auld wumman! *(MRS CRAIG lifts the poker and advances on TOWSER)* I tellt ye I'd come back.

CRAIG *(Alarmed)* Disarm her, Kate, for God's sake. She's nae respect for genius.

POUTER Ye'll never kick another ba' for Rangers, Towser.

TOWSER Ah showed them, didn't ah? *(To HUNTER)* Did ye see me gie that wee Celtic fellow the head?

HUNTER Towser met Troy Celtic brake-club and went intae battle right away.

KATE The baboon! I'm surprised at you, Father. Bringing him here.

TOWSER It's Towser, Kate! Towser Graham! The bashin centre. The bonny wee lad wi a right an' left foot drive that's got hate in each boot. Gie's a kiss.

MRS CRAIG *(Hysterical)* I'll lip ye wi this!

(She lunges at him with the poker. TOWSER dances back. The men grab him.)

TOWSER *(Bellows)* Bring oot yer ten men and yer fancy ludger! Double-cross Towser Graham, wad ye?

(The door opens. A police SERGEANT appears, a CONSTABLE following him.)

SERGEANT Ah want you, Graham.

TOWSER C'mon and get me, ye Hielan stoat. Ah'll blatter the heather oot o' yer hair.

(He struggles. The policemen get a half-nelson on him. The women cling to each other. MR CRAIG is dancing in bed. Through the doorway comes THE PROVOST. He is small, shrewd and alert; slightly greying. He peers over steel-rimmed spectacles. He has an ever-ready trick of patting everyone he talks to. At heart, he is a hard man of little scruples.)

PROVOST You're no' taking Towser to jail! Think o' the match, Sergeant! We've nae reserve centre-forward.

SERGEANT If he was Lord *Goad* o' the Hielans, he's goin inside.

KATE Democracy rule in Clanmarnock, hooray!

TOWSER Put the hard word on him, Provost. Towser in the nick on Cup Final day! Some hope!

PROVOST Shut up, ye sook an' blaw.

TOWSER Sook an' blaw! Me? The hope o' Rangers.

PROVOST Ah'll be personally responsible, Sergeant. Ye can tak' the Provost's word, surely?

SERGEANT He's been creatin a disturbance an' annoyin' the lieges. Ye ken the law, Provost, as weel as me, I hope?

TOWSER Whit sort o' Provost *are* ye . . .

SERGEANT Ask him *that* when ye come afore him on Monday. You'll batter yer big heid against a cell wa' this weekend. Come on!

(TOWSER is dragged, bellowing and kicking, through the doorway)

POUTER Now we've only the ten men. Holy Mackerel, it's twenty meenits o' the kick-off.

HUNTER Whit about a reserve?

POUTER The only reserve we've got'd qualify for an Auld Age Pension. Provost, the boy! Mind? The boy I told you about!

MRS CRAIG Whit d'ye want wi my boy? If it's not an inconvenience to all of ye, I'll trouble ye for the privacy of my kitchen.

HUNTER There, there, Mrs Craig. Haud on a wee.

KATE I'm ashamed of you, Father, bringing that beast in here.

HUNTER There's charity for ye! The whole o' Free'd Ireland wis chasin Towser. He'd hae been razored, knifed, bottled. Ye gave him sanctuary, Mrs Craig, that's what ye did.

PROVOST *(To POUTER, ignoring MRS CRAIG's truculent invitation from the open doorway)* I've seen mair flesh on an ice-cream wafer.

POUTER When he stripped for Scotland in his first international, Alec Jackson was under nine stone.

PROVOST He's awfu' young-lookin. Ye'll need a wean's napkin in the hamper.

MRS CRAIG If there had been wean's milk in your Towser's bottle, he wadnae be where he is. Will ye leave my house, please?

CRAIG Haud your tongue, wumman. This may be a suspicious day in the Craig household.

POUTER Alec Jackson wis seventeen and had two international caps.

HUNTER Tommy had a cap when he was fifteen. Captained the Scottish Schoolboys, didn't ye, Tommy? As ye say, he's young; but youth's the time for splendid endeavours.

PROVOST If he wis a quintuplet an' could get us oot o' this pickle, ah'd play him.

POUTER Come here, Tommy.

PROVOST So ye were a guid yin at schule?

TOMMY What d'ye mean?

POUTER Fine ye ken whit he means.

HUNTER Guid! Tommy's a find, Provost, worth more than a hamper o' new boots.

MRS CRAIG Sit down to your broth, Tommy.

PROVOST Has he got big match temperament?

HUNTER If Tommy wis in Hollywood, they'd gie him the Hollywood Bowl. In temperament he's like an electric eel in an ice-box – what the moment demands.

PROVOST It's a risk.

HUNTER Ah'm a student o' the game, Provost . . . Player's Friend ye micht say. Whit aboot his signature? *(To CRAIG senior)* Ah, John, you an' me'll hae nae protests or suspensions *sine die* on questions o' illegality.

PROVOST *(To POUTER)* Signature! The boy's been on our books since he left schule. Hasn't he, Pouter?

POUTER Yin o' our colts, ye might say. *(Ready for the twist)*

HUNTER *(Reproachfully)* John Craig! Ye never told me Tommy was a signed player. I thought he was unattached. If I was welcome at his christening, ye might think ah'd be welcome at his signing-on.

CRAIG Dod, an' this is a' news to me.

POUTER Ye've got boots, haven't ye, Tommy?

CRAIG Studded or barred. I bought both the time I won four aways in Murphy's pool.

MRS CRAIG Sit down to your dinner, Tommy. An' you, mister, use your boots to carry you back over my doorstep.

HUNTER As the boy's manager I'd like to see the papers. Documents, ye might say. There's always documents at a signing-on or a transfer.

PROVOST *(To HUNTER)* You and your documents. Tommy, you'll strip! Ah'll take a chance.

TOMMY Play centre-forward for Rangers? Do you mean it?

HUNTER Demand a signing-on form, Tommy. It's legal.

PROVOST *(To TOMMY)* This very minute.

KATE Substitute for Towser Graham. There's honour for ye.

PROVOST Substitute nothing. If he's got it in his feet he can be successor to Towser.

HUNTER We'll call this a try-out, Tommy. If you're a sensation we'll demand documents.

CRAIG *(In agony of excitement)* String! Will anybody gie me a bit string? An' auld bootlace even. Boots! Tommy, ye'll be late for the kick-off. *(Dives under the bed. Reappears holding aloft a pair of old boots, misshapen and clay-clogged)* Your *boots*, Tommy.

KATE What about your books?

TOMMY Thanks, Father. I couldn't get the feel of new ones.

> *(Goes up to POUTER who is standing in anxious impatience at the door. As he passes KATE, she turns aside in silence. MRS CRAIG turns sadly away and faces MR CRAIG. He goes off in excited dash, shoving his arms into his jacket.)*

MRS CRAIG This is a bad day's work for you, John Craig. There'll be no blessing on it.

CRAIG *(From the door)* If ever ye prayed for your son, pray now. Pray he'll score – aye, even if it's only one goal.

ACT I

Scene 2

Late the same evening. The Craigs' kitchen. A paraffin lamp on either side of the mantelpiece lights up the kitchen. It looks warm, comfortable, a home where shared affection defeats poverty and hardship. The kitchen is tidied, the supper dishes decorously arranged on the table. The bed blankets are folded over ready for the sleepers. MRS CRAIG is lying back in the 'faither's' chair; a smooth-rocking, spacious, wooden chair with padded arms and back. At the table, TOMMY is reading the evening paper. He is clearly bored by it.

TOMMY I suppose it's Morning Meeting again tomorrow, then Bible Class, then Night Meeting. God had it in for us when he gave us Sunday, eh?

MRS CRAIG Six days shalt thou labour . . .

TOMMY And on the seventh do all thy work.

MRS CRAIG 'Keep it holy.'

TOMMY Holy? It's a wonder I don't sprout wings.

MRS CRAIG That's almost blasphemy.

TOMMY But Mother, surely once is enough? Why can't we be like other civilised folk? Our meetin makes me feel auld Mr Logan can't get me into Hell quick enough. Anyhow, I don't believe in Hell. Neither does Kate Hunter. She says even God couldn't think up a better Hell than Clanmarnock on Sunday.

MRS CRAIG (*Worried*) Don't dare let me hear you make mockery o' God's Word. Kate's a fine lass, but ye know what the preacher said: 'A little learning is a dangerous thing.'

TOMMY One minute you tell me to *read, read, think* for myself, and now you say . . . I don't know, if it's not a hymn book it's the Bible or *Pilgrim's Progress*. I wish they'd put Bunyan in Barlinnie Jail. When Erchie Campbell's father got sixty days hard labour, I asked him did he feel like writing a book like Bunyan? He said he didn't believe there was any jail in England or Scotland where ye get supplied with writing paper an' ink.

MRS CRAIG John Bunyan was a *saint*.

TOMMY He gives me nightmares.

MRS CRAIG That's enough. I'll have no smart talk from you.

(*KATE comes in*)

KATE My, my! Cottar's Saturday Night without the Cottar.

MRS CRAIG (*Grimly*) Did ye see him doon the road, Kate?

KATE He's outside telling Tom Arnott the story of the great match. He's funny, Mr Craig, always good-natured.

TOMMY Except when his pool coupon is burst.

KATE How's the paper, Tommy?

TOMMY Rotten. It's almost as bad as the *Christian Herald*.

KATE Dope for the people.

MRS CRAIG Now, Kate, I'm no' saying your Socialist stuff is any better.

TOMMY I think I'll come to the Socialist School wi you, Kate.

MRS CRAIG I'll Socialist School ye.

KATE You'd be a reactionary in our school, Tommy.

MRS CRAIG What's a reactionary?

KATE Anybody who believes in something you don't.

MRS CRAIG If I had an escort o' Glasgow polis I'd be afraid to go into one of thae places. Just as such as I'd be afraid to go into a Catholic chapel.

KATE Feart they might kidnap you and take you to a nunnery, Mrs Craig?

TOMMY Imagine Mother a nun!

KATE Oh, I'm sure you get no more harm there than you get at the Brethern; Catholics are not all bad.

MRS CRAIG They're foaled by the same mare.

KATE The girl who sits next to me at the university, Elspeth Macdonald, is a Highland girl, and a Catholic. If all Protestants I know had a tenth of her goodness, I'd begin to believe in a heaven upon earth.

MRS CRAIG A Catholic! Oh, Kate!

KATE Don't forget, a Scots Catholic.

MRS CRAIG I never heard of such a thing.

KATE Elspeth's family have always been Catholics, and they've lived in Stornoway for centuries.

MRS CRAIG Stornoway? Ah! Maybe the missionaries never got as far as there.

KATE I hate and detest this religious bigotry. People are so busy fighting for mansions in the sky, they're content with middens on earth.

(TOMMY has picked up a book. KATE glances at the title.)

KATE Hello, Tommy! Jevons? Did ye need logic at Rangers' Park this afternoon?

TOMMY There's nothing wrong with football.

MRS CRAIG Except when men make a god of it and gods of each other.

KATE It's a point of view, Tommy! Your mother sees football as a rival attraction to religion. I see it as antisocial. Nobody has a right to exploit foolish credulity. Look at the fortunes spent on it – the pools, children robbed of food to provide money for gambling risks.

TOMMY We get football at school.

KATE Aye, as a game.

TOMMY *(Bitterly)* I suppose now you're at the university, rugger *(Almost snarls the word)* will be your game.

KATE My game's the same as yours was yesterday: an escape from the sordid horrors of the Raw, a chance to live less like an animal, the sight and smell of poverty always before you.

(MR CRAIG enters as KATE starts talking. He listens, then comes forwards.)

CRAIG Ye're on the right track, Katie – with Law as your sword.

KATE I'll no' wait, like Littlewood's Legions o' Micawbers, for a coupon to turn up, Mr Craig. I'll work.

CRAIG Work! I knew thae lessons wad fool ye. Tommy, my boy, the bashin centre-forward.

MRS CRAIG Remember, Tommy, 'Beware when men praise you'!

TOMMY I wish you'd stop spitting texts at me, Mother.

MRS CRAIG I'd sooner see you take up the sword of the Lord and of Gideon. Think of Cameron and Peden, men who lifted their eyes to the hills and saw the face of God. Get back to your books, Tommy.

CRAIG Books! Tommy, you played like a coming international. Like ten coming internationals.

KATE A footballers' outing, in fact.

TOMMY I hardly ever touched the ball.

CRAIG You scored the only goal. A beauty it was.

TOMMY The ball ran for me.

CRAIG That's the spirit, let the ball do the work. A good workman relies on his tools.

TOMMY I just saw the chance and swerved past the centre-half.

CRAIG Ye hear that? *Swerved!* Ye cannae hit a swerve. Now then, wife, whit's that about a good an' faithful servant? Supper? I wish we had a fish-supper – even fourpence worth o' chips.

KATE I'll go.

MRS CRAIG Yes: I'll gie fourpence for a paper bagful o' greasy Tally's chips!

TOMMY Here, Kate, get four fish suppers. *(Hands half a crown. There is general amazement.)*

CRAIG Have ye turned coiner?

TOMMY I got five shillings from the Provost. Here, Mother. *(Hands her half a crown)*

CRAIG Five bob! I tell you, there's money in the game.

MRS CRAIG No good ever came of easy money.

CRAIG Only four fish suppers. Let me tell you, Tommy – an' I'm older and wiser than you – the man who works wi his hands is a fool.

KATE There's no disgrace in honest craftsmanship. It's when the craftsman is exploited.

CRAIG That's the lawyer in ye, Kate. Only Trade Union MPs, ministers and lawyers talk about the dignity of labour. Show me one of them who'd give up his job for hammering or digging. Wad Kate take a job in a mill as a weaver? No her.

KATE You should've been a lawyer yourself, Mr Craig.

MRS CRAIG I can see the serpent's hood on him now.

TOMMY That's a backhander at Kate.

MRS CRAIG Kate kens fine what I mean.

KATE Five shillings is a miserable instalment for a body.

TOMMY I hated taking it.

CRAIG Hated? Five shillings for yon goal? Look, Tommy, forget the weemin. You want to be an engineer? That's five years at a few bob a week. An' then what?

TOMMY It's not easy money I'm after.

MRS CRAIG There's no easy road to where you're going, Tommy. It takes courage and self-denial. Think o' Dr Livingstone.

CRAIG I'm sick of Livingstone. He went to Darkest Africa when Darkest Clydeside was round the corner. Man, I've heard tell of players getting as much as five pounds a week, and I'm only talking of third-raters, *not* geniuses!

MRS CRAIG Easy money means a bad conscience.

KATE Think of the specimens we know – Towser!

TOMMY Kate, you're prejudiced – like Mother.

MRS CRAIG We want to have pride for you, not pity.

CRAIG Pity!

KATE Football's a cemetery for high hopes.

TOMMY Talk about prejudice. Think of Paterson of Rangers, a doctor. R. S. McColl, a millionaire, they say . . .

KATE Exceptions. Look at the others, from Lanarkshire and Ayrshire: golden calf today, slaughtered goat tomorrow. Be honest, Tommy, which would you rather have: an international cap or your B.Sc. degree?

TOMMY Both. Given the chance, football can help me to the other.

MRS CRAIG (*Reading*) 'His truth shall be thy shield and buckler. A thousand shall fall at thy side . . .'

(*A scrambling and rattling outside. RAB HUNTER comes in. He speaks slowly and utters each word as though repeating an oath.*)

HUNTER They're efter him! It's God's truth, John. They're efter him. (*To KATE*) Ye're there, Kate.

MRS CRAIG (*Flustered*) Who's efter him, Rab Hunter? Tommy's been at his books all evening. You ken fine he never takes up wi the Raw gang.

HUNTER It's Snatcher MacEwan, John.

CRAIG Snatcher MacEwan? Ye mean o' Drumont Rovers?

HUNTER Himself.

CRAIG What did I tell ye, Tommy? You're spotted.

MRS CRAIG If this is more of that football I'd rather see him tarred.

HUNTER My advice, Tommy, if I'm asked, is – speak him cannily. He's as slippery as a mackerel.

KATE Probably lives on the same food. You shouldn't have brought him here, Father.

HUNTER I met him in the Drumstone Arms.

KATE You would.

HUNTER I was playing dominoes, Kate. He spends money like a man wi the backdoor key to a bank. 'A glass an' a pint all round,' says he, like you an' me wad say on a Friday, 'Half an ounce o' thick black'.

CRAIG Does he want Tommy to sign?

HUNTER On the dotted line.

CRAIG A pen – quick! Have we got a pen? The ink – put some water in that auld bottle.

HUNTER That's where I come in. We're neighbours an' friends, John. Tommy's your boy, but I'm a student o' the game, not just whit they ca' a fan. You must demand a whack!

TOMMY A whack!

HUNTER Aye, a whack. Not a penny less than five pounds. Take it under the table, let him leave it in the china dog, but get it: (*Glowering suddenly at KATE*) legal or unlegal.

CRAIG Five pounds! Bring in Santa Claus!

(*HUNTER goes to the door. Whispers to all, 'Remember, five pounds!' Enter MacEWAN. He is middle-aged; a managerial Napoleon, and looks the part with his carefully displayed gold watch chain. His heavy overcoat pockets are bulging with newspapers.*)

MacEWAN Good evening! Hullo, Tommy! I'm MacEwan of Drumont Rovers. I saw your goal. Not a bad effort.

HUNTER Nut a bad effort? It was a blinder. A Craig Special, ye might say.

MacEWAN One goal doesn't make a player, Mr Hunter.

HUNTER It was an opportunist effort that showed a football brain.

MacEWAN Give the boy his due. He's got the right idea.

MRS CRAIG I hope so.

MacEWAN Ah, Mrs Craig. Tommy's a credit to ye.

MRS CRAIG What d'ye want wi my boy?

MacEWAN I want – if he's the lad I think him – to give him a future.

MRS CRAIG Who gave you tomorrow?

KATE (*To TOMMY*) They may be brief yesterdays, Tommy . . .

MacEWAN You get me wrong, Mrs Craig. It's true I've got Hielan blood, but I'm nae spaewife. It's a future in football I mean.

MRS CRAIG Football, football, football! Is the world daft? Is there no higher purpose for a boy than that he will get booting a bit ball?

CRAIG This is my affair. Mine and Tommy's.

HUNTER That's right, John.

MRS CRAIG Like a sheep before his shearers is dumb.

TOMMY Please, Mother, be quiet.

MacEWAN Now, Tommy lad, I don't like to hear a lad give rough tongue to his mother. Play the whistle, ye ken.

KATE He'll now tell you that 'A boy's best friend is his mother'.

CRAIG His mother thinks everybody a sinner who isn't a Brethern.

MacEWAN Not bad thinking, either. That was the teaching my mother gave me.

MRS CRAIG It's a blessing to hear someone speak gratitude for the Word!

MacEWAN *(Giving KATE a dirty look)* This is Tommy's testing time. His chance. I don't think – coming from you – Tommy's likely to go the way of all flesh; either by bottle, blonde or brunette. Football, I admit, may not always be a steady crutch, but it can be a useful walking-stick.

CRAIG A true word.

HUNTER Claverley couldn't have said it better in his column.

KATE And what has this likely lot got to say about it?

TOMMY Kate, I'll be years here. What can I do? Do you want me to spend my life in the backroom? You know, better than anyone, I need money.

KATE This is a body-and-soul transaction.

MacEWAN Tommy, my club will put no obstacle in your way of advancing yourself. We'll help you.

TOMMY I'll go. I'm going to Drumont, Mother, not to Australia.

MacEWAN An hour on the train, Mrs Craig. He can be home every other weekend. Trust me!

MRS CRAIG I will. But I'm telling you I'll have no underhand work in my house. If the boy goes, he'll go as I hope he'll come back; in honesty; no under-the-table tricks or leaving it in the china dog . . .

MacEWAN China dog?

MRS CRAIG If my boy is worth money, he'll take it openly. Give it him in front of his father and me.

KATE Enter the philanthropist.

MacEWAN Mrs Craig, I don't know how you could have thought otherwise. It's not usual, of course, but certainly I'll give Tommy a . . . well, an honour token. How much? *(Swiftly stepping between MRS CRAIG and RAB)*

HUNTER I'd say . . .

MacEWAN Now, what figure would ye have in mind, Mrs Craig?

MRS CRAIG Twenty pounds.

(KATE laughs; the others gasp)

TOMMY Mother!

MRS CRAIG Twenty pounds, not a penny less.

CRAIG There ye go again. Your tongue . . .

MRS CRAIG I'll say fifty pounds in a minute if anybody angers me. I have your word, Mr MacEwan.

MacEWAN It's a lot of money . . .

MRS CRAIG It's a life you may be buying. God forgive me.

(*MacEWAN busy with his pocket book. There is a loud rapping at the door. MacEWAN is alarmed and begins feverishly counting the notes he takes from his pocket book. He fears competition.*)

KATE This'll be Towser to proclaim abdication . . .

CRAIG Maybe he's been bailed out.

MRS CRAIG Bailed out? Wi the whisky he was drinking they'd need the pumps from the pit to bail him out . . .

MacEWAN I don't think I'd worry, Mrs Craig. Let whoever it is wait. We'll just settle that little bit o' business . . .

HUNTER I know. (*Wildly excited*) I knew ye were spotted, Tommy.

TOMMY It's another manager. The scouts were all at the match, I bet.

MacEWAN Scouts fiddlesticks. I was the only manager at the match. There wasn't a scout this side o' the border at the game. I know. Now then, Mrs Craig . . .

(*The door opens. It is CLAVERLEY.*)

CLAVERLEY When I heard that voice I knew there was no need to wait.

MacEWAN Now then, Bob, I'm surprised at you. This is a private house. Surely there's some limit to your snoopin? Ye can wait outside. I'll be through in a minute. If, mark ye, if you're civil, I'll maybe give ye a bit paragraph for your column . . .

CLAVERLEY From scenes like these auld Scotia's grandeur springs. The cosy but-and-ben, the kindly gudewife and gudeman, neeborly friends, and, wi wolfish eye on the lamb, stands the civil, well-spoken citizen. Sometimes he's a master, a laird maybe or the MP, advising a sodger's life or puttin the lad in touch wi an Emigration Scheme. Whatever the bait, the hook's aye below.

CRAIG Bob McColl . . . CLAVERLEY!

CLAVERLEY I'm still Bob McColl to you, John. Hoo's a' wi ye?

HUNTER Dod and it's proud and pleased we are to see ye, Bob. Ye come like thaw in April. Ye'll be able to settle a point in dispute between me an' the Provost – whit's the procedure about signin on a boy frae juvenile to junior? An unattached boy, mind ye . . .

MacEWAN Maybe ye'll have anither room, Mrs Craig. I've got a train to catch.

(*MRS CRAIG is staring at CLAVERLEY, a sudden gay smile on her lips*)

MRS CRAIG Bob, Bob, have ye nae pity for your frame?

(CLAVERLEY runs a hand over his sagging chin and gives a wry look at the shapeless folds of fat where once was a waistline)

CLAVERLEY Ah've been out to grass since I last saw ye, Meg. But *you!* Meg, a *sight* of you is like the chink o' gold to a miser. If John'll o'erlook a bit sentiment from an old man wi a young memory, the line that fits is, 'red, red rose that's newly sprung in June'.

MRS CRAIG *(Winsome in her rebuke)* Haud your tongue, Bob. The years havena clipped it. Ye were never slow nor canny when ye got to word-spinning.

CRAIG Word-spinnin! The gab ye mean, wife. Just plain gab, an' I don't care if Bob McColl is editor o' the Bible.

CLAVERLEY Give ear to him, Meg? Is that speech not a token o' true love? John's as jealous as a Stewart! Forbye he's the laddie ye gave the silver penny.

MRS CRAIG 'Deed, your heart was soon mended. It's little look of the stickit lover there is about you, Bob McColl.

CRAIG Blast and bleezes, can ye no' keep your Annie Swan deleeriums for another day.

KATE It's true, Tommy. He's as jealous as an auld cat.

CLAVERLEY Tommy? Man, John, I waited for an invitation to the christening. Sez I to myself, musin, when I heard the news that Meg had a boy, surely that old skinflint'll gie me a crumb o' consolation and ask me to be godfather . . . Hullo, Tommy, your hand, son . . .

CRAIG Watch there's no' a burr in his hand, Tommy. That yin'd switch . . .

MRS CRAIG Quiet, John. Ye're ready enough to cry 'Welcome' to anybody else who's able to mouth the word 'football'. Tommy, Mister McColl's a gey old friend o' mine. Your father and he were once like bothers born . . .

CRAIG Wad ye believe it ? If we fought once we fought fifty times.

CLAVERLEY That was when we got to the courtin stage, Tommy. Before that, your father was quite human. When he saw I had an eye for a bonny lass, he made Clanmarnock too hot to hold me.

(TOMMY laughs and returns the handshake warmly)

CRAIG Hell itself'll be too hot to hold ye, Bob, after what ye wrote about Clanmarnock this morning. Man, d'ye get paid for yon? Auld Sarah McClarty looked in her teacup and saw a truer result than you.

CLAVERLEY Had I known Tommy Craig was going to play for *us* . . .

CRAIG US! Didn't I tell ye, Tommy, he has a face would get him into a Masons' Lodge.

CLAVERLEY Why not *us?* Am I not Clanmarnock born an' bred? Wasn't I to be godfather to Tommy but for your crabbed conceit?

HUNTER Ye can be a better godfather this night than ye ever hoped to be, Claverley . . . Dash it, *Bob*, was your own name not good enough but you must get yourself ane out o' a dictionary?

MacEWAN *(Heartily)* I see I did ye an injustice, Bob . . .

CLAVERLEY Mr McColl, even Claverley, at a pinch, but no' Bob to you, MacEwan.

KATE Ah, what Towser calls 'the needle' appears.

CRAIG What did I tell ye? Every time I see him, it's like lookin at a new moon wi a bad coin in my pocket.

MacEWAN Don't mind Claverley, Mr Craig. We're old rivals . . .

CLAVERLEY Rivals?

MacEWAN *(Hastily)* Mrs Craig, if you and Tommy'll just come into the next room . . .

CLAVERLEY Meg, let me do myself and you a favour. I'll go into the next room wi Tommy and the *Snatcher* . . .

CRAIG Snatcher! D'ye hear him? He's trying to insult the gentleman . . .

CLAVERLEY I'd need the venom o' an adder to irritate his skin . . .

MacEWAN Toots, Mr Craig, Claverley's always touchy when he sees himself beaten to a signature. Ye see, he's our old friend, not a reporter only. Many a manager owed his discovery to Claverley. I'll say this for him, he's got an eye for a likely-lookin footballer.

CLAVERLEY I've got an eye for this lad, as you'll discover. Don't forget I've still got the receipt for the last likely-lookin footballer you and me went after.

MacEWAN Didn't I tell ye, Mr Craig? There's no grudge like that borne by a scout who's once lost a player –

CLAVERLEY You never lost the player. You got him. It was the player got lost.

HUNTER If this is what the football writers call 'negotiatin', the sooner I'm a scout the better. I could buy and sell ten players wi less talk. Look, Bob, I'm Tommy's manager –

MacEWAN *(Coldly)* There's no need for managers or long-lost godfathers. Tommy, ye'll come to Drumont? *(To MRS CRAIG)* A moment ago we were agreed, you know, Mrs Craig.

CRAIG Of course he'll go, Mr MacEwan.

HUNTER The documents, man, the documents. I appeal to you, Bob.

CLAVERLEY Meg, let me handle this, please!

HUNTER Negotiate, John, negotiate. Man, will ye no' listen to the expert?

MacEWAN Tommy, the word's yours. What is it to be? I've promised to look after you.

CLAVERLEY That's a promise, Tommy, believe me! You might as well go for a walk wi a man-eatin tiger. Meg, I implore you! Tommy! Give me two minutes alone wi MacEwan and I'll –

MacEWAN Sorry, Claverley, some other time. The deal's arranged. *(To MRS CRAIG)* Twenty pounds it is . . .

CLAVERLEY John Craig, you're a stubborn, prejudiced old crab. God forgive ye for this night's work, for Tommy won't and I won't.

CRAIG You keep out o' this, Bob, that's all I ask.

MacEWAN And there you are, Mrs Craig. It's in your hand. And to prove my good faith, I'll name the terms now. Three pounds a session, two pounds a week for the close season.

KATE Tommy's Magna Charter.

HUNTER Quiet, Kate. The terms are generous, as generous as Fister McNaughton got from Auchenshuggle Rangers.

MRS CRAIG Ye'll no' listen to Mr Claverley, Tommy?

TOMMY What's the use, Mother? I'll never get another –

CLAVERLEY Be advised by your mother and me, lad. See, I'll swear to your mother to find you a club and watch your interests.

MacEWAN Tommy, is this fair to me? I ask you, Mrs Craig, on the word of a rival –

CRAIG Ye canna back out now, wife. The lad's as good as signed –

KATE He's not in the slave market.

TOMMY Mother, we've had all this out. I don't want to be ungrateful to Mr Claverley, but I can't wait. I can't take a risk of losing.

MRS CRAIG You're content, then?

TOMMY Yes, Mother.

(She hands him the notes and MacEWAN puts a pen into his hand. TOMMY signs. CLAVERLEY comes forward and shakes hands with MRS CRAIG.)

CLAVERLEY Maybe it'll work out, Meg. Maybe because he's yours. I'm over-anxious.

MRS CRAIG I feel as Joseph's brethren must have felt when they sold him to the Ishmaelites. For my sake, Bob, you'll keep an eye on him.

(CLAVERLEY nods and pats her gently on the shoulder)

CLAVERLEY Better still, I'll keep an eye on the Snatcher. *(Goes out. As he passes CRAIG, with kindly bitterness he says:)* You're wab-footed, that's what you are, John Craig. But, man, ye'll aye be Jock Tamson to me. Goodnight.

CRAIG Nae ill will, Bob. Ye know my tongue.

MacEWAN Goodnight, Mrs Craig. Report on Monday, Tommy. We'll fix the bonus money then. *(Goes out)*

CRAIG *(Gazing at the money still lying on the table, whispers)* Tommy, son, there's gold in your boots!

ACT I

Scene 3

Two months later. The CRAIGS' kitchen, Sunday morning. MR CRAIG is in bed. On a chair, by the bedside, lie a pile of Sunday papers. There is a noticeable difference in atmosphere and setting. This may be traced to recent prosperity, evidence of which is a wireless-set of cheap wood and flashy facings on a dresser, right, between the fireplace and the door wall. Between the door, left, and the bed against the wall, stands an American organ. MRS CRAIG comes in at the door.

CRAIG Ma pipe tastes like stewed, taury rope. *(MRS CRAIG ignores him)* Hand me the bottle o' Iron-Brew that's under this bed. Ma throat's as hot as a plumber's lead ladle.

MRS CRAIG Snorting and gabbling like a pig . . .

CRAIG Haud your tongue you wi your nag, nag, nag! You never was better off in your life.

MRS CRAIG Wait till Tommy hears about you an' Rab Hunter and the Arms.

CRAIG If ye don't hand me that Iron-Brew!

(MRS CRAIG gropes under the bed and hands him a huge glass bottle filled with fiery-coloured aerated water. He drinks from the bottle, making a horrid gurgling noise, at the sound of which she makes nauseated grimace.

RAB HUNTER comes in. As he enters, MRS CRAIG sits down at the organ and plays a bar or so of 'Stand up, stand up for Jesus'.)

CRAIG My Goad! This is worse than Merryflatts, the Glesga asylum. Rab, I think I'll hae a drap o' Epsom Salts. They're beside the sink.

(MRS CRAIG goes out)

HUNTER I'll tak' a sip, too. My need is like yours, John Craig. Christianity! Huh! Imagine having to walk three miles to get a hair o' the dog that bit me. Kate gave me a livener, but wi little grace.

CRAIG She *did*?

HUNTER Aye, that's the best o' having a freethinker in the house. Kate's a great ane on free will. She said if I wanted to make a sink o' ma stomach, it was ma stomach. But tell me – d'ye see the screed about *our* boy in the *Evening Times*?

CRAIG Tak' a load off your feet. *(Points to a chair)*

HUNTER 'A cert for a cap,' says John o' Groats.

CRAIG Claverley says Tommy's 'the Napoleon of soccer'. Meanin football, I suppose? – 'Soccer'!

HUNTER The *News of the World* says Tommy 'has the classic style' –

CRAIG The man on the wireless says Tommy's 'like a *bally* dancer'. Is that bad?

HUNTER Bally dancer? Um! Mebbe he didna' mean anything. These wireless lads are awfu poor at speakin English. But did ye read the *Sunday Dispatch*? It says if he can acclimatise himself and blend his craft wi English speed, any first-class English club will mortgage their goal-posts to get him.

CRAIG Tommy'll stay in Scotland. We've exported enough brain to England.

HUNTER As a student o' the game, I consider that a narrow view. The game benefits frae intermarriage – the speed o' a Bastin, the guile o' a James, that makes for combination.

CRAIG When Tommy comes here this morn I'll sound him. Hand me a bible – *quick*, afore the wife comes.

(HUNTER hands him a pile of Sunday newspapers.

MRS CRAIG comes in from the bedroom. She is dressed for the Morning Meeting, plain black coat and simple hat, a Bible in her hand, no gloves. CRAIG makes a frantic grab at the newspapers. MRS CRAIG gets them first.)

MRS CRAIG When Tommy sees you, maybe he'll no' be so eager to listen as to talk – give *you* a piece o' his mind. To think I'd live to see the day when ma man would look and act like a pig in a strange sty. As for these – the sewage o' mind and soul *(Begins stuffing them in the fire)*, divorce, murder, scandal. Whit they canna' rake up from broken homes and broken lifes, they invent. Well, they'll no' stain my house, not even as floor mats. Anybody who thinks they'll be read here might as soon hope to see a spittoon on my table. If you've found God in a bottle an' ba', John Craig, I'll see you'll no' want for other example.

(KATE appears)

KATE Good morning, Mrs Craig. My, you'll soon be leaving us for Hollywood!

MRS CRAIG If he carries on as he's going, it's that Holloway place, the women's jail the papers are aye speakin about.

(She again starts playing 'Stand up, stand up – ')

CRAIG If she doesn't stop playing that thing it's me'll land in a home.

MRS CRAIG Aye, for inebriates.

KATE I hear Tommy is coming.

MRS CRAIG Poor Tommy! He little kens what sad results his goodness has brought.

(A knock at the door. The latch is lifted and MRS McCLARTY, a buxom, panting, elderly woman, whirls into the kitchen.)

MRS McCLARTY *(To CRAIG)* Bed-ridden, John? *(CRAIG groans and turns over on his side)* Maggie Craig, are ye daft? Five shillings to ma Teenie. It's me who knows it'll go on the pictures, Peg's Papers, fish suppers, an' never a crust or cloot for the weans.

MRS CRAIG She said the wean hadn't had milk for a week –

MRS McCLARTY Ah'm her mother and should know. If ye gave her Nestle's Milk factory, she'd sell the milk and let the weans lick empty tins. An' yesterday, Tam, the Co-op butcher says ye bought that Annie McEvoy an' ashet of pie. Since your Tommy started playin fitba' there's no' a hungry mouth in the Row. I tell ye, it's waste. An' look at yourself – a coat that's as windproof as a crochetted window-screen –

CRAIG Gie her a pulpit, somebody.

MRS McCLARTY Ah'm the only one hereabouts who'll tell *you* what boat you're on.

MRS CRAIG It's nae loss what a friend gets, Sarah – I gave Teenie the five shillings because it might as well go to her as to the Clanmarnock Arms.

MRS McCLARTY It takes a steady hand to haud a fu' cup, I've always said. I'm no lookin far, but I can see a hand couldn't haud a fu' teaspoon. Aye, it's a sad day when a weak heid an' a tank belly are joined in unholy wedlock.

CRAIG Will ye say what ye want, ye auld clapper tongue, an' get back to your sin midden.

(MRS McCLARTY advances towards the bed)

MRS McCLARTY Talk to me like that, Craig, and I'll claw that rope ye call a whisker off your face. Maggie an' me was school-mates and after that worked side by side in the mill. That was afore Maggie went for what she ca's a closer walk wi God. Though I canna' see how getting hauf-drooned in a watter tank – immersion or whatever they ca' it – an' cawin yourself a Brethern, brings ye closer to God. Listen to me, Craig, when Maggie turned her back on yon fella Bob Claverley, and gave you seven-and-sixpence out o' her menage money to pay the weddin certificate, my hert sang 'The Flooers o' the Forest'. Marryin you, I prophesised, wad be as bad as bein clapped in the Black Hole o' Calcutta. Wi Bob Claverley, an' him the great man on the newspaper, she'd be as cosy as a queen.

KATE Poor Mr Craig! You're his Annie Laurie this morning, Mrs McClarty. For you he'd lie doon an' dee.

MRS CRAIG Don't *you* take his part, Kate.

HUNTER An' whiles twal' penny worth o' nappy can make a body fu' and once happy –

147

MRS McCLARTY That's it. By the look o' him, he's had a skinful o' naptha.

KATE There's the kirk bell, Mrs Craig, you'll be late.

MRS CRAIG Dear me, I clean forgot to put on –

KATE On you go. Tell me an' I'll put things straight.

MRS CRAIG It's a broth and a bit steak and kidney pie, Kate. The vegetables are in the sink, a' ready, the pie's to go into the oven.

CRAIG For God's sake take McClarty wi ye.

HUNTER If McClarty goes to Kirk she'll be excommunicated – suspended *sine die* at least, as the bag o' yeast might say.

MRS McCLARTY You God-less auld sepulchre. I'll bag o' yeast ye if you misca' my priest. Father Grant, next to Maggie, is the only Christian in Clanmarnock.

CRAIG Did ye no' bring your flute, ye auld papish blether?

MRS CRAIG Never mind him, Sarah. That's the heathen talking.

MRS McCLARTY Off ye go, Maggie. Say a bit prayer for him, though I'm thinking St Peter himself couldn't put in a good word for that auld rogue. It's a good job I'm no' thin-skinned or I'd bash him wi that Iron-Brew bottle for his lip about Father Grant. *(MRS CRAIG is at the door)* I'll stay and watch the dinner.

MRS CRAIG Have I got a collection – *(Fusses in her glove to discover coins)*

MRS McCLARTY Away to your singing, Kate. I'll see to the dinner.

(They go off. CRAIG rising up in bed:)

CRAIG Slide, ye two-faced auld witch. 'Naptha', says she, an' the auld soak got a gill an' a pint from me last night, an' shared a three-cross-double wi me on Wednesday.

MRS McCLARTY Haud yer tongue, auld man. Ah'm the best frien ye ever had. Ye should be on your knees thankin God it's Sarah McClarty has the real Christian idea o' what's what for a man on a Sunday morn, see?

(Flings open her shawl – displays two large bottles of John Haig whisky. The men are at once astonished and ecstatic.)

CRAIG Gie me it! Just let me look at it! Ah could bite the neck off it.

HUNTER The wumman's a fair Jesuit!

MRS McCLARTY Nae dirty insults from you, Rab Hunter.

CRAIG Ach, Sarah, he means the clever way ye bamboozled Maggie.

MRS McCLARTY Either we tak' a dram thegether like civilised folk, forgetting Party and Creed, or me an' the bottle'll tak' the high road.

CRAIG Sarah, where you go, I go, your bottle's my bottle. If ye had an Inquisition at your elbow and that bottle in your grip, it's me wad follow you frae here to Dublin. *(Sings)* 'Follow, follow, I will follow Sarah. Even *unto* Dublin I will follow on – '

McCLARTY Tak' a lip o't, then.

CRAIG *(Drinks from the bottle)* It's nectar, Rab!

McCLARTY Oot to the water-closet and you'll find twa screw-tops o' Youngers –

(RAB goes out dazed)

CRAIG Ye havena robbed a poor-box, Sarah?

MRS McCLARTY 'Deed no. In a way, you're responsible.

CRAIG Me? Don't tell me I've taken to no' letting my left hand ken whit ma right hand's doin?

MRS McCLARTY *(Drinks, then offers bottle)* Here, anither, before the Clanmarnock ghost comes back. Ah'll tell ye: it was Tommy, young Tommy, the tousiest wee centre-forward.

CRAIG Tommy?

HUNTER *(Coming back in)* Dod, an' Sarah's right, John. They were coolin in the cistern. Smart woman.

MRS McCLARTY Here, wet your whistle. Aye, John, Tommy! Ah drew him in the Row Sweep. That hat-trick he got yesterday brought me twenty-four shillings. I nabbed half a crown o' the five shillings Teenie got frae Mrs Craig. Two bottles o' Haig, two screw-tops, an', sez I, ma auld crony John an' me'll slake oor thirsts while the others are away marching to Zion.

HUNTER Sarah! Ah'll start a subscription for a monument to a camel, two thirsty travellers, an' you, standing like Rebecca at the well, handin oot glasses an' pints. Man, it'll be biblical to look at!

CRAIG A toast! Here's tae the shamrock, St Patrick – a good Scotsman by the by – an' Sarah McClarty, the Florence Nightingale o' Clanmarnock. *(Leaps up in bed, his shirt-tails flapping about his bare legs)*

HUNTER A song! A song frae Sarah!

MRS McCLARTY Ach, it's Kate ye should have.

(RAB shudders)

HUNTER She'd gie us the 'Internationale' or that ither dirge, 'the Rid Flag'.

CRAIG Let's have something cheery, Sarah. A warning, though, nae 'Steer my Barque to Erin's Isle' or 'Up to the Knees in Orange Bluid'. It's your bottle, but, by King Billy, it's my hoose.

MRS McCLARTY Are ye insultin me? Since when did Sarah McClarty forget what was due from her, even when in a but-an'-ben in a Scot's miner's row? *(Sings)* 'All around my heart I'll wear the green, white an' yellow –

CRAIG Another word o' that an' I'll –

HUNTER He's right. It's the Lord's Day, nae –

MRS McCLARTY Yer pleasure then, ma heather-eatin jocoes.

CRAIG By Cromwell! The woman wad anger a saint. At one step she's a

149

Samaritan, the next she's a Jezabel, smacking her chops wi blood in her eye.

HUNTER *(Sings)* 'We'll buy a rope an' hang the Pope . . .'

MRS McCLARTY *(Fiercely)* Another note, one more dirty word, an' ye'll be saying 'Good morning' to your father, the Earl o' Hell, Rab Hunter.

HUNTER My best respects, Sarah. I wis at fault. Ye canna help bein what ye are.

(MRS McCLARTY screams in angered affront and flourishes a bottle)

CRAIG Blisterin damnation on ye both, is it a wake ye're after? Let's twang the loud harp in friendliness. Your pleasure, Sarah.

HUNTER Sing 'The Nameless Lassie'.

MRS McCLARTY I'll praise no illegitimate.

CRAIG I've got it, Sarah – 'The Bonny Wells o' Weary'.

MRS McCLARTY Ach, John, man, it's no' my song. Ye'd get the words here, but for the air ye'd have to go outside.

(CRAIG leaps out of bed. MRS McCLARTY yells bawdy delight and makes a smack at his legs.)

CRAIG Air? Listen to me, ah'll make this damned hurdy-gurty speak.

(Seats himself at the organ, his legs pedalling furiously. With one finger he makes melancholy melody. MRS McCLARTY strikes a posture and sings in a not unpleasing voice. RAB's head droops in drunken sympathy with song and singer.)

MRS McCLARTY 'Come let us climb old Arthur's Seat,
     Where Summer suns are gleaming,
     Where bonnie lassies bleach their claes
     A' – '

(They join together in the chorus)

ALL   'The bonny Wells o' Weary,
      The bonnie Wells o' Weary,
      Come let us spend a summer day
      Beside the Wells o' Weary – '

(MRS McCLARTY stops singing. She listens attentively to RAB, who goes on singing.)

HUNTER 'The bonnie Wells o' Weary,
     The bonnie Wells o' Weary,
     King Billy slew the Papish crew
     Beside the Wells o' Weary – '

MRS McCLARTY Ye treacherous Orange get! Sing sacrilege in my face, wad ye? Here's your answer – *(Crowns him with the steak and kidney pie)*

(The door opens. TOMMY enters. He stands in amazement, anger and disgust on his face. CRAIG reels from the organ stool and makes a grab at his trousers. RAB stands swaying, desperately tearing pie-crust and meat from his hair, face and eyes. MRS McCLARTY takes in the new TOMMY at a glance – low-cut baggy plus-fours of loud, almost ludicrous check.)

MRS McCLARTY God bless ye, Tommy boy, your hat-trick was a miracle. Man, the Duke o' Argyll himself couldn't look more like a gentleman.

TOMMY Get out –

MRS McCLARTY Ach, Tommy lad, me an' the auld yin an' the ghost was having a bit o' a terr – a celebration like.

CRAIG *(Drunkenly)* That's it, Tommy, just a bit song an' laugh –

TOMMY Whisky!

HUNTER A whole bottle. A God's blessing to auld bodies who canna mak' the three-mile limit. You know, Tommy, 'bona fide traveller' they ca' it. Ye've got to prove you've travelled three miles afore ye qualify for a drink. That's Scotland.

(CRAIG is scrambling into his clothes – draws on boots and jacket)

TOMMY Get out!

CRAIG Now, Tommy, that's nae way to talk to visitors.

TOMMY You too, before my mother gets back. If you weren't who ye are I'd decorate the place with you.

CRAIG An' me your father? Is that a way to show respect –

TOMMY Get out, I tell you, while I can keep my hands to myself – and that, that trollop –

MRS McCLARTY Trollop? Me? Tommy Craig!

(CRAIG hustles her out of the door. At the door he turns and in maudlin sadness says:)

CRAIG To think the day would come when I'd say a son o' mine was too big for his boots.

MRS McCLARTY Ye never said a truer word, John Craig. Too big for his boots. That's what he is.

(They go out, RAB singing 'Come let us spend a Summer day'. TOMMY sits wearily on a chair and buries his head in his arms folded upon the table. KATE appears at the door. She looks at him, understanding and sympathy on her face. She goes forward quietly.)

KATE They were all right when your mother left, Tommy. I came back to see everything was all right. Sarah McClarty must have –

TOMMY How long has he been like this?

KATE Oh, he's not bad, Tommy. Poor devil! Like my father, he isn't fed for boozing. Years of idleness and semi-starvation. Suddenly money to burn, friends by the hundred, all saying 'Hullo, John, have a dram. How's the boy?'

TOMMY My mother?

KATE She thinks it a judgement on her for having sold you to the Ishmaelites.

TOMMY That's daft!

KATE Your mother's conscience is as sensitive as a compass needle. Every word she hears about you and football is a jag at her heart.

TOMMY What have I done? She should be grateful.

KATE She *is* – about you. Her worry is, how long before the gold bug gets you. She looks at your father and is afraid.

TOMMY I'm all right. I'll talk to her before I go back tonight.

KATE Tonight?

TOMMY Yes. Tonight, Kate! I'm the last-minute choice for the Norway trip –

KATE Norway?

TOMMY The SFA Norwegian Tour, silly. Congratulate me! The Selection Committee decided late last night at Carlton Terrace. Imagine – Norway! MacEwan didn't want me to come home this weekend.

KATE You're going?

TOMMY Going? Can a duck swim? It's an honour! Snatcher took me to Forsyth's last night. He got me a complete kit, these (*Displays plus-fours in mannequin pose; half caricature, but vanity is not concealed*), two suits of pyjamas, a dressing-gown – you should see it, tassels, silk-facing – a Burberry and a hat – snap-brim. They're outside in the car. I wanted my mother and you to see them.

KATE Car?

TOMMY I forgot. Hamish (*He says the name with relish*) Strachan, one of our directors, drove me over. A nice man, Kate, you'll like him. He's a director of Tan Brae Whisky, but not a fraction of swank in him. Never batted an eye when he drove into the Row – I watched him.

KATE Did you expect him to swoon? As director of Tan Brae Whisky he's probably grateful for places like the Row and men like your father and mine.

TOMMY I thought you'd like to see the sort of folk football brings me in touch with.

KATE Oh, Tommy, I'm sorry. I'm getting as bad as your mother. I mean, prejudiced. Tommy, it's for you I'm worrying.

TOMMY I'm trying hard to be a credit.

KATE I'll bet you're a fair terror to the girls of Drumont, Tommy – plus-fours, silk dressing-gown –

TOMMY You're the first to see the plus-fours.

KATE All you need is a golf course.

TOMMY I'm learning golf, too, Kate. We were at Gailes on Wednesday for part of our special training. We get special baths and massage.

KATE It's a beauty they'll make you, Tommy –

TOMMY The *Record* has asked me to do a 'Tommy Craig' article each week – I'll get more money for that. And Dobbins, the tobacco people, want me to sign an advert – you know, 'Tommy Craig says – "I smoke Dobbins Gold Leaf cigarettes night and day" '. I'll get paid for that. Look, I brought you this, Kate. *(Hands her a neat red Russian-leather pocket-book)* I saw an Edinburgh beauty with one, it's a season-ticket holder, purse and diary in one.

KATE Tommy! It's real Russian leather. It's lovely. And what *taste!* Who's been coaching you?

TOMMY Look, Kate, it's got the dates of Law Terms and –

KATE Oh, Tommy! You know me better than I know myself, I think. Never a day since we were at school but we've been together.

TOMMY D'ye remember the day we went to Loch Lomond?

KATE And you made tea from a Boy Scout's kettle and tried to fry sausages on a biscuit-tin lid!

TOMMY We were high up on the heather and you read *John Splendid*. We pretended the mountainside was swarming wi Campbells, black an' red.

KATE When we heard the sound of the pipes drifting up from the tinker-camp by the lochside, you ranted like Rob Roy, 'My foot is on my native heath, my name's McGregor!'

TOMMY An' that first trip down the Clyde, when we saw Ailsa Craig. The peaks of Arran.

KATE The Paps o' Jura.

TOMMY You danced a reel with me and we were named the best couple on the deck.

KATE That was when we were coming through Rothesay Bay.

TOMMY I took you aft to show you the Cloch Lighthouse.

KATE And you gave me a keepsake –

TOMMY My first medal – the one I got for the Academy versus Govan High School.

KATE Look, Tommy. *(Lifts the silver chain from her neck and shows TOMMY the badge attached)*

TOMMY Remember your promise?

KATE Wheesh! That was a long time ago.

TOMMY We passed Govan and were coming near the Broomielaw. You whispered, 'I'll keep it for ye, Tommy.' I kissed you, the only time I ever kissed you.

KATE We planned to go to the university together, you to be another Lord Kelvin, me to be your legal advisor. Oh, Tommy, we were poor daft dreamers, but we were wonderfully happy. Even the Row looked lovely that night. I lay in the dark, through my window the moon was high and we were back in Arran, the slag-heap was Goatfell. No ugliness, no hungry scraping, no terrifying fears about what would happen next day – the threats of butcher or factor! – just wonderful serenity, laughter and love.

TOMMY We can have a house in Arran. The club would get it for me this summer.

KATE The club! No, Tommy. I'm feart, feart the club's got you, Tommy.

TOMMY But Kate, I'm getting over fifteen pounds a week *now*. Wi benefit money, extras from newspaper articles, bonuses –

KATE No, Tommy, our dream's over. Love never looks twice. You have your football – I have my work.

TOMMY But I'll help. *(Quickly)* I know, Kate – I'll give you Oxford as a wedding present.

KATE Oxford!

TOMMY Pay the fees for you to take that English degree.

KATE Please, Tommy. It won't work. If you were studying . . .

TOMMY Studying? When I get fifteen pounds a week for playing. Snatcher says he can't risk a breakdown – You know, too much studying – nerves – puts a player off his game.

KATE What would marriage do to your nerves? Did you ask Snatcher that, Tommy?

TOMMY Don't mock, Kate. I want you. I've always wanted you – I need you.

KATE No, Tommy. There would be me, Snatcher MacEwan – Mr Strachan – your father, my father, the *Record*, Dobbins Gold Leaf, the special training. If I marry you I'll be marrying somebody else's gold mine.

TOMMY I won't be playing football all my life.

KATE Maybe you'll have reason to fear that one day, Tommy. Tommy, let me ask my uncle, John McLintock, you know, he's a civil engineer, to take you into his office.

TOMMY I know what it is: a professional footballer isn't good enough. It's an inkwell or a ledger you'd marry.

(KATE brushes past him. At the door she turns and faces him.)

KATE You're like the others before you who stepped up from the Row. Perfection in promise.

TOMMY I want to be a whole man.

KATE So you mortgage yourself to a ball – a bit of inflated pigskin. *You* chase *it* and *it* hunts *you*. Don't you see, Tommy? *You're* the ball, don't fool yourself. A bad game and you're out of the team, out of the spotlight. It's passover Saturday for you. I want a name-plate that is permanent, not one that's 'Home and Away' a lot.

TOMMY Come down to earth, Kate. I'm good at the game, I know that, whatever you say. I don't need a B.Sc. degree to tell me that I'll get more for my Benefit Game than I'd get for two years' work as an engineer. I'm offering you as good a life as you've got any right to expect, for all your university ideas.

KATE You're offering me a gamble, Tommy. But I want more than that. I want love and happiness. We know that unemployment and the Means Test can do a lot of funny things to marriage, however lovely its beginning.

TOMMY There ye go again. It's a raven not a linty I should call it.

KATE Call me what you like. I'm not putting on handcuffs as your mother, or Mrs McClarty and my mother did, Tommy. I'm feart for the risk.

TOMMY Feart! It's swank that's at the bottom of this. You'd sooner have a fifty-bob week engineering clerk than a fellow with guts.

KATE Swank, you call it? Swank to prefer ideas to what you call guts? I won't marry a pair of football boots anyway!

CURTAIN

END OF ACT I

ACT II

Scene 1

One month later. A room in St Mungo's Hotel, Glasgow. The room is furnished in heavy Victorian fashion: a long broad mahogany table, solidly upholstered chairs on either side, a large armchair at the top centre. At the fireplace are two large low-seated armchairs. The windows, right, look out on St Enoch's Square. A fire is burning in the grate. When the curtain rises the room is empty. Immediately after the rise of the curtain the door opens – left – and a young man sticks his head round the edge of the door. In a loud whisper intended to reach someone behind him, he says:

YOUNG MAN This looks like the auction room.
VOICE Get in, then.

(The YOUNG MAN is given a shove. He stumbles into the room and is followed by two other men, BOB CLAVERLEY and TONY SPALDING of the London Morning Telegram. *The reporter thrust into the room is McSPORRAN, Sports Feature Writer on the* Daily Post. *McSPORRAN is a London-Scot, and consciously the superior of CLAVERLEY, who, in his eyes, is a provincial hack whom one humours, partly because of pity for his unspectacular professional status, but mainly because, hack or no hack, he is on his own hunting ground and can follow trails hidden from the keenest Fleet Street eyes. SPALDING is snobbishly tolerant of both CLAVERLEY and McSPORRAN. An Oxford man, he is resentful of the importance given editorially to Association football. SPALDING is a rugby man and despises soccer, not on athletic considerations, but because of its mass popularity. In manner and dress SPALDING aspires to aloof classification. His Hawes & Curtis suit, Buhl suede shoes, monocle and Oxford University tie are defensive props against being classified as a CLAVERLEY, even a McSPORRAN.)*

CLAVERLEY Take off your shoes, boys, we're on holy ground.
McSPORRAN Spill it, Bob, what time are they due?
CLAVERLEY Ten-thirty, but I think they'll be late. The English party were in the lounge until four o'clock this morning.
SPALDING What's the blood money likely to be, Claverley?
CLAVERLEY Six thousand? Your guess is as good as mine. It's not the Scottish Highlands that's being transferred, it's Tommy Craig. Tommy Craig, uncrowned King of Scotland, the wee devil in blue, the boy who puts the jag in thistle. Six thousand, why, ye'd get a deer forest, a couple of Hebridean poets an' a wheen of Scots MPs for that figure, but not Tommy

Craig. Let me tell you, by the time news of Tommy's transfer reaches Fleet Street the figure'll look like Mae West's payroll on night-shift.

McSPORRAN Certainly he's worth a record fee. When you see Craig, Spalding old man, you're looking at rare football genius.

SPALDING I'm told he's a teetotaller and non-smoker! It's historical – an English manager's dream!

CLAVERLEY Either of you sent over a story this morning?

McSPORRAN Speculate on this? Tuts, Bob. *(He is stringing BOB and being ingratiating to SPALDING)* Guesswork would be sacrilege, wouldn't it?

CLAVERLEY It's a scoop, then?

McSPORRAN What a break for United! Tommy's first game'll be a classic. Think of the gates! United playing Arsenal at Highbury and Tommy Craig's first appearance. There'll be a ninety-thousand gate . . .

CLAVERLEY Ninety thousand! Tommy'll think he's back in school football. Ninety thousand! We get that gate at matches on the Merchants' half holidays.

SPALDING Oh, we might arrange for royalty to be present . . .

CLAVERLEY When ye talk of classic 'gates' take a look at the Hampden figure – one hundred and forty thousand for an international, for an Old Firm, Rangers–Celtic Cup Final round about the same.

McSPORRAN After all, Bob, football's not yet a national industry in England.

SPALDING There are rival sports, you know. Thank goodness England still enjoys games free from the taint of the money machine. *We* still play games for sport, y'know.

CLAVERLEY For instance?

McSPORRAN Oh, come, Bob, you know perfectly well that you envy the Englishman his cricket spirit – the game's the thing.

SPALDING Twickenham is still paradise to the amateurs . . .

CLAVERLEY Wimbledon, too, I suppose? Wimbledon – home of the racqueteer. Let me see the purist in sport, Mr Englishman. Lizzie-called-Elsie arrives wi a rabbit-skin coat and a forearm like a village blacksmith. She leaves in chinchilla, a first-class ticket for Palm Beach, Monte Carlo, or New York in her racquet-bag. Her face is good in Bond Street shirt shops, her vanishing freckles are the theme-song for the professors of Ponds. For chaperon she gets herself a banker who makes a footballer's friend look like Dr Barnardo. There's cricket – Gentlemen versus Players. They've got in ahead of the Creator at Lords, dividing the sheep from the goats – though which is goat and which is sheep only? A Player who's not a Gentleman could tell. When they send a team to play the Australians, the Aborigines have got to go out on the field in armour-plated suits because the bowling looks like Mills bombing. As for the rugby purist, now, there's self-denial for you. From the hacking pitches of the Welsh borders, Cornish pits, Severn dockyards, come the rugger-buggers – as your Oxford intellectuals call them, all passionately eager to prove the game's the thing. So you get Welshmen playing for England; English sons of Scottish mothers playing for Scotland; Irish medical students making rugby a backdoor to the Services; stockbrokers, distillery and brewery touts rising from the scrum to the directors' boards. I've even heard tell of academic honours being won on the rugby playing fields.

SPALDING Slander, absolute slander, Claverley.

CLAVERLEY Tell me, Spalding, what's the normal transfer fee that enables a suburban boy to travel from, say, a two-guinea-a-year subscription, to the millionaire hide-outs in the South of France or California?

SPALDING You know perfectly well that a first-class player may add to his income by improved commercial contacts.

CLAVERLEY That's good! 'Improved commercial contracts'! That's what ye call it when a tennis player, a rugby player, a cricketer or a golfer starts stepping heavenwards into the bankbook class. When a footballer . . .

SPALDING No comparison. The white slavery we will see this morning. I ask you, more than six thousand pounds. That's the sum to be paid for a gutter-rat because he has skill in ball-kicking.

CLAVERLEY Gutter-rat?

SPALDING And that six thousand pounds is probably only half the sum the Snatcher will collect for the transfer. Sport? McSporran is right – it's an industry.

McSPORRAN Goodness, now we're sunk! Spalding, you're starting Bob on a rare hare.

CLAVERLEY Sometimes, Mr McSporran, when I read your back-heelers at home-keeping Scots, I'd write your obituary, opening with the obvious quotation from 'The Lay of the Last Minstrel'. Wasn't it 'Willie Whitewash' they called ye in the Edinburgh coffee howffs?

SPALDING Now you're being unkind, Claverley.

CLAVERLEY I apologise. But McSporran knows I've little patience with highfalutin Anglo-Scots patronage. I'm all for a one-team man. Support your team and wear the colours, say I.

SPALDING Typical soccer spirit. No side but your own.

CLAVERLEY And what's wrong wi that spirit? I've yet to meet the Englishman resident in Scotland who's willing to call himself a Scots-Anglo.

SPALDING For all that, Tommy Craig will go to England to be the idol of English football crowds.

CLAVERLEY Yes, but let Tommy Craig fail to deliver golden goals and see what happens. Fleet Street analysts will have him on the X-ray table, body and soul. Let him but sidestep from the training diet – a glass of beer, a bit of a fling with the girls – and the Pharisees will train their inky arrows on him. And that's why I'm fashed for him. I'm feared he may go the way of all football flesh. I was told, last night, Tommy's had a row with his lass. I don't like that. No more do I like the idea of his being led by the nose by Snatcher into the bull-ring, for MacEwan will sell him as a butcher would a side of beef.

McSPORRAN Oh, Tommy will get his cut okay, Bob.

CLAVERLEY Cut? MacEwan'll mince him.

SPALDING When did a Scots footballer resign the right to his cut?

CLAVERLEY No wonder England knows even less about football economics than about theology. Tell me, since the first player ever transferred for money – before that, they were transferred on the feudal system – when has a player had a fair cut? He gets the maximum eight pounds a week and a whole lot of honour. I've seen boys go from Scotland to England who were gate-money attractions, in comparison to whom the biggest West End actor idol looked like a man selling Derby tips. The star actor's minimum is hundreds of pounds a week. The footballer gets a two-quid bonus for a cup final. I tell you, if Tommy's paid on gate-money estimates, he'll leave here feeling like Carnegie. But not on your life! They'll give him the maximum and tell him he can wear plus-fours every day as proof that he's off the dole.

(The door opens. TOMMY enters, sees the reporters and draws back, but is pushed forward. We hear SNATCHER's voice.)

MacEWAN Don't be nervous, Tommy. The gentlemen'll no' eat you, even though they are English. *(Enters, sees the reporters)* Damn and blast, is there no privacy?

CLAVERLEY Ye should have hired the Sahara. I'm told one feels very close to God out there.

MacEWAN This is an intrusion.

CLAVERLEY Spill it, *Mister* MacEwan.

McSPORRAN Got that gold-rush feeling, Tommy?

(TOMMY smiles shyly. He is on rather friendly terms with the reporters, but is awed and uncertain because of MacEWAN's attitude.)

SPALDING You'll sign, Tommy? We'll do you proud south of the border.

TOMMY I'm not to talk.

CLAVERLEY A mouse in a trap an' no squeal! I'll write to Aldous Huxley.

MacEWAN Over here, Tommy. *(TOMMY goes over to him)* Now, boys, have I ever sold ye a pup?

CLAVERLEY We're no' English managers, Mr MacEwan.

McSPORRAN Personalities apart, Bob! The Snatcher, that is, Mr MacEwan, always gives a square deal. At least, he does us. You wouldn't fool Fleet Street, Mac?

SPALDING That's true. Mr MacEwan shared Craig's signing-on for Drumont.

CLAVERLEY With all except Tommy.

TOMMY What d'ye mean?

MacEWAN Bob, you'll go too far one of these days.

CLAVERLEY The name is Claverley, *Mister* Claverley.

MacEWAN Ye've too damn much to say.

CLAVERLEY Would ye rather I printed it?

MacEWAN Gentlemen! You must understand. This is a delicate moment – a very delicate moment. A wrong word now, and you know – *(Holds his hands out expressively, deprecatingly)* I know I can trust the *gentlemen* of Fleet Street.

McSPORRAN Give me a line for the evenings, Mac.

SPALDING Just a word about the negotiations.

MacEWAN Please, gentlemen, I'll not deny that there are negotiations, but at the moment I can only hint. Sir Joseph might think me garrulous. And you know our national reputation for silence. Besides, it *might* be a false alarm. I don't want to let you down badly.

CLAVERLEY We'll take the lift.

MacEWAN I'll tell ye what, boys. I'll meet you in the lounge the minute I'm –

CLAVERLEY *(Sings)* 'I'll meet ye on the lea-rig'. You know perfectly well you telephoned the transfer and price – your price? – to your pal in Fleet Street.

MacEWAN That's a damned lie!

CLAVERLEY Be careful! It's been a long wait, Snatcher. I warned you in Clanmarnock for the last time.

MacEWAN My solemn word, gentlemen. I'll meet you in the lounge.

(Impatient, nervous, tense, MacEWAN takes the two reporters, an arm of each, and leads them to the door. As he does so, BOB signals to TOMMY, and leads him swiftly to the door at the far end. SNATCHER is hidden behind the open door, pleading, arguing, promising.)

CLAVERLEY I'm talking fast, Tommy. Listen, I'm your friend. What did your mother get when ye signed for Drumont – twenty pounds? Well, MacEwan promised the Provost he'd give her fifty. I ferreted that out when it was too late to stop the ramp.

(SNATCHER comes from behind the door, sees TOMMY and clears the space in a jump)

MacEWAN Ye auld weasel, McColl. Tommy, what was he saying?

(BOB laughs, swings open the door, beckons, and DICK GRAVES enters. GRAVES is a well-set man, aged forty, smartly dressed, kindly featured, and talks in a gentle voice of subdued Lancashire accent.)

CLAVERLEY Just this: Tommy, meet my old friend, Dick Graves, a football oddity – a *gentleman*-manager. Dick – this is Craig.

TOMMY *(Respectfully)* Pleased to meet you, Mr Graves. I've read about you and Rovers.

GRAVES Not much to our credit, I'm afraid, Tommy. We've had a bad patch. You know, loss of confidence. A crop of injuries. Bad gates.

CLAVERLEY Maybe Tommy will be your sunbeam.

MacEWAN This is very unprofessional, Dick Graves. I'm amazed.

CLAVERLEY We see surprise in your eyes!

MacEWAN I told ye my last word at one o'clock this morning.

GRAVES I'm sorry, MacEwan, but Claverley –

CLAVERLEY Yes, me, Snatcher. Am I no' the perfect impediment? Tommy, lad, you're in the market, but not quite the slave market. You've the power of choice. If ye don't want to go, say so.

TOMMY One club's the same as another.

CLAVERLEY One club isn't the same as another. There are clubs I wouldn't trust wi a mower – they'd steal the edges off the teeth. There are other clubs I'd let sign on my daughter – if I had one. Dick's club is one of them. Don't forget Snatcher's a manager – he's not God.

MacEWAN You keep other managers out of this. Tommy'll be guided by me. He's my boy. Who discovered him? Who brought him into the game?

CLAVERLEY Einstein MacEwan.

GRAVES After all, MacEwan, Sir Joseph Pettingell is not the only bidder in the market. I'm ready to make an offer.

MacEWAN Chicken feed!

CLAVERLEY Let's hear what the cockerel says! Tommy, Mr Graves wants ye to go to him. I give ye my word, it's a good club. You'll get a fair deal. You'll be happy.

TOMMY I'm willing to go to Mr Graves. After all, I'm a player.

MacEWAN You're *my* player, Craig. Get out, Claverley. This is a private room. For the last time, Graves, your offer is no good. It suits neither my club, my boy, nor me.

CLAVERLEY Tommy!

TOMMY What can I do? I'm not a lawyer. Mr MacEwan tells me I'm bound to him.

GRAVES Mr MacEwan's perhaps right, Tommy. You're his player.

CLAVERLEY The willing lamb.

GRAVES I can't tell you how happy I'd be to sign you, Tommy.

MacEWAN I'll remember this morning's work, Bob.

CLAVERLEY So will Tommy, puir devil.

TOMMY I gave my word, Claverley.

GRAVES Good luck, Tommy! You're a great player. I hope the ball always runs for you.

(They go out)

MacEWAN Blast that old mole.

TOMMY He means well.

MacEWAN Means well! Take it from me, Tommy, there never was a newspaper-man did any good to a player. He was after a cut. I know, Graves promised him a backhander.

TOMMY I don't think so. He was only doing his best for me.

MacEWAN Doing his best for himself! I tell you, it's a cut he's after.

TOMMY I feel as if I'd lost the ball.

MacEWAN Now Tommy, I don't know what he whispered to ye. What's more I don't care. You owe me something, Tommy. But for me you'd still be guarding your mother's fireside.

TOMMY I'm not ungrateful, Mr MacEwan – don't think that. Maybe it's just that I'm a bit flustered. So much is happening to me. I get in bad.

MacEWAN Tuts, Tommy! Who said anything about getting in bad? I just want loyalty and co-operation.

TOMMY In bad with others, I mean, Mr MacEwan. My girl –

MacEWAN So that's the rub. She's against the transfer, Tommy, eh? Afraid she'll lose you. Now I see the light.

TOMMY No, not quite that.

MacEWAN You play wi me, Tommy. Once the English press starts boosting you, it'll be blondes and bonanza for you.

(As BOB and GRAVES leave, two men enter: SIR JOSEPH PETTINGELL, Chairman of Coaltown United, successful Lancashire mill-owner, who has acquired an impressive St James's Club exterior and superior manner, accompanied by ALDERMAN RAMSHAWK)

SIR JOSEPH Good morning, MacEwan. We're a few minutes late. I had other important business. With me, at any rate, football is still only a hobby. Ah, Craig!

RAMSHAWK Damn reporters. Your local rags ferreted out Sir Joseph and me last night.

SIR JOSEPH But we kept our part of the bargain, MacEwan. We gave no interviews. What puzzles me is how they found out we were in Glasgow.

MacEWAN In this town they can hear ye think! I'm disgusted with the behaviour of the Press, Sir Joseph.

RAMSHAWK Let me warn you, young fellow. Don't let press talk put big ideas into your head.

SIR JOSEPH A good sign. I'm all for the lad who appreciates his position.

MacEWAN To his face I'll say it: Tommy's not a forward boy. He's gallus enough on the field, though, eh, Tommy? Down the centre every time. A two-footed player from whistle to whistle.

RAMSHAWK Tush! We've got his credentials. Let's have a bit of *speed* now. Sir Joseph and me want to be on the midday for Manchester. *(To TOMMY)* You're packed and ready, I hope?

MacEWAN As trig as a registered parcel, Sir Joseph. *(Moves towards the table, keeping distance between himself and TOMMY. Produces documents.)* All in order, sir, as you'll see.

SIR JOSEPH The figure is yours, I see.

MacEWAN I told your scout –

SIR JOSEPH Oh, yes! We've agreed, but I thought perhaps our arrangement with you – ?

MacEWAN A bargain's a bargain, Sir Joseph. I'm honouring my word. The boy's here, and it's not you need be told he'd be welcome elsewhere.

RAMSHAWK Let's hope he'll be worth the money. *(To TOMMY)* We'll have no hanky-panky at United. We expect twenty shillings in the pound.

MacEWAN Tommy, sign here. Man, it's the fortunate boy you are, going to United.

TOMMY I'm not quite sure.

MacEWAN Tommy!

SIR JOSEPH Ah! Trouble? Now, lad, let's understand each other. This transfer is strictly above board.

TOMMY I hope so, sir. You see, I just want to be clear about myself.

RAMSHAWK He gets eight pounds a week, the maximum, the club have arranged a soft job on the side, and he's not quite clear! A month or two ago he was unemployed.

TOMMY I'm only anxious about fair dos – my rights!

MacEWAN Your rights! My God, Tommy, don't tell me you're getting swell-head. I told Sir Joseph and the Alderman you were a quietsome boy, and now this!

TOMMY I'm sorry, but I've got nobody to advise me. Surely it's reasonable to ask?

MacEWAN Of course it's reasonable to ask, but Tommy, we can't waste Sir Joseph's and the Alderman's time. This is important. Come on now, boy, I'll explain everything later.

TOMMY It'll be too late then.

RAMSHAWK Too late! What does he mean? I tell ye, Sir Joseph, some of these youngsters talk as if they were film stars.

SIR JOSEPH Come, Craig, you surely don't want to give me a bad impression.

MacEWAN Don't forget, Tommy, it's Sir Joseph, United, and –

TOMMY *(Desperate)* Can you not see what I'm driving at? I don't want to be unreasonable, but I must *know* – I'm signing and don't know *what* I'm signing.

RAMSHAWK In God's name – what is it you want to know?

TOMMY I – I'd like to know the figure.

MacEWAN Tommy Craig! Have ye gone daft? The figure! What next?

SIR JOSEPH Good gracious! MacEwan, this is very unsportsmanlike. One would think we were conspirators.

TOMMY *(Desperately)* And while I'm at it – what do *I* get?

RAMSHAWK Damned blackmail.

MacEWAN You're right, Alderman. Tommy, you're a disgrace to the game. How *much* do you get!

> *(The door opens and BOB CLAVERLEY slips in, unobserved. He drops on his knees and, crawling across the floor, goes under the table, where, notebook placed before him, he takes a verbatim note of the talk.)*

TOMMY Well, how much *is* my transfer fee? Surely you don't blame me for asking?

MacEWAN Now, Tommy, leave all that to me. I'll see you're looked after.

TOMMY *(Now truculent, though nearly tearful, too)* Like you looked after my mother!

MacEWAN What! So that's what Claverley was doing – filling you with clip-clash slander! Yes, Tommy, *slander*. I hope you realise that.

RAMSHAWK Blackmail, I call it.

SIR JOSEPH I hope you realise the possible consequences of your attitude. If the Association get to hear of this!

TOMMY Blackmail? Is it blackmail for me to ask a share of the blood money? He's got his. I daresay you've got yours.

SIR JOSEPH Really, MacEwan, this is most embarrassing.

MacEWAN Tommy, boy, if ye'll leave me to deal wi the business side.

TOMMY The way you dealt with my transfer from Clanmarnock? If I'm to be sold, I want to know my price. If I sign this paper, what happens to me? I'm sent across the border like a trussed hen.

RAMSHAWK Maybe you'd like *fifty-fifty* of the transfer money?

TOMMY All I'm asking is to be told the transfer figure. I know what happened last time I signed on for a club. This time my share won't be on the table, in the china dog or in my boots.

MacEWAN If you don't behave yourself –

TOMMY Behave myself! I'm sold, body and soul, and because I ask the price I'm called blackmailer and slanderer. What do you call *yourselves*? Let me call in somebody to advise me. Let somebody else read the paper. Claverley's outside –

SIR JOSEPH Another word and we'll call off the deal.

TOMMY You'll call it off? Oh, I'm sick of the whole business. My girl was right – I'm just livestock.

RAMSHAWK I thought this was all fixed, MacEwan?

MacEWAN Don't forget you're a signed Drumont player, Tommy. You boast you've never played in the reserves – how'd you like a season in the stiffs?

(There is general splutter and protest. Rage and tears are in TOMMY's *voice.)*

TOMMY You'll put me in the reserve team, if I don't sign?

MacEWAN To hell with you. You'll be lucky if I let you play even there.

TOMMY *(To SIR JOSEPH)* You and your talk of playing the game! *(To RAMSHAWK)* You, with your soft job on the side. This is one registered parcel you don't collect. I'm through.

MacEWAN Tommy, I can fix anything!

(BOB appears. There is splutter and protests when he emerges from below the table.)

CLAVERLEY Aye, you're some fixer.

*(**GENERAL TALK**: 'Disgraceful!' – 'I'll report you to the SFA!' – 'Your editor will hear of this!')*

MacEWAN From this hour, Claverley, you're barred Drumont ground.

CLAVERLEY Wi Tommy out of the team and me barred the press-box, Snatcher, it's a grave-digger you'll need, not a groundsman.

MacEWAN Tommy, don't be hasty. Sir Joseph.

CLAVERLEY Stick to your guns, Tommy.

MacEWAN Come with me, Tommy.

TOMMY Not a foot!

CLAVERLEY The goose has stopped laying, Snatcher! How would you advise Tommy if he were your son, Sir Joseph?

SIR JOSEPH I've got nothing to say to you. I never talk to the Press.

CLAVERLEY No, that needs thought and caution. Not like telling a raw lad he's a blackmailer and a slanderer when he asks reasonable questions – questions concerning the sale of his body.

MacEWAN You're at the bottom of this, Claverley. Tommy was willing to sign until you talked to him. I'll break you for this.

CLAVERLEY Yes, Snatcher, I told him.

TOMMY Name your sum, and, if Mr Claverley advises me, I'll sign.

SIR JOSEPH You're being badly advised, Craig.

RAMSHAWK This morning's performance will put a black mark to your name in every boardroom in England. I'll see to that.

MacEWAN Tommy Craig, your blood be on your own head. You'll soon learn football players are ten a penny.

CLAVERLEY D'ye hear that, Sir Joseph! How's that for a fair price? I'd make a bargain wi the Snatcher on those terms right away. You might get a referee, a couple of linesmen, and a half-dozen directors thrown in, the pocket money Snatcher's thrown at you.

(TOMMY make a move towards the door)

TOMMY I'm for the Miner's Row. That's a slave market I know.

CLAVERLEY Man, MacEwan – he means it. I'll bet ye could eat his boots. One minute, Tommy.

(TOMMY waits. The others stand hesitant. Conscious of loss of dignity, SIR JOSEPH leads the way out at the doorway.)

MacEWAN Tommy! Think of me. I'll be the laughing-stock of football.

RAMSHAWK *You'll* be the laughing-stock of football? – what about me?

CLAVERLEY Somebody going to squeal?

MacEWAN Talk to him, Bob. For my – for old time's sake. I gave a hint o' the deal to John McAdam. By now it's in the *London Daily Express* as *official.*

SIR JOSEPH My God!

CLAVERLEY There, there, Sir Joseph. Don't worry. What's one *exclusive* more to the *Express*? Just another stork in Stornoway.

(They go out)

TOMMY What a mess!

CLAVERLEY What d'ye expect? Surely you've been long enough in the players' dressing-room to know football's a game played by more than a ball and twenty-two players?

TOMMY Did you hear them? *(Tearfully sarcastic)* My nerve – asking for a rake-off! That Ramshawk talked as if I was a leper. *(Suddenly)* But, oh Bob, I'm out of the game for good. MacEwan'll never let me kick another ball in first-class football. You heard what he said?

CLAVERLEY I heard.

TOMMY What chance have I? It's true what Ramshawk said – a month or two ago on the dole, now I'm getting a small fortune in wages.

CLAVERLEY Aye, and last week fifty thousand Henrys went through the turnstiles to see you score three goals. They howled themselves hoarse wi 'Good wee Tommy' and other clishmaclash praise. Forget it, Tommy. You did right. Ye were a *man* asking for your rights. If you were worth twelve thousand pounds to United, not counting Snatcher's backhander, ye were worth a faring for yourself.

TOMMY MacEwan said he thought he could squeeze two hundred for me.

CLAVERLEY MacEwan! God! The man makes Shylock look like a spendthrift.

TOMMY *(Heartbroken)* Well, it's me for the hard road. I'll be on my way back to Clanmarnock. 'The Napoleon o' football', 'The Uncrowned King of Scottish Football' in the stiffs. That's what they'll do to me. But I'll beat them to it. I'm through with football.

CLAVERLEY I'll get you something – a bottle o' beer –

TOMMY No – I never touch the stuff.

CLAVERLEY Not even a wee port?

TOMMY No. I'm for home.

CLAVERLEY Gosh! What else is there to drink? A – (*Swallows hard when he says the word*) a coffee?

TOMMY No. I tell ye, I'm for home.

CLAVERLEY Tommy, I'm for helping you. Every *reporter* in football's out there waiting for ye. I've got it – *tea*! (*Anxiously*) Ye like tea, surely?

TOMMY Oh, all right.

(*BOB looks at the bell above which hangs the legend 'Waiter'*)

CLAVERLEY Dod, if I ask a waiter for tea, he'll think I've got DTs and bring a doctor! – Promise ye'll wait here, Tommy?

TOMMY Oh, I'll wait.

CLAVERLEY Button your lips if any ill-mannered, inquisitive reporter comes in and finds you still here. If he's got an Irish fur coat on, ye'll ken he's from Fleet Street. Tell him ye don't speak English. He'll believe ye. Tea! Whit d'ye have wi it – soda?

TOMMY For God's sake, Bob!

CLAVERLEY Ah'll be your Abigail, Tommy. (*Rushes out*)

(*TOMMY walks over to the window. He stares out in moody dejection. The door opens. KATE comes in. She is carrying a newspaper.*)

KATE Tommy!

TOMMY Kate!

KATE I couldn't let you leave Scotland without a Flora Macdonald at your going.

TOMMY Stop mocking, Kate.

KATE Tch, Tommy! I had to come and say goodbye. I must say you don't look like a man with the world at his feet. Listen. (*Reads*) 'A sad blow comes to Scots football today. This morning Tommy Craig signed transfer forms, and on Saturday will play for Coaltown United, leaders of the English First Division.'

TOMMY I'm not going.

KATE You're not going?

TOMMY I'm through.

KATE But the papers – twelve thousand!

TOMMY If it says twelve million, I tell you, I'm still not going. I'm out of football for good. They put a price on me, Kate, and I put a price on myself.

KATE It's not true! You'll never give up football.

TOMMY Football's given me up. The English director says my name'll be *mud* in every boardroom in England. Snatcher threatened to keep me in the stiffs – the second eleven.

KATE But they can't do that to you, Tommy. (*Looks at the paper*) 'Tommy Craig, football's greatest living artist.'

TOMMY That was yesterday.

KATE I'm proud of you, Tommy.

TOMMY Proud.

KATE Yes. When MacEwan threatened you, the real Tommy spoke up – the Tommy Craig whose ambition stands higher than goal-kicking.

TOMMY Let's face it. I liked the life, the flattery, even when I wasn't fooled by it. If I'm two-footed, I'm two-fisted as well. I'll get a job in the pit.

KATE Listen, Tommy, my Uncle John knows about you. I told him about us. If you go and see him, he says he'll fix things so that you can become apprenticed to his firm.

TOMMY I can't let you be my meal-ticket.

KATE Why not? Tommy, it's you I'm thinking of. Football's a lazy life. You're not lazy. Oh, Tommy, don't you see? Our dreams are coming to life. You said we should always be together.

TOMMY You're nearly where you want to be, Kate. I'm back at the starting post.

KATE I could help, Tommy. You've no idea what a good coach I am *now*. Uncle John says he would talk to you about a job that would fit in with your football career. He knows how hard you worked at the night-classes. He's willing to pay you two pounds a week.

TOMMY Two pounds a week! We could go into digs in Glasgow.

KATE Not me, Tommy Craig.

TOMMY Do you mean to stay on in the Row?

KATE We could always get our back bedroom. I'd settle with Mr Rab Hunter for a reasonable rent.

TOMMY We'd be among our own.

KATE We'll be the happiest couple in Clanmarnock.

TOMMY Make it Scotland, First Division towns included.

KATE And when you get your degree, we'll share a *suite* of offices. You'll engineer contracts and I'll engineer payments.

TOMMY That reminds me – 'Contract' – a ring! I've got enough left.

KATE Portia can wait. When I choose my ring and tell you the price, you'll know the real meaning of transfer fee! Oh, Tommy, we're daft! First it was a boat-deck, then a kitchen, and now a hotel morgue. In the end we'll maybe get married in a Woolworth's!

TOMMY Five minutes ago I felt as though I'd taken a dive from the Tron Steeple on to Argyle Street pavement.

KATE If I kiss ye this minute –

TOMMY *Kate!*

KATE And they told me you could always rise to the big occasion.

(*KATE makes a shyly bold affectionate gesture. BOB comes in carrying a tea-tray.*)

TOMMY Bob!

CLAVERLEY 'A pot of tea for two,' sez I. The waiter sez, 'Take it easy, Mr Claverley. Two bottles of Bass is the normal cure. Don't you be led away by newfangled notions.' I'm disgraced!

TOMMY I said: I'm through with the game. I mean it.

CLAVERLEY I don't blame you, Tommy. You'd a raw deal.

TOMMY Thanks for the tea, Bob.

(GRAVES has followed CLAVERLEY into the room)

GRAVES I don't want to butt in, Tommy. Bob told me what happened. I want a word with you.

TOMMY Did Bob tell you I'm through with football? The football label passed out half an hour ago. I've got other plans – at least, *we've* got other plans, haven't we, Kate? Bob, meet Kate – Miss Hunter. Kate, you remember Bob Claverley of the *News*, an auld Clanmarnock billy, and Mr Graves from England.

KATE Tommy, if we're going to see my uncle . . .

TOMMY Yes, Bob, we've got big business on.

GRAVES 'Big business'? You're not fixing up?

CLAVERLEY And why not? That stuff about black-balling him! Tommy's too good.

KATE Tommy's out of football.

TOMMY I've got a chance to become a civil engineer. I'm going to take classes at the Technical College.

GRAVES Well done! I wish you luck, Tommy.

CLAVERLEY A nice little romance? *(KATE nods)* Tommy and Kate! Damn it – it's a Clanmarnock Special, Tommy.

TOMMY Forget it, Bob. I'm not *news*.

CLAVERLEY Not news! Tommy Craig's romance not news? Coming on top of this morning's story it's a football classic.

KATE Football's got no place in our plans.

CLAVERLEY No' many lassies would say 'the back o' my hand' to the sort of dowry Tommy could get ye from football.

GRAVES I could start the wedding bells with a nice backhander somewhere in the four figures.

TOMMY Four figures?

KATE Are ye coming?

TOMMY Kate! Four figures would see us both right.

CLAVERLEY *(Sings)* 'You in your small corner and I in mine . . .'

KATE Remember MacEwan!

GRAVES Once Tommy's with us, I know you'll apologise for that remark, Miss Hunter.

KATE Apologise – me? Tommy! Are you coming?

TOMMY Be reasonable, Kate.

GRAVES If it's Tommy's studies, Miss Hunter, I give you my word my chairman, Sir William Sutton, a man of honour, will arrange matters so that Tommy will start work at Manchester Technical College right away.

TOMMY Bob, are the other terms good?

CLAVERLEY You'll be worth a small fortune in three years.

GRAVES Miss Hunter, I beg you to believe Tommy will be all right with us.

KATE It's Tommy I'm worried about, not you. Look at this morning. One minute and to him football made every other form of crookedness look like a nursery game. You come along and flap a few banknotes under his nose. At once the righteous philanthropist is the real man in the game. One month in England and –

TOMMY I'll think I own a bank. You're unfair, Kate.

CLAVERLEY With *you* alongside him –

KATE Me? Oh, I'm thrown in with his boots, as moral and spiritual control. Are you coming, Tommy?

TOMMY Kate! A thousand pounds.

CLAVERLEY Here are the papers, Tommy, and don't worry about MacEwan. Dick's fixed him.

TOMMY I'll sign. *(He signs)*

> *(KATE picks up her handbag, gives a bitter look at the prospectuses, and goes quickly out of the room. TOMMY cries her name and makes a half-hearted effort to follow her. DICK and CLAVERLEY sit down.)*

ACT II

Scene 2

Six weeks later. A dressing-room at Coaltown Rovers' ground. Through a doorway we get a hint of a bath-room beyond. The room is Spartan-like in its furnishings – a broad wooden seat runs all round the walls. But large and expensive-looking towels and sponges; excellent lighting; costly floor matting. The producer can decide how many players should be present. There is a telephone in a corner of the dressing-room. A notice on the wall beside it says: 'No Personal Calls'. Youths in gym slacks and sweaters stand about. They are resting from training exercises. One rather pleasant-voiced youth sings soulfully 'South of the Border'. A trio is formed.

On the great square table in the centre of the room a young man lies flat, face downwards. 'TINY' RAFFERTY, a huge man of, say, seventeen stone, is giving him a rub down – slowly, laboriously, with one hand, his free hand clutching a sponge. The player is JOE WITHERS, captain of Rovers, a deep-voiced, solemn-faced Yorkshireman, who has the respect and admiration of everyone on the field or off.

JOE Tiny, lad, I've been on the rack for twenty minutes. You'll strain yourself and stiffen me.

TINY Stay there. On Saturday you went for a ball as if there was lead in your boots.

TAFFY Why pick on Joe? Tommy, our flying Scotchman, looked like a legless man.

JOE Shut up, Taffy, or we'll buy you one of those stupid hats Welsh women wear.

TAFFY I have a voice to use – thoughts to express.

PADDY Hire a hall! You're sore because you haven't had a goal in two matches.

TAFFY Have I had a pass? Has anybody given me the ball once? Just *one* pass?

PLAYER I've got two passes for the Hippodrome you can have.

JOE 'Spotter' in the *Herald* says our collapse is due to old-fashioned training.

TINY The weasel-faced, ink-mouthed rat! I've trained two Cup-winning teams.

(The PLAYERS chant in good-humoured chorus)

TAFFY 'I've trained the league championship team three times running . . .'

PADDY '. . . When football was a game and players were craftsmen.'

PLAYER 'I took four teams on the continent, France, Germany . . .'

PLAYER '. . . Italy, Holland.'

ALL 'And now I'm expected . . .'

TINY Shut up, you imps of Satan! Now I'm told to get foam baths, ultra-pansy ray . . . 'Psycho-paralyse them', says the Spotter, 'like they do in Vienna'! Like they do in Vienna! Huh! God bless me, where is Vienna and its psycho-analiars? Ask me that?

ALL Where is Vienna, Tiny?

TINY I'm a trainer, not a horoscope. If that Spotter fellow comes near my dressing-room I'll stuff fourteen rolls of cotton wool and a league handbook down his throat. Then he'll know something about training. Brine baths, electric massage! Get your clothes on, you misbegotten League of Nations loafers. *(In aside)* Oh, Paddy, did ye hear of anything for tomorrow?

(PADDY nods vigorously)

PADDY *(Whispers)* Over here, Tiny. If that hungry Welshman hears, he'll wire Wales and ruin the price.

(They go off into a corner. JOE leaps down from the table, a huge towel wrapped round his middle. As he reaches his 'hook' – at a spot next the door back centre – the door opens and at once there is earnest silence when the sound of angry voices is heard.)

1st VOICE We want fresh blood, Mr Chairman.

JOE He means *our* blood.

2nd VOICE As Vice-President of the Supporters' Club, Mr Chairman, and speaking with the respect due to you, I want to register the personal conviction that some of our players aren't pulling their weight.

PADDY He thinks we're a boat-crew.

GRAVES As manager of the club, I resent the inference that any of our boys are slacking. A more hard-working team –

VOICE What about the great Craig?

GRAVES The boy's struck a bad patch. He'll find his feet once he's acclimatised.

VOICE As oldest member of Supporters' Club I think Tommy Craig's greatest player today – with feet or without feet.

JOE Good old Milestone! Shut door, lad, we know the rest.

PLAYER Blimey! It's like being in a concentration camp here. 'Do this,' says the Press. 'Play your natural game,' says the Press. 'Why not a goal-scoring machine,' says the Press. 'Concentrate on the Cup,' says the Press. These supporter mugs read it all and in the end fancy they know as much about football as the Press.

PADDY They're right there. Every time I read a report of a match I've played in, 'twas my astral body was playing and me at home wearing a straight-jacket. How was your Press last weekend, Joe?

JOE Slipping! One picture, two 'Stolid Joe' headlines, one 'rale Yorkshire tike', and one gossiper, 'I fear me age is taking its toll'. You'd think I was as old as Tiny! I expect I asked him fifty-fifty for a signed article.

PADDY Why are they picking on Tommy?

JOE Some racket.

PLAYER It stinks. Let's face it. Tommy's put us into the semi-final.

PADDY Yes, but he's acting queerly. Look, he's missed training again. That's not like Tommy.

JOE It's weeks since he came up to the recreation room. Dick tells me he's asked to be excused going for special training.

PADDY I don't blame him for that. Lord! How I hate the museum specimens we get lined up with at those blasted hydros. D'ye know, Tiny's right. If some sausage-eating or spaghetti-guzzling croak said players shouldn't walk when off the field, they'd have us going in bath-chairs! Has anybody seen Tommy?

JOE No.

(GRAVES comes in the door)

GRAVES Hullo, Tiny. I've brought you a little present. You'll be the envy of every trainer outside Roedean.

TINY A present? It's not another of them 'Get Fit on Carrots'? And what the hell's Roedean?

GRAVES It's a school for girls. See, boys, look what Aunt Agatha's brought Tiny.

(Throws open the door and discloses a large-sized shining sun-ray cabinet)

TINY What is it? A newfangled American coffin?

(Shouts from all of them – 'Sun-ray!', 'Oh, Tiny, what a wonderful figure you'll soon have!')

JOE I'm captain. I'm first for sunburn.

TINY Look here, Dick –

GRAVES It's a farewell present. Where's Tommy?

TINY Farewell – ?

(TOMMY comes in)

TOMMY Sorry I'm late, Dick . . . Tiny. Hey, Tiny, that'll make the Arsenal one look like a night-lamp.

(Two assistants carry the cabinet into the bath-room)

GRAVES I'm just telling Tiny and the boys, Tommy, it's a farewell present.

TOMMY Farewell?

JOE Ye don't mean – fired?

GRAVES At the last Board meeting I thought the Directors were being unreasonable about our League form. I threw in my resignation. It was expected, of course. This morning they accepted it. My successor's here now. *(Goes into the outer room, says loudly)* Come this way and meet the players. *(To TOMMY)* Keep your chin up, Tommy-Boy, meet the new manager, Mr MacEwan.

TOMMY Snatcher!

MacEWAN Hullo, boys. I'll meet you individually later in my office. Craig, of course, I know.

TOMMY Dick, I want to be put on the transfer list.

GRAVES I'm sorry, Tommy.

MacEWAN I'll deal with that, Craig.

GRAVES Steady, Tommy.

TOMMY How can I play for him, Dick?

GRAVES Tommy, you never played for me – you played for the club and love of the game.

MacEWAN From all reports he hasn't played too well for either.

JOE Tommy's played well, hasn't he, boys?

(They nod and growl angrily)

MacEWAN I'm manager now. I'll judge who's playing well and who's not playing well. And I'll have something to say to the player who misses training. Craig, I want to see *you* on the track, stripped, at ten o'clock tomorrow morning.

(Goes out)

PADDY Now I know why you left home, Tommy.

TOMMY I left home for the same reason as the rest of you – for money.

GRAVES The score is 1–1, Tommy. He beat you at Clanmarnock, you beat him to here. Why, lad, you're lining up fresh for the second half.

TAFFY Is he what you call a Red Clydesider, Tommy?

TOMMY There's more red blood in a black pudding than in that. But Dick, it's near the close season. Your wife?

GRAVES I'm all right, Tommy. Don't worry. I got a year's money, and I know a club –

TINY I suppose it'll be me next, for it's an electrician they'll need here now they've got that thing.

GRAVES I can reassure you, Tiny. MacEwan's footballer enough to respect practical experience more than handbook stuff.

TOMMY So long as you don't gyp him on 'brandy for injuries', carry the hampers yourself, do a blackleg on the porters, and don't drink the olive oil.

PADDY When next season opens, my sixth sense tells me none of us here – except perhaps Tommy – will even be memories to MacEwan.

GRAVES Nonsense! Snap out of it, boys! MacEwan's a good manager, and a sound judge of a player. You'll win the Cup.

JOE Yes, that'll be a great moment, hearin him say, 'Mr Chairman, the man who won the Cup for Rovers left a fortnight before the semi-final.'

GRAVES Listen to me, lads. There are many clubs who boast the palsy-walsy spirit. When we've had tough times we've said so and looked and been sick. You're no angels, I know.

PADDY I want a certificate to that effect.

GRAVES There was never a mean word spoken, officially or unofficially, between us. When Tommy came on the Bally-Hoo express, you gave him a glad hand.

TAFFY It took us weeks to learn his language.

GRAVES My goodbye to you is: 'Keep the comedy and cut the criticism.' You'll find it pays.

TINY I wish you'd tell that to the Spotter.

GRAVES Come up to the house tonight, boys. We'll have a singsong.

JOE Girls?

GRAVES Graves is the name, not Goldwyn. Okay – if you bring your *own*. Tommy, you coming?

PADDY Ha! Now hear from the Vanishing Man.

TOMMY I'll even sing, Dick.

TAFFY Over my dead body.

PADDY You sang once for us, Tommy Craig. What was it? 'The Nameless Lassie'! Ugh! The title was the only considerate part.

TOMMY I'll –

JOE I'm captain. No song from Boy Craig.

(*TOMMY goes into the bath-room*)

GRAVES Well, see you tonight.

(*The door opens back and MacEWAN enters. He hands TINY a typewritten script.*)

JOE The team for Saturday?

(*MacEWAN nods. And goes out. There is a hubbub. They group round TINY.*)

TAFFY Maybe he's afraid we'll forget there's a match.

PADDY Maybe I'm the goalie.

TAFFY That's your right position – goalkeepers are always mad. Well,

Tiny? Has he picked *you* as right-half? Ye can read the results quick enough.

(*TINY, reading, seems slightly dazed. He stares at the paper, then his gaze shifts to DICK.*)

TINY Dick, we can't do this to the boy.
DICK Do what? What boy?
TINY Tommy's out of the team. Dropped – (*There's a shout: 'Dropped! Tommy!'*) 'Disciplinary action for Craig's missing training and falling off in form.'

(*The PLAYERS go out singly or in twos and threes. The TRAINER and JOE go into the bath-room. BOB CLAVERLEY comes in through the players' entrance to the dressing-room. MacEWAN comes in again, obviously to savour the sensation.*)

MacEWAN (*Snarling*) What brings you here?
CLAVERLEY You!
MacEWAN Who let you in?
CLAVERLEY Never let it be said, *Snatcher*, I started you off on your English career wi a sacking.
MacEWAN I've got nothing to say.
CLAVERLEY You'll soon learn the language. English is easy – *graft* a good word to start with.
MacEWAN Get out!
CLAVERLEY 'Educated Scots' – that's what they ca' Anglo-Scots – swear that England has a refining influence on Scotsmen. Maybe you haven't been here long enough to get refined.
MacEWAN I told you once before, you're barred.
CLAVERLEY But I saw every match you didn't want me to see. Besides, that was Drumont. I'm not barred here. I'm great pals wi Dick.
MacEWAN Don't give me that stuff. You've weaselled out –
CLAVERLEY (*Contemptuously*) Your pal sent you the tip last Thursday. You wired for the job on Friday. You came south yesterday with me. Only I didn't like to be seen on the same train as you: I've got to use the train service a lot. In thirty years the railway police have never seen me in bad company. Mind if I use the phone?

(*Goes to the phone, ignoring SNATCHER's wrath*)

MacEWAN God! Claverley, I'll forget patience.
CLAVERLEY Poor Snatcher. I'm what they call a blackmailer, eh? Talk! Trunks, please!
MacEWAN It's true. *I'm* here. Your friend's out.
CLAVERLEY Glasgow 4321.
MacEWAN And that's all *you'll* get. Oh! Ye can say I'm looking forward

to getting the best out of my young protégé Craig. You blackmail me, I'll get a second best out of him.

CLAVERLEY When you came in, I thought he'd get the best out of *you*. Anyhow, that'll be the impression in my *exclusive*. Hullo, Bob here. Right! I'll hold on.

MacEWAN *Exclusive*! I'll – *(His hand over the mouthpiece)*

CLAVERLEY *Exclusive*, I said, Snatcher. And by Bellahouston I mean it! This is the first time – I hope it'll be the last time – I put the screws on ye, Snatcher.

(DICK GRAVES comes back into the room. Grins when he sees BOB.)

CLAVERLEY But when did it happen?

GRAVES Wangled yesterday, Bob. He took over twenty minutes ago.

CLAVERLEY Twenty minutes – seventeen minutes' risk I've taken on you, Snatcher. I'll have it for the late-night final, Snatcher. Ye'll no' keep till morning. Dod, that'll be a good epitaph for ye!

(The door bursts open. TOMMY rushes in, followed by JOE, PADDY, TAFFY, all trying to restrain him.)

CLAVERLEY Man, it's the spaewife in me! *(Beginning to talk into the telephone, his voice drowned by the uproar)*

TOMMY You called me a gutter-snipe once, Snatcher.

MacEWAN You still here?

(The others look startled but TOMMY goes on)

TOMMY You were right, maybe. But *you* took me from the gutter. D'ye mind the night you stood in our kitchen and did a bit of Bible-punching? When you put twenty pounds in my mother's hand and kept thirty in your pocket? The day that you took me to St Enoch to meet the United directors? Not a word about money. I was too green to ask.

MacEWAN You'd no right. You were and are a player.

TOMMY How much were you getting out of that deal? What was your percentage on twelve thousand pounds?

CLAVERLEY *(Dictating loudly)* 'The meeting between MacEwan and Tommy was like the meeting of father and son.' Quote: '"A moving moment," said Mr MacEwan.'

(DICK goes round the table. TOMMY advances on SNATCHER, who edges away from him. His expression is laughable. He is enraged by CLAVERLEY and TOMMY.)

MacEWAN Put down that telephone, Claverley!

CLAVERLEY *(Into the telephone)* Hold on! *(To SNATCHER)* You prefer the photostatic plate?

MacEWAN Listen to me, Craig! By selling you to the United –

TOMMY Selling is right!

CLAVERLEY *(Into the telephone)* Quote: ' "Just Jock Tamson's bairns," ' unquote, 'said the Snatcher, the stern disciplinarian giving way to the emotional Scot.'

MacEWAN By God, Claverley! I'll thole a lot –

TOMMY You'll thole this. I'll play for the Rovers.

MacEWAN Ah! That's civil of ye.

TOMMY So far I've had a square deal from the club. The man who brought me here advises me to stay, but I'm not going to be made a monkey.

MacEWAN Monkey! What did I look like at St Mungo's when you walked out?

CLAVERLEY *(Into the telephone)* A minute! *(To SNATCHER)* Give me another paragraph of this Stanley–Livingstone stuff, and I'll tell ye I was there. You remember?

TOMMY Why am I in the stiffs on Saturday?

MacEWAN Because I'm manager.

GRAVES Believe me, Snatcher, Tommy's playing well. He practically carried us into the Cup.

MacEWAN You're there, Graves? I suppose you'll be wanting to move your bits o' odds and ends. The morn'll do. Ye can have the place to yourself. I'm having my new office in the Director's room from tomorrow.

CLAVERLEY 'MacEwan says,' quote: ' "Managers must move with the times".'

TOMMY Am I in the team on Saturday?

MacEWAN You know the team!

CLAVERLEY Continue quote, fresh paragraph: ' "A manager must be a little Napoleon, a little of Freud, and a lot of Machiavelli," said Mr MacEwan, who is scholar as well as sportsman.'

MacEWAN If you print a word of that stuff!

CLAVERLEY I'm no Crainer, Snatcher. One of the marvels of modern journalism is, a reporter is relieved of the responsibility of actually printing what he writes.

MacEWAN *(To TOMMY)* The interview is over. Get out.

TOMMY Then I'm not playing –

MacEWAN You'll be on the ground.

TOMMY Am I playing?

MacEWAN It's a long time since you've seen a match?

TOMMY What do you mean?

MacEWAN You'll help the trainer on the touch-line, as his assistant.

GRAVES By God, you're bitter, MacEwan.

TOMMY I'll stuff the sponge down your throat before I sit –

(There is a wild anguished yell, the door is flung open, TINY appears, grabs the telephone)

TINY Exchange – a doctor. Quick, a doctor!

(Sensation)

GRAVES What the devil?

TINY A doctor! Quick, get anyone! By God, Dick, that sun-ray cabinet –

(BOB picks up the telephone from the ground where it lies sprawling. TINY is dashing back.)

TINY The boys had gone. Joe comes back. 'I'll have a touch o' sun, Tiny,' he says, and kids me into shutting him into the thing. 'Tomorrow I'll have a set o' new glands,' sez he.

GRAVES What happened?

TINY I got into my corner with the *Evening Herald* to see what was likely – to see if there was any likely new juniors.

MacEWAN And then?

TINY When I looked round he was dancing about in the damned thing, hammering on the panes and looking like a lobster with St Vitus' dance.

(DICK rushes out followed by TINY. SNATCHER attempts to follow him – TOMMY holds him by the sleeve.)

TOMMY You're not going to do this to me, MacEwan?

MacEWAN Aye, and a damned sight more, Craig.

TOMMY We'll start level, then. You got in first –

(Hits him hard and SNATCHER disappears through the bath-room door)

CLAVERLEY *(Still talking into the telephone)* Quote: 'I realise, of course, that my job is not going to be a picnic', end message. Johnnie, black that story of the sun-ray machine. Get Anderson to put it on a block on the front page. Tell him – he's got brain and imagination – the body'll be home any day. And wire five – no, I feel like plucking berries harsh and crude – ten pounds to me at the General Post Office here. Tonight? Of course. Am I a hermit as well? *(Hangs up the receiver, looks at TOMMY thoughtfully. Then begins thumping the receiver violently)* Miss – a doctor, quick! He's to come to the Rovers' dressing-room immediately.

(Walks forward to TOMMY; slowly, and with affectionate hand on TOMMY's shoulder, says:)

Tommy, Tommy, now ye *can* go and burn your boots!

ACT II

Scene 3

The Rovers' dressing-room on a Saturday, ten minutes before kick-off. The PLAYERS are nearly all dressed in shorts, etc. TINY is busy answering noisy requests: 'A knee bandage, Tiny', etc.

PADDY Hey, Tiny! I'll be arrested if I go out in these shorts.

PLAYER You should be arrested for going out.

TAFFY Seen Tommy, Joe? *(JOE gives denial by pathetic gestures)* Hey boys! Not a word to these newspaper fellows.

PADDY I'd like to – *(Makes a fierce kick)* Man alive, one of them comes to my digs at one in the *morning* and says – as if saying 'Your autograph, please' – 'I suppose it's the usual story, Paddy, booze and blondes!?' And he was so full of MacEwan's booze he tried to lean on me.

JOE I could've got twenty quid from a fellow. He said his game was *rugger*, *really*, but he knew the right way to treat soccer. Would I take twenty and give him the *inside story*.

PADDY What did you do?

JOE Taught him something about *soccer* that'll make him think *rugger* a game for baby girls.

TINY I wish Tommy would show up.

TAFFY Why the hell should he? He's having a raw deal.

JOE Tommy on touch-line would be like duck out of water.

(TAFFY goes to the door and looks out)

TAFFY Here's Tommy! And *is* he stewed! There's a crowd following him.

ALL Stewed!

PADDY That's the finish!

(TOMMY enters)

TOMMY *(Sings)* 'Push it up the centre, pass it to the wings,
        You know we've got wee Tommy Craig,
        He'll do the very thing.'

(TINY shoves him roughly into a corner. The other PLAYERS look serious. They crowd around.)

JOE *(Whispers)* Go easy, lad.

PADDY Tiny! Something to straighten him?

TOMMY Well, pals, all set? There's only a few of us left. And I won't keep till Easter. *(Gets up. Is unsteady on his feet.)* Tell the assistant-trainer our trouble. *(With bravado)* Joe! Got your knee bandage? Paddy, smelling salts?

180

Paddy, a little spearmint for you. Tommy Craig, assistant trainer, passes the sponge. *(Getting out of his coat and into a white jacket)* Some say, good old Tiny!

PADDY And how did you become a trainer, Mr Craig?

TOMMY Bumped the manager.

TINY Come on, drink this. *(Gives TOMMY a spoonful of olive oil)*

TOMMY Good old Tiny! One of the best – speak as you find 'em. Boys, to you! To Snatcher, the sheep-stealer!

(The door opens. SNATCHER MacEWAN stands in the doorway. He takes in TOMMY's condition, even though the PLAYERS group round him quickly.)

MacEWAN All set, Tiny?

TINY Yes, sir.

MacEWAN And you, boys?

(Dead silence. Even PADDY is awed.)

Stand aside.

(Reluctantly the PLAYERS stand aside. TOMMY is looking a little strained, but by a terrific effort he masters a bucolic display.)

Suppose I ordered you to strip?

TOMMY Suppose?

MacEWAN You'd be a credit to your club –

TOMMY If I had one eye, one arm and one leg, I'd still be a greater credit to my club than you – double-crossing, slimey-tongued Judas. If you say a word to me, cast an eye at me, or let the foulness of your body near me, I'll rip you from navel to thrapple. Get out!

(TOMMY makes a movement, slow, but deadly menacing. SNATCHER steps back toward the door.)

MacEWAN *(With pathetic attempt to cover his fear)* Good luck, boys. Play your usual game.

(A man's head peeps round the door. We see his open-necked shirt collar and the top of a black blazer.)

MAN Ready, boys? We're on.

TAFFY *(Almost weeping)* Tommy boy, you're daft, but –

PADDY Glory to God, Tommy! For the honour and joy of that moment, I'd give you all the cups and medals in football.

JOE What's mine's yours, Tommy – but oh, canny wi the tongue.

TINY That was the ref, Joe. Out you go.

(JOE leads the way. The PLAYERS troop out single file, their studs and bars making loud noise. TINY picks up his jacket, puts it on, stuffs a bottle of embrocation into his outside pocket, picks up a bottle of water, hands it to TOMMY with a sponge.)

TINY Come on, Tommy, son. You can take it.
TOMMY *(Looking piteously at his luggage)* I hope so.

(They go out.

A moment later a MAN comes in and lays on the table, centre, plates of sliced lemon. He goes out and reappears with two trays laden with bottles of ginger beer. These he shoves under the table and goes out. TOMMY comes back, flings himself into the room, tears off his coat, hurls it into a corner, and, with an expression of fiendish rage upon his face, goes round the room kicking angrily any loose article in his way. The MAN goes out. TOMMY comes to a sudden halt opposite a cupboard on the wall, right, near the door. Opening it, he searches feverishly and at last discovers what he wants – the brandy bottle, kept for emergency needs. He uses savage force in uncorking the bottle and begins drinking. The first draught is long, but not ridiculously so. He sits on the form underneath the cupboard. The door opens and KATE enters, nervous but determined. She is smartly dressed: a loose tweed coat, small shapely green hat, stout but not mountain-climbing brown leather shoes, and brown leather gloves.)

KATE Tommy. *(He takes another drink, unheeding)* Tommy!
TOMMY Tell MacEwan to come and take me out.

(KATE turns swiftly round, sees TOMMY and the empty bottle. TOMMY's eyes are glued to the floor.)

TOMMY Tell him to come. This time I'll *break* his jaw.

(Lifts the bottle, and, as his hand rises, throws his head back. He sees KATE, and rises to his feet slowly but steadily, mesmerised. He is maudlin in manner, nor is his voice too drunken in tone.)

KATE Tommy, oh, what have they done to you?
TOMMY Made a name for me. You *knew* they would. If you're come to say 'I told you so' *(KATE makes a swift gesture of denial)*, let me say it first. *(Lapses suddenly into familiar dialect)* You're bonny, Kate. Now get out. Get out! Away ye go!
KATE Tommy, I came in pride. I heard from Bob Claverley. He said you were wearying to see me.
TOMMY Claverley! His nose is in everything. Leave me, Kate.
KATE I saw ye throw the sponge at that brass-necked big-mouth. I was on my way down to take my hand across his mouth!

(He gapes)

TOMMY *(In a whisper)* That was the Row in ye, Kate.

KATE It was not! I'm just angry. Anyway, it's expressive. *(Pause)* I love you, Tommy!

TOMMY Eh?

KATE More than anything in the world.

TOMMY All I've given you is the back of my hand. And you love me.

KATE Wheesht, Tommy.

(TOMMY takes her in his arms)

TOMMY *(Brokenly)* I'll kill him, Kate.

KATE Wheesht, Tommy! We'll be over the border an' awa and you need never set eyes upon him again.

TOMMY *(Ignoring)* You're a lawyer at last!

KATE You knew?

TOMMY I had my ear to the ground. *(Pause)* You heard all about me?

KATE My heart split, Tommy.

TOMMY I know, Kate.

KATE Let me see you before I go back. *(TOMMY makes a sign of denial)* Just once, Tommy?

TOMMY Forget me, Kate. I'm bad luck. Quick! It's half-time. They're coming back. *(Shoves KATE outside)* Bless ye, Kate. Goodbye! Kate, I'll remember ye.

(TINY comes wheezing into the room. His eyes search for TOMMY. He gasps. TOMMY is staring at the door through which KATE went, tears lining his cheeks. TINY throws off his jacket and begins furiously rolling up his sleeves. We know TINY has seen KATE.)

TINY Twelve-and-six that sponge cost me. That's fifteen bob off your wages. Why the hell couldn't ye throw the pail?

(Through the open door we hear the jeers, catcalls, and cheers of the crowd)

TOMMY She's lovely, Tiny.

TINY Dick told me she was. He must have had a stutter that day. With her at your side, Tommy, you could say 'trash' to a million MacEwans. Here they come. Flash that across your face.

(TOMMY wipes his face. The PLAYERS come trooping in, all quietly curious about TOMMY, but perspiring, breathless and gloomily disturbed by the score. TOMMY picks up the plates of lemon slices.)

JOE Thanks, mister.

TOMMY Nae bother, nae bother.

TAFFY And me, assistant trainer.

TOMMY *Mind*, I'm not saying you were *ever* a great player, but, ah, when –

(The PLAYERS stand in unusual inaction, delighted at the old TOMMY's return. Keeps moving from player to player.)

You had the greatest centre since Hughie Gallacher *playing* next to you. No names, please. Read last week's team. Then you *looked* like a player. *(To goalie)* You must be tired picking that nasty ball out of the net. I'll ask Mr MacEwan to give me a horse-band and we'll suspend you from the crossbars. Then you can swing an' bend, dip, and see what you can find. Nae bother!

PLAYER Tommy, who was that fellow you slugged?

(TOMMY stops dead. TINY turns like lightning on the PLAYER.)

TINY A big-mouth like you – *(Then a decision is made)* Help yourselves to lemon. I was proud of Tommy.

(PADDY and TAFFY jocularly but sincerely each take an arm of TOMMY's)

You should have seen him. This big-mouth – hired, if I'm a judge – started when Tommy came onto the track with me: 'Why don't ye throw in towel?' – 'Twelve thousand pounds for catching cold on a bench!' – 'Ye were better coal-diggin than goal getting!' Even the crowd began to say 'put a sock in it'. Then he gabs: 'What's the sponge for? Sucking?' Before he could say 'sponge' again, Tommy grabbed him and began stuffing the sponge into his mouth. He left him with the sponge half in and half out of it. Fifteen bob he's docked for that sponge.

(There is a startled cry from the other room, back centre. TINY grabs TOMMY.)

This'll be MacEwan. He saw it all. Now keep your temper, Tommy. Better still, shut up. I'll do the talking.

(A COMMISSIONAIRE bursts in. He is in terror.)

COMMISSIONAIRE My God! Mr MacEwan! He's in there! He's – he's –

JOE Don't say he's dead. That'll be too good to be true.

COMMISSIONAIRE He was locked in the sun-ray cabinet. His face is covered with blood. He's taken a terrible hammering.

TINY *(Hurrying forward)* Joe, tell the referee. Tell the police.

(The others crowd behind TINY)

PADDY Tell the band to play 'Hallelujah'!

TOMMY Dead! Not him – there's not enough heat in hell to roast MacEwan!

(Goes to the locker, opens it, helps himself to a long drink)

PADDY Dear Lord, Tommy! Are ye stone mad?

TOMMY Here's to MacEwan on the hot-plate.

(At that moment the PLAYERS crowd back from the door, a uniformed INSPECTOR stalks through them. He looks at PADDY, then at TOMMY.)

INSPECTOR You two don't seem curious to know what happened in there!

PADDY If we did, you'd say we were morbid. So what?

INSPECTOR Irish, eh?

PADDY See the bomb in my hip-pocket?

INSPECTOR I thought so.

PADDY *(In a whisper)* Tommy! He *thinks*, too!

TOMMY Look here, bloodhound, we're players and this is our dressing-room.

TINY That's all right, Tommy.

INSPECTOR *(Turning to TOMMY)* And who are you?

TINY Tommy Craig, our centre.

INSPECTOR Ah! The fellow who –

PADDY Tiny, get that fellow out of here.

JOE That's right. He's not coming in here with his 'Who are you?' and 'The fellow who – '.

INSPECTOR This is a serious matter. The manager of this club has been found in the sun-ray cabinet.

(BOB CLAVERLEY comes in at the players' entrance. Sees TOMMY.)

CLAVERLEY Oh, there ye are, Tommy!

INSPECTOR Who are *you*?

PADDY There must be a password.

CLAVERLEY Who? Me?

INSPECTOR Yes, you.

CLAVERLEY Oh, me! Ask Tommy, ask Tiny – ask my million readers. I'm just a ministering angel.

END OF ACT II

ACT III

Scene 1

One week later. The Craigs' kitchen. MR and MRS CRAIG are seated opposite each other at the fireside. RAB HUNTER is standing by the window. The evening papers lie in untidy heaps upon the table.

CRAIG The *Daily Mail* says there was gossip about dissension among the players.

HUNTER Gossip! Gossip – that's what kills the sporting element in the game. A player can have nae private life.

MRS CRAIG Not a line from Tommy. He must be suffering terribly, for that Mr MacEwan was a big man to him. I mind Tommy telling me he was the biggest man in football. Puir man! I can see him, standing where you're standing, Rab, *(RAB jumps)* giving me his word he'd be like a father to my Tommy.

HUNTER They're sayin' doon the road that MacEwan wasna the fine man we thought him.

MRS CRAIG Ah'll not believe that. Did I not hear him say to Tommy, 'Never give your mother the rough side of your tongue'?

CRAIG Rab and me'll just walk doon the Row an' hear.

MRS CRAIG You'll not set foot over that door. Dear sakes, man, are ye utterly lost to decent feeling?

HUNTER John's right, we might hear a bit of gossip that'll ease our minds about the boy.

MRS CRAIG Ye'll hear nae good in the Clanmarnock Arms.

CRAIG There ye go again, 'Clanmarnock Arms' – who says we're goin to the Clanmarnock Arms? Ye've a mind like a polisman, wumman.

MRS CRAIG I wish I'd the hand of a polisman. Look at ye! The pair o' ye, eyes like coloured marbles. Since this business began, ye've drunk enough whisky to satisfy fower Burns Clubs. Where ye get the money from –

CRAIG Will ye stop naggin, wumman? If it wasna' for you an' the likes o' you, pubs wad be empty. It's – it's *escape*. That's what sends quiet-gaun men like Rab an' me to the pubs, isn't it, Rab? Come on, speak up, man, ye've plenty to say about persecution ootside.

(The door opens and SARAH McCLARTY comes in. She is ominously subdued in manner.)

MRS CRAIG Come in, Sarah. Guidness me, are ye ill?

MRS McCLARTY No, Maggie.

(Goes forward to MRS CRAIG and lays a hand gently upon her shoulder. CRAIG turns to vent his irritation on SARAH.)

CRAIG Oh, ye're there, McClarty. An' whit bad news do you bring? Maybe you saw us in the Arms – maybe you think a dram turns a decent man into a combination o' Burke and Hare?

MRS McCLARTY Ah've just come frae the Arms, John, man.

CRAIG 'John, man'! Christmas crackers! Don't tell me ye've seen the light?

HUNTER Ah'll never believe *that* o' Sarah. John the Baptist couldn't convert Sarah McClarty.

MRS McCLARTY Ye long drink o' melancholy! God gie me patience, Maggie.

MRS CRAIG Tuesday, Sarah! An' you in that place?

MRS McCLARTY Maggie, come awa' doon wi me. Ah want ye to take a look at the wean. It's, it's –

MRS CRAIG Sarah! Ye've heard something. It's about Tommy!

CRAIG Whit did I tell ye? When McClarty was born the ravens lost a witch bird.

MRS CRAIG Sarah McClarty! It *is* Tommy.

(There is loud jeering from outside. TOMMY's voice is heard in drunken challenge. MRS CRAIG runs forward to the door. CRAIG and HUNTER stand aside. SARAH grips CRAIG by the sleeve.)

MRS McCLARTY Get oot there, ye fool. Tommy's hame, fightin fou. He came into the Arms so drunk he couldn't stand. Ah wantit to get Maggie oot of the road.

(CRAIG and HUNTER step towards the door. They are too late. TOMMY is on the threshold. He is terribly drunk.)

TOMMY *(To his father)* Hullo, auld yin. How's the coupons?

MRS CRAIG Tommy! Oh, Tommy, son!

(TOMMY stares stupidly at his mother. He makes a spectacular attempt at joviality.)

TOMMY It's Mrs Craig herself! The bonniest wee woman in the Row.

MRS CRAIG Tak your coat off, Tommy.

TOMMY Aye, Mother, the boy wi gold in his boots is hame. The tousy wee centre-forward, Sarah. The artist, Rab, the first-class football brain.

CRAIG You're a bonny specimen. By God! I'll spray your guts over the pavement!

MRS McCLARTY John Craig!

MRS CRAIG John. *(To TOMMY)* Your father's upset, lad.

TOMMY And what's biting you, sir? D'you not know me? I'm the boy who paid your farin at the Arms. I'm the boy who made you feel the weariness o' the lang Scots miles on a Sunday. Sit down! Aye, we'll sit down together, just you and Rab and Sarah an' me. We'll tak aff our dram like honest sportsmen. *(He produces a whisky bottle)* Glasses, Rab, glasses. We'll drink to the Napoleon of Scottish football. We'll drink to my father, the man who picked my first club.

CRAIG *(Grabbing the bottle and smashing it in the fireplace)* That's where your whisky'll go. Get out. I'm ashamed o' ye. Get back to your cronies. Get back to England where they made a man o' ye. I said there was gold in your boots, it was lead you needed.

TOMMY D'ye know what they sang when I left Coaltown? *(Sings)* 'We'll hang Tommy Craig from a sour apple tree.' 'An English Cup medal,' says you; it's a gallows dance they'll give me.

MRS CRAIG Tommy! Whit are ye saying? It's the drink. Say it's the drink. It's the Devil's word ye're speaking.

CRAIG Get out, get out before I lift my hand to ye.

TOMMY *(Brutally)* Lift your hand to me? You! *You*, you'd hit Tommy Craig? I'll dight the fireside with your face. That's where ye'd be at hame, in the whisky scupperings.

MRS McCLARTY For God's sake. Tommy Craig! You're mad. It's your *father* you're talking to.

TOMMY Mad, Sarah? I'm what they made me. The boy wi gold in his boots. That's me. I'm what he made me. 'Easy money,' said he. 'Grab yourself a gold-mine. Get into football.' Well, here I am. Look at my millions!

(KATE comes in the door and stands behind TOMMY)

MRS CRAIG I said there wad be no blessing.

CRAIG I'll kick him frae ane end o' the Row to the ither.

(RAB grabs CRAIG. He and SARAH pin him against the bed.)

MRS CRAIG Tommy, go ben to the bedroom.

TOMMY Not me. I'll not stay where I'm not wanted. Did ye hear him? – *he'd* kick me?

MRS CRAIG Oh, Tommy, he didn't mean what he said. Your father's not himself. He's upset.

TOMMY Upset! I give him lashings o' money. He blows and brags and boozes an' then tells me he'll spray my guts on the pavement. There's a fine father for ye.

MRS CRAIG Oh, Tommy, wheesht. My heart's breakin.

(TOMMY sways a little. His hand goes wearily across his forehead. MRS CRAIG puts a comforting hand upon his sleeve. At her touch he turns and looks at her face. The agony there unmans him. He clutches her to him and buries his head into her shoulder. Sobs rack him. Through his sobbing comes the story.)

TOMMY Everywhere I went, a detective. They stood outside my digs.

When I went to the ground, two of them followed me. They waited outside. Oh, Mother! – they think I killed MacEwan.

MRS CRAIG You're hame, Tommy. You're hame. That's all that matters.

CRAIG Come on, boy, sit doon by the fire. Sarah!

MRS McCLARTY Rab, fill the kettle. It's a cup o' tea he needs.

(TOMMY is led to the armchair. He sits, his head buried in his hands. His father begins unlacing his boots. KATE comes forward and taps him on the shoulder. MR CRAIG looks up and moves aside to let KATE untie the boots. KATE motions to her father to take SARAH next door. TOMMY is mumbling.)

TOMMY I hated MacEwan, Mother, I admit that. I told the police I hated him. But I never killed him.

MRS CRAIG Son, ye don't need to tell your mother ye never harmed him.

TOMMY But I hit him. I hit him. A dozen people saw me hit him. It was just after that they found him.

KATE Mr Craig, take Mrs Craig next door.

(TOMMY looks up, suddenly alert. He shoves KATE away. His voice becomes harsh.)

TOMMY Leave me alone! I'm going.

MRS CRAIG Let him be, Kate. Tommy, stay with me. Stay with your mother.

KATE I'm the lass he jilted, Mrs Craig. I've got a word or two to say to Tommy Craig.

(KATE signals to MR CRAIG over TOMMY's shoulder. MR CRAIG whispers into MRS CRAIG's ear. Reluctantly she allows herself to be led out of the door. TOMMY is stumbling over his boots, searching for his coat and hat. KATE goes to the bedroom door, shuts it firmly, and faces TOMMY.)

KATE Did your friend Hamish, the whisky distiller, bring you home? Or, maybe you fell in wi Towser? Towser's been at this door every day since you left. When he's drunk he says you robbed him of a crown. When he's sober he's all anxiety to know how his old pal Tommy is doing. Yes, you're his 'old pal' now. He even forgives you for stealing *me*.

TOMMY He can have his crown now.

KATE And me, I suppose.

TOMMY Kate!

KATE Whisky and defeated football dreams have made him maudlin mad. 'Like a bull at a gate I was,' he cried. 'Could batter my way through a batallion o' full-backs.' And then, 'But Tommy had the craft, Tommy had brains in his boots.' Maybe Towser's right.

TOMMY Where's my hat? I came home thinking –

KATE A bonny homecoming. I little knew how near the truth I was when I named you Towser's successor. The great Tommy Craig! I wonder ye didn't bring a piper with you.

TOMMY Get out of my way, Kate. I'm going.

KATE Why did ye come back? Were ye afraid we'd miss something of your success? Did ye think your mother couldn't be spared the sight of you drunk?

TOMMY I don't want to talk to anybody. My hat –

KATE Come here. Let me look at you. What a sight!

(She goes into the bedroom and comes back carrying a basin full of water, which she places on the table. TOMMY has dropped into the seat again and is sitting with his face in his hands. KATE takes him firmly by the shoulder. He goes with her to the table and she shoves his face and forehead into the water.)

KATE Maybe ye'd like a trainer and a sponge and your orders.

TOMMY I'd like to sleep.

KATE Not till I've finished with you. *(Rubs his face with a rough towel, the water is dripping round his neck. He gives a shuddering grimace.)* It's a nurse you need, not a trainer.

TOMMY For God's sake, Kate, leave me.

KATE I've been daft long enough. Last time I left you – well, take a look at yourself.

TOMMY You're a good lass, Kate. But I'm done.

KATE Stop snivelling, Tommy! One minute you're a fighting man, next minute you're a bubbly-jock.

TOMMY It was the murder. That was the finish. No! There was a lot beside that.

KATE Out wi it. Was it women?

TOMMY Women? Women! No, it wasn't women. It was flattery, vanity, stupidity, cowardice, and a whole lot of hate. MacEwan hated me. He never forgave me for robbing him of his rake-off. When he came to Coaltown he had one ambition, to see me in the gutter. That was easy. I helped him send me there.

KATE How?

TOMMY Before he came, I spent all my spare time – I'd plenty of spare time – studying. Then MacEwan came on the scene. He took it out of me in the ground. His pal, the Spotter, put paragraphs in the paper that made me look like a loonie who'd slipped his chain. I'd be playing well, and when the reports appeared they read as if I was hen-toed, knock-kneed, headless, and had sinkers for boot studs.

KATE So you looked for sympathy?

TOMMY I used to go out with Izzy Montagu. He knew what I was up against.

KATE And what did Izzy, the bear-leader, do?

TOMMY We'd go to the dogs. Once or twice he ran me over to Blackpool. He always had something on. He knew everybody in Coaltown.

KATE Except Snatcher!

TOMMY He –

(*MRS CRAIG appears at the door. She is carrying a cup of steaming tea.*)

MRS CRAIG Drink this, Tommy. It's just made.

TOMMY (*Suddenly bellicose*) I don't want tea. I should never have come here.

KATE It's too late for that. Drink the tea.

MRS CRAIG (*Breaking down*) Oh, Tommy, what have they done to ye?

(*MR CRAIG appears in the doorway*)

TOMMY Stop snivelling at me. It used to be texts.

KATE The cockerel's home to crow on his own midden.

CRAIG Drink the tea, Tommy, son, it'll do ye good.

TOMMY Good! Tea! I like that from you. Remember the last time I came home?

CRAIG I was off my heid, Tommy, lad.

KATE Shame on you, Tommy Craig.

MRS CRAIG Oh, Kate, it's no' Tommy. It's that cursèd drink.

CRAIG He's right, Kate. I deserve it.

KATE He's no right to talk.

TOMMY I've no right to talk. I've no right – who did the talking when I –

CRAIG I did, Tommy. It was me from the beginning. I should have left ye to your books. But it's not too late now.

MRS CRAIG Ye can forget football, Tommy.

TOMMY (*Miserably*) I'm finished, Mother. It's too late I tell ye.

KATE There's Sarah calling you, Mr Craig.

(*MRS CRAIG goes into the bedroom and is followed by MR CRAIG. As MR CRAIG passes TOMMY he touches him gently upon the shoulder.*)

CRAIG Do you feel better, Tommy?

TOMMY My head's like a pit-head.

KATE You're not cut out for social life.

TOMMY That day you saw me. That was the first day. I was mad at MacEwan. Then when I heard about the murder and saw the look the policemen gave me, I went daft. Reporters came. I got scared of the questions they asked me. Then they began chasing me. One fellow wanted to pay for my defence. 'Sign me on,' he said. I tell you, Kate, I'm –

KATE You're all right, Tommy. What a good thing we've got a lawyer in the family. Forget the vultures. You've been a fool, but that doesn't make you a murderer. Remember, I was to be your legal adviser.

TOMMY If I'd listened to you, Kate!

KATE If I'd listened to you. I was smug.

TOMMY Smug?

KATE And a snob. You see, I had the bungalow mind.

TOMMY And I was all plus-fours and Bentley.

KATE With your fifteen pounds a week from Lord Beavermere and your Dobbins Gold Leaf and my seven-and-sixpence.

TOMMY I don't mind no football, Kate. Honest, I don't. If only I could forget MacEwan.

KATE That'll right itself, Tommy.

TOMMY Think of the Row, what they're saying.

KATE I've been thinking of that. Tommy, we must get away.

TOMMY *We*?

KATE Yes, *we* – all of us. Your mother and father. My father.

TOMMY But how?

KATE That job with my uncle's still open. I'll see him.

TOMMY A job? Get away from the Row?

KATE We can get one of the new houses.

TOMMY You mean one of the Glasgow Housing Scheme?

KATE Yes – away on the other side of the city, on the Paisley side. We'll be on the road to the coast.

TOMMY One with a garden front and back?

KATE And a bathroom, Tommy, now you've got the habit!

TOMMY And electric light?

KATE Is this a proposal, by the way?

TOMMY I clean forgot.

KATE Even a Socialist and a freethinker –

TOMMY Kate, will ye really have me?

KATE My dear, I'll never let you go. Oh, Tommy, I was the most miserable lassie in Scotland when you took your boots to England.

(They are embracing when the bedroom door opens and MR and MRS CRAIG appear)

MRS CRAIG Kate!

KATE Yes, Mrs Craig?

MRS CRAIG Is he sleeping?

KATE Come and see.

MRS CRAIG Quiet, John. Oh, Kate, what have they done to our boy, Kate!

KATE He's signed on again!

CRAIG *(Joyfully)* A transfer. Tommy! Tommy, ah wouldn't take first prize in Murphy's Pool in exchange for this minute.

TOMMY Not even a ticket to Wembley?
CRAIG Not if ye gave me Wembley to bring back with me.

(A knock on the outer door)

KATE It's my father. Oh, let me give him a surprise.
CRAIG Surprise? Ah gave him six to four against this happening years ago. He'll be ready to collect.

(MRS CRAIG goes to the door. She opens it and BOB CLAVERLEY and DICK GRAVES walk in.)

CRAIG Outside! I tell ye, Claverley.
TOMMY Let him stay, Father. He can't –
CRAIG Not a step. He was my shadow at school.
CLAVERLEY *His* shadow, Margaret? He flatters himself.
MRS CRAIG What do you want, Bob? My boy's hame and he's having no part wi you or your football again. He's by wi'all that, thank God!
CLAVERLEY *(To GRAVES)* He looks –
GRAVES Tommy, when you disappeared from Coaltown, I got terribly worried.
CLAVERLEY Worried! He was frantic.
GRAVES I heard that –
TOMMY I was acting like a fool, Dick. I was – look! *(Points to the smashed bottle)* That's the answer.
KATE Not all, surely, Tommy?
TOMMY Oh, yes! Not all. Bob, you want a story?
CLAVERLEY I want no more stories from you, Tommy. All I want to know is that you're home. *(Looks at MRS CRAIG)* Dick and I made you a promise, Tommy. We just wanted to keep it. That's why we chased after you, to see you had the right address.
GRAVES I'm glad he's come home to you, Mrs Craig.
MRS CRAIG To me?
KATE See, Tommy. You're not even worth a story now.
CLAVERLEY Oh, hullo, Miss Hunter. How're the briefs coming?
KATE That's your story. I've got my first big brief. *(Looks at TOMMY)*
GRAVES My hand, Tommy! Man alive, what a pity there's not an English Cup medal to go with the bride-cake. I'm back with Rovers, you know!
MRS CRAIG *What's* that?
KATE And why not?
TOMMY Kate!
KATE That's what you would like, Tommy, wouldn't you?
CRAIG An English Cup medal! I'll run an' tell Rab.
TOMMY My last game.
MRS CRAIG Are you mad, Kate?

KATE Mr Claverley, tell us the truth. There are ugly stories about Tommy.

CLAVERLEY Now, Miss Hunter!

KATE Answer me. You're usually fond of questions.

CLAVERLEY Well, you know what happened at Coaltown. Scandal breeds scandal. Gossip, ye ken. But –

KATE But everybody says, 'Tommy Craig has dropped out of football – why?'

GRAVES Nobody in the team.

KATE The *team*! You made Tommy a name to millions. They idolised him. Now they slander him. They suspect him. They whisper vile rumour. If he disappears, the scandal remains, for ever.

CLAVERLEY Oh, Miss Hunter – it'll be forgotten.

KATE Not in football legend. Not while your files remain.

GRAVES What do you propose, Miss Hunter?

KATE I want Tommy back in the Cup Final team. But there's a condition attached.

GRAVES The condition?

KATE He trains at home.

CLAVERLEY Dick?

GRAVES Report at Wembley, Tommy! One hour before the kick-off.

CLAVERLEY A telephone! Dash it, I forgot this is Clanmarnock. The last time I sent a story from here – a smasher it was, too – I sent it by carrier pigeon.

(*SARAH McCLARTY's voice is heard in a wild scream. Everybody looks in alarm to the kitchen door. Against the window is silhouetted the bulky frame of a man.*)

GRAVES My God!

MRS McCLARTY (*Her voice is pitched in high rage*) An' who the devil are you? Prowling about in the dark, skulking against the wall, scaring the wits out of honest home-keeping folk?

VOICE (*Recognisably English*) I'm a police officer.

MRS McCLARTY Police officer? I'd say ye were the Gestapo. And what the blazes d'ye want here?

CLAVERLEY It's the Coaltown Inspector.

(*TOMMY collapses into the armchair. The others stare at him. MRS CRAIG and KATE stand over TOMMY.*)

ACT III

Scene 2

The players' dressing-room, Wembley Stadium. It is 2.45 p.m. on the day of the FA Cup Final. There is the same confusion of noise and scene as at Rovers' dressing-room, with added tension brought on by the knowledge that, outside, 80,000 fans, mostly partisan, are shouting themselves hoarse in a fever of expectancy. As the PLAYERS stand, sit, hop about in undressing and getting on football kit – brand new, except for the tired, shapeless boots – TINY and DICK, and extra trainer helpers, move from one to another with almost womanly solicitude. Every now and then the door, left centre, opens, and TINY lets out a howl of exasperated protest. Occasionally, a bowler-hatted, rosetted official peeps round the door, whispers to the COMMISSIONAIRE-SERGEANT on duty, produces a card with self-conscious majesty, and is admitted. But once inside he, too, is affected by the atmosphere and, beyond a 'Good luck, Paddy, Taffy, Joe, Dick', is content to gaze in awed worship and hope. Through the window comes the noise of community singing – 'Abide with Me', 'Land of Hope and Glory', 'On Ilkley Moor Baht Tat'. There is sudden whispering among the PLAYERS. PADDY asks the question agitating their minds:

PADDY *(Plaintively)* Dick, for God's sake, is he coming?
DICK Yes.
JOE Did anyone meet the train?
DICK Yes, damn you, Joe! Can't you see I'm sick as you are, wondering!
TAFFY He might've sent a wire.
TINY Shut up, Taffy.
TAFFY Well, anything might have happened. That Inspector was at Bushey this morning, looking like the mouse that swallowed the cat.
JOE They couldn't arrest him today, Dick?
DICK I don't know, Joe.

(The door opens, MILESTONE appears and is promptly barred by the COMMISSIONAIRE. DICK goes out.)

PADDY They say the turf is as good as a Galway stretch.
JOE I wish they'd let me sign cheques the way they ask for my autograph.
TAFFY Why don't you – then you'd have a good long stretch before you, too – but not in Galway.
PADDY Did you read the dead-heads, our old friends, Lionel, Frederick, Trevor and John – the four apostles?
JOE 'If Coaltown don't lose they'll win.'
TAFFY If the ground is dry it'll suit us; if it's wet it'll suit the other fellows.

PADDY An' if it's damp?

JOE There's always high winds at Wembley.

PADDY They make me sick, Fleet Street! They know more about football in a girls' reformatory.

TINY *(Roars)* Football! I thought I told you football was barred here!

DICK *(Comes in)* I did what you said, Tiny. I talked to the police at Clanmarnock. I couldn't make out what the fellow said at first – he talks the lingo worse than Tommy.

TINY *(Roaring)* Where is Tommy?

MILESTONE Tommy left for here, he said. Miss Hunter was with him. They turned out the town band, but none of the Scots fellows saw him go on the train.

DICK It's my fault. I shouldn't have agreed to let him train at home. I'll be fired before the Cup Final yet! The Directors are croaking like a school of crows.

PADDY You don't think the Inspector – is?

DICK No. I saw him at Euston. He looked like a man who'd lost insomnia and caught sleepy-sickness.

(Door opens)

VOICE The King's arrived!

DICK *(To nervous-looking youngster)* That's settled it. Alf! – strip. You'll play.

PADDY *(Standing on a form, shouts)* Dick, he's here. Standing just outside. Oh, saints help us!

DICK *(Hysterical)* Who's there?

PADDY The Sergeant from Coaltown. The Inspector's shadow.

(DICK sits on the table-edge in weary resignation)

DIRECTOR *(Comes in)* What's all this, Dick? There's a rumour Craig's double-crossed us again.

(DICK jumps to his feet. There is angry protest from the PLAYERS, led by PADDY and TAFFY. JOE leaps across the room.)

JOE Outside, you!

DIRECTOR Me? Joe, d'ye forget –

JOE Forget nothing! Tommy's our pal. We're his club-mates.

DIRECTOR I'm a Director and my concern's the Cup.

JOE An' we've got to win the bloody Cup – two quid for us and a lot o' jaw-work for you.

DICK Joe's right, Councillor. I can't have my players upset on the whistle.

DIRECTOR *Your* players! Our twelve-thousand-pound centre dodging police while –

(TINY slams a sponge across his mouth. JOE bundles him out of the door. As he does so, TOMMY flings himself into the room. We get a glimpse of KATE.)

KATE *(Through the doorway)* Play as if you were at Hampden, Tommy.

(The door slams. The PLAYERS are clamouring round TOMMY. TINY grabs his coat – underneath is his jersey.)

TOMMY Is it all right, Dick – ?

JOE Boy oh boy! Tommy, we'll tear the turf.

TOMMY I came by road. *They* were on the doorstep all day yesterday. Warned from England, I was told. Oh, Dick!

PADDY The –

TAFFY Language in the dressing-room, please.

DICK Don't talk, Tommy. I knew you wouldn't let me down.

TINY Wash your mouth with this, Tommy.

TOMMY No, nothing. One of them's outside, Dick. I saw the look he gave me. Like a gamekeeper on to a fox.

DICK Another word of that, Tommy, and I'll – I'll drop you! Nobody's going to harm you.

PADDY We'll burst up. Hey! *Quiet! (A cat is seen slinking along the edge of the window)* I'll brain the man who whispers –

(There is a sudden tense silence. The door opens. TAFFY makes a leap and claps his hand over an official's mouth. All stand in an agony of hope. Even TINY, who is lacing TOMMY's boots, stops, the lace stretched and upraised in his hand.)

PADDY Puss, puss, puss! Psss!! Come to Uncle Paddy. I'll give you a million cows, mice as sweet as the lips of the queen of all the cats. Ah! Got him!

(There is shouting from the PLAYERS. PADDY rushes over to the hamper and gently lays the cat inside.)

VOICE Gentlemen, the King is in the Royal Box.

PADDY *(To the hamper)* You bet he is!

TAFFY I'll bet *it's* neutral.

TINY Joe, your mascot!

(JOE grabs a huge black-and-white Mickey Mouse)

JOE *(To the goalie)* Yours – *(Hands him a mallet)* Don't use it on the referee.

DICK Well, boys, it's here! You know what I want from you: keep it on the ground, first-time passing, start holding it when you see them fainting, and – find your man every time. Come on!

PADDY Get between us, Tommy.

(As they go out through the door, KATE steps quickly in and hands TOMMY a sprig of heather)

KATE It's from Ben Lomond, Tommy. I picked it myself.

CURTAIN

The curtain is lowered to indicate the time lapse between the kick-off and the first interval. When the curtain rises, TINY and the PLAYERS come hurrying in.

1st ASSISTANT What a performance! More football in an automatic machine. Sheer sacrilege to call it a Cup Final.
TINY He hasn't a kick in him.
1st ASSISTANT Did you hear that chorus as he came out? – 'We'll hang Tommy Craig from a sour apple tree.' It hit him like a back-heel from an elephant.
TINY He's running about like a cow stung by a thousand flies. Quick! Not a word.

(The PLAYERS come trooping in, listless, leg-weary, steaming and gasping, all dead beat. DICK follows them in.)

DICK All into the bath-room. Tiny, that champagne open?
TINY It's open, but it's arsenic they should get! Cup-finalists? Why, I've trained –

(JOE steps up to TINY)

JOE A word about Crystal Palace and I'll make you think the only training you ever did was with goldfish. I'll hold you in that tub until you spit mussels.
TINY In you go. I'll talk to you later.

(The PLAYERS troop into the bath-room, followed by the TRAINERS carrying trays and glasses and champagne bottles. As they walk in, they eye TOMMY with comprehending but reproachful eyes. TOMMY rises.)

DICK Tommy! Not you.
TOMMY I know. I'm letting them down. I'm a passenger.
DICK You take the words out of my mouth, but I'd never have spoken them, Tommy. If I thought it would help, I'd say, 'Don't go back.' I can find a hundred alibis.
TOMMY And not one good one.

DICK Champagne's not your tonic, Tommy. It's a word, and it's not in my dictionary.

TOMMY It's in mine – coward. Dick! It was that song! That feeling you get when you're in for a bad day – you know it, every player knows it. Wild fear in the head, and ghastly emptiness from the middle down. 'Hollow legs' they call it. I'm a shell, Dick. I could no more play that ball than do a handspring on the top of the flag-pole. I'm done.

(There is a loud knocking at the door. BOB's voice is heard.)

CLAVERLEY I'm a reporter and, of course, reporters are barred. That's why I'm going in. *(Bursts in)* So! *(To TOMMY)* You're there? Man, you're a disgrace to Clanmarnock – you're a disgrace to Scotland. Most damnable of all, you're a disgrace to *me*, for I gave you a column and a half this morning, namin you wi the best – McColl, Gallacher – an' this is the thanks I get. 'Cradled in Clanmarnock, football's greatest nursery,' I wrote, and you're playing as if you were still in the nursery!

DICK Bob! Are you mad, or drunk?

CLAVERLEY 'Both,' they'll say, when they read my running commentary on that first half. 'Too much Russell and Palace Hotels for auld Bob,' they'll say. *(The PLAYERS are coming out, and glare at DICK and BOB in stupefied anger)* But I'll lay your bogey, my lad. Nae bashing, footless centre-forward's going to ruin my record as a picker. *(Turns swiftly to the door)* Come in, Inspector. *(The INSPECTOR enters, half apologetic, half grinning)* Is that the fellow? *(Pointing to TOMMY. DICK steps forward in fierce anger. The PLAYERS look ugly and ready to rush BOB and the INSPECTOR.)*

TOMMY Thanks, Bob! I'm sick of it all.

CLAVERLEY Sick? Give him a glass o' champagne.

(There is a panic-stricken shout from the doorway)

VOICE Rovers! The referee's waiting and he's mad. There'll be an official protest.

CLAVERLEY Tommy, son, get out and play and never let MacEwan's name worry you again – tell him, Inspector.

INSPECTOR This morning I arrested a man named Towser Graham. The man Towser made full and frank confession. He murdered the late Archibald MacEwan. He was drunk, he said, and went to see MacEwan about a debt – an old grudge. MacEwan had promised him a club in England – the club Craig plays for. They had an argument. Graham says he saw red, bundled MacEwan into the cabinet, slammed the door and left. He heard Craig had been arrested and gave himself up.

PLAYERS Tommy!

DICK Out! All of you –

TOMMY I – I'm going to be sick.

CLAVERLEY Not till I've interviewed you on how it feels to get an English Cup medal. Gie him another champagne, Tiny.
TOMMY Here, *you* take it. That's a drink for reporters and directors. They're better judges of it than of football.

(TOMMY runs out. CLAVERLEY stands smiling, looking round the dressing-room, and, taking shrewd stock of the case of champagne, says aloud:)

CLAVERLEY Duty says I should climb back to my pigeon-hole in the press-box. Sense and good taste tell me there's not a damned word will be written there I couldn't quote from memory as accurately as I could report the speeches the two chairmen will make at the banquet tonight – 'We deserved to win' – 'We were unlucky to lose, but were beaten by a team of grand sportsmen'. Anyhow, I can get the goals from the boys – that'll be the real story. Tommy's right. *(Drinking)* The player's always right. This is the place for the expert. *(Goes to the champagne case and takes out a bottle and opens it. Talks aloud in kindly reminiscent tone.)* Champagne and the Cup. The two together. Man! – how many Cup Finals have I seen? How many behind-the-scene sensations? But Tommy's is a cracker! Towser hating MacEwan and proud o' Tommy. Me having the bulge on MacEwan all these years wi that forged cheque. It's a reporter's dream! An' a reporter's dream is usually a player's nightmare. Man, it's no' canny drinking alone.

A ROAR: Goal!!

(Long-drawn-out, a mingling of joy, wonder and acute sorrow)

CLAVERLEY *(Complacently)* Tommy's started. *(Goes to the door and opens it)* Who's scored?
VOICE *(Vibrant)* Craig. A beautiful solo effort.
CLAVERLEY That phrase, my man, perfect prose! I'll steal it. *(Quotes)* 'A beautiful solo effort.'

ANOTHER ROAR Goal!!!

CLAVERLEY *(Going back to the door)* Hey, mister, whit happened?
MAN Craig again. He broke through on his own, nearly burst the net. What a player!
CLAVERLEY *(Still drinking)* 'Broke through on his own.' 'Nearly burst the net.' 'What a player!' Man, we're a nation o' prose writers. If I stay here, maybe somebody'll coin a phrase. *(Goes to the door)* Hey, mister, you, let's celebrate. Come awa' in.

(A MAN comes in at the door. He is shabbily dressed, but on his waistcoat, attached to a black cord chain, gleams a gold medal. BOB, his back turned to the MAN, staggers over to the champagne case. The MAN steps forward, eyes BOB curiously, picks up the umbrella, smiles,

as though sight of the odd-looking little man has brought pleasant thoughts.)

CLAVERLEY A dram, a man, as we say back where the very lamp-posts are potential football critics. It's no' the real thing, but it'll do.

MAN The last time we drank that stuff, Bob, I handed it to you.

CLAVERLEY *(Turning swiftly)* A ghost! My God! *(Looking at the champagne)* You're no' doing a Hamlet on me, I hope.

MAN Remember Sailor Stokes?

CLAVERLEY Remember him? Sailor Stokes? The best winger England ever had – the Hammer of the Scots! Sailor – the only sea he ever sailed in was a sea of popularity! But what a player! Had he been born in Scotland, I'd say 'genius'.

SAILOR An' the Cup was the English Cup –

CLAVERLEY My Auntie Maggie, it's Sailor himself!

SAILOR Four times I carried it from the Royal Box, then onto the coach going to Wharncliffe rooms, home to the civic banquet, and –

CLAVERLEY Tell me, Sailor, what's England's Glory doing standing in the alleys at Wembley?

SAILOR I couldn't get a brief. I got *one* from the old club but gave it to my kid. He's never seen a Cup Final.

CLAVERLEY Have *you* seen anything of the match?

SAILOR Not a kick. A fellow at the gate recognised me and slipped me in, but I couldn't brass-face it past the inside barrier.

CLAVERLEY If there's one there's a thousand dead-heads inside – and I don't mean only editors' wives, children and sweethearts.

SAILOR Oh, I'm not beefing, Bob. It's the game.

CLAVERLEY Tak the bottle. If the FA bought ye a vineyard, Sailor, they'd still be stingy.

SAILOR They do lads better in Scotland, Bob?

CLAVERLEY You're havering. There they give meaning to Malcolm's words in *Macbeth. (Strikes an attitude)* 'And here from gracious England have I offer of goodly thousands – ' *(Makes a sudden fearful silence)* Gosh, if I'm heard quoting Shakespeare . . .

SAILOR Here's to happy memories –

CLAVERLEY Happy memories! Dear heaven, Sailor, the thrills you gave them – there was that Inter-League match at Maine Road, Manchester – the *big* international at Hampden when our folk called ye a second Cumberland, and on Tyneside, when Colin Veitch – God bless him! – said, 'Given a park, two goalposts and a balloon, ye could beat twenty-one Scotsmen on your own.'

SAILOR Yes, I daresay, Bob. On my game I was good.

CLAVERLEY Good? Ye were the Shakespeare o' football. And ye can't get a ticket?

A ROAR Goal!!!

SAILOR *(Excitedly)* There's another, Bob! *(Then, anxiously)* Oh, Bob, your report! Don't – you're not out of the game, too? It's a goal, Bob!

CLAVERLEY Aye. It's Tommy. Ask!

SAILOR *(Rushes to the door)* Who scored?

VOICE Craig! A forty-mile-an-hour drive from outside the penalty area.

CLAVERLEY Area! Man, Sailor, even the vocabulary never alters. Another bottle! It'll never be missed.

(A POLICEMAN comes rushing in)

POLICEMAN Hey, what's this? Who are you?

CLAVERLEY My, my – another detective.

SAILOR *(Humbly)* I was invited in –

POLICEMAN Champagne! I'll attend to you in a minute.

CLAVERLEY *(To SAILOR)* Reward at last, Sailor. Ye got fourteen international caps, four Cup medals, and now you're getting attention. *(To the POLICEMAN)* What's biting you, Lord Trenchard?

(A scuffle and TINY comes in, tears streaming down his cheeks)

TINY It's Tommy, Bob! He's got a packet. *(Suddenly recognising SAILOR, grips his hand)* You *know*, Sailor –

CLAVERLEY Where is he?

TINY They're bringing him – *(Quickly efficient)* Lend a hand, Sailor, old-timer.

(SAILOR throws off his coat. He has no jacket underneath. His shirtsleeves are cut off at the elbow, there is half-an-inch gap between his shirt neck and the collar, a wisp of cotton serves as tie. He clears the table of rubbish in a sweep, and soon has blanket and headrest in position. Two St John's AMBULANCE MEN enter. Outside there is a continuous roar. As TOMMY is laid on a stretcher on the table, one man says:)

AMBULANCE MAN It's all over.

(TOMMY sees BOB)

TOMMY *(Whispering)* Aye, it's all over, Bob.

(BOB looks first at the DOCTOR who has followed the stretcher, then at DICK, who has also come in. The DOCTOR nods silently at BOB.)

CLAVERLEY Oh, Tommy, lad! *(Affecting heartiness)* Ye're no' deid yet!

TOMMY *(Suddenly and bitterly)* No, but I might as well be. *I know.* They sang 'We'll hang Tommy Craig – ' when I went out. They cheered me when I came off – did ye hear that, Bob?

CLAVERLEY Alan Morton never got louder.

TOMMY A year ago they said I was the uncrowned King of Scotland. Then they said I was the best expert since the fellow who started the Bank of England. Last week they said I was a disgrace to the game. *(KATE comes in)* It's two years since I left the pit, Bob. All I've got is plus-fours and a stumer leg. A limp for life. Oh, Bob. The fellows who've come up to me at the players' entrance and said I was the Boy Wonder! Now I'm on the Main Drag! I'm no' due a benefit, Bob. It's me for the Dole again. *(Suddenly quiet)* Will I get a medal, Dick?

CLAVERLEY *(Bitterly)* Here's a fellow'll give you one, Tommy. He's got four. Sailor Stokes.

TOMMY Sailor Stokes, the wizard winger?

CLAVERLEY Right out of the book –

SAILOR For that hat-trick, Tommy, they'll give you Coaltown.

KATE Coaltown? Not for him! Tommy, I've been sitting in the Director's box. Look, here's our rent and class fees for the next three years. *(Waves a cheque)* The Chairman gave it to me. He says he owes it to you, personally –

TINY We'll have a star benefit for you, Tommy.

KATE I'll have your boots gold-plated.

DOCTOR *(Seeing signal from the doorway)* Now, now, there's too much talk here! *(Nods to St John's AMBULANCE MEN, who throw blankets over Tommy. Then gently:)* Would you care to come along, Mrs Craig?

TOMMY *Mrs* Craig!

DOCTOR That's the ambulance. Now don't you fret. We'll have him back to you in a week or two –

(The PLAYERS come trooping in. JOE hands TOMMY a medal. They put the Cup in his arms, and follow him out. BOB and SAILOR are left in the room.)

SAILOR That's one way of going out of the game, Bob.

CLAVERLEY Come on, Holy Loch, I've got a' the words to telephone. Come on, Sailor, you'd better describe the goals for me. Whit was it? 'Magnificent solo effort' – 'A great burst through the middle' – 'A forty-mile-a-minute drive from outside the penalty area' – Ah nearly forgot, 'The goalie never saw it'! *(To SAILOR suddenly)* And my exclusive interview wi Tommy. *(Quotes, musingly)* 'It was the team, not me,' said Tommy, speaking through great physical pain. 'I'm proud to have won an English Cup medal, but prouder to have worn Rovers' colours. I'm sure the best team won. If I'm out of the game for good, I'll always think back on the happiness the game gave me.' Sailor, have I no' the imagination and command o' words? It's true, ye see, I'm a genius among football reporters.

CURTAIN

THE LAMBS OF GOD

A PLAY IN SEVEN SCENES

by

Benedick Scott

The Lambs of God was first produced at the Theatre Royal, Glasgow, in August 1948. Details of this production do not survive. When the play later went on tour, renamed *This Walking Shadow*, the cast was as follows:

A POLICE OFFICER, *with ideas* . . . . Andrew Keir
KATE McSHANE, *has been around* . . . . Eveline Garratt

The Gossips: MRS DYKES . . . . Irene Barry
MRS McKAY . . . . Maisie Hill
MRS THOMSON . . . . Sybil Thomson
MRS McDOUGALL . . . . Marjorie Thomson
MRS WATT . . . . Bertha Cooper

The Boys of the Village: BOOL McKAY . . . . Ivor Kissen
CHICK DYKES . . . . Russell Hunter
JAKE THOMSON . . . . Carl Williamson
BERT McDOUGALL . . . . Reginald Allan
HARRY WATT . . . . Anthony Currie

DICK MARSHALL, *the lonely one* . . . . Jack Stewart
ALEC STEWART, *takes his fun where he finds it* . . . . Andrew Keir
MRS McPHEE, *a decent hard-working body* . . . . Alrae Edwards

The Hopefuls: JIMMIE McPHEE . . . . Roddy McMillan
MOLLY BROWN . . . . Betty McGregor

Produced by . . . . Robert Mitchell
Décor . . . . Tom Macdonald
Stage Manager . . . . Helen Dibley
Wardrobe Mistress . . . . Julie Wallace

The setting throughout is that of Mercer's Vennel in the town of Drumnoull in Central Scotland. The action passes in a sequence of daylight and moonlight scenes and covers a period of several weeks in the summer of a year in the 1930s. As regards the flight of time, the audience should use its own imagination. Time sequences will be suggested by lighting changes and music.

Scene 1

Moonlight.

OFFICER Oh – hullo, Kate. Out for an airin?

KATE Oh – it's you? Hullo. Just that.

OFFICER Aye. It's a fine night for it.

KATE It is that.

OFFICER Aye, a fine night. A grand night for it! Ever since I came on duty a coupla hours back, I've been thinking – up one side o the street and down the other – rattlin door handles, tryin window shutters – it's the very night for it – it's i' the air.

KATE It often is – these long deep nights o summer. You feel lazy and content – and yet – and yet life's runnin sweet and swift at the heart o it all.

OFFICER What an understandin lass you are, Katie. No wonder the men seldom turn their blind eye i' your airt! Still it is, more often nor usual. And no only i' the clear nights o summer time. Every night o the year for somebody or another. Think o it i' winter – making the grey life around you gleam like gold for a while. Or i' spring – the sudden lift to your heart when it beckons to you. Even i' the fa' o the year – if only for half an hour – shieldin you wi its warmth from the decay that's a' around.

KATE You've been to the Alhambra this week?

OFFICER *(Unabashed)* No. I read a lot. And think a lot champin round the quiet streets.

KATE Too bad. And you could be content at home i' your own bed.

OFFICER 'Deed no. I've got immune to the scent of my own blankets. It hasn't varied these ten years back.

KATE That so? Night shift must have its charms for you.

OFFICER Oh, aye, it has its compensations. I'll admit that. There's many the excitin scent in the streets – after the good are bedded down!

KATE So I've heard.

OFFICER *(Admiringly)* Aye, you would. You would be i' the way o hearin, I'm thinking.

KATE *(Smoothly)* Sure. I get around.

OFFICER You should wi what you've got.

KATE D'you think so?

OFFICER 'S fact. You've had your fine times before now, Katie. And it is fine – is't no?

KATE *(Casually)* Sometimes.

OFFICER Aye? Sometimes? Still – we can't choose a' the time. Got to take what the Lord sends us.

KATE Hardly put it that way – masel.

OFFICER Well. Maybe no, but you see what I mean?

KATE Sure, there are times when you give – because you feel like it. Other times you give because others feel like it.

OFFICER Right. And very well put too, Katie. You can't be selfish if you depend on other folks to meet the lawin. Got to come and go a bit.

KATE Oh, sure.

OFFICER 'S fact. So it is. You've had your fine times, Katie, and no harm done. Providin you aye steer clear o the docks, of course. Seamen are no particular what they bring back from foreign countries!

KATE So I've heard tell.

OFFICER Look! Just look, Katie! Does that big beamin moon up there no jist put you i' the right mood for it?

KATE The devil if it does! The moon and me have never been butties. Fact is – it kinda gives me the shivers. Away up there – watching. Aye watchin.

OFFICER Aye, it's aye on the watch. But it doesn't tell, Katie. It's discreet. And no easily shocked – it's seen so much.

KATE Mebbe. But it jalouses too much. For my liking. Gimme the flicker o lamplight. It's cosy and familiar. It doesn't seek you out – or follow around. You can move away out o its glare – and it lets you bide i' the shadows.

OFFICER Aye, very true. Still – it's a grand night. Well, well, I suppose I'd better away and rattle the doors i' Cutlog Lane. Would you no like to take a stroll up the lane wi me? It's fine and quiet there at this hour o night.

KATE *(Laughs easily)* I'll take your word for it. Goodnight.

OFFICER *(A shade regretfully)* Aye – well – goodnight, m'dear. *(He proceeds down the Vennel and KATE goes towards the High Street)*

(Enter MRS McKAY and MRS DYKES at their windows)

McKAY Lost anything?

DYKES *(Starts)* What? H'oh! It's you. I might've known. If it isn't Thomson – it's McKay!

McKAY And if't's no Tamson, it's Dykes!

DYKES I thought I 'eard voices?

McKAY You've still got the touch, Dykes. You did it. It was Kate McShane and the bobby on the beat, away up Cutlog Lane.

DYKES *(Eager)* Together?

McKAY No. Him. She's away on the prowl, but you missed yersel. They had a fine crack thegither. A' about the moon and the docks and the blankets on the man's bed.

DYKES You don't say! Is she takin h'in washin' now?

McKAY *(Snorts)* Suit her better! No – he was ettlin for five minutes, but she wasn't i' the mood.

DYKES Allow 'er. She'll give nothin away – that one. She's Scotch.

McKAY Dammit all – why should she? As I masel once said to McKay – if it means that much to you – how about givin something worthwhile in return?

DYKES *(Gives her shout of a laugh)* And did he?

McKAY I've still got his fee on my finger. Philanthropy's a' very well for them that has the siller. Though God knows, now we're at it – there's damn few wi siller i' this town that sets up tae be philanthropists. The wherewithal but seldom goes wi the warm heart! And another thing, Dykes – you Sassenachs are no over-prone to give away much yersels, but the wide side o your tongues!

DYKES Hooh! Is that so?

McKAY It's a fact. However – I agree. A sly besom. Far as she's concerned we're but sparrows peckin for crumbs on a schnorrer's doorstep.

DYKES I know. I've tried.

McKAY I've heard you.

DYKES H'i daresay. But we can guess!

McKAY No proof, but we'll get it, Dykes – we'll get it!

DYKES We certainly will, McKay, we certainly will.

McKAY No that it's any o our damn business, come to think o it.

DYKES *(Righteously)* Everything that goes on in the Vennel is our business, McKay, h'everything!

McKAY Oh – that reminds me. I was making my way to bed about half an hour ago – and I heard feet come along the street – fell quick like – and more nor one pair it seemed – but before I could throw up the window they'd turned into our close – I just caught the tail-end of a suitcase –

DYKES *(Agog)* You don't say? Who . . . ?

McKAY *(Emphatic)* And they went into McPhee's. Been expected too. The door wasn't locked. They went in too quick for that.

DYKES Are you sure, McKay?

McKAY I'm never very far out It wasn't McDougall's – that I know. *(Tartly)* I've been at McDougall for weeks to oil that damn squeaky door of hers – but no – she likes hearin it – thinks it sounds hospitable.

DYKES Hooh, *her*, but who could it be? To the McPhees?

McKAY Well – who d'you think?

DYKES *(Getting all worked up)* You don't mean – ?

McKAY I'm never very far out. You'll see the morn.

DYKES Beth? Surely to God *she'd* never venture back here?

McKAY *(Snorts)* Her? My private opinion is – and it's been made fairly public up and down the Vennel – she's capable o anything.

DYKES Agreed – agreed. There was more than one?

McKAY Seems so to me.

DYKES Surely to God 'e hasn't come 'ere with 'er?

McKAY She wasn't alone.

DYKES Well – your breath would blow me down flat?

McKAY 'Deed and it wouldn't. This isn't pay-night. Mark my word, Dykes, there's something wrong. Something byordinar i' the wind – they're no just through for a holiday wi the old folks.

DYKES I'm all the way with you, McKay! You got something.

McKAY Not yet, but I will, before the morn has aged me half a day.

DYKES And I'll give you every h'assistance.

McKAY Well – I hear McKay blowin away like a' the trumpets this side o the Jordan – I'd better get in and remind him the Happy Land is still far far away. Is Dykes bedded?

DYKES *(Scornfully)* H'oh 'im. Hours ago. And sat snorin hours before that by the fireside. No company at all.

McKAY Well – the poor man's got a hard day's darg behind him and before him. Are you no thinkin o gettin beside him?

DYKES It's many the night since *that* gave me any pleasure. Besides, Charlie isn't in yet. Is Willie?

McKAY *(Snorts)* Oh – them! Hoolets. That's what I call them. Set them a damn sight better to get out o their scratchers i' the morning and look for work.

DYKES H'oh – come now, McKay. Be fair to the boys. There's no work to be 'ad in Drumnoull. Charlie tells me.

McKAY Then how the hell do they no get out o it! Believe them if it pleases you. A rabble o feckless, heart-lazy liars – that's our sons. Well – I'll away. *This* time. *(Sniggers)* Better no stand there by yoursel, the bobby should be back any minute and if he's still struck by the moon – you'll mebbe find yoursel rowed in his blanket and carried away to the Docks. No that Dykes himsel would be over-much vexed but the Vennel would take it out of your bugle!

DYKES Well!!!!!

(McKAY retires. After a few minutes glancing around, DYKES also retires. The gang – BOOL, CHICK, JAKE, and BERT – come into view singing 'A rovin', a rovin', Ah'll gang no more a rovin' . . .' This culminates in the crescendo, 'I'll go no more a rovin'!' Simultaneously, McKAY's window clatters up and DYKES appears in her doorway.)

DYKES H'i declare!

McKAY *(Shouting)* What the ruddy – !

(Silence)

BOOL Oh – the old 'un. *(Affably)* Hullo, Maw.

McKAY What a carry on!

BOOL *(Innocently)* We was jist havin a bit o a sing-song, Maw.

McKAY *(Breathing heavily and making a deal more noise than the sing-song)* Sing-song! Oh – a sing-song, was it? You good-for-nothing fag-end o your father's eisen! I – I – d'you think we all lie abed till the sun has warmed the street corners for us?

BOOL Och, now, Maw. Control yourself!

McKAY Ooooooh!! Give me patience – God give me patience! Gin I wis near enough to draw the back o my hand from that wide mouth . . .

BOOL Now – Maw. Don't shout – it's late, you know.

McKAY You – you – come up the bloody stair! D'you hear? This very minute. What a carry on! *(Pulls head in and slams window)*

BOOL *(Unabashed – perches on an old well and chants)* 'The sergeant he paid nothin for it, but he came furthest ben o . . .'

DYKES Now, now, Willie. Don't h'aggravate your ma like that. It ain't nice.

CHICK *(In his usual polished manner)* And what the hell are you still up for?

DYKES 'Ow dare you talk like that to me, Charlie! 'Ave you no respect either for your mother?

CHICK Oh, don't give us the patter.

DYKES H'of all the cheek – you should be ashamed, Charlie Dykes.

CHICK Oh – give your tongue a rest.

DYKES Yer father's son – h'all over. That's what you are.

CHICK You should know.

DYKES I should – shouldn't h'i? To my h'everlastin shame an' sorrow – I should have known better.

CHICK Oh, for Nick's sake – save it for the old man.

DYKES I've got a good mind to lock the door on you. You – you h'ignorant h'upstart! See if I don't!

CHICK See if you do, you'll rouse up the whole ruddy Vennel.

DYKES 'Ell do I care. You and your father. Two of a kind – two of a kind, that's what I say. *(Goes in slamming door)*

JAKE Well, well – who woulda thought a bit of song would cause such a randy.

BERT We did, Jake, wis that no the idea?

BOOL Oh, Bert, surely we didn't mean to wake the Vennel i' the wee sma' hours.

CHICK Oh, no, we jist thought we'd have a ruddy good try.

(HARRY and DICK saunter in from the High Street)

HARRY (*Laughing*) We heard you comin up the High Street.

CHICK (*With the usual half-contemptuous friendly manner of his dealings with the gang*) Folks who work, you know, have got to get a little shut-eye sometimes.

BERT (*Grins*) That so – Dick.

CHICK (*Whose dislike of DICK is most cordially returned*) Well – of course, Bert – *we* had only tuppence-worth o chips to get round, no fish-suppers.

BERT (*Pleasantly*) Bloated plutocrats – regularly employed. That's what they are.

BOOL Mind you comrades – I don't envy them. My philosophy o life –

DICK (*As he strolls along the street towards Cutlog Vennel*) . . . Stinks!

HARRY (*Laughing*) One up for Dick!

CHICK He's a smart guy all right. But it's no the first time he's slipt and cut himself.

DICK (*Swinging round*) What the hell do you mean?

CHICK (*Pushing out his chin*) What could I mean?

DICK (*Stepping forward*) See here, Dykes.

BERT (*Butting in*) Take it easy, boys.

DICK Well – ! What could I do? Nothin, far as I know.

(*DICK walks away again*)

JAKE (*Murmuring*) Touchy swine.

BOOL (*Likewise*) For Nick's sake, don't cross the awkward devil.

CHICK (*Truculent*) So what? He should get round the corner where he belongs.

BOOL Funny, he didn't give up the house when his old lady signed off.

HARRY She told him no to – before she died.

CHICK How do you know?

HARRY He told me.

CHICK (*Sneers*) You're far in, aren't you?

HARRY (*Staring*) Am I?

CHICK Well paid for it?

HARRY (*Edgy*) What d'you mean?

BERT (*Hurriedly*) Oh, for Nick's sake! (*Then normally*) Sensible, I think. Keepin the house on – better on your ain than lodgins any day.

CHICK Sure. A landlady might cramp his style.

JAKE A bit lonesome, I'd think.

BOOL Me too. I wouldn't know what to do with myself – if I'd two rooms and a kitchen to do it in. I'd fa' a victim to solitary habits! You know what I mean, boys.

BERT Sure, I share the same lavatory on the stairheid.

(*KATE comes in from the High Street and passes*)

CHICK & BOOL *(Together, respectively)* Hello, Kate. Night night, Katie!
KATE *(Going towards the close)* Hullo, there. *(She comes face to face with DICK at the close-mouth)*
DICK *(Smoothly)* Fine night, Miss McShane.
KATE *(Curtly)* There are blots on the landscape. *(Goes up the close)*
DICK Ach – don't be too hard on yourself.
JAKE *(Sniggers)* He doesn't rate high in that airt, either.
CHICK Nor she in his.
BERT Can't blame *him*. By Nick, no! Got it in for her all right. And some day – given half a chance – he'll crack her wide open. Seven and a tanner a week for going on five years!
JAKE *(Sniggers)* And nine still to go. Better him nor me!
HARRY *(Alert)* How? Was that . . . ? Oh, the kid! But what had she . . .

(DICK begins to stroll back again)

BERT Shut up, Harry.
DICK Here comes a cop.
BOOL Oh – it wasn't me! *(Pretends to hide behind the lamp-post)*
CHICK Ruddy fool! *(To DICK)* So what? There's no law against standin roon a lamp-post.
DICK *(Blandly)* There should be . . . wi your kind.
CHICK *(Pushing out the chin)* Look here, Marshall . . .
BERT Quiet there!

(POLICE OFFICER passes through High Street)

BOOL He was just burstin for a crack wi us. I'll bet he's lonely.
BERT *(Laughs)* Oh – take him away up Cutlog Lane.
BOOL He hasn't got what I take. Now Harry . . .
HARRY *(Laughing)* . . . You go to blazes.
BERT *(Making a move)* Far as Bool is concerned . . . no a bad idea. I'm off to bed.
BOOL *(Skipping along)* Wait for me, Bert. I'm scared going up that stair masel. Katie might be lurkin about.

(They go up No. 9 together)

JAKE *What* a carry-on! *(As DICK hands him a fag)* Oh – you know what young Pat McPhee was tellin me this mornin?
CHICK How the Nick could we?
JAKE *(Huffily)* Okay, okay. I can save it. Just a bit o gossip.
CHICK *(Grinning)* Oh get it off your chest, Jake.
JAKE Oh. Well. Pat was tellin me, Jimmie's lost his job i' Glasgow, and the old man has told him to come home for a while. He's expected any day now.
CHICK That a'? Now . . . had it been Beth who'd lost her job –

212

DICK *(Disgusted)* Heaven help her if ever she shows face hereabouts. They'll tear her apart.

JAKE Well – anybody who does what she did.

DICK *(Contemptuously)* There's damn few o you with any room to speak. She was just unlucky.

CHICK *(Sneers)* That so? Some are.

DICK *(Turning on him)* Meaning?

CHICK *(Half truculent – half expostulating)* Can I no open my trap without being accused o settin it for you?

HARRY *(Rushing in)* Been away two-three years, hasn't he?

JAKE Think so.

HARRY I mind. He's two years older than me. Makes him about twenty now?

CHICK Thereabouts. Decent kid, Jimmie. The quiet sort. Never had much to say. No like some brought up in the Vennel. But mebbe Glasgow'll have brought him out.

JAKE Sure. Another one out o the Vennel on the Buroo.

DICK Tough luck on his old man. Three to feed already.

CHICK Shoulda chucked gettin 'em sooner than he did.

JAKE Oh, rather! But I'd like to see Beth appear at the close-mouth some morning. Skin and fur, boys – skin and fur!

CHICK For Nick's sake. You've got your old girl beat to a frazzle. *(Going)* And *that's* sayin something.

(Door slams behind him)

JAKE *(Stung)* Some blasted night I'll – I'll hit that swine between the eyes. *(Going towards No. 11)*

DICK *(Ironic)* Better chib him, Jake – it'll be safer.

JAKE *(At door)* I will, too! *(Goes in)*

HARRY *(Laughs)* What a bunch.

DICK Y'woulda been no great loss had the stork dropped 'em down the Foundry lum.

HARRY You know, Dick – considerin what you think o them – it beats me why you hang around. You don't even live i' the Vennel!

DICK *(Smiles at him)* First close round the corner. Two stairs up. *You* should know.

HARRY *(Edgy)* I – I – of course. *(Recovers)* Daft. Well. I suppose I'd better slip away up No. 13.

DICK What's a' the hurry?

HARRY Hurry? Round about one o'clock? I've work to go to the morn.

DICK So've I. You can skip it.

HARRY *(Laughs)* Tell that to my Auntie Liz. Holy mackerel! I can hear her.

DICK That naggin bitch. Tell her to raffle herself.

HARRY Often feel like it.

DICK It'll come. Some day.

HARRY And out I'll bounce on my behind.

DICK *(Softly)* So what? You can always come round and share my bed. Couldn't you?

HARRY *(Edgy)* I – I suppose so.

DICK Sure thing.

HARRY Well. I – I'd better get goin.

DICK *(Quietly)* Seems you've been avoidin me a' night, young 'un.

HARRY *(Pretending surprise)* Avoidin you? Holy smoke! Hardly been out o step since eight o'clock. You took me to the Alhambra – had a daunder through the park – met the gang – had chips. Don't be daft, Dick!

DICK *(Watching him – still quiet)* Mebbe no exactly avoidin. But every time we looked like being left by oursels – you seemed edgin to be elsewhere – i' the crowd.

HARRY Ach – go away. You imagine things. Honestly!

DICK Mebbe. Mebbe no. I'm no a thought-reader – but when someone's – close to me . . . *(Breaks off)*

HARRY But you've done nothin – I . . . What's wrong, Dick? I just can't follow you.

DICK *(Still outwardly casual)* No? What's worryin me is – what's up wi you?

HARRY *(Still trying to bluff)* Nothin. I keep on tellin you. Damn all! I – I just said I'd better get home.

DICK *(Shrugs)* What's the rush? Come on round, young 'un. We'll have a cup o char.

HARRY *(Losing his grip)* No – no – honestly, Dick. No at this time o night.

DICK *(Pulling at his arm)* You've been later. Come on.

HARRY *(Pulling away)* No. I'll come up some other night – mebbe the morn – honest I will – but –

DICK Come on round for half an hour.

HARRY *(Pulling free)* No. Ach don't – don't –

(DICK stands quietly looking at him – Harry turns his head away)

DICK What are you scared about?

HARRY I'm no scared. You know that. I – I just don't want to. Tonight.

DICK *(Still quiet)* I see. Runnin out on me.

HARRY *(Petulant)* Don't give us that. You know it isn't true.

DICK *(Suddenly flaring up)* Why the hell can't you be honest? Don't I deserve that much?

HARRY Ach – there's no use talkin.

DICK *(Controlled – bitter)* No? I'd rather talk than think. You can control things better. *(Quietly, tensely, yet always with a calculated undercurrent grappling for sympathy)* There's an eternity o time for turnin mysel outside in – round the corner. And no-one to take stock. To hold in evidence against me – or use as a future good conduct medal. Who wouldn't be me? Folks envy me – don't they? Sure. I've got everything. Everything. And nobody to share it wi. Nobody – o my own. Responsible for nobody. Accountin to nobody. Well off? I don't know I'm livin. Isn't it the God's truth?

HARRY *(Moved)* Dick – stop it. For Nick's sake.

DICK Folks o one's own. You take 'em for granted – when you have them. They may nag and irritate and interfere at times – get in the way when you want to feel free and independent-like – asking awkward questions and expectin honest answers – laying down the gospel accordin to *their* young days – when you want to live it accordin to yours. But – they're your folks. They belong – and you belong – for keeps. You're close to them – in the quiet places o their hearts and minds, in the sweet and small things o their lives – the steadfast moments, the best and lastin moments. When you're down in the dumps, they understand. When you're jumpin sky-high, their hearts quicken too. But me. Me! I can do without a' that. It passes by and leaves me unmoved. What am I losin? Damn all. Human companionship comes to me at street corners is – or lounging across the bar at the White Horse. Once it moves on – I drift out o sight. And the bloody blindin loneliness o it!

HARRY Give over, Dick. For heaven's sake. You mean more nor that to – to me.

DICK You're showin it – aren't you? If God – *(Suddenly tired)* ach, what's the use – passin the buck even to Him gets one nowhere. It may – at the final reckonin – but no here – no among the passers-by. I'm sorry, kid. You believe me, Harry – don't you? I – I didn't mean to crowd you into one o my dark corners. Honest – Blame me – if it helps. But – don't hold it against me – don't hate the sight o me. Not always anyhow. I – it meant something to me. And I shan't forget.

HARRY *(Rallying him)* Ach – shut up, Dick. You dunno what you're sayin. *(Catching him by the arm)* Come on. Let's go.

DICK *(Making to pull himself away)* No. If that's the way you feel.

HARRY *(Persisting)* Come on – it's gettin late.

DICK No, kid. You'd better get home.

HARRY *(Slipping his arm through DICK's and pulling him towards the High Street)* Come on – we'll be here a' night. For Nick's sake, what made you blow up? *Come on!*

DICK Ach. *(They go out)*

(Slow fade out)

Scene 2

Daylight. DICK MARSHALL rides in on bicycle. Props it against shop window and, as he turns, ALEC STEWART comes out of the shop.

DICK There you go, Alec.
ALEC Oh – hello. Oh – *(Hesitates, glancing round)* Dick, would you do me a favour?
DICK Be glad to.
ALEC I'll have to be gettin back. *(Produces letter)* Would you post this registered letter for me?
DICK Sure.
ALEC It's – it's to – to Lizzie Bradley in Glasgow. A – an old cousin o mine. I send her a sma' thing occasionally. See?
DICK *(Putting letter in pocket)* I see.
ALEC *(Jocose)* But it wouldn't do to let herself know. *(Jerking head in direction of his wife's shop)*
DICK *(Nods)* I get you. Cheeroh.
ALEC *(Going)* Cheeroh, Dick! And thanks!

(DICK goes into shop. MRS McPHEE and JIMMIE come from close and move towards High Street. She is carrying shopping-bag and, taking out purse, hands JIMMIE money.)

McPHEE Take this, Jimmie.
JIMMIE Ach, its all right, Mother.
McPHEE Here – you can't be without a smoke.

(DICK comes out of shop)

DICK Hello, Mrs McPhee, how's things?
McPHEE Oh, hello, Dick. Not so bad.
DICK Good! And – is this our James?
JIMMIE *(Grinning)* Hello there!
DICK *(Eyeing him up and down)* Well – who'da thought it?
McPHEE Aye. He's changed – hasn't he?
DICK You're tellin me.
McPHEE Well – I'll away, Jimmie. *(She goes)*
JIMMIE Right-o, Mother.
DICK Somebody's certainly tellin me.
JIMMIE I hardly thought you'da bothered to recognise me at a'.
DICK How come?
JIMMIE Well – you seldom appeared aware o my existence before I went away.
DICK Far's I can mind – you was just a quiet wee squirt. No lookin much and sayin less.

216

JIMMIE *(Laughs)* Thanks – handsome!

(They grin at each other – or maybe make a pass at each other – in obvious friendship)

DICK You've certainly blossomed out.

JIMMIE Well – best part of three years.

DICK In the big city too. Havin the time o your young life.

JIMMIE You've got me wrong, Dick. I'm no the kind that sets much store in havin – a fine time.

DICK Oh, *no*! *You*'ll find Drumnoull damn dull – after Glasgow. You won't stick here long.

JIMMIE Don't expect to, for other reasons. A job will be easier to get there.

DICK Oh – sure! You stick to that reason, kid – it's good. But you'll have to go slow with the talent while at home.

JIMMIE Easy matter – that. Women play little part in my life.

DICK *(Softly)* So? How come?

JIMMIE *(Laughs)* Just not interested. Mebbe I've seen too much of the trouble that follows in their wake.

DICK *(Sober)* I wouldn't let what's happened get me down, kid, if I was you. You've your own life to play with.

JIMMIE *(A shade grim)* That's just it. I don't intend playing with it. What happened in our family taught me *that* much.

DICK Oh – why the hell did you go after her? What good did it do?

JIMMIE Somebody had to. The old man couldn't throw up his job. Somebody had to make shift to find her. When I did – best thing seemed to be to stop by her. She needed somebody in her condition.

DICK You – a kid of seventeen!

JIMMIE *(Easily)* Surprising how quickly you grow up when you've to shoulder somebody else's responsibilities.

DICK Ach – so bloody unfair. Look what it's snaffled from you. Three years . . .

JIMMIE Oh, it wasn't Beth I thought of. It was to help the old folks.

DICK M'mm? How did you leave her? Okay?

JIMMIE *(Grimly amused)* I didn't. She's here. And the kid.

DICK *(Stares)* In the Vennel?

JIMMIE Came back with me, last night.

DICK Heaven help your mother when it leaks out.

JIMMIE *(Sober)* It already has. What could I do? After being paid off, she wouldn't stay by herself.

DICK Beth has certainly played merry hell with the McPhee family.

JIMMIE *(Bitter)* Somebody played merry hell with her.

DICK *(Eyes him keenly)* Has she ever said who?

JIMMIE *(Shrugs)* Never asked. No more nor we did then.

DICK Probably good reasons for sayin nothin.

JIMMIE She has. They come every week in a registered letter from Drumnoull.

DICK *(Starts – but says nothing)* Oh??? *(Pause)* Listen, kid – don't let this rotten mess get you all twisted up inside.

JIMMIE I try not to. But I'll take damn good care it doesn't happen to me.

DICK *(Grins)* You're not as dumb as I always imagined.

JIMMIE *(Likewise)* You never imagined anything. A pimply-faced wee squirt.

DICK You sound peeved. Looks as if I'll have to make up for it now.

JIMMIE *(Not sure)* I – I wish you would, Dick.

DICK Eh?

JIMMIE I can't see myself running around with the gang.

DICK Oh – them! No. Okay. It's a deal. *(Struck)* I only hope to God I don't run you off the straight and narrow.

JIMMIE *(Laughs)* No fear of that, you're safe enough.

DICK *(Softly)* I wonder? *(Then, casually)* Oh – what did Beth call herself in Glasgow?

JIMMIE *(Shakes his head)* A regular old wife, Dick! She skipped by as a Mrs Bradley.

DICK *(Shrugs)* Bradley? Fair enough! *(St John's starts to chime the half after eleven)* Dear God – listen! I told the boss I was just slipping out for fags – be back in two puffs. *(Rushes for his bike)* Be around tonight?

JIMMIE I suppose so.

DICK *(Grins at him as he swings off)* Better be – squirt!

JIMMIE *(Sauntering down street after him)* Cheeroh – handsome!

(Enter MRS McKAY and MRS THOMSON)

McKAY *(Without glancing around)* You should take something for it, Tamson. Or no open your mouth so often.

THOMSON *(In no way offended)* Fine day, McKay.

McKAY Get your share o it.

THOMSON Can't complain.

McKAY *(So surprised that she stops rug shaking)* Well-ll! Oh – here she comes.

(DYKES has now appeared in her doorway)

DYKES H'oh – it's you kickin up a dust.

McKAY Aye – it's me. *(Vigorously shaking her rugs)* And there's a damn lot more in them than I thought.

DYKES And it's h'all goin into my 'ouse.

McKAY Then shut your door.

DYKES *(In no way put out)* Thomson, did you ever know such a woman?

THOMSON Oh – her bark's worse nor her bite.

DYKES Not so sure o that – I've seen her showin her teeth.

McKAY I was dragged up in a hard school, Dykes, and by the look o them – so wis my rugs. Another shake or two and there'll be little left but a hantle of fluff, floating down the Vennel. *(Stops)*

DYKES That's life, McKay – 'ere today and where tomorrow?

THOMSON Goodness knows. I sometimes wonder. Wherever it is we can hardly be worse off.

McDOUGALL *(Suddenly appearing at close-mouth behind them)* There you go again. The Book o Doldrums, Chapter 13.

McKAY It's you – McDougall.

McDOUGALL As large as life. I'm movin in on Teenie. Been in the shop the day, anybody? What sort o mood is she in?

DYKES She was very sharp with me this morning, h'i must say.

McKAY *(Sly)* How much is there down against you in the book?

DYKES *(Annoyed)* No more than most.

THOMSON She goes beyond the score at times, I think. She knows fine how we're all placed.

McDOUGALL Well, well – I suppose she's got to pay for her stock. And if she doesn't get the cash in . . .

McKAY *(Tartly)* She can delve in her stockin!

DYKES And she won't get to the bottom of it in a 'urry.

McKAY What maddens me is goin in there and bein civil.

McDOUGALL Askin how's her back the day?

McKAY And if she had a better night last night?

DYKES As if we cared a damn.

McDOUGALL And a' for a loaf and a tin o sardines. Or something.

THOMSON Aggravatin's no the word for it.

McDOUGALL Especially when she says – 'Can ye no make do wi half a loaf' and 'D'you no think sardines a luxury just now?'

THOMSON *(Greatly daring)* It's a wonder she doesn't say something about your drop o beer, Dykes.

DYKES *(Outraged)* What? I've walked down this street at noon and at dusk for twenty years with my jug – *h'and* h'i'll continue to walk h'it and may God preserve the person that tries to stop me!!

THOMSON *(Drawing back)* Oh – I didn't mean that you'd no right – far from it. Nobody has any business.

McDOUGALL *(With malice aforethought)* That's right. Live and let live. Here's McPhee.

(Enter MRS McPHEE)

McKAY Fine day, McPhee.

McPHEE It is that. Fine.

McDOUGALL How's your leg the day?

McPHEE Oh – it's a bit easier thanks.

219

DYKES *(Effusively)* Thank God for that, Mrs McPhee. H'i sympathise. Sciatica's a nasty thing.

THOMSON Very true. And how's a' wi ye the day, McPhee?

McPHEE Oh – fine, thanks – fine.

McKAY See you've been to the butcher's.

McPHEE Aye, I wis round for something for the dinner.

THOMSON *(Meaningly)* Aye, no doobt you would be wantin something extra the day.

McPHEE I – I have a lot of mouths to feed.

McDOUGALL *(Pleasantly)* 'Deed an' ye have, Jeannie.

McKAY *(Tired of all this finesse)* See you've gotten Beth hame?

McPHEE Aye. She – she's back.

THOMSON I hope it wasn't a shock to you?

McPHEE No. Oh no. We – expected her. With Jimmie.

DYKES Now, isn't that nice.

THOMSON So it is. A fine time of the year for a holiday too.

McPHEE So – so it is.

McKAY Well – after all this time away – she'll be stoppin two or three weeks.

THOMSON Oh, I hope so. I'm lookin forward to seein her.

McPHEE She – she'll be bidin a wee while anyway.

DYKES Now, isn't that grand?

THOMSON And how is she?

McDOUGALL *(Bowling them over)* Looking fine! I was speaking to her on the landing this morning. *(Blandly ignoring glares)*

McPHEE *(Nods)* So she wis sayin, McDougall.

McKAY *(Snorts)* First we've heard of it.

THOMSON And how's the bairnie?

McPHEE *(Little more sure)* Fine – fine. A bonny wee thing. Her grandfather's fair taken with her.

DYKES *(Heartily)* I'm sure he will be. God bless 'im an' the little darlin too. The first grandchild.

THOMSON Amen to that.

McPHEE *(Seeing a way of escape)* Well – I'll away and get on.

THOMSON 'Deed aye, a body can't put off time in the forenoon. Goodness knows I sometimes wonder how I manage to get through a' that's to be done.

(McPHEE goes into her house)

McKAY Dod aye. I should be gettin on myself.

McDOUGALL *(With a certain satisfaction)* Well. That's that. No much there for you.

THOMSON I wonder at McPhee bein so tight. How can a body sympathise when she'll no tell what's ado?

DYKES It's h'exasperating.

McKAY No – didn't commit herself too much. Now what brings that besom back here after a' this time? That's what vexes me.

THOMSON And to think – after three years we still don't know the man's name.

DYKES Yes, Thomson, that's what strikes me.

THOMSON They are bound to know.

McDOUGALL *(Laughs)* An awful thought! Might be anybody in the Vennel. Even our own sons or our neighbours' husbands.

(General consternation)

McKAY That a joke?

McDOUGALL Mmmm? No! A remark we can all take to our hearts, mysel as well. It might be anybody, McKay – and don't jalouse I know more than the next.

McKAY Mebbe no. But what did you mean by holdin out on us? Meeting *her* on the stairheid *(Snorts)* jist by chance!

McDOUGALL *(As she moves to shop)* Oh, when it comes to gossiping about the Vennel – I can't claim absolution, but I'm real sorry for Jeannie McPhee. A decent hard-working soul that's done small harm to anybody. *(Goes into shop)*

McKAY *(Sneering)* The sympathetic neighbour. Gettin' a' the titbits for herself.

THOMSON That's no right o McDougall.

DYKES Not playing the game.

(Enter MRS WATT – buzzing along from No. 13 in full spate, superior titters and all)

WATT Good morning to you, you're all real busy-like.

DYKES And where are you off to, Watt?

WATT Oh, I'm jist slippin to Teenie's to see if she has any custard.

McKAY *(Aggressively)* Don't bother to slip – march in wi a clatter. She'll no consider custard a luxury for you.

WATT *(Sniggers)* Well, if I'm willin to pay for it . . . *(Skips away)*

(McKAY picks up rug and attacks it with venom)

McKAY Give me patience. God, give me patience wi that woman. It's a sma' thing to pray for – patience. Or else!

THOMSON Is that no nasty o her?

DYKES Throwing h'our poverty h'in h'our faces.

McKAY *(Shaking hell out of rug)* It's no our poverty bein thrown in our faces, it's being slapped across the trap wi her prosperity.

(McDOUGALL comes out of shop. McKAY rests from her labours.)

THOMSON Goodness knows she can afford small luxuries.

McDOUGALL *(In full spate)* Oh dear – oh dear. You'll have to show more responsibility to me, Mrs McDougall. I've got to meet my travellers' accounts every week, you know. *I* can't get credit for ever, you know. And you know your account is runnin up – runnin up – runnin up. *(Normal)* I declare to heaven she made me half believe it's grown steeper nor the spires o the kirk o St John's.

McKAY *(Heartily)* Advise her to jump the steeple after it. It might cure her backache.

McDOUGALL Get thee well behind me! *(With satisfaction)* However – I got a loaf, a bit boiled gammon, and two-three odds and ends. I don't mind a sermon if I get my deserts at the end o it.

DYKES *(Skirls)* That's 'ow to look h'at h'it.

McKAY *(Snatches up another rug)* Patience, women – patience!

(WATT returns)

DYKES Well? Get it?

WATT *(Complacently)* Of course. If I didn't get what I wanted from Teenie, I wouldn't be slow of shifting my custom.

McKAY *(Dazed)* Just like that?

McDOUGALL *(Laughs)* Often feel like patronising another grocer's myself. But I'm no sure what *that* would get me.

WATT Well, of course – she's no runnin a business for the charity of it – is she?

THOMSON *(Huffily)* I'm no complainin. But I've never passed her door this many a year.

McDOUGALL In good or bad times. I agree, Tamson.

WATT Well, I'd better away. Making beef olives for the dinner. I don't want *them* to burn. Too expensive a dish for that. *(She titters off)*

THOMSON Dear me – you're right there. Beef olives!

DYKES *(Likewise stunned)* Beef h'olives!!!

McDOUGALL And why not? She's a man, a sister, and young Harry, a' bringin in the wherewithal. It's the reward o a well-doing family.

THOMSON *(After a second – giving her time of getting out of earshot)* Well – goodness knows, that's one thing *she* can't brag about.

McKAY *(Snorts)* McDougall's a' there. Allow her. Nobody in the Vennel is better than she for holdin out a poor mouth to look upon the bright side. She can get a damn lot more out of that shop than you nor me.

DYKES McKay, I've thought that often.

THOMSON And you'll mind too – though I'm far from envying anybody their good fortune – McDougall himself has a pension from the war that's bound to help.

McKAY It helps him to raise his elbow.

DYKES And she's not far behind.

THOMSON And look at Robert. Going out at night helping his good-brother to whitewash kitchens, and drawin the dole. Now, that's no fair.

DYKES Shouldn't be allowed. It's breaking the law. Our boys don't do that.

McKAY They're too damn lazy.

THOMSON Oh, now, McKay. *(Turning to go)* Well, it's neither boiled gammon nor beef olives – I'll away and hot up yesterday's kale.

DYKES Now Thomson, don't grumble, don't complain. I wouldn't say no to a drop of your good broth.

THOMSON *(Ignores the hint)* Complain? Me, Dykes? That's the last thing anybody could lay at my door. *(Goes off)*

McKAY It's the first thing the Vennel would throw in her teeth.

DYKES With justification. The woman's face is never straight.

McKAY Like a Christmas card – aye greetin. An' what the so-and-so has she got to grumble about? Tell me that? Himsel and Molly workin?

DYKES And h'every penny 'anded h'over. Not a bigger 'enpeck in the Vennel. An' look at that poor kid, scrubbing, ironin, cleanin – every night. After 'er day's work. It's a shime.

McKAY A lassie o eighteen turned into a skivvy. So that *she* can gossip from sun-up to sun-down.

DYKES A bleedin shime.

McKAY And that big lazy devil, Jake, neither work nor want.

DYKES A puppy. If h'ever there was one. Better dressed than some working regular.

McKAY The apple o her eye. Always was. And the way he talks to his father – she backs him up.

DYKES McKay – know what? My 'eart bleeds for that poor man. No 'ome life at all. If that pansy was mine I – I'd show him different.

(BOOL and CHICK stroll in from the High Street)

BOOL Oh – hullo, Maw! Doin your rugs?

McKAY *(Snorts)* If you wasn't a lazy good-for-nothing sod, you'd be doing them for me.

BOOL *(Pretends to be aghast)* What – me? In the middle of the Vennel shaking rugs? Oh, Maw – think of my manhood.

McKAY Your what?

DYKES *(Skirling)* Now, Willie, you haven't proved that yet, have you?

McKAY Heaven help the limmer that lets that loud-mouthed coof tumble her. *(Gathering up her rugs)* What brings you in about anyhow?

BOOL My stomach.

McKAY *(Going)* The pity of it – as old Mother Hubbard used to say.

(BOOL goes cheerily up close behind her. DYKES turns to indoors, CHICK following.)

CHICK *(To DYKES disappearing)* Hey! Old 'un – what about a bob for Woodbines?

DYKES What?

(As they go, JIMMIE McPHEE saunters in by way of Cutlog Lane and meets MOLLY BROWN coming in by way of the High Street)

JIMMIE Hullo – it's – it's Molly Brown?

MOLLY *(Shyly – she's that kind of girl, remember)* Hullo, Jimmie. I – I knew you at once.

JIMMIE *Did* you? Takes me all my time to recognise *you!*

MOLLY Oh? Why?

JIMMIE You – you're different. Last time I saw you, you wis only a school kid.

MOLLY Ach, you wasn't much more.

JIMMIE Wis I no? Guess we've both grown up.

MOLLY I – I would have recognised you anywhere.

JIMMIE Aye. You spotted me right away.

MOLLY Surprised?

JIMMIE Sure.

MOLLY Why?

JIMMIE Don't know.

MOLLY *You've* changed in some ways. But – you're just the same.

JIMMIE Funny – you're the only one who seems to think so. With everybody else I've – blossomed in the dust.

MOLLY Oh – well. Mebbe *they* think so.

JIMMIE But not you?

MOLLY You're just as – as I imagined.

JIMMIE Oh – sure. And I bet this is the first time in years I've crossed your mind – because I happened to come in sight.

MOLLY *(Earnest)* No, Jimmie, that's not the way of it. I've thought of you more nor once.

JIMMIE *(Sounds bucked)* Have you? How come?

MOLLIE Just because.

JIMMIE Because what?

MOLLIE Because.

JIMMIE Don't give us your patter.

MOLLY Ach, I get small chance for that kind of practice.

JIMMIE Ach, now, Molly – Don't crowd me. I've got eyes in my head.

MOLLY Meaning?

JIMMIE Not flattering myself, but I see something other fellows don't.

MOLLY It wasn't patter – I wasn't just passing the time.

JIMMIE You really mean it, Molly?

MOLLY Why not – Jimmie?

JIMMIE You actually did give me a passing thought?

MOLLY Well – we've – known each other a long time.

JIMMIE Sure. Ever since we was kids. Heavens – I'm just beginning to realise that. Funny.

MOLLIE *(Perhaps realising things are moving rather quickly)* And how are you, Jimmie?

JIMMIE Okay. And you?

MOLLY *(Laughs)* Oh – as long as I'm working I'm not a burden.

JIMMIE I get you.

MOLLY Of course, I'm a worry and responsibility – so easy for an orphan to take the wrong turning.

JIMMIE Oh, sure. Does she think you go too often to the jigging?

MOLLY The *dancing*? I've as much chance as a garden party at Hollywood!

JIMMIE *(Stares)* Do you never get off the chain at all?

MOLLY Not so's you'd notice it.

JIMMIE *(Crafty)* What does your boyfriend say to that?

MOLLY Nothing.

JIMMIE *Nothing*?

MOLLY He – he hasn't turned up yet.

JIMMIE Oh? – Does she scare them all away?

MOLLY Mebbe – mebbe it's more than Auntie's fault.

JIMMIE Explain yourself.

MOLLY Mebbe I've already got somebody in my mind.

JIMMIE I see – you're not the sort that goes linkit in the park in the moonlight.

MOLLY Too many in the Vennel strolled that way.

JIMMIE *(Suddenly coming down to earth)* God – you're right there.

MOLLY *(Quickly)* Jimmie – I'm sorry – I wasn't thinking.

JIMMIE *(Smiles)* It's okay.

MOLLY It was thoughtless of me.

JIMMIE It's okay.

MOLLY *(Rather breathless)* I – I thought it was fine – the way you – went after your sister and – and stood by her all this time.

JIMMIE Oh – that.

MOLLY Few brothers would. But it's – it's just what I would have expected you to do.

JIMMIE *(Grins)* Heh!!!

MOLLY It was a fine thing you did. She should think a lot of you. I – I know I would.

JIMMIE Where did you get this opinion of me?

MOLLY *(Drawing back)* I – I'll better away for my dinner – time's gettin on.

JIMMIE *(Eager)* When'll I see you again?

MOLLY *(Softly)* Sure you want to?

JIMMIE Can hardly wait.

MOLLY You're chaffing?

JIMMIE *(Suddenly serious)* Mebbe aye, mebbe no. Remains to be seen.

MOLLY *(In a little rush)* Oh – I – I'm glad you're back.

(Turns quickly and goes into THOMSON's)

JIMMIE *(Calling)* I'll be waiting. *(Stands looking for a second and then goes up close whistling cheerily)*

(DYKES comes out with her jug in hand, followed by an angry CHICK. HARRY comes in from High Street on way home.)

DYKES Not one bean – won't give you nothin. You'd take my last penny.

CHICK *(Lounging in doorway)* Oh, give it a rest.

DYKES What? *(As she passes HARRY)* The living spit of his father to my shame and sorrow. *(Goes off)*

CHICK *(To HARRY)* Got a fag?

HARRY *(Grinning, hands one over and passes by)* Don't rile your maw.

CHICK G'an nick yourself.

CURTAIN

Scene 3

Daylight. MRS WATT comes along the street and goes into shop. MRS THOMSON comes to door and watches her. After a second, KATE McSHANE comes out of close.

THOMSON Oh – there you go, Katie.

KATE *(Turning – pleasantly)* Oh – hello, Mrs Thomson.

THOMSON And how's things wi you the day?

KATE *(Shrugs)* Sib to yesterday – and this time last week – and very likely this time next month.

THOMSON Dear me, aye. It's a poor existence we lead these days. You'll no have heard o anything suitable like? No prospects yet?

KATE Not a thing.

THOMSON Goodness knows what's to become o us. I sometimes wonder.

KATE It's a fact. Nothing turned up for Jake yet?

THOMSON *(Shaking head)* The poor lad's tried everywhere. I'm woe for him – trampin round the town day after day.

KATE *(Tongue in cheek)* Aye. It's no very cheery.

THOMSON It's disheartening, Katie. So it is. It passes my understandin how he manages to keep up his spirits.

KATE Still, you're no so bad. Your man and Molly's working.

THOMSON Oh, we manage, Katie. Wi a struggle. I never let on to himsel just how hard it is at times.

KATE No?

THOMSON Oh no. That's no in me. Goodness knows I don't grumble. No like some o our neighbours. *(Nods her head at DYKES's closed door)* I'm no one to be spiteful o anybody, Katie, but I sometimes wonder how I keep the rough side o my tongue from that Sassenach!

KATE *(Glancing around)* Mrs Dykes?

THOMSON Oh – she'll no hear us. She's lyin down. How any workin woman ma age can take to her bed every afternoon like she does – it beats me! But there – have you ever seen the inside of her house?

KATE Me? No.

THOMSON A disgrace. A fair disgrace. Even for the Vennel. My heart goes out to the poor man. A canny, quiet-spoken creature. And such a grand job too in the Corporation Cleansing Department! The poor man can't turn around in his own but-and-ben without a volley of Sassenach oaths. And if there a plate handy . . . *(Throws up her hands)*

KATE Wonder he stands it.

THOMSON He can't make a better of it. Now. And that big gomeril of theirs. He's no lookin for work, Katie. I know that fine. Lounges about Graham's Billiard Saloon a' day. And never a civil word out o him.

KATE No use for him masel.

THOMSON Who has? The poor man has a heavy burden between the two. And away to the English Kirk every Sabbath morning! Of course she got a ton o coals last winter.

KATE *Did* she?

THOMSON Och – she's aye gettin, Katie – aye gettin. That coat o hers came aff the back o Mrs Pinkerton – the jewellery wife. And stumpin down the street twice a day wi a jug o beer! Seems to me – the less complainin you do – the more you try to struggle through on your own – the less thought o.

KATE Often that way, Mrs Thomson.

(*JIMMIE McPHEE strolls in from High Street, hesitates on seeing two women at close and parks himself by the lamp-post*)

THOMSON No – I keep my worries to mysel, Katie. Himsel's safe enough – But if Molly was to be thrown idle – or – or anything, I – well, she'd just have to fend for hersel. My dead sister's bairn too. But what could I do? I've my own to think o. Goodness knows, seems there'll be no brightness for us this side o the grave.

KATE (*Gravely*) Shouldn't think there'd be much the other side.

THOMSON Mebbe no. It's hard to tell. But we'd be away from it all.

KATE Oh well, Mrs Thomson – till then it's just – (*Shrugs*) lift up your heart and struggle up the hill.

THOMSON Awful true. And a very fine thought too. Well, I'd better no keep you, Katie – likely enough you'll have someone to meet?

KATE (*Carelessly*) Nobody in particular.

(*She strolls down street to JIMMIE. During their conversation MRS THOMSON pops in and out eyeing them.*)

KATE Hello – it's – Jimmie McPhee?

JIMMIE How's things, Katie?

KATE Oh – middlin. I heard you'd turned up.

JIMMIE Lost my job. Thought I'd come home for a while.

KATE Tough luck. Most of us are in the same boat.

JIMMIE So I hear. Are you . . . ?

KATE Been on the dole for months.

JIMMIE Too bad.

KATE (*Shrugs*) I get by. With a push.

JIMMIE Still got the attic?

KATE One thing I thank Providence for. As long as I can meet the rent I – I feel kinda safe.

JIMMIE Still – that can't be easy.

KATE Oh I'm not so bad. I saved a little in the dry days.

JIMMIE Good for you.

KATE Glad to be back, Jimmie?

JIMMIE Well – in a way. In another – no.

KATE Sure. Where you've been – you can go your own gait. That's no easy in Drumnoull.

JIMMIE *(Laughs)* You've said it! *(Taking out cigarettes)*

KATE *(Producing her own)* You'll need them. Here – have one of mine.

JIMMIE Oh – right-o. Thanks. *(Lights up)*

KATE Thanks. You've filled out.

JIMMIE Think so?

KATE Bet you'll turn many a head. If not already.

JIMMIE You've got me wrong, Kate.

KATE Listen to him! But you was aye the quiet sort.

JIMMIE Mebbe still am.

KATE Sure. Aye the worst – when you get started. *And* a way wi you.

JIMMIE *(Laughs)* You'll get me scared of mysel.

KATE No you. It's me – and my likes – who'll have to watch our step.

JIMMIE Now, Kate – you're not easy to come by.

KATE Think so? If you've come back fancy free?

JIMMIE What d'you think?

KATE M'mm – find out. Oh – *(Change of tone)* – Saw you in Sam's the other night.

JIMMIE Havin a coffee? What sort of company was I keepin?

KATE *(A shade grim)* Real cheap.

JIMMIE *(Surprised)* Eh?

KATE You was with Dick Marshall.

JIMMIE Oh – Dick? He's all right.

KATE Mebbe. For his own kind. You're not.

JIMMIE What makes you think that?

KATE I get around. So does he.

JIMMIE Where's the harm?

KATE Depends on where. And the purpose.

JIMMIE No doubt.

KATE *(With a show of friendliness)* Jimmie – I say what I think – Even if it gets me in the bad – And I like you. You're a decent kid.

JIMMIE Thanks!

KATE As far as your kind's concerned – Marshall's poison.

JIMMIE *(Protests)* Wouldn't say that, Kate. I've nothing against Dick. 'Fact, he's provin a damn good pal.

KATE Mebbe. On the surface. To further his own book.

JIMMIE Fail to see what he could hope to get out-a playin up to me!

KATE No? No, Jimmie? *(Shrugs)* Well – mebbe you haven't filled out so much after all. If you don't – I'll bet he does. He's deep – that one. With a heart as black as sin. And I'm speakin for your own good!

JIMMIE Okay, Kate. Decent of you. I'll not forget.

KATE I hope so. *(Glancing along)* Heavens! – that woman's out again.

JIMMIE It'll be annoyin. Seein – and no hearin.

KATE Let's aggravate her by saunterin round the corner. *(They move off towards the High Street)* She was sayin Jake's walked himsel off his feet lookin for a job. Can she mean round the tables in Graham's Billiard Room?

(They go off laughing. THOMSON watches them go, then turns to go indoors. No. 7 opens and DYKES appears.)

THOMSON Oh – you've got up?

DYKES I 'ave. Anything in the wind?

THOMSON Watts's been in by with Teenie this half hour and more.

DYKES Be going h'over the books together.

THOMSON I wonder at Teenie being so nasty just now. *She* can't be hard put to it. That shop's been a gold mine for years! And Alec – a foreman in the Brewery – bringing in independent of it.

DYKES It's h'always surprised me what 'e saw in her. A big upstanding man like 'im.

THOMSON Oh, he knew fine what he was about when he married Teenie McGrath!

DYKES A man like him needs something to 'ave a bit o proper fun with. Not a dried-up stick. She's older than 'im – ain't she?

THOMSON Goodness me, aye! She's no far behind masel. And he's but forty.

DYKES It ain't natural, Thomson.

THOMSON Well – it's no for me to turn over things that's mebbe but spiteful gossip. There's far too much o that sort o thing I sometimes think. But they say in the Brewery that he's no beyond a squeeze here and a tickle there – on the quiet.

DYKES Ah?

THOMSON Oh – I've heard some stories, Dykes. Whether true or no I can't tell!

DYKES Know what, Thomson? *I'd* believe them!

THOMSON And wi my own eyes – a year or two back – I've seen him at the street corners in the summer nights bandying words wi some o the lasses – Simpson's daughter, Jennie McKay and Beth McPhee.

DYKES You 'ave?

THOMSON Oh – there's been many the wink about Alexander Bradley Stewart!

DYKES You don't surprise me. I know the look o h'old Adam when I see it!

THOMSON And I've seen him having a barney wi Kate McShane. But recent too.

DYKES Don't blame 'im. What use is a woman with the backache to h'any h'upstandin man?

THOMSON Something in that, Dykes.

McDOUGALL *(Suddenly appearing in close-mouth)* No wonder my ears are ringin! *(Obviously annoyed)*

DYKES *(Stares)* What's wrong wi you?

THOMSON You seem out o sorts?

McDOUGALL It's no often. I'm fair scunnered.

THOMSON What's wrong – what's wrong?

McDOUGALL Into the middle o the week – and that stair o ours isn't washed yet!

THOMSON G'way? Whose turn will it be?

McDOUGALL Need you ask?

DYKES McKay?

THOMSON Now that's no right!

DYKES H'it's not the first time!

McDOUGALL It's happened before.

DYKES What's 'er reason?

McDOUGALL Too much bother.

THOMSON She shouldn't get away wi that. Will you no speak to her?

McDOUGALL Me?

THOMSON Oh, I wouldn't let her get away wi that. I'd speak to her.

McDOUGALL *(Bluntly)* You'd do a hell o a lot less.

DYKES *(Judiciously)* She's a difficult woman.

McDOUGALL I'm no ettlin to be bawled out before the Vennel.

THOMSON Goodness knows, she's no particular what she says. Did you hear her and himsel last Friday night?

DYKES 'Ear them? Had you been at the other end of Drumnoull you'd still 'ad a ringside seat!

McDOUGALL We hardly take notice nowadays. It starts on Friday night when he comes in wi a drop more in him nor she has and rumbles through a' the weekend.

DYKES What a life!

THOMSON Nag, nag, nag at your own fireside. Poor man.

DYKES And when she starts on Willie.

McDOUGALL Bool – he's well nicknamed. Nothing but what the spoon puts in. And that's damn little.

DYKES Look 'ow h'impudent she is with Teenie too. As if she 'ad any right to any more credit than the next!

THOMSON And look at the brazen way she pokes her nose in other folks' affairs.

DYKES She gets results, Thomson – I must say that for 'er!

THOMSON *(As if her own method has been slighted)* No doubt. There's a way o doin it though. Without givin offence.

McDOUGALL *(Laughs)* Oh aye. Saw you practisin on Kate McShane a while back.

THOMSON *(Huffily)* Oh, come now, McDougall – we just passed the time o day. *(Normal)* No prospects of a job yet. I'd like fine to know how she manages to keep that attic roof over her head.

McDOUGALL In the way we manage oursels. By payin that old bloodsucker of a factor.

DYKES But Thomson's put 'er finger on the thing that's puzzling me. No-one can go as far as she does on the Buroo money.

THOMSON Stands to reason.

McDOUGALL Then reason it out. If wishes was wild horses the Vennel woulda had her on the streets long ago. It's my belief she has a pay-poke up her sleeve. Likely enough a married man, who hasn't enough to squeeze at home. And mebbe no very far away.

DYKES I met 'er in the Co-operative yesterday morning. Two lamb chops.

THOMSON Oh, she goes to the Co-operative for *everything*! I know that. Even her groceries. She never darkens Teenie's door!

McDOUGALL Who's to fa' oot wi her for that? But it'll be a long time before you an' me, Dykes, 'll dine on lamb chops in the middle of the week!

DYKES H'or the end h'of it. McDougall, know what? There's no damned justice in this world.

McDOUGALL Dae you tell me so?

DYKES This country is the last outpost on God's fair earth of the Few!

THOMSON The Few?

DYKES The Few! The Haves! The lordly ones who inherited soil, the workin man, 'usbands. The 'aves. The 'ave don't toil – *but* they 'ave! The 'ave-nots toil – *but* they don't have! Never was so many h'exploited by so few!

THOMSON *(Dazed)* Is that a fact?

DYKES And 'ow did our Lords and Masters come to possess the fruits of the workin man's h'industry? By their h'ancestors grabbing here and snaffling there while the common man, the workin man was not h'edicated enough to realise 'ow he was being diddled!

THOMSON But the Law?

DYKES *(Scornfully)* My good woman. The workin man does not need laws to protect what 'e hasn't got! Laws are made to keep 'im in 'is proper place. And to leave to Caesar the cakes and h'ale 'e would not h'otherwise 'ave without taking h'off 'is jacket!

McDOUGALL *(Sniggering)* And what's the remedy?

DYKES H'until the h'upper classes h'of this country are rooted h'out h'and h'utterly destroyed . . .

THOMSON *(Aghast)* Surely you don't mean Leddy Scoonieburn?

DYKES 'Er? H'i spit h'in 'er face!

THOMSON Oh, I wonder at you, Dykes. A real leddy that's done a lot o good in Drumnoull since she became our MP.

McDOUGALL *(Innocently)* Was it no her that got the soup kitchen set up in the Town Hall?

THOMSON It was. A real nice leddy. And awful sympathetic. Goodness me, I heard her mysel at a meetin sayin how worried she was at a' this unemployment in the town.

DYKES *(Snorts)* She 'ad h'every reason! 'Er 'usband's got shares in the Brewery, the Dyeworks, the Linen Factory, h'ain't 'e?

THOMSON Oh, you're goin too far, Dykes. Rootin out Leddy Scoonieburn! She's awful sympathetic.

DYKES Her voice sounds the proper note all right – but does 'er blinkin 'and h'ever h'extend h'it? The deserving poor are h'always with us, says 'er ladyship – we must h'open the soup kitchen 'alf h'an hour earlier on three days a week.

McDOUGALL And the undeserving among us? Do their bellies no rattle as loudly?

DYKES You don't h'understand the h'ins and outs, McDougall. Know what? If they're undeserving that's their h'own fault. If they're the crawling kind that's h'always dutifully grateful for damned small mercies – h'it's the fault of the depression. Or something.

THOMSON Oh, I don't know, Dykes. If a body's no well doing –

DYKES Thomson, know what? You talk like the sort who go out h'in their bare feet to vote Conservative at a general h'election! What separates the goats from the sheep? A liking for most o the things that makes life worth living! A pint down the hatch now and then, a tanner treble wi the street corner bookie, something new from the shilling-a-week man, h'and the last not all paid off, a bit fried steak on Friday night with the week's rent still h'unpaid, turning h'over in bed on Sunday morning and all the bells of Christendom reminding you where you should be. H'all that. And a lot more. A bloody lot more.

THOMSON Well – there's a limit, you know.

McDOUGALL But who sets it?

DYKES H'exactly! There's a limit. Does the Scoonieburn woman and 'er tribe go by h'it? Not ruddy likely! They gamble and booze and guzzle and muck about. And who calls them to 'eel?

McDOUGALL No the Kirk anyway. It's too busy tryin to keep the Sabbath day holy – and blamin the workin class for its failure.

THOMSON But *they've* got the wherewithal!

DYKES Thomson – know what? You can spot the truth without realising h'its h'implications!

THOMSON *(Shade huffed)* I'm no so backward as a' that, Dykes. What can we do? All said and done.

DYKES We should h'organise.

McDOUGALL What?

DYKES H'organise. We should lay down the tools with the job unfinished and march!

THOMSON March?

DYKES *(Firmly)* We should march. March on the beaches, march on the streets, march up the hills. We should march forward with banners!

THOMSON *With banners?*

DYKES With banners.

McDOUGALL *(Wickedly to THOMSON)* Like the Army of the Lord.

DYKES Mark my words. The day will dawn. The workin man is being h'edicated. And *that* is the biggest mistake *they* ever made!

THOMSON Who?

DYKES The 'aves. Because – when the clear call comes – the working man will be ready. 'E will march forward –

McDOUGALL *(Sly)* With banners?

DYKES Or without. And then – and then – if the 'aves have what the 'ave-nots 'ave not – and want – then the 'ave-nots will take from the 'aves by right of might what the haves 'ave and the 'ave-nots 'ave not – and want. And *then* when the have-not 'ave what the have-nots 'ave not – then – when the master becomes the working man and workin man becomes the master – *then* –

WATT *(Dashing out of the shop in a great flurry)* Oh! Leddy Scoonieburn's round in Brown Street!! She's in the wash-house turnin the mangle for Nellie Johnstone!!!

(She dashes off towards the High Street)

THOMSON *(All agog)* G'way? Oh come on round – she'll have a crack wi us!

McDOUGALL Jings – aye! We can't be out o this!

(Both set off in a hurry)

DYKES *(Drawn in spite of her politics)* If she'd only shown a little more *practical* sympathy.

(McKAY's window goes up with clatter and out she pops)

McKAY What's wrong – what's wrong?

THOMSON *(Shouting back)* Leddy Scoonieburn!! Turnin the mangle for Nellie Johnstone!!

McKAY *(Gasps)* God give me patience – what a carry on! *(Pops in without staying to pull down window)*

(They disappear. And after a second or two McKAY appears at close-mouth, and waddles hurriedly after them, smoothing her hair, etc., as she goes.)

CURTAIN

Scene 4

Moonlight. The street is empty except for JIMMIE McPHEE kicking heels by lamp-post. BERT McDOUGALL comes out of close and moves towards him.

BERT Hello, Jim.

JIMMIE Hello, Bert. Lookin for the gang?

BERT No. Off to give my good-brother a hand for an hour or two. White-washin.

JIMMIE Better nor hangin about the billiard rooms.

BERT Sure. Aye two-three bob for my pocket. What's on your mind?

JIMMIE Don't know. Yes. I – I promised to meet Dick.

BERT Goin to the Alhambra?

JIMMIE Expect so.

BERT Lucky lad! Nobody ever thinks I'd like a night out. Cheeroh!

(He goes. JIMMIE saunters along towards close, steps back as THOMSON's door opens and she appears dressed for visiting, with MOLLY in doorway.)

THOMSON I'll away, Molly. See and no be sittin doon wi a book or something. There's a' that ironin, mind. I can't be expected to do everything.

MOLLY I'll attend to it, Auntie. Have a nice time.

THOMSON *(Stops)* Goodness me! Away to visit a poor woman that may never stand on her feet again.

MOLLY I – I just meant she'll be pleased to see you.

THOMSON No doubt. There's many the sick bed I've been welcomed at. *(Moving off in direction of High Street)* I'll no likely be back till the last tram. Now see an' no put off time.

MOLLY Oh, no, Auntie. Cheeroh.

(DYKES, jug in hand, appears from her house)

THOMSON *(Waiting)* Oh?

DYKES *(Moving along street)* You're h'off?

THOMSON Aye. I needn't ask where you're goin.

DYKES *(Skirls)* H'all one to me! *(Passing JIMMIE. To THOMSON:)* And 'ow is Mrs 'annigan?

THOMSON *(As they move out of sight)* Oh just hangin on – hangin on.

JIMMIE *(Moving quickly forward)* Molly!

MOLLY Oh, Jimmie – you shouldn't. Somebody might see us.

JIMMIE Did you get a tellin-off for bein late the other night?

MOLLY *(Smiles)* No – no to speak o. I – I said I – met a girl who worked beside me.

JIMMIE So you did – mind? You pointed her out.

MOLLY *(Dubiously)* I didn't spend an hour in the park wi her.

JIMMIE Would you rather you had?

MOLLY Oh, Jimmie! But – I'm scared. If she should find out!

JIMMIE Ach – where's the harm? Does she think to smoor a' the brightness out o your life?

MOLLY You know fine what like she is.

JIMMIE But what can she do? She'd yap a lot! But is my reputation as bad as that?

MOLLY It's – no just you.

JIMMIE I see. Orphans are so easily led off their feet – especially in the park.

MOLLY I'd better go. Somebody might come along.

JIMMIE It's early yet!

MOLLY I can't stand here, Jimmie.

JIMMIE Well – let's go for a dauner.

MOLLY Oh, no! No, Jimmie, I couldn't. Really. I – I've things to do.

JIMMIE She'll no be back till after eleven.

MOLLY *(Swithering)* Mebbe no – But – no, Jimmie – I daren't.

JIMMIE Don't want to come. That it?

MOLLY You know that's no true. I do. But –

JIMMIE If we're goin to allow *her* to come between us –

MOLLY I don't want anybody to – to do that! But – but we might be seen.

JIMMIE *(Coaxing)* It's a slim chance. Let's risk it. Molly? We'll keep to the quiet end of the park.

MOLLY I – there's so much to do.

JIMMIE Won't take you a' night. Molly?

MOLLY Maybe I could get through the ironin in an hour or so. Before she gets back.

JIMMIE I'm sure you could, sweetheart. Just for an hour. By ourselves. Hidden away from a' the lave o the world. Come on, Molly. *(Pulls her into his arms)*

MOLLY *(Struggling)* Let me go – let me go – Jimmie – Somebody –

JIMMIE *(Holding on)* To hell wi the somebodies! Are we to lay waste o our happiest hours in fear o folks who don't matter a hoot? You're mine – aren't you?

MOLLY *(Low)* Need you ask?

JIMMIE *(Likewise)* As I am yours. As I feel I've always been. As I'll always be. Yours – Just yours – Oh, Molly –

MOLLY Jim – *(A moment, then)* It's been lonely without you.

JIMMIE M'mm? Sweetheart.

MOLLY And waitin – waitin – wondering if you'd ever come back.

JIMMIE Guess somebody was watching out for us. Mebbe – mebbe a wee leprechaun sitting up aloft.

MOLLY Think so?

JIMMIE Wouldn't surprise me.

MOLLY Bless him! I'd like to thank him for't.

JIMMIE Best to do that by being happy together.

MOLLY We could be. If they'd leave us alone.

JIMMIE (*Rallying her*) Listen, you sweet little coof. We're goin to be. We'll make it so! Through a' the golden days that stretch ahead o us. Nothing – nor nobody's goin to keep us apart! From now on. See?

MOLLY I wish I could think so.

JIMMIE Oh, faint heart!

MOLLY But – Jimmie – it's this, this slippin out when nobody's about. Aye in fear o meetin someone who'll – talk. And lyin aboot where you've been. It – it's no the right way.

JIMMIE Do I like it? Or want it this way? It's for your sake! We have nothing to be ashamed of. What I feel for you – and you for me – it's no hole and corner stuff. It holds a' the promise and brightness, a' the sweetness and glaumrie o life we're ever likely to reap in this world! It needs no lies or shadiness to keep it burning.

MOLLY You – you talk like a wanderin bard, Jimmie!

JIMMIE (*Muffled, lips on her hair*) Aye. Songless for years. (*After a moment, drawing away*) Hurry, Toots. Slip on a coat.

(*MOLLY goes indoors. After a moment, returns.*)

JIMMIE (*Gaily*) Already? Scared I'd change my mind?

MOLLY No. No you. That's one thing I feel sure of.

JIMMIE From now on.

(*As they move off towards Cutlog Lane, HARRY WATT appears from No. 13*)

JIMMIE Hello, you!

HARRY (*Staring*) Oh, hello!

(*Stands staring after them. MRS McKAY comes out of close.*)

HARRY (*Still staring*) Hello, Mrs McKay.

McKAY It's yoursel, Harry.

HARRY (*Going towards High Street with her*) Out for your constitutional?

McKAY You can call it that, son. It'll take me no farther than the White Horse.

HARRY (*Chuckles*) Oh, of course, Friday night.

McKAY (*Feelingly*) Thank heaven for that. Been slower nor ever o coming round this week.

(*They pass from view. DICK MARSHALL appears, glances up to*

McPHEE's window, then goes up close whistling. Comes out looking exasperated, turns towards High Street and encounters KATE McSHANE.)

DICK *(Smoothly)* Ah? Lookin for somebody, Kate?
KATE *(Curtly)* You go to hell.
DICK There are one or two things I've got to do first.
KATE *(Indifferent)* I wish you luck.
DICK Coming from you – that does buck me up.
KATE Couldn't care less.
DICK *(Still smooth)* You will – Believe me, Katie, dear – when the time comes.
KATE *(Sneering)* Should I seek polis protection?
DICK Well – you're on fell good terms wi them. Especially the huskies on the night-shift.
KATE *(Stung)* Listen you – if you're trying to anger me . . .
DICK Is there reason I should?
KATE *(Controlled – sneering)* You think there is.
DICK *(A little more edgy)* You're tellin me.
KATE *(Laughs)* You fancy I'm scared o the likes o you? Or anything you can do?
DICK *(Barely holding temper)* We might get round to it.
KATE *(Laughing)* What a hope – what a ruddy hope!
DICK *(Giving way)* Don't be so damned sure! Even the slickest o us –
KATE Was that said from the heart?
DICK *(Roughly)* Listen you –
KATE *(Now in command)* If you'd been a man at a', Marshall, instead o what you are – you'd-a gotten over your ill-will long ago.
DICK *(Bitterly)* I've a long memory.
KATE For heaven's sake! Let it sleep!
DICK You forget there's a little something very much alive – to bring it aye fresh to mind.
KATE Do you bear it a grudge too? What has it done?
DICK *(Flaring up)* Not a thing – not a bloody thing! Except bear my name.
KATE As it should.
DICK You're a liar!
KATE You couldn't deny it.
DICK You knew – you knew!
KATE What?
DICK You bore witness against me!
KATE The least I could do.
DICK You knew. Yet you swore!
KATE I believe her.

DICK As one cow from another!
KATE *(Beginning to lose coolness)* She was my pal!
DICK *(More controlled)* A Dock Street tart!
KATE She blamed you.
DICK And you backed her up.
KATE You went about the house!
DICK *(Flaring up again)* What if I did?
KATE For what reason?
DICK You –
KATE Did you tell that in court?
DICK You –
KATE Could you tell it?
DICK You –
KATE Could her young brother?
DICK Liar!

(KATE goes into close. DICK wheels towards High Street. She watches him go. After a second, ALEC STEWART comes out of shop and locks door. KATE moves forward.)

KATE *(Softly)* Alec.
ALEC *(Wheeling round)* Oh!
KATE *(Urgently)* I saw the light. Been waitin. I must see you.
ALEC *(Glancing round, mutters)* This – this is no wise.
KATE Just a minute.
ALEC Somebody might come along.
KATE There's something I've got to tell you.
ALEC Well – meet me tomorrow at –
KATE *(Impatient)* It'll wait no longer.
ALEC If we're seen together.
KATE *(Mood increasing)* We can be passin the time o day, surely?
ALEC That's no what they'd take out o it.
KATE So what?
ALEC *(Trying to edge away)* I really haven't much time.
KATE It'll no take long.
ALEC But –
KATE Come into the close.
ALEC *(Reluctantly following her)* Damn it, it's no wise.

(To end of scene they remain just inside the close)

KATE *(Losing control)* So what? Who cares?
ALEC *(Surprised)* Damn it, Katie, what's got into you?
KATE Alec, you – you care for me?
ALEC *(Becoming himself, taking her into his arms)* Of course! Don't be daft. *(Releases her)* I'd better away, Katie.

KATE *(With more spirit)* I'm no finished yet.

ALEC *(Nonplussed)* We've been so careful to now.

KATE Have we?

ALEC Don't you think so? No a breath of gossip?

KATE *(A shade bitter)* Sure. We've been canny.

ALEC You see?

KATE About gossip.

ALEC Then why be rash and – and risk things now?

KATE *(Dry)* It's a point.

ALEC Eh?

KATE Whether we've been rash or no.

ALEC I can't fathom you at all the night.

KATE *(Softly)* No?

ALEC No like yoursel at a'.

KATE Mebbe good reason.

ALEC *(With show of masterfulness)* Come now, Katie. It's no like you to be so flighty. *(Pats her shoulder)* I'll need to go now. She'll be –

KATE *(Bursting out)* As if I cared a damn what she's wonderin.

ALEC *(Hurriedly)* Don't get angry now. Somebody might –

KATE Or anybody else!

ALEC *(Trying to smooth her down)* There, there, love. We can't stand a' night argy-bargyin. And a' about nothing, I'll wager!

KATE *(Urgent)* Alec – listen – There's something –

ALEC *(Irritated)* Well, for heaven's sake out wi it! And let me out o this.

KATE *(Flaring up)* That's a' that's worryin you. To slip away before you're seen.

ALEC Would it do us any good?

KATE What if we was?

ALEC You'll ruin everything. A' these months being so circumspect.

KATE *(Grim)* And mebbe now – even more so!

ALEC Glad to hear it! You're goin about it in an antrin way

KATE *(Catching him by shoulders, tensely)* Alec, do I mean anything at a' to you?

ALEC *(Holding her – himself again)* You mean the whole wide world to me.

KATE Do I – do I?

ALEC *(Humouring her)* Without you, Katie – life would come to a standstill.

KATE *(Clinging to him, brokenly)* Oh, Alec, Alec.

ALEC There now. Everything that means anything at a' begins and ends wi you.

KATE You mean that?

ALEC I swear to it!

KATE Do I mean more – more nor she does?

ALEC Her? What use has she ever been to me? You know that fine.

KATE But she's your wife. I'm no.

ALEC *(Releasing her – going cold)* We can't make a better o that.

KATE *(Earnest)* Can we no? No, Alec?

ALEC *(Impatient)* Oh, come, Kate. What maggot's this?

KATE Has she more right nor me?

ALEC Look now, Kate. Time's runnin on –

KATE Alec – do you love me enough to show it? That's what it's come to.

ALEC Eh?

KATE *(Urgent)* We could go away together. Edinburgh – Glasgow, anywhere. You could get a job anywhere.

ALEC *(Stupidly)* What – what?

KATE *(Mood increasing)* We could get out o it – that way. Some place where nobody knew us. Or cared. We could pass as married, and nobody the wiser.

ALEC *(Perturbed)* I – I wasn't just thinking o –

KATE *(Brusquely)* Mebbe no. No more nor me. But we gotta think – is *now*.

ALEC *(Suddenly aware and afraid)* You – you mean?

KATE We're caught, Alec. Caught – hard and fast.

ALEC *(Losing head)* My God! My God in heaven! *(Catches her roughly by shoulders)* Are you sure, woman? Are you *sure*?

KATE *(Quietly, watching him)* I've seen the doctor.

ALEC *(Releasing her)* God! What'll I do? What'll I do? What a helluva mess! *(Raging at her)* How could you be so careless? How *could* you?

KATE *(Still quiet)* Me?

ALEC Aye – you! You knew better nor that. How could you land me in this mess? God – what'll I – What a ruddy mess to land a man in!

KATE *(As before)* What about me? Am I no in it? Am I layin the blame a' on you? What about me?

ALEC Ach!

KATE Is it just yoursel that's worrying you?

ALEC Had I ever for one minute thought this again . . . *(Breaks off)*

KATE *(Staring)* It's happened before?

ALEC *(Roughly)* What if it has? That *you'd* be so damned stupid –

KATE *(Breaking in angrily)* I *was* damned stupid! You're making that clear – now!

ALEC Don't give me that! You knew what you was about. You wasn't but a lass fresh in her teens.

KATE Suppose I put mysel in your way? Offered mysel?

ALEC *(Sneering)* You didn't hang back over-much. Nor take much time to give in.

KATE Sure. My fault. I led you on.

241

ALEC *(Sulkily)* You knew I was a married man.

KATE *(Sneering)* You forgot it fell easily.

ALEC *(Cooling down – dour)* Ach. Is there no way we can get out o it?

KATE *(Calmly)* You're the man o experience.

ALEC *(Annoyed)* Don't stand there jibin. *(Calming down)* Can it no be seen to yet? Is there time?

KATE *(Slowly)* Mebbe. I – never thought o it in that way.

ALEC *(Snapping)* Then you'd better begin now!

KATE Think so?

ALEC *(Trying to be reasonable)* Come now, Katie. Misca'in each other'll no get us far.

KATE *(Grimly)* It's got me further nor I expected. In understandin.

ALEC *(Keeping a grip on himself)* Damn it all. If something can yet be done – there's no much risk wi it. For you.

KATE *(Coolly)* Oh no? It just put Jenny Laird i' Brown Street under the ground last back-end.

ALEC Ach. A strong healthy lass like you.

KATE Put that right out o your mind, Alec. No even for you.

ALEC Now – look here.

KATE Waste o breath.

ALEC Don't be so bloody dour! What are we to do then? Tell me that?

KATE *(Shrugs)* Face up to it.

ALEC I'll no tell *her*! Put that out o *your* mind!

KATE I might.

ALEC If you dare – by God! – if you dare.

KATE *(Shrugs)* She's nothing to me.

ALEC She's my wife. An' I mean that to stand.

KATE Oh!

ALEC I'm warnin you!

KATE *(Angrily)* You'll no shut my mouth!

ALEC I'll deny it!

KATE You – you –

ALEC And who'll believe *you*? Your word against mine? I' the Vennel? They lippen on her for a lot, mark you. And do they think so mighty much o you? And we've been circumspect. You admit that? *(She makes no reply, just looks at him)* Nobody yet jalouses.

KATE You – you swine!

ALEC Just try blamin me – just try it!

KATE *(Letting go)* And what does a' your fine words amount to? A' the lovin words and routh o kisses? A' the vows and the promises? Lies – lies – lies! A rotten shilpit coward. A coward and a swine. Do you hear? You're scared your fat soft life wi that wizened stick should be disturbed. Oh – you're safe wi her. Her big handsome Alec. It's been a fine sop to your rotten selfish vanity – set up on a pedestal while she fetches and carries. Her grand upstandin Alec. Her man! My God! What ever made me fancy I saw a man in an empty gutless bag o lust!

ALEC D'you want to alarm the street?

KATE *(Reckless)* The hell do I care – *now*!

ALEC *(Alarmed)* I'll away.

KATE *(Grabbing him by the arm)* No you don't! You're no leavin me to fend for mysel.

ALEC *(Almost tearfully)* I'm no ettlin to do so. If only you'd be reasonable, Katie!

KATE *(Beat)* I – I – God knows I'm no sure what I should be.

ALEC Come now, Katie. What needs we quarrel? *(Puts his arms around her)* After the fine times we've had together!

KATE Oh – Alec.

ALEC And mebbe again.

KATE If I could only think what to do.

ALEC What made you so careless-like?

KATE Oh. *(Shrugs)* Suppose because it was you.

ALEC *(Fondling)* Daft wee thing.

KATE If only we could slip away –

ALEC *(Hurriedly)* No to be thought o.

KATE *(Getting weepy)* Oh – Alec.

ALEC There, there.

KATE You – mean so much to me.

ALEC I know – I know. But look now, Katie. Stop greetin. It's gettin late. And we're still i' the middle o it. You must do something, Katie. God in heaven – *(Breaks off)*

KATIE *(Thoughtfully)* If only I could find somebody to – to –

ALEC *(Eagerly)* Aye – aye! That's an idea.

KATE Think so?

ALEC Dod aye! Some daft young gomeril. There'd be no lack o money, Katie. Mind you that!

KATE If I could pin it on somebody.

ALEC Even though you married him.

KATE Even though?

ALEC *(Pulling her back to him)* T'wouldn't make any difference between us, Katie – would it now?

KATE No – *no*! You know that.

ALEC Of course. You and me – we suit each other fine. Oh, God! Katie – I must be goin. She'll be thinkin I've met wi an accident – or something. Meet me Friday night? Eh? Usual place.

KATE A' right, Alec.

ALEC Now don't worry. You'll find a way out. We'll have many the laugh over this yet. Goodnight, m'dear,

KATE *(Heavily)* Goodnight, Alec.

(She goes up the close. He turns to go down the street. DICK MARSHALL appears.)

DICK Oh – you're late on the go?

ALEC Aye, Dick. I – I've been doin a few odd jobs i' the back shop for Teenie.

DICK I see.

ALEC I – I came out by the back door.

DICK *(Blandly)* Handy. You can slip out real canny.

ALEC So you can.

DICK *(Presumably thinking it out)* And you didn't even need to come out No. 9. Two palings and a couple-a back-courts and you're into my own close round the corner.

ALEC *(Laughs. Unsure)* Puttin ideas into my head?

DICK *(Dry)* You're a bit older nor me, Alec.

ALEC Meanin?

DICK They're a' there already.

ALEC *(Laughs, then)* Oh – by the way, Dick. That registered letter – did you post it?

DICK Eh? Oh – to Mrs Bradley – your cousin, wasn't it, i' Glasgow? I did. *(Searching his pockets)* Why?

ALEC Oh nothing. I – I found out it wasn't necessary to send it to – to Glasgow after all.

DICK Sorry to hear that.

ALEC Doesn't matter. No harm done.

DICK I'm damned if I can find your receipt!

ALEC Don't bother. It's a'right. Well – I suppose my supper'll be waitin.

DICK Lucky man. And Teenie brimmin over wi a' the day's news i' the Vennel.

ALEC *(Laughs)* 'Deed no. It's a thing she rarely turns over. Folks get married, have bairns, even pass on – it's an old song before I hear o it.

DICK That so? No scandal at a'?

ALEC Devil a bit!

DICK Better keep you posted after this. Wouldn't do if somebody out o your past ran slap into you – and you a' unprepared.

ALEC No likelihood a that. There's very little o my past wi its roots i' the Vennel.

DICK Oh? Or your present?

ALEC *(Laughs)* Nor my future!

DICK *(Murmuring)* You should sleep sound.

ALEC *(Going)* I do. Goodnight to you. And thanks!

DICK *(Looking after him)* Night. And thank *you* – for everything.

(He wanders along the street, looks up at McPHEE's window, and goes

up the close. BERT McDOUGALL and HARRY WATT enter from the High Street.)

BERT . . . Some supper and off to bed.
HARRY Appears to be a' ahead o me too.
BERT Where's the gang?
HARRY Heaven knows!
BERT McPhee's off to the Alhambra wi Dick Marshall. I know that.
HARRY Oh?
BERT Rather did your eye in there.
HARRY He's welcome.
BERT Well – cheerioh.

(Disappears up close. HARRY hangs around aimlessly. After a second, DICK comes out of close, glances at HARRY without expression and would move on.)

HARRY Oh – hello, stranger.
DICK (Without warmth) Hello.
HARRY Lookin for somebody?
DICK Should I?
HARRY Well – you're lookin a bit lost.
DICK So what? Is it your concern?
HARRY (A little bitter) Oh no. Your affairs don't concern me – nowadays. (More controlled) Do they – Dick?
DICK They don't. You can skip it.
HARRY Oh. Been prowlin around on your own?
DICK I'm used to it.
HARRY But – you – you don't like it much though – do you?
DICK (A shade rough) What the hell are we gettin? Listen – if you've anywhere to go – don't let me stop you.
HARRY Changed days.
DICK (Casually) The world wags on.
HARRY (Bitter, goading) Your world does. Though it gets jammed by a spanner now and then.
DICK (Rough) Come clean.
HARRY (Sneering) Pity you didn't get to the Alhambra the night. It's real good this week.
DICK Oh?
HARRY No doubt he thought there'd be more fun i' the park. Wi Molly Brown.
DICK (Making a grab at him) Listen, you little –
HARRY (Savagely) Lemme go! – Lemme go! – (DICK releases with a shove that almost throws him off his balance) And it isn't the first time either. He's

245

aye hangin around at dinner time too – and five o'clock. For her coming hame.

DICK *(Threatening him)* Beat it – *beat it*! Or by Nick I'll –

HARRY *(Scrambles up, muttering)* Okay, okay. *(Goes quickly out by the High Street)*

(DICK, in not at all a pretty passion, glances up and down street, starts, presumably seeing someone coming by way of Cutlog Lane, looks round, and hastily nips in shop doorway. JIMMIE and MOLLY come in view.)

JIMMIE Well – here we are again!

MOLLY I'd better no wait. Goodnight, Jimmie.

JIMMIE Okay. When'll I see you again? Tomorrow night?

MOLLY No sure. It – depends.

JIMMIE Well – can I wink as you pass by?

MOLLY *(Dimples)* I'll look the other way!

JIMMIE You will – will you? If you dare – *(Breaks off)*

MOLLY What?

JIMMIE I'll no say.

MOLLY Jimmie!

JIMMIE Keep your pecker up, old girl. We'll win through. You'll see. Even though I am but a daft young gomeril.

MOLLY *(Whispering)* Goodnight – my dear.

JIMMIE Goodnight, sweetheart.

(She goes in and closes the door. JIMMIE, very pleased with life, looks around, whistling, goes into close. DICK steps out of shop doorway. JIMMIE, in entry, presumably changes his mind, turns round and spots DICK.)

DICK And where the hell have you been?

JIMMIE *(Aback)* Oh!

DICK Thought you were to meet me at eight?

JIMMIE Oh!

DICK You forgot?

JIMMIE *(Hurriedly)* Aye – aye – I forgot.

DICK Where you been?

JIMMIE Eh – i' the house.

DICK A' night?

JIMMIE Sure. I – I was readin.

DICK You don't say? What?

JIMMIE Oh – a – a book. Of course. *(Trying to appear more at ease)* Don't be daft, Dick!

DICK Did you no hear me whistlin up the stairs?

JIMMIE N-n-no! Did you?

DICK Back o eight.

JIMMIE N-n-no. I – I didn't hear you.

DICK Must-a been deep in the book. Or was the kids kickin up a row?

JIMMIE *(Brightens)* Eh – aye, they were. A bit.

DICK No doubt. *(Quietly catching him off guard again)* What was it?

JIMMIE Eh? Was what?

DICK The book. A love story?

JIMMIE *(Trying to laugh it off)* Drop the patter. Can you see me head over heels in a love story?

DICK *(Dry)* Now you mention it – I wouldn't swear but what you are the very type for it.

JIMMIE Sorry, Dick. Honestly. 'Twas a shabby trick. I – I just clean forgot.

DICK Oh – okay. What do we do now?

JIMMIE No almost bedtime?

DICK If you feel that way, your looks belie you – you're wide-eyed.

JIMMIE *(Uneasy)* Guess it was the book!

DICK Sure. Let's go round to Sam's.

JIMMIE Ach. No i' the mood for that joint. It's too rowdy at this hour.

DICK Well. *(Eyes him for a second, then)* Come on round to the house for a cup o tea.

JIMMIE Okay!

DICK *(Moving off. Casually –)* Did you reach the last chapter?

JIMMIE Eh?

DICK The book. The love story.

JIMMIE *(Laughs)* Oh – that! No. The best bits are still to come.

DICK *(Softly)* I wonder.

(Slow fade out)

Scene 5

Moonlight. JAKE THOMSON discovered lounging by the well. DICK MARSHALL enters, somewhat hurriedly, black-browed.

JAKE *(Rising, saunters forward)* Hello!
DICK Oh – Jake. Seen Jimmie?
JAKE No since this afternoon.
DICK I – I mean just now?
JAKE Nobody's been about these ten minutes. Lookin for him?
DICK He – he was wi me a while back.
JAKE *(Curious)* Anything up?
DICK *(Taking a grip of himself)* What d'you mean?
JAKE Nothing – nothing much. Just thought you – looked a bit annoyed.
DICK Fact is – we – had an argument round i' the house. He – he cleared out.
JAKE Mebbe walkin it off. Certainly didn't come this way. *I* wouldn't worry. Not enough go in him – for me.
DICK Mebbe.

> *(MOLLY comes out of the house with a pail in her hand)*

JAKE Oh – Molly – the old girl home yet?
MOLLY No. She said last tram. *(Goes up close)*
DICK Visitin?
JAKE Moanin at a sick bed. She's good at it.
DICK I see. *(Nods towards the close)* She's blossomin out – that one. Trickly little piece gettin.
JAKE Who? Oh – Moll. Think so?
DICK *(Full of worldly good-fellowship)* No eyes in your head? High-stepper too. Or I'm no judge.
JAKE *(Interested)* Think so?
DICK Bet somebody'll make a pass at her one o these nights. If they haven't already.
JAKE *(Sniggers)* Doubt it. They'd better go easy there. Any muckin about – and she'll land i' the street. The old girl wouldn't stand for't. She's made *that* plain enough.

> *(MOLLY comes out of close and re-enters the house. They watch her in silence.)*

DICK That'll no stop some lusty lad from tryin his luck. And she'll respond. She's gettin that way.
JAKE Oh? *(Pricks up his ears)*
DICK Nice kid, too. Aye – you've certainly got something there, Jake. Beneath your own roof!

JAKE Eh? Oh – sure!

DICK Come off it, Jake. You're lookin too damned innocent. Bet you've had a squeeze before this. A' on the quiet.

JAKE *(Protesting)* Me? Heavens no –

DICK *(Can hardly believe it)* No?

JAKE No me.

DICK No even a kiss or two when you're by yoursels?

JAKE God no – I never thought o –

DICK Lord – you are slow. Fancied *you'd* more gumption in you.

JAKE *(Huffily)* I'm just as keen as the next for a bit o fun. Just never thought o her i' that way.

DICK *(Shakes his head wondering)* You'd go a long way hereabouts before findin as temptin a cherry.

JAKE *(Thinking)* Think so?

DICK *(Laughs)* Sure. Couldn't go wrong there.

JAKE Oh?

DICK *And* ripe for the pluckin. Notice the wee bit swagger in her walk? *(JAKE just stares. Amused, ironic)* No – *you* wouldn't.

JAKE *(Getting annoyed)* Well – damn it all!

DICK *(More and more amused)* Oh Jake! What a lad. There's many who'd change places wi you for a night.

JAKE How come?

DICK Heavens! A' at your own leisure. Every chance under the moon. You're sleepin, man!

JAKE *(Shrugs, bluffing)* I've looked her over once or twice – I'll admit *that*. I just don't fancy it.

DICK No?

JAKE Daresay I *could* get it any night I wanted.

DICK Think so?

JAKE *(Cocksure)* Sure thing!

DICK *(Bursts out laughing. Offensively)* Come off it! Never entered your head!

JAKE *(Getting huffy again)* Just didn't think o it.

DICK And you'd better no start thinkin.

JAKE How no?

DICK Doubt if you'd ever get past the thinkin. Mebbe just as well.

JAKE What way that?

DICK *(Goading)* Ach – confess, Jake. You haven't the guts.

JAKE Don't be so damned sure!

DICK Stick to your jiggin. It's safer. And leave that sort o ploy to your betters.

JAKE I'm no so slow as a' that.

DICK No? Just the very devil o a rip for it? *(Laughs)* Okay, Jake. Forget it. Probably wise no to fool around where your old girl's on guard.

JAKE *(A bit mollified)* No daft a' thegether.

(DICK hands him a cigarette. They light up. Then –)

JAKE Oh! Look what's comin.

(McKAY and DYKES appear in view, wending their merry way home from the White Horse. They pass the two by the lamp-post and, gradually, reach the close.)

McKAY . . . Best night we've had for long enough.

DYKES H'i've never laughed so much.

McKAY That Barney Ross. What a carry on!

DYKES Split me sides, I did!

McKAY Long as it was only your sides!

DYKES The things you say, McKay! A grand night it's been.

McKAY Does a body good.

DYKES H'exactly! To get away from it all.

McKAY Once in a while. After a', what credit do we get for knockin our pan out?

DYKES Devil a bit. Working our fingers to the bone. Day h'after day. And no more thought o than the gossips who clutter up the close-mouths. Day h'after day.

McKAY Devil a bit. A' taken for granted.

DYKES You know what, McKay? If I 'ad my time over again – there's not a blinkin man alive who'd tie me to 'is chariot wheels!

McKAY Nor me either!

DYKES Slavery. That's what it is. Wedded bliss!!

McKAY *(Snorts)* Men!! A lot o fushionless coofs at the best o it. Even i' bed.

DYKES *That*? An h'over-rated pastime!

McKAY What does it bring you? A parcel o ignorant ungrateful brats. The minute they're able to stand on their own feet – it's me an' the old folks'll never meet again on the bonnie, bonnie banks o Loch Lomond!

DYKES The Truth out of Heaven itself! Look at my Lily – after all I did for 'er!

McKAY *(Snorts)* Never looks your airt –

DYKES McKay, know this? Up to the very night of the wedding 'e 'ad his bag packed to slip off. But I kept my eye on him.

McKAY Well believe it. Wasn't much o a catch anyhow.

DYKES Is any h'of them?

McKAY And look at my Lizzie.

DYKES I haven't seen 'er down the Vennel near you this year!

McKAY Damn good job for her! If I hadn't told *him* damned straight where his heart lay – she wouldn't have a man on the dole right now!

DYKES And what was 'e – h'after all?

McKAY What's any o them, come to think o it? Look at our braw lads. The truth now, Dykes – will they ever work?

DYKES Never in their natural. Heart-lazy.

McKAY No sense o responsibility. Never a thought for old age creepin up on their poor mothers – nor that it's time we should be sittin noddin by the fire wi a wee thing for comfort on the table within reach.

DYKES Selfish – that's what!

(JIMMIE McPHEE, we shall soon realise, has been somehow shaken out of his usual placid self. He comes up by way of Cutlog Lane and tries to slip past them up the close, but McKAY bars the way. He pointedly ignores JAKE and DICK by the lamp-post.)

McKAY *(Pugnacious)* And here's another o them!

JIMMIE Oh?

McKAY Aye – oh! Comin home here and campin down on your poor old father. Has he no enough mouths to feed?

JIMMIE *(Curtly)* That hardly concerns you.

McKAY And your poor mother. When I think o what that poor body's had to face this while back –

JIMMIE *(Butting in)* Who asked you to think o it?

McKAY I have some thought for my neighbours.

JIMMIE *(Nastily)* Most o them could well spare your interference.

DYKES The impudence!

McKAY Are you to be another spendin your days i' the Billiard Rooms? That's what I want to know!

DYKES That's just what we want to know!

JIMMIE *(To DYKES)* You would. Ask that o your son. I've been workin these past three years. He's hardly done a day's darg since he left school.

DYKES If my Charlie was 'ere!

JIMMIE He's round i' the High Street. Up against Cavillini's fish-shop window. Tryin to get off wi the dames. That's the hardest o *his* day.

McKAY And that fly-by-night sister o yours – what's she doin here? Sittin indoors a' day long?

JIMMIE Aggravatin you?

DYKES What?

McKAY Her that can't name the father o her by-blow!

JIMMIE How do you know?

McKAY Can she?

JIMMIE *(Coolly impertinent)* Can you?

McKAY Me?

JIMMIE Is that no what's worryin you?

(Somewhere hereabouts KATE McSHANE slips out of close behind

McKAY and stands down beyond the old well. MOLLY has appeared in the doorway of THOMSON's. DICK and JAKE have edged nearer.)

McKAY *(Beginning to bawl)* I'm tellin you – had she been a daughter o mine –

JIMMIE You've nothing to boast o there. She was lucky you managed to fasten *hers* on some poor coof.

(BOOL and CHICK appear up the street)

BOOL Wheeeeeeeeh!

DYKES Charlie! If you 'eard the cheek –

CHICK *(Unmoved)* Probably deserved it. Get in and shut your trap!

JIMMIE You've a lot to be proud o. The lot o you. Suppose by gossipin about the McPhees you think to scoor the dirt on your own doorsteps!

(From here, everybody talks and moves in a mêlée)

McKAY Damned if I don't draw my hand from –

BOOL Hey, Maw –

DICK Jimmie –

JIMMIE *(Shaking him off)* Had enough o you for one night –

BOOL Come on, Maw – up the stair –

McKAY Let me be – I'll tell him –

DYKES Impudent puppy – Charlie – 'ow dare you –

CHICK Get inside –

(DICK shrugs and strolls off)

McKAY *(To BOOL)* Damn you –

BOOL *(Pulling her into close)* Don't be daft, Maw – come on.

DYKES Charlie! – *(He hauls her indoors)*

THOMSON *(Running along the street)* My goodness – my goodness! What's ado? What's ado?

JIMMIE *(Snapping)* Nothing byordinary.

THOMSON But what's up? What started it?

JAKE *(Grabbing her by the arm)* Come on. Bedtime.

THOMSON What are you about, Jake? Pullin *me*! What's ado? What's ado?

JIMMIE No bein able to manage their own families i' this street – they try to run other folks'. That's all.

THOMSON Dear me. Well, thank goodness that can't be said about me anyway.

JIMMIE *(Nasty)* Mind if I disagree?

THOMSON *(Gasps)* My goodness!!

JAKE *(Pulling her away)* Come on – come on.

THOMSON Well I never! What impudence! Did I deserve that? *(To MOLLY)* And what are you doin wastin your time? Inside wi you.

(The door slams, and only JIMMIE and KATE are left. She moves forward to him at close.)

KATE *(Amused)* Well! Never imagined you had it in you, Jimmie.

JIMMIE *(Grins, rueful)* No?

KATE What got into you? Wherever have *you* been the night?

JIMMIE Through hell!

KATE Oh? Trouble up the stair?

JIMMIE Eh? No – oh no.

KATE Where you been?

JIMMIE Oh – let's forget it.

KATE Something must have upset you. To bawl out old McKay.

JIMMIE No before time.

KATE Oh sure. But you was the last I thought to do it. Still, did I no say you quiet lads had the gumption?

JIMMIE *(Laughs, a shade grim)* Ach – don't give me that, Kate. Two-three times the night I've been accused o lackin it.

KATE Certainly appear to have been up against it. Smoke?

JIMMIE Thanks. *(Lights up)* God, and I have. Started too well, the night. Had too much promise.

KATE Who spoiled it for you? Beyond old McKay.

JIMMIE Ach – skip it. Heaven knows I want to.

KATE Okay by me. *(Then, casually)* Were you i' Sam's the night?

JIMMIE No.

KATE Haven't you had any supper?

JIMMIE Eh – had a cup o tea.

KATE Where?

JIMMIE In – in Marshall's.

KATE Oh? I see. Was that where the night started gettin a bit grim and out o hand?

JIMMIE *(Grins, rueful)* Oh – suppose I had it coming to me.

KATE Did you no guess? What was i' store for you?

JIMMIE Lord, no. Or I'd taken a different gait.

KATE *(Still quiet)* I tried to warn you, Jimmie.

JIMMIE I mind. Daresay I'm still a bit dumb.

KATE He's clever. That one. Been around for a while. And no wi his eyes shut.

JIMMIE *(Laughs)* Like me?

KATE I didn't mean it that way. You know that, Jimmie. And what's the next move?

JIMMIE There won't be. Far as I'm concerned.

KATE Good. *(After a second)* Kid – d'you think it – it pays dividends – being decent and straightforward?

JIMMIE Heaven knows! I'm beginnin to wonder.

KATE Look at me. No workin – no means but the dole – and because I've – saved a sma' thing – without tellin the Vennel – I'm labelled street-walker.

JIMMIE *(Grins)* Does it worry you?

KATE It hasn't – till lately.

JIMMIE Why the change o heart?

KATE Ach – well – For instance – Somebody like yoursel, Jim – I wouldn't like them to look askance at me.

JIMMIE Don't worry. You're about the only real friend I've got here.

KATE Thanks, kid. That means a lot to me. *(More brightly)* Y'know, there *is* something – different about you, Jim.

JIMMIE Patter, Kate – patter! I've had some the night.

KATE Neither him nor the gossips are worth the thought.

JIMMIE *(Getting worked up)* God knows it's difficult. Look at my old folks – They had five to bring up – And fed and clad us better nor most – Mother never had much interest outside her own brood – She'd neither time nor inclination to seek for truth at the bottom o her neighbours' wells! And the old man has worked a' his days – without spendin a' his nights in a pub – And just when things shoulda been gettin easier for them – when they shoulda been getting a bit credit for lives well spent – Beth goes and makes the Vennel's bogey!

KATE Jimmie –

JIMMIE *(At close-mouth)* What have they done? What has the lave o us done? That we should be marked out?

KATE *(Going to him)* Don't you see? It's because your folks have been well-doin – have kept their trouble to themselves. But don't you –

JIMMIE Oh, it's no mysel. I can get by. But when I see them jibin away at my mother – a' under the cloak o neighbourly sympathy!

KATE Had she been the sort to hit back . . .

JIMMIE But she's no! She can't lift her head above Beth's slip.

KATE Ach – she had a helluva nerve comin back here!

JIMMIE To stir it up again! I warned her. But no. *(Crying out)* Oh – damn them all to hell!

KATE *(Gripping his arm)* Jim . . . !

JIMMIE The ruddy fool that I am – to go for that old bitch the night.

KATE Do her good!

JIMMIE No do my mother much good the morn.

KATE *(Shaking him gently)* Let up, kid.

JIMMIE What a helluva night! Oh, Kate. *(Somehow her arms are out, and he sinks into them)*

KATE Give over.

JIMMIE Damn him –

KATE Okay.

JIMMIE *Damn him*!

KATE *(Whispering)* Sure.

JIMMIE *(His hands are wandering over her, though he does not quite realise it)* And damn *them* to hell!

KATE *(Playing with his hair)* Ach, Jim – if you could loosen up for half an hour.

JIMMIE *(His head on her shoulders)* Seems to me I've been lettin go for hours. And pourin it a' out on you!

KATE I don't mind.

JIMMIE No?

KATE No. I'm glad.

JIMMIE How?

KATE Because – it's you.

JIMMIE Oh.

KATE Forget it a', kid.

JIMMIE How can I?

KATE By doin something better?

JIMMIE What?

KATE *(Kissing him)* This.

JIMMIE No – no –

KATE *(Holding him close)* It's easy.

JIMMIE What?

KATE To forget.

JIMMIE Is it?

KATE *(Kissing)* This way.

JIMMIE *(Responding recklessly)* Oh damn them a'!

KATE Jimmie –

JIMMIE *(Growing bolder)* Damn them a' to hell!

KATE Jim – no here – no here –

JIMMIE Aye – aye –

KATE No, no – up the stairs –

(Quick fade out)

Scene 6

Moonlight. Except for JIMMIE McPHEE loitering by the lamp-post, there is no one about. After a second, DYKES, whose voice can be heard, comes out, bawling back presumably to her husband. She is carrying a jug.

DYKES . . . Call *me* a Sassenach so-and-so! And what are you? You 'ighland stott, that's what you are! You *h'and* your son. Looking at you – and looking at 'im – nobody could h'accuse me of taking my marriage vows lightly. More's the pity! I'm going to the White 'orse. You can go to 'ell.

(She stumps down the street and, as she passes JIMMIE, she glares at him, and tosses her head without speaking. He grins, and looks after her, then saunters down until he reaches THOMSON's window, and whistles softly. After a moment, the door opens and MOLLY appears.)

MOLLY Oh – Jimmie.

JIMMIE Hangin' around. On chance. Coast clear?

MOLLY *(Nods)* Her and Mrs Finnigan's away to the Alhambra.

JIMMIE Oh – Friday night. I'd almost forgotten. A' days are becomin alike to me.

MOLLY *(Keenly)* Gettin tired o bein at home?

JIMMIE The weeks are flyin in.

MOLLY I expect – one o these days – you'll be makin tracks for Glasgow again.

JIMMIE Been idle long enough.

MOLLY *(Nervous)* If only you could get a job i' Drumnoull!

JIMMIE I've tried. And no nearer nor two months ago.

MOLLY It doesn't seem so long since you came back.

JIMMIE No? No. *(Pulling her to him)* Coming for a walk?

MOLLY Oh I can't. They'll be home by nine.

JIMMIE Oh? *(Releasing her. Cold.)* Okay.

MOLLY *(Hesitating)* Jimmie.

JIMMIE Well?

MOLLY You – you haven't been yoursel these two-three weeks back.

JIMMIE *(Grim, amused)* Oh? Who've I been?

MOLLIE Oh – it's – it's just as if a – a cloud came down around you – every now and then. What's wrong?

JIMMIE Nothing. Perhaps I – I've been thinkin. It's a ploy no for the young in heart.

MOLLY I – I don't follow you.

JIMMIE Whatever it is – it's done wi.

MOLLY *(Tension increasing)* Jimmie – what are you talking about?

JIMMIE Heaven knows. Nothing. Don't remind me o it. *(Pulling her to him)* It's wastin time.

256

MOLLIE Oh – Jimmie.

JIMMIE Come to think of it – you haven't been very bright yoursel lately.

MOLLIE *(Nervously)* Have – have I no?

JIMMIE Nobody i' the house been interferin wi you? More nor usual!

MOLLIE *(Suddenly pushing him away)* I' the house? Who – who'd interfere wi me there? Why do you think that? What made you say that?

JIMMIE *(Stares)* Good Lord, Moll – come off the high horse. *(Then, he laughs)* Worryin at the thought o me goin away?

MOLLIE *(More normal)* A – a wee bit.

JIMMIE *(Pulling her to him)* Don't you see – the quicker I get settled – start earnin – and savin – the sooner we can be together.

MOLLIE I – I wish you could take me away now. This very night.

JIMMIE *(Rallying her)* Don't be daft, sweetheart. Nothing could make me happier. But how could we? Where could we go? How live? Even though I did get a job right away. T'wouldn't be easy.

MOLLY I wouldn't care how hard the way – if we were together – away from this place – and everybody that surrounds us and – and threatens our happiness.

JIMMIE There you go again. Don't be fanciful, Molly. Nobody's threatenin our future.

MOLLY No?

JIMMIE Like to see 'em try it.

MOLLY It doesn't do – sometimes – to – to challenge Providence.

JIMMIE But why should Providence have it in for us? What have we done? But pledge our troth. And that was under a half-moon – no a night a skulkin clouds.

MOLLY Mebbe – mebbe. But every day that goes by makes me feart a' the more o losin you.

JIMMIE Never i' this life.

MOLLY If only we could get away. I – we'd be safe. Mebbe I could find something to do!

JIMMIE I'm old-fashioned. My wife'll have her job – me mine. But we won't clock in at the same factory.

MOLLY But time will go by – days fa' into weeks – weeks drift into months – an' – and mebbe the months devoured by years.

JIMMIE No – no if I can help it.

MOLLY And it's such a frail thread that binds two people together – and a long, long stretch o miles between. Anything may happen while – while – *(Breaks off)*

JIMMIE *(Quietly)* While I'm away? I see. You can't trust me?

MOLLY *(Crying out)* No – no you. It's no you I'm thinkin on.

JIMMIE Do you think then my faith in you is no deep nor strong enough?

MOLLY I know that fine. But – but sometimes – one breaks faith – breaks faith without meanin to . . .

JIMMIE *(Perturbed)* Molly – Molly – what's wrong? Tell me – Who's been gettin at you?

MOLLY Nothing – nothing's wrong. Why do you keep on askin me that? What could be! What could you have done – or me – or me either? What could be wrong wi me?

JIMMIE *(Suddenly, listening)* Quiet!

(MOLLY runs indoors. He moves to edge of pavement. KATE appears at close-mouth.)

KATE Oh – Jim.

JIMMIE Hello.

KATE That a'?

JIMMIE Eh?

KATE Avoidin me nowadays?

JIMMIE *(Stares)* Lord – no. What made you think that?

KATE I'd an idea.

JIMMIE *(Laughs)* Off the mark.

KATE Glad to hear it. It *was* worryin me.

JIMMIE Sorry, Kate. It wasn't i' my mind.

KATE What is?

JIMMIE Oh – nothing much.

KATE *(Quietly)* No? You and me, kid – we've got beyond a nod i' passing. Have we no?

JIMMIE *(Uneasy)* Suppose so.

KATE Jimmie – it wasna – what's happened that's made you – shy away?

JIMMIE *(Shrugs)* I wasn't aware I had.

KATE Well – mebbe t'was a fancy o mine.

JIMMIE Ach – you women are aye havin them.

KATE We've other things as regular. More's the pity for some o us.

JIMMIE *(Staring)* Don't follow you.

KATE No? No, Jim? After that night? Guess I'm no so wide-awake as I thought either.

JIMMIE What – what's a' this?

KATE You don't aye escape scot-free, you know. No the woman anyway. Jimmie, don't look like that! It – it goes right through my heart!

JIMMIE *(Slowly)* Are you tryin to tell me? – God!

KATE Don't take it so bad, Jimmie. We're no the first. Nor likely the last.

JIMMIE Does that help?

KATE *(Putting up a tremendous show of a poor girl lost in a fog)* Don't nag, Jim. Please. I – I couldn't bear it. I didn't want it this way for mysel – or for you. You believe me? Don't you – Jim?

JIMMIE *(Grudging)* I'm no blamin you.

KATE But I do! I'm older nor you. It's – it's my fault.

JIMMIE Oh, for heaven's sake!

KATE Oh – don't look so – so – so down. I've been thinkin more o you nor mysel!

JIMMIE *(Heavily)* Right now I'm thinkin o my old folks.

KATE I know – I know well that.

JIMMIE Oh God.

KATE If we could only spare them.

JIMMIE As if they hadn't enough.

KATE We've got to, Jimmie. We – we can't bring this down on them. It – it would be – be wicked.

JIMMIE How? How is it to be done?

KATE We – we could go away together. I – I've a hundred pounds i' the bank. Enough to keep us till you got a job.

JIMMIE Go – go away – together?

KATE *(Momentarily forgetting her simple girl role)* D'you understand what I'm sayin?

JIMMIE No – no. It's a' running round and round.

KATE *(Holding herself in)* I knew – I knew it. Knew you'd go to pieces. Kid – for a' our sakes – pull yoursel together!

JIMMIE As if they hadn't borne enough.

KATE There's nothing I haven't thought o already. Again and again. After Beth and a'. Dear God – if only we could recall that night. I – I've been beside mysel this day or two, no knowin what to do – the best for a' o us. I – I loathed the thought o dragging you into it. And your old folks. But what can I do? If I could face it alone, I – I – I'd rather take to the river.

JIMMIE *(Alarmed)* For heaven's sake.

KATE *(Simply)* It'd be the finish. A way out for everybody. The quietest way. It's – it's no only ourselves who'll suffer. There's the – pain we'll cause others.

JIMMIE They've had enough – they've had enough.

KATE More nor enough. Neither you nor me's so blind selfish as no to see that! More nor enough. If – if only I had the guts. It – it would be the easiest way out.

JIMMIE You mustn't think o that, Kate! For heaven's sake – no that.

KATE *(Hopeless)* No. But – how the Vennel will ring wi it! They – they'll crucify me!

JIMMIE For the love o heaven – give over. Don't need you to tell me they'll take it out o your bugle. And mine. And a' connected wi me!

KATE But – but if I'm – left to face them alone.

JIMMIE *(Roughly)* Who's askin you? You'll drive me daft!

KATE *(Appealing, touching his arm)* But what are we to do, Jim?

JIMMIE *(Shaking her off)* Ach – I don't know! For the love o heaven – go away! Go away!! D'you hear? Leave me alone! I've gotta think! Go away and leave me i' peace!

(He turns and goes quickly down towards Cutlog Lane. KATE looks after him, shrugs casually, laughs softly, and goes up the close. After a second, MOLLY comes out and looks around. MRS DYKES returns.)

DYKES 'Ello, Molly. Your auntie out?

MOLLY The picters.

DYKES Gettin away from it h'all! And why aren't you out, too, this fine night?

MOLLY Oh – I – I had to mind the house.

DYKES H'it won't run away. A girl of your age should be out 'aving 'er fling.

MOLLY Auntie wouldn't like that, Mrs Dykes!

DYKES Bosh. Only young once. Look at that good-for-nothing son of 'ers. H'all the funs that's going.

MOLLY *(Starts)* He – he has that.

DYKES 'Eaven help the girl who falls in with 'im.

MOLLY Oh!

DYKES *(Skirls)* But of course 'er Jake wouldn't do a girl wrong. Now would 'e?

MOLLY I – I – I . . . *(Her voice dies away)*

DYKES *(Going)* She'll never think so any'ow. If I know 'er!

(MOLLY, looking upset, glances up and down the street. JIMMIE returns.)

MOLLY Jimmie.

JIMMIE Well?

MOLLY I – I was thinkin. I'll mebbe make an excuse to slip out for an hour tomorrow night.

JIMMIE *(Indifferent)* Oh – will you?

MOLLY We – we could go for a walk.

JIMMIE Mebbe.

MOLLY Jimmie – what's wrong? You sound – funny?

JIMMIE Funny?

MOLLY Queer like.

JIMMIE *(A shade rough)* We had a' that the night already. Startin again?

MOLLY *(Drawing back)* Oh – I'm – sorry. I didn't mean to offend. If – if there's something worrying you – mebbe – mebbe I could help.

JIMMIE *(With a splutter of a grim laugh)* Help? You?

MOLLY Goodness knows I'm told often enough I'm o sma' account – thoughtless and stupid. But I understand you better nor – nor mebbe you think.

JIMMIE Oh? What sharpens your wits when they have to deal wi me?

MOLLY Mebbe – because you're so much i' my thoughts. Mebbe. I don't rightly know.

JIMMIE Aye – mebbe.

MOLLY You can laugh, Jimmie. But I know when there's something troubling your mind.

JIMMIE For the peace o your own – you'd better no delve too deep i' mine.

MOLLY There is something!

JIMMIE *(Getting wild)* No – there's no – if there is – it's no your affair – ach, mebbe it is – I don't – No – I'm raivelled! I'm like you. My brain's sma'-bookit. I never thought this – this sort o wedge would be driven between you and me! *(He grips her by the shoulders, and as she listens MOLLY becomes increasingly distraught)* Molly – whatever happens – I – I didn't let *you* down – You know that – It – it hurts me too. Mebbe more so – Because it's you – you that's – I didn't let you down – It was aye you – Wi me – Closest to me – Nobody else – Just you – you –

MOLLY *(Beginning to cry)* Jimmie – Jimmie . . .

JIMMIE You was right. I was too cocksure. Too sure that we – we was different. Doubtless Providence accepted our challenge.

MOLLY You know – you know . . .

JIMMIE Aye – I –

MOLLY It wasn't by my will – As God is above us – It wasn't by my will. He – he had the door locked – I – I tried to fight him off – He was stronger nor me – I – I pleaded wi him – He – he just laughed i' my face – He – he was like a madman – Stark mad –

JIMMIE *(In dawning horror)* Who?

MOLLY Auntie and Uncle John was out. He –

JIMMIE Jake?

MOLLY He swore he'd – he'd get me if – if I told them.

JIMMIE You? You too? Dear God in heaven . . . !

MOLLY Oh Jimmie – don't think ill o me. It wasna my fault. I – I never did a thing to make him fancy that I'd – that I'd – You know I'm no that kind.

JIMMIE No – no –

MOLLY Oh the bitterness o it – Naggin away at me this week back – My mind can't reach beyond it – Nothing behind it that I can reach back to – Nothing ahead that I can look forward to – And aye you were there – i' my mind wi it – a' mixed up wi it –

JIMMIE Weeesht – weeesht.

MOLLY I – I didn't play you false, Jimmie. I swear it – I swear it. It – I didn't will it –

JIMMIE I know fine. It – it was something that just happened.

MOLLY But why me? Why me? To bring this down on you – you –

JIMMIE Oh the bloody swine.

MOLLY You'll never forgive me.

JIMMIE Ach – stop it – stop it. What is there to forgive?

MOLLY I'll never forgive mysel. Never . . . never . . . never . . .

JIMMIE God – I'll kill the swine.

MOLLY Oh no, no – Jimmie. You mustn't – She'd find out –

JIMMIE So what?

MOLLY And what would become o me? It's bad enough if – if – oh I'm scared – scared –

JIMMIE Eh?

MOLLY Frightened o what might happen. And she wouldn't believe – He'd deny it –

JIMMIE Hasn't the guts for anything else!

MOLLY She'd put me out – and where could I go?

JIMMIE Oh God – God.

MOLLY I've nobody – nobody. No even you now . . .

JIMMIE Molly?

MOLLY I don't blame you – For – for changin – When a' that we – we hoped for . . . I can't look to you – to – to care –

JIMMIE *(Low)* If something's gone deep enough in you – it can't be pulled up and destroyed through a moment's wanchance.

MOLLY It's all gone now – the sweetness, the glaumrie –

JIMMIE Be quiet –

MOLLY The brightness, the promise, a' the lovely days that seemed to stretch ahead o us.

JIMMIE Be quiet – be quiet, Molly.

MOLLY It's you I'm thinkin o – more nor mysel.

JIMMIE *(Hearing an echo)* Eh? Oh God! *(Releases her)*

MOLLY If we could get away, I'd make it up in a hundred ways, Jimmie. You'd never regret it.

JIMMIE Oh give over.

MOLLY A' my life.

JIMMIE No – no –

MOLLY If we both haven't changed – we – we could put it behind us – in time. Oh I know we could, Jimmie.

JIMMIE *(Low)* I can't – I can't –

MOLLY Then you have changed – you're only pretendin no – You – you don't want me – now. Now that –

JIMMIE Oh for heaven's sake.

MOLLY Nothing would ever come between us you said. *Nothing.* From now on.

JIMMIE *(Dour)* I spoke out o my turn.

MOLLY You never meant – It wasn't as if I – I swear it, Jimmie – I –

JIMMIE *(In a sudden roar)* For Nick's sake!!!! *(Calming)* Sorry. Let's – let's leave it for a while. I – I feel beat to the wide. I – I just can't think. Don't know where we're goin – or even if I care. Oh for heaven's sake, stop cryin – stop – stop – stop it!! *(Pulls himself together)* Don't worry, sweetheart. I'll mebbe – I –

(She turns and runs into the house. He goes into close, obviously in two minds what to do. MRS THOMSON and MRS WATT come from the High Street.)

WATT Oh I like fine a night at the picters.

THOMSON It's real enjoyable.

WATT So it is. And it takes you out o yoursel.

THOMSON Goodness me aye. And a body needs taken out o themselves nowadays – It's the only way to keep your head.

WATT That's very true.

THOMSON *(Halting by her door)* Have you been this week?

WATT *(Titters)* Oh we've been twice since Monday.

THOMSON G'way?

WATT We're doin a show tomorrow night too. The Repertory Theatre, you know. Of course, our seats are booked.

THOMSON G'way?

WATT Well, I'll away and see to the family's supper.

THOMSON Goodness aye – our work's never done.

(They both disappear. JIMMIE is still at the close-mouth. DICK MARSHALL hoves in sight.)

DICK *(Unsure, restrained)* Oh –

JIMMIE *(Quietly)* Hello.

DICK You're a – stranger.

JIMMIE Aye.

(A pause)

DICK How's things?

JIMMIE So-so.

DICK Still no workin?

JIMMIE No yet.

DICK Too bad. How – how's everybody upstairs?

JIMMIE Fine. *(Grim)* She's still here.

DICK Oh. *(Pause)* I – I thought you'd been moving out before this.

JIMMIE Thinkin o it.

DICK *(Still making heavy weather of it)* Never see you in Sam's these nights?

JIMMIE No.

DICK Leadin a quiet life?

JIMMIE Did I ever do anything else?

DICK *(After a second)* Well – I – I expect you're wishin I'd push off.

JIMMIE *(Casually)* Why?

DICK Eh?

JIMMIE No reason to move because I'm here. And I'm stayin.

DICK Oh! *(After a second)* Been to any shows lately?

JIMMIE No. *(He moves forward)*

DICK Eh – smoke? *(Offering one)*

JIMMIE Thanks. *(They light up. He takes a deep puff.)*

DICK Looks like the first you've had for a while.

JIMMIE It is.

DICK Oh? *(Then)* Wonderful how a smoke seems to – to brighten you up.

JIMMIE *(Bursts out laughing)* Oh – give over, Dick!

DICK *(Grins)* It *is* a bit uphill. *(More normal)* Well – what'll we talk about next? The latest scandal i' the Vennel?

JIMMIE *(Grim)* There'll probably be a brand new one ready to break any day now.

DICK Oh? Is that just – passin the time – or a look into the future?

JIMMIE *(Flaring)* Why the hell should I know what's coming next?

DICK Okay. *I* was only passin the time.

JIMMIE Good. Let's keep it that way.

DICK Jimmie – mebbe you and me . . . Well, what's past is behind us – Before that – I wasn't such a bad pal to you. I could still be one.

JIMMIE *(Disgusted)* Heavens – my mind must be as open to the public as the Corporation parks!

DICK Eh?

JIMMIE Can be read, seen through – even by lamplight.

DICK I'm no interferin out o curiousity. If there's anything I –

JIMMIE *(Butting in)* Sure. You can shut up.

DICK Oh – sorry. I thought you could mebbe tell me what – what you couldn't very well take upstairs.

JIMMIE *(Laughs, grim)* You're right there!

DICK What is it – Jimmie?

JIMMIE *(Airily)* Ach. I'm mebbe thinkin o gettin married – and shy o breakin the good news.

DICK *(Gasps)* Married? You?

JIMMIE *(Brutally)* Why no? Wouldn't be a bigger shock nor your own.

DICK *(Stifling an impulse to hit back)* Suppose you cut the cracks – and spill it?

JIMMIE Why should I?

DICK Okay. It hasn't anything to do wi me. Agreed.

JIMMIE Sure thing. *(Then, staring)* No – But – Oh mebbe you had something to do wi it – Now that I mind –

DICK Eh? Me?

JIMMIE Aye. You. Rather a lot too. She warned me about you, see? And – and when you came up to expectations – she got me on the retreat. Sure.

DICK For heaven's sake – out wi it!

JIMMIE Kate McShane. The last night I was round the corner wi you.

DICK *(Gasps)* No – No! Holy smoke! You and – and her? That night? After – you left me?

JIMMIE *(Grim)* Guess something shook me out o my normal that night.

DICK *(Stung)* Dear God – no – no!

JIMMIE There it is.

DICK And she – she's . . . ?

JIMMIE Got to be made an honest woman.

DICK She's blamin you?

JIMMIE The reasons appear sufficient.

DICK *(Grim)* You may think so. I know different.

(KATE appears at the close-mouth)

JIMMIE *(Staring at DICK)* Eh? *(Spots KATE)* Oh?

KATE *(Moving forward coolly)* Am I i' the way?

JIMMIE *(Embarrassed)* Eh – eh?

KATE Interrupting something?

JIMMIE Wh–at?

KATE You look kinda awkward.

JIMMIE Do – I?

KATE Thought you'd given *him* the breadth o the street?

JIMMIE I – I just spoke.

KATE Find it necessary – the night?

JIMMIE *(With more spirit)* What are you hintin at?

KATE *(More in sorrow than in anger)* Jim – I hate to see you mixin wi –

JIMMIE Where's the harm?

DICK *(Caustic)* I doubt if mixin wi my kind would lead him into the pitmirk playin around wi your kind has.

KATE *(Starts. To JIMMIE)* Oh. You – you told him? Oh Jimmie – how could you – how could you? Betray me i' that way? *Him* by anybody?

DICK *(Smoothly)* I see what you mean.

JIMMIE *(Irritated)* How can we – keep it quiet?

KATE We can – we could have! There was no need for anybody – but you and me to – know. Until we were clear what to do.

DICK Oh?

KATE You know fine what *he* is. And to stand and listen to him black-lyin me – puttin suspicion i' your head – was that fair to me, Jim? After what we've been to each other?

JIMMIE *(Shortly)* He hasn't said a word about you.

KATE *(Taken aback)* Oh! Oh – I – I'm a' upset, Jim.

JIMMIE No the only one.

KATE *(Watching him)* You – you're speakin different to me than you did a while back.

JIMMIE Mebbe feelin different.

KATE How? How could you? Are you forgettin we – we're in this together? And – and the folks behind us we – we must think o.

JIMMIE I'm no forgettin anything.

KATE *(Softly)* And – and your promise?

JIMMIE Eh?

KATE You'll – you'll stick to your word? I – I'm countin on you, Jimmie. I – I trust you – as I've always done. You can't let me down!

JIMMIE *(Dour)* Did I say anything to the contrary?

KATE Then – then it's settled?

DICK *(Softly)* What is?

KATE *(Urgent)* Jimmie? *(He makes no sign of replying to DICK; she turns to him, defying him)* We're goin away together. Gettin married.

DICK *(Blandly)* Why?

KATE *(Stares)* Why?

DICK *(Shrugs carelessly)* Aye – why?

KATE *(Just holding her temper)* Why do folks get married – as a rule?

DICK *(In that irritating, mocking way that gets under her skin)* There's several reasons – I thought 'em all out at one time – Love or money is the most usual. But i' your case – neither need be considered.

KATE No?

DICK No. He has none o the second for you – you have none o the first for him.

KATE What makes you so sure?

DICK I get around.

KATE So did I – for a while – till I realised where it was leadin me.

DICK *(Mockingly interested)* And you stopped i' time?

KATE *(Between her teeth)* I did.

DICK Who'd – thought it?

KATE It happens to be true. *(With a great show of candour)* You may hate the sight o me – May even have cause – God knows I may have been wrong – I was a harum-scarum i' my teens – daft and thoughtless. I may have done you an ill turn – But there's nothing I can do now – wi a' the goodwill i' the world – to – to make recompense – or, believe me, I would! – Wi good heart! – So why keep it up against me? Why try to stab me now when I'm – I'm just another defenceless fool o a woman?

DICK *(Entirely unmoved)* Aren't you jumpin ahead?

KATE No. I know you. I've been conscious for years o your shadow. If you can wreck my life – you'll do it. But why? Why no be a man and stand aside? It's no your affair. I'm pleadin – aye, pleadin wi *you*. That should be no sma' satisfaction – that I should be brought to such a pass – that I should be afraid – mortally afraid o you. It's no only mysel – though I've no kith or kin to – to shelter me – if *he* fails me. It's for his sake too – For mercy's sake give me credit for what I feel for him! And that's the naked truth –

though he should leave me to rue it for the lave o my days. And there's his folks too. We can't spare them. If it comes out.

DICK *(Entirely unmoved)* Nice patter. *Very* nice patter. And he's listenin. He heard you okay. You may be right! It's hardly my concern. If he's ready to throw away his life – on you. Well!

KATE *(Breathes deeply)* Well?

DICK *(Smoothly)* But why blame him?

KATE Eh?

DICK That's the interestin point.

KATE What is?

DICK *(Casual)* I shoulda thought a girl wi your grasp o realities woulda chosen somebody more – substantial. After a' – havin got around as far as you did – before you realised of course where it was leadin you! – A very interestin point *that* – I'd like to discuss it some time wi you – But I'da thought it unlikely that a handsome face would make *you* fall.

KATE *(Angrily)* Listen –

DICK Can it be he was the only one available who could bring a little golden ring wi him?

KATE *(Swinging round to JIMMIE)* Jimmie – D'you think no better o me nor to listen to this?

JIMMIE Aye – I've had enough.

DICK *(Shrugs)* By a' means – go ahead. It's easy, y'know, for women to father their bairns where the fancy pleases them. Some men set great store in that sort o achievement – God knows why. But I wonder if Alec'll no be vexed at such a reflection on his prowess?

KATE Oh!

JIMMIE What are you givin us?

DICK Was he no a long, long way ahead o our young friend here?

KATE *(Tight-lipped)* Jimmie! I'm warnin you. He's just tryin to drive us apart wi his dirty tongue!

JIMMIE Let him carry on –

KATE Just his rotten way o gettin his own back – on both o us!

JIMMIE *(Grim)* He'll get what's comin to him shortly.

DICK Take it softly, kid. I can give as good as I get. If you want to make a bloody fool o yoursel – don't mind me. *(Then: spitting it out)* But first ask her when she broke it off wi Alec Stewart!

KATE *(Starts, simulates amazement)* Alec – Alec Stewart? *(To JIMMIE)* He's drunk wi spite! Jim – have you ever seen me wi Stewart? Heard our names mentioned together?

JIMMIE *(Slowly)* Can't say I have!

KATE Alec Stewart! Good heavens! I can hardly tell you when I last passed the time o day wi the man! I hardly know him! *(She bursts out laughing)* It's – it's – he's mad – mad!

JIMMIE *(To DICK: quietly)* Finished?

DICK (*Now less casual, more decided*) How'd you think she manages to live?

JIMMIE I've an idea.

DICK He's been keepin her for months.

KATE (*Furious*) It's a damned lie!

DICK Meetin her two-three times a week.

KATE It's a damned lie!

DICK Whiles slippin her into the back shop.

KATE You – you swine!

JIMMIE (*Alarmed*) For heaven's sake! You'll warn out the street.

KATE Are you believin that – that black-hearted swine?

JIMMIE (*Calmly*) If he can't prove it –

KATE How can he? He hates us both. That's his game. Sowin suspicion.

JIMMIE No need to get roused. If he can't – where's the harm?

KATE (*Probably suppressing a desire to hit him between the eyes*) Is it nothing to you? What I'm called? It's lies – I tell you. Nothing but!

DICK When did you see him last?

KATE Months ago – months ago!

DICK Was it no but a week or so back? (*Jerks towards the shop*) In there one night?

KATE What?

DICK (*Sneers*) A shadow's an ill thing to get rid o.

KATE (*To JIMMIE: urgent*) No – no – It's no true. Jimmie, listen – The man's nothing to me – Never has been – God – he's years older!

JIMMIE Why get so worked up if it's just Marshall's idea o a joke?

KATE Because he has it in for me. Would do any mortal thing to get a crack at me. And you – you're lettin his poison seep into you.

JIMMIE Give me credit for some common sense.

KATE Had you any – you'da told him long ago where he got off.

JIMMIE Oh?

KATE Don't be so damned dumb, Jim. Surely to heaven your own experience has proved what he is. D'you think – after what passed between you – he's still full o the milk of lovin kindness? He hates you as bitterly as mysel. He's tryin to break up your life – and mine. He's hittin at you i' the only way he can – through me.

JIMMIE Kate: be honest wi me.

KATE I've aye been that.

JIMMIE Has there ever been anything between you – and Stewart?

KATE I hardly know the man!

JIMMIE Has there?

KATE No, Jim. No – I swear to it. So help me, God.

JIMMIE (*Moving forward: to DICK*) Will you take that back?

DICK No.

JIMMIE I'm warnin you.

DICK No.

JIMMIE *(Making for him)* We've had enough.

KATE Hit him between the eyes, Jim!

DICK Just one thing more.

JIMMIE *(Grappling with him)* Get the hell outa here.

DICK *(Throwing him off)* Easy now.

JIMMIE *(Diving back at him)* D'you hear?

DICK *(Pulling registered letter from pocket)* Have a look at this.

JIMMIE *(Halts, stares)* Eh?

DICK *(Tosses it to him)* Recognise the address?

JIMMIE Where – where did you get this? *(Sharp)* What's this to you?

DICK Nothing. I was asked to post it. Several days ago. And conveniently forgot. I think – if you open it – it might help us along.

(A pause. KATE nonplussed and uneasy. DICK smoothly amused. JIMMIE tears open letter, extracts two or three pound notes and a letter which he glances over.)

JIMMIE God in heaven!

KATE Jim . . . ?

DICK *(Blandly)* Alec's weekly love-offering to Beth.

KATE *(Completely giving herself away)* What – Alec? And Beth McPhee? *(JIMMIE raises his head and watches her)* It's no true – no true! It can't be – I won't believe it.

DICK No?

KATE Another o your damned trickly lies! I won't believe it!

DICK *(Nodding towards JIMMIE)* He does.

KATE *(Swinging round)* Oh!

JIMMIE *(Angry, bitter)* You're another damned liar – aren't you?

KATE Jimmie.

JIMMIE Give yoursel away – didn't you?

DICK Alec likes to keep things nice and quiet. But Kate's no like Beth. She wants a husband – no a by-blow. She prides hersel on havin got around – and she's sensitive o the Vennel havin the last laugh.

KATE *(Furious)* Damn you – damn you for an interferin swine!

JIMMIE *(Disgusted)* And I was to be the gowk. God, what a ruddy blind fool!

KATE *(Tartly)* Don't congratulate yoursel too soon! You're no by wi it!

JIMMIE What? You can't – ?

KATE No? We've never been seen together. Him and me. It's your word against mine. Marshall's doesn't count. It's his against Alec's.

DICK *(Sneers)* Your word.

KATE *We've* been seen often enough. *(She laughs)* And you haven't kept on the gossips' side! You'll mind that. And if you want to drag your old folks down a bit further . . .

JIMMIE *(Groans)* Oh God.

KATE I'm ready!

DICK *(Calmly)* I might take a hand.

KATE You've done your worst.

DICK I'm no so sure.

KATE Proud – aren't you?

DICK Fairly satisfied.

KATE You'll no move Alec.

DICK He's no above it.

KATE Think you've got us licked?

DICK Well on the way.

KATE I'm no.

DICK No?

KATE You'll see.

DICK It's your move.

KATE I don't give a damn now.

DICK You never did.

KATE What right had you to butt in?

DICK You should know.

KATE Gettin your own back?

DICK Been a long time i' comin.

KATE Don't pretend it's because o what happened years ago.

DICK *(Beginning to lose his smoothness a little)* No?

KATE And you know it.

DICK Oh – do you?

KATE I got what you couldn't.

DICK *(All the more deadly because he manages to keep a grip on himself)* For nearly five years I've waited and bided my time – Waited for the day you'd be delivered into my hands – Waited for the day I could tear you apart and break you – Nothing would give me greater pleasure than to see you i' full flight wi all the old cows i' the Vennel at your heels – Thought for nobody – no even him – would stop me from pinnin you down and watchin while the black blood oozes out o you – I've waited patiently to pay you – repay you i' full measure and interest for what you did – Did you ever stop to think o what you wantonly smashed for my mother when you fathered your pal's bastard on me? When you brought down on her the malice and jeers and spite o the Tenements? When you made me a joke and a byword at the street-corners? No – *no*. It mattered not a damn what you did to her – to me. I swore I'd get you – and the longer I had to wait the greater the interest that's piled up – And I've got you – got you where I've long wanted you – And so help me, God – be it the last thing I do i' this life – I'll finish you – finish you – finish you – *(Losing complete control, his voice rising on a hysterical note, he dives at her. She backs away in terror, while JIMMIE, aghast, rushes forward,* *to pull him back)* And get to bloody hell away from me or I'll do it right now!!!

(*KATE turns and runs up the close. DICK shakes JIMMIE off, his hands jerk up to cover his face. JIMMIE drops back silently.*)

DICK *(After a second, controlled, glances at JIMMIE, a shade embarrassed)* Some day I'll wash it out o my system.

JIMMIE Appears to me I'm washed up right now.

DICK How?

JIMMIE You heard her.

DICK *(The weariness dropping from him gradually)* Words – fine loud words – and nothing behind them. She'll say damn all. She's beat – and knows it. She accuses you – he's roped in. She daren't risk that – to lose her hold over him. He's generous wi his wife's cash. And – you know, they *have* been damned clever! She'd have a job pinnin it on him.

JIMMIE *(Morosely)* We'd have the same difficulty.

DICK Hardly. The Vennel wouldn't lick its chops over you. But Alec – there's a juicy morsel!

JIMMIE How did you tumble to it?

DICK Known for long enough. Aye on the prowl, you know. And when *he* gave me the letter and you told me what Beth called herself – well . . . And I counted on Kate losin her balance when *she* knew. I'll bet she's already had it out wi him! 'Twould do her no good – spillin it. He'd scoot behind Teenie.

JIMMIE Oh – I dunno.

DICK He's an old hand at findin a way out o his little fixes, don't forget. *(JIMMIE starts)* Even though she did lose her head and bawl you out, you've still a trump card. Beth.

JIMMIE What could she do?

DICK After the way you stood by her? Good God, has she no sense o gratitude? Would she let him do the dirty on you too? If she threatened to expose him –

JIMMIE *(Dour)* I'm no bringin her into it.

DICK Don't be a damn fool! Least she could do.

JIMMIE No!!

DICK In a showdown – we couldn't avoid it.

JIMMIE We?

DICK *(Blandly)* Oh come, come – you're no to put my nose out o joint by becomin a martyr.

JIMMIE Well – then. She's out. So's he.

DICK What?

JIMMIE And you shut your trap.

DICK What the hell?

JIMMIE Bringin him in – and her – See? The old folks are goin to be the biggest sufferers. And I won't have it.

DICK But – if Kate blames you?

JIMMIE I'm the loser. Now don't let's have any more argument. My mind's made up.

DICK But –

JIMMIE You'll get your own back another time.

DICK You're a ruddy fool, Jimmie.

JIMMIE Then I'm livin up to their estimation. That's a'. *(Change of tone)* Dick – I – I'm no ungrateful. I won't forget what you did.

DICK Little to thank me for – seems to me. If you're goin through wi it. Only shown you what she is. How they roped you in.

JIMMIE Aye something.

DICK No so sure. You might have made the best o it – otherwise – till you found her out for yoursel. As a' married folks do i' time. That's what keeps most marriages alive and kickin. If the expectations o one kind are no realised it puts more pith i' the other kind. But at least you wouldn't have started off wi everything mapped out on the kitchen blankets.

JIMMIE No? *(Slowly)* Mebbe isn't my intention ever to share the blankets.

DICK *(Stares)* Eh?

JIMMIE Is Drumnoull no the central railway station i' Scotland?

DICK *(Starts)* And wi a grand selection o trains at a' hours o the day. For a' the airts!

JIMMIE *(Coolly)* Sure.

DICK But, young 'un – don't you see? We've got it – we've got it! Beat it – beat the hell out o it! Right now. If you slip through her fingers – *that* way – if you're no here to bawl out – she's cornered!

JIMMIE How come?

DICK What use are you as a daddy if she can't produce her marriage lines? That's what she's ettlin for – to save her face. Listen – *(Diving into his pocket to produce a wallet from which he takes several pound notes)* You've got Beth's two quid – I can give you three or four. Thank the Lord this was pay-day! Now we're gettin somewhere!

JIMMIE *(Amused)* In a damned hurry to get rid o me.

DICK Keep to the point. It's the way out.

JIMMIE No so sure. That she'll say nothing.

DICK What if she does? I'll – *(Breaks off, then quickly)* She'll no. Wager on that.

JIMMIE *(Quietly)* Have you got something else up your sleeve?

DICK *(Innocent)* Eh?

JIMMIE Once I'm out o the way. Your way.

DICK *(Sardonic)* Jimmie – aren't you misjudgin me? What could I do without you to back me up?

JIMMIE *(Eyeing him grimly)* A body can never be sure what you'll bring out o the hat.

DICK *(Serious)* Young 'un – I'm only thinkin o you – and the folks upstairs – I wouldn't do them an ill turn. Honest. But I know – damn it all! It's beyond argument. You out o reach – and she's sunk.

JIMMIE *(Slowly)* Ach – well. Wonder what she'll do? Kinda sorry for her.

DICK *(Is not)* Her? Hell mend her! Here – *(Gives him the cash)* Don't sleep on it. You might start worryin about lettin poor Alec down. Ach – they'll pin it on another coof. *(He laughs)* Mebbe Bool McKay. Who knows? Or even Jake Thomson!

JIMMIE *(Suddenly remembering)* God!

DICK Eh?

JIMMIE Oh heavens above! I forgot – clean forgot.

DICK *(Wondering)* What now? What's upset you?

JIMMIE It's no use. I can't do it.

DICK What is it?

JIMMIE It's Molly.

DICK *(Exasperated)* Holy smoke! Love's young dream lost i' the fog. Pull yoursel together, kid – for heaven's sake! You can write – can't you? Tell her you cleared out to – to get work. This is no time for fond farewells.

JIMMIE You don't understand. I – I've got to be near her. For a while – anyway. She – she needs somebody.

DICK She's got the Thomson gang.

JIMMIE It's – it's me she needs. I – I've got to stay put and – and look after her.

DICK *(Staggered)* Eh? Dear God – don't tell me – don't tell me – I don't think I could survive it! Is she . . . ?

JIMMIE We – we don't know yet.

DICK Oh? The waitin's aye the worst bit, isn't it? Well – certainly no half-measure wi you. Painstakin. Explorin every avenue.

JIMMIE Me? Wish to God it had been!

DICK Eh?

JIMMIE Jake.

DICK *(As it dawns on him, low)* Christ!

JIMMIE Tripped her up.

DICK *(Wheels away from him: in horror and self-disgust)* No – no! God forgive me.

JIMMIE The bastard.

DICK God help me.

JIMMIE I could kill him.

DICK No – no. Me.

JIMMIE Eh? *(Noticing DICK's perturbation)* What's the matter?

DICK Nothing – nothing. Don't mind me. Often go like this. *(Bitterly)* I'm thinkin Conscience can call a man by dirtier names than coward.

JIMMIE *(Not understanding)* I'd feel one if I cleared out right now.

DICK *(Returning: edgy)* In heaven's name, why? What can you do? Is it your blame? What *can* you do?

JIMMIE Not much. I know. At least be near her. If the worst comes.

DICK Aren't you forgettin that hellcat upstairs?

JIMMIE Oh God.

DICK *(Still nervy, emotionally keyed up)* When did it happen?

JIMMIE About a week ago.

DICK Then Kate's claim'll be registered long before hers. Do you intend to marry Kate and stand by to comfort the other one?

JIMMIE I don't know what I intend doin.

DICK *(His sense of humour gradually controlling his emotion)* Oh – kid! You've either got to face it out wi Kate – and a' that means to your mother and father – *and* Molly – or get to hell out o it!

JIMMIE How can I – how can I?

DICK Stayin won't help. On the contrary.

JIMMIE What's to become o her? Jake wouldn't admit it. You know what his mother is.

DICK Even wi a gutless pouff like him there are ways and means.

JIMMIE And who's to see to it?

DICK *(Grimly)* Puttin the fear o death in him wouldn't lose me a night's sleep. It would make me sleep a' the sounder! Listen, young 'un, leave it to me. I promise you. He'll toe the line. Should it – be necessary. *(Sardonic)* Though frankly – wi Jake – I can't imagine him capable o ringin the bell! And if it's no needed – no harm done.

JIMMIE *(Deeply)* No harm done.

DICK *(A trifle shamefaced)* Oh – sorry, kid.

JIMMIE The lousy bastard.

DICK *(Quiet)* Jimmie – you – you still fond o her?

JIMMIE How should I no be? Did she ettle for it? 'Course I am. To think o her goin through hell – and me – me – Can't do a thing – Nor even be near her – to comfort – to shield her – And surrounded by that gossipin mob o hellcats –

DICK I know, kid. But she won't be alone. She's got me.

JIMMIE You? Why you?

DICK *(Brusque)* Ach – Mebbe because I've a tender spot for the young and innocent – Mebbe because o what she means to you – Mebbe there's another reason – Let's no delve too deep – My reasons sometimes astonish even mysel. But – I'll look after her, kid. Honest.

JIMMIE Dick . . .

DICK Okay. And later on, if you still feel the same, well – what's sixty miles? Coupla hours in a train!

JIMMIE You mean?

DICK When you're ready, so'll she be – to come to you. The Best Man'll see to that.

JIMMIE *(Moved)* You – you – I –

DICK *(Brusquely affectionate)* I know – I know – Man to Man the world o'er. Here. *(Gives him the money again)*

JIMMIE Thanks. I – I –

DICK Shall brothers be for a' that. The Inverness express stops for a drink round about half past four on its way to the Second City.

JIMMIE *(Grins)* I know.

DICK *(Likewise) You know?* Then what the hell are you standin here for?

JIMMIE Determined to run me out o Drumnoull without waste o time – aren't you?

DICK *(Suddenly quiet)* Am I? Mebbe the risk o continually meetin you i' the streets would be too much for my conscience – it might keep on remindin me o happenings I'd rather forget.

JIMMIE *(Puzzled)* I can't follow you.

DICK You're no losin by it. *(Catching him by the shoulders for a second, then, smiling)* Goodnight – squirt!

JIMMIE *(Smiling back)* Goodnight – handsome!

(DICK watches him go, his whole body sags dejectedly, as if all the bitter self-disgust and torment, all the tragic unhappiness and inherent loneliness of his inversion had of a sudden been thrust upwards by his overburdened conscience, and for one stark moment the mask falls; with a tremendous effort he pulls himself together and turns to go. McKAY's window clatters up.)

McKAY Oh – it's you. Thought I heard voices.

DICK *(With an effort)* So you did. I was just havin a bit crack wi myself.

McKAY *(Leers at him)* Is that a fact? And what conclusion did you reach?

DICK None. There can be none. No i' this life. But tell me – you that's seen so much and talked so much more about it – If there be a Creator at the beginnin o Life – and a Judge at the end o it – should Man stand by himself at the Judgement bar?

McKAY *(Eyes him keenly, then astonishingly gentle)* You've reached that stage, have you, Dick? Well – well – Listen here – And mind I'm never very far out! I came to the Vennel forty years ago come Candlemas as a blushin bride – And that's a fact! Heaven knows I had cause to blush when I saw what I'd let mysel in for! – But if Life has scaled my heart, yet and a' it's taught me this much – If we're a' God's children, then He's very little to boast o – and even less to condemn! Life's no to be resisted – And there are some He sent out to tackle it in polished hides – and others i' fine-drawn stuff that rips a' too soon i' the struggle. And whose fault is that? It's no aye the weak, Dickie, who fail to resist – often and on it's the strong in heart who accept, who are ready and willin to pay the lawin. Never fear but what the left hand's drawin back'll no be balanced by the right hand's comin forward! *(Normal self)* And now – whatever ploy you've been up to, son – away home to your bed and put it a' behind you. *(Snorts)* No that you'll no do it a' again!

DICK *(Laughs)* Mother McKay – I think I'll adopt you!

McKAY And how no? You and me would get along champion!

DICK Well – I'll away. Goodnight.

McKAY Goodnight, Dick.

> *(He goes. She looks after him and shakes her head. DYKES's door opens and she comes out.)*

DYKES *(Glancing up)* H'oh – it's you!

McKAY Aye – it's me.

DYKES I thought I 'eard voices.

McKAY You did. Me – and Dick Marshall. He – *(Stops, then)* he's away home to his bed.

DYKES It's a fine night. Moonlight.

McKAY And lamplight, Dykes. And in a wee while the bobby wi *his* lamp. Plenty o illumination.

DYKES For what?

McKAY You stump me there.

> *(A movement at THOMSON's door)*

DYKES *(Abruptly)* H'oh – come out, Thomson.

THOMSON *(Doing so)* I thought –

McKAY Nothing much goes past you – is there?

DYKES God knows you don't miss much yourself, McKay.

McKAY Do you?

DYKES H'oh no. There's not much we miss.

THOMSON *(Glancing up and down the Vennel)* I sometimes wonder.

> *(Quick fade out)*

Scene 7

Moonlight. The Vennel is asleep.

Then suddenly the quiet is rent by the unearthly wailing of a couple of cats. After a moment, this dies down to a distant murmur.

Someone, discernible as JIMMIE McPHEE, appears at the close-mouth. He is wearing a raincoat, and carries a small suitcase. As he moves out, he apparently sees someone approaching from the High Street, and nips back into the close out of view.

The POLICE OFFICER strolls up, moves into the close, and lights up.

The cats commence again, mounting to a terrific crescendo.

From nearby, a dog barks loudly, once, twice, in angry protest. At once, the cats are silent.

The POLICE OFFICER swears softly, throws down his fag-end and moves off in the direction of Cutlog Lane.

After a second, JIMMIE reappears, glances cautiously right and left, then makes off hurriedly towards the High Street.

As he moves out of sight, the thin far-off wail of a passing train is heard.

The clock of the Kirk of St John commences to strike four o'clock.

The curtain falls.

ALL IN GOOD FAITH

A PLAY IN THREE ACTS

by

Roddy McMillan

All in Good Faith was first performed at the Citizens' Theatre, Glasgow, 5 April 1954, with the following cast:

ROBERT BRYSON . . . . Paul Curran
AGNES BRYSON, *his wife* . . . . Marjorie Thomson
JADIE BRYSON, *their eldest son* . . . . Roddy McMillan
NICOLL BRYSON, *another son* . . . . John Cairney
ALLAN BRYSON, *youngest son* . . . . Alex McAvoy
RENA BRYSON, *their daughter* . . . . Mary Walton
COLIN, *Mrs Bryson's brother* . . . . Andrew Keir
PETER, *Rena's boyfriend* . . . . Ronald Fraser
ROBERT MARR, *a lawyer* . . . . Fulton McKay
TINA GIBB . . . . Madeleine Christie
THE GANCHER . . . . Lea Ashton
THE CRAITUR . . . . Abe Barker
Handers/Hangers-on . . . . John Carlin
Charles Johnstone
Alistair Wilson
James Nairn
Clark Tait
Andrew Laird

Directed by . . . . Michael Langham
Set design . . . . John Wilson
Stage Director . . . . Lea Ashton
Stage Manager . . . . Rita Burr
Assistant Stage Manager . . . . Jessie Barclay
Wardrobe Mistress . . . . Mrs MacAdam
Scenic Artist . . . . Joy Stanley
Piano . . . . Arthur Blak

ACT I

Scene 1

The action of the play takes place in the present, in a tenement kitchen – any district in Glasgow.

Downstage right wall there is a fireplace. Above that a door leading to the room shared by Jadie, Nicoll and Mr Bryson. Adjacent to that door, in the back wall, is the door of the room used by Colin and Allan. Window middle of back wall. To the left, almost in the corner, is the door leading to a lobby and an outside stairhead door. Standing against the left wall is a chest of drawers, upon which rests a small cupboard. Below that, in the left wall, is a set-in bed. The time is a Friday evening about 7 p.m.

ALLAN Hey, Ma, where's ma drawin instruments, Ah left them in this drawer last week?

MRS BRYSON Whit instryments is that, son?

ALLAN Ma T-square and compass and set-squares, Ah put them here last Friday.

MRS BRYSON Oh is that that big widden thing and that other wee sharp thing – Ah shifted them, the sharp yin wis tearin ma sheets – wait noo, where did Ah put them?

ALLAN Ach hurry up, Ma. Ah'll be late fur the night-school.

JADIE Aye hurry up, oul-yin. Let the boy get smartly off the mark – ye no' see he's gaspin tae get ladled intae this ingineerin gem o' his . . . ye want tae turn it up, young yin, night school!

NICOLL Aye it's aboot time ye wur gettin the length o' the jiggin, Allan. Dae ye merr good than gettin yur nut stuffed wi that muck. That right, Jadie – the old Honolulu Blues, eh?

JADIE First timer, Nick! Walk two and twinkell, Hallo!

NICOLL HALLO!

   (They shake hands and laugh)

MRS BRYSON Oh shurrup, ya per o' clowns. Never mind them, son. Try that tap long drawer, Ah think that's where Ah put them . . . good. Noo aff ye go, son. Never heed whit they say, you stick in, ye'll be gled o' it some day.

ALLAN Ah'll away then, cheerio.

   (He goes off)

MRS BRYSON It's a sin the way youse two carry on wi that lauddie. As brothers ye should try an' gie him a wee bit encouragement.

JADIE Encouragement for whit? You and Colin egg him on as if he wis gonny end up a heid bummer o' some kind.

MRS BRYSON Better than eggin him on tae playin billiards or runnin aboot dancin daft.

JADIE Ach the wey Allan gets intae that night-school stuff's no the gem at a' . . . workin a' day and then studyin at night. Oh ho, his heid's away, definitely!

NICOLL Aye definitely! He might learn all about the ole Pie Arr Squared or somethin but he'd be a dead gaub if it came tae pottin the darkie in a black ba' final.

(NICOLL and JADIE laugh together)

MRS BRYSON Oh aye, laugh go'n, wi yur fly talk; a sensible buddy couldnae understaun a word yese say; snooker and diggin up a bob or two. It's a' yese think aboot.

(NICOLL pots an imaginary ball across the kitchen table)

JADIE Nice play, brother – ma dough's on you.

(They laugh again)

MRS BRYSON Aye, aye, yur good at that. An' as fur you sittin therr dozin, can ye no' speak up fur Allan?

MR BRYSON Ach . . . Jadie and Nicoll are right. The boy's wastin his time.

MRS BRYSON At least he's workin – an' wan day he'll hae a trade at his hauns.

MR BRYSON An' whit's he want a trade fur; whit's a tradesman these days? They bunged that mony dilutees intae his gem durin the war, the Clydeside's loaded wi chantyrasslers noo. Servin his time . . .

NICOLL Monkey-work!

JADIE Aye, an' if the boy should nod the wrang way at the gaffer meantime, he'll find hissell doin army time at the double.

MRS BRYSON Nothin o' the kind. They've promised tae wait till the lauddies have their five years finished before they even think o' callin them up.

NICOLL Five year o' punishment an' two year in the army. Enough tae give ye the duodenial ulsters – like me.

JADIE Like you! The army musta been bughouse tae let you kid them intae believin that. Hey day, any dilutee doctors in the army?

NICOLL Not at all, brother. All guaranteed certified gents that put me on the road tae the pension.

JADIE All certified first-class mugs. Too much stretchin ower the billiard tables in the canteen gives you a short strain that these eediots think is a duodenial ulster, worth an X-ray an' a ticket back tae yer mammy.

NICOLL Ah'm an invalid. Ah've got a pension tae prove it.

MRS BRYSON Invalid, pension, listen tae it! If yur ulster's as big as yur pension ye'll live tae be as fly as this other pensioner here. Ye're a pair, the two o' ye.

MR BRYSON Aw hey, go easy, Aggie, go easy. Ah'm drawin a genuine retired man's due. Ah'm nae invalid.

MRS BRYSON Well, away and look fur work! In fact three o' yae wid dae well tae get yersels work.

JADIE Aw are ye startin that again. Ah tell ye Ah've been over at the buroo every day fur the last month. Nothin wanted but navvies an' tottie-hawkers.

NICOLL Ah'm delicate, Maw.

MR BRYSON Ach. Ah'm jist tired.

MRS BRYSON Are yese no' ashamed that yese are being kept by a lassie, a ludger, an' a boy wi merr spunk than the three o' ye thegither?

JADIE Aye aye, we know, we know. The rose o' the bag-work, and the two gallant gaubs. Ah pey ma wey too ye know.

RENA Aye aboot six weeks in the year.

JADIE Are ye deaf; ye nutt hear me tell yese all that there's nothin doin at ma gem.

RENA An whit's your gem, bee-baw-babbity?

JADIE All right, all right, funny honey. Ye'd think ye wur earnin a binder tae hear ye. Ah could fiddle merr at the boys-fur-rags.

RENA Well fur God's sake buy a bugle.

MRS BRYSON Ach fiddle fiddle faddle. Ah'd rether have Rena's an' Allan's wages, alang wi Colin's ludgin money, an try tae keep things gaun kinna daicently, than a' yur fancy, fiddled, dug-up . . .

JADIE Now now, Maw, many's the time Nick here's won an odd copper or two and ye've been gled o' it.

RENA Aye an' many's the odd copper that Nicoll won has been played back the next night, an' no a word sidey-weys aboot it.

JADIE Listen tae Bedelia here; the plumber-boyfriend must be knocking up the overtime when you're so snidy.

NICOLL Aye an' Ah'll gamble ye Peter's floggin the odd pun o' lead noo an' again, tae keep her wee heart up.

RENA You mind yur jaw, Junior!

MRS BRYSON Noo, noo, nane of that. Keep Peter oot o' it.

RENA Ah never mentioned him.

(COLIN enters from the room)

COLIN How about a lick o' that boot-polish now, Agnes?

MRS BRYSON Aye sure, Colin, if Allan's left any; he lays it on thick.

JADIE Clear the wey an' slap it on fur the night-school.

COLIN That's the way fur him, Jadie boy.

JADIE Oh you're another.

NICOLL Ah suppose you went tae night-school tae learn how tae scoot water tae a hole-borer.

COLIN Naw, but if Ah had Ah might not be labourin now.

JADIE Naw, ye'd be on the Parish!

(The BOYS laugh and COLIN smiles)

MRS BRYSON Never you heed them, Colin. Ah'm gled fur your ludgin money . . . yur in luck, there's a wee scrapin left in the tin.

COLIN That'll do me.

MR BRYSON *(Yawning)* That you, Colin, where are ye makin fur the night?

COLIN Oh the usual Friday night howff Ah suppose. Ah think Ah'll manage a pint or two. Will we be seein you in John's?

MR BRYSON Ye never know – if the wife's in a good mood.

COLIN Ah'm sure she'll see ye all right.

MR BRYSON She was bawlin me out five minutes ago.

MRS BRYSON Aye an' ye deserved it. He lets these hooligans here say whit they like tae Allan.

COLIN Still, Agnes, Ah'm sure ye'll no' let yer man down fur the want o' a pint eh?

NICOLL Hope she disnae let me down either. How about half a dollar, eh, Maw?

MRS BRYSON That's enough!

NICOLL Two bob then.

MRS BRYSON An' whit's gonny feed ye next week?

NICOLL Two bob'll no ruin ye.

MRS BRYSON Naw, but it'll buy hauf the tea next Thursday.

NICOLL Wur entitled tae a copper or two surely.

MRS BRYSON Oh aye ye're entitled! Did ye get cigarettes the day or did ye no?

NICOLL Aye, but this is different – this is pocket money.

MRS BRYSON Pocket money! Ha-ha!

NICOLL Ach come on, Maw, come on. Ah might win a few bob at the billiard hall and Ah'll see ye right fur the hauf o' it.

MRS BRYSON Aye if ye don't go tae a late-night at the dancin. Here, but that's the last ye get oot o' me this week.

(NICOLL grabs the money and takes his jacket from behind the chair)

MRS BRYSON Right enough between billiards and dancin ye cannae afford, yur heid's turned.

JADIE Aw, lea' the boy alane. They tell me he's doin well at the snooker; he's takin them all tae town. Mind, Nick, if ye dae knock up a few pence, ye know where tae find me.

NICOLL Sure, Jadie. Thanks, Maw. So long!
JADIE Wire in, boy.

(NICOLL goes out)

MRS BRYSON Well we can a' sit back noo and wait for the money rollin in.
RENA Aye, blue moons an' things. It's about time Ah wis gettin oot masel.
MRS BRYSON Ye seein Peter the night, hen?
RENA Aye. *(She rises and lifts her coat off the set-in bed)* This coat's seen it's day. Time Ah had a new yin.
MRS BRYSON Oh aye, it's time we a' had somethin, hen.
RENA Nae chance o' another credit line fae oul Baird yet?
MRS BRYSON No till the last yin's cleared, Rena. He's a patient oul sowl fur a tick-man, but he's no giein us lines fur the good o' his health.
RENA How much is there tae pey on the last line yet?
MRS BRYSON Too much tae start thinkin aboot a fresh yin.
RENA Ach . . .
MR BRYSON Never mind, Rena, hen, wan o' these days, ye never know . . .
RENA Aye, you'll back ten winners in a row an' we'll be floatin.
MR BRYSON Naw, maybe no' as much as that – ten in a row wid run ye a queer fortune – but ye never know. See us ower the noon *Record* oot ma jaicket pocket, hen; the back o' the door therr. Have a look at the morra's form.
JADIE You back three in a row the morra, owl yin, an I'll be yer sweetheart the morra night.
MR BRYSON Ye want tae try backin a couple fur yersel.
JADIE Naw, naw – Ah'd rather stick it ontae a king in a pontoon school.
RENA Where's this paper ye asked fur?
MR BRYSON Inside pocket – that's it stickin oot.
MRS BRYSON Ah hope ye think that Ah'm gonny see ye all right fur yur three-cross, or yer roll up, or whitever ye call it.

(In the meantime RENA has bent down to pick up the ticket which has fallen to the floor, from her father's inside pocket)

RENA Whit's this that's fell on the flerr? A ticket o' some kind.
MR BRYSON Let us see it . . . Never you mind whit it is . . . give us it ower here quick.
RENA Awright, jist asked ye.
MRS BRYSON Whit kind o' ticket is it?
RENA Well it's no a pawn ticket anywey.
MRS BRYSON It better no' be.

MR BRYSON Give us it ower here Ah tell ye, ye've nae right haulin it oot anyhow.

RENA It came oot alang wi the paper. Och ye're a right narky oul . . .

(She moves to hand the ticket over)

MRS BRYSON Jist a minute, haud on, haud on; Ah'll have a look at this great ticket.

RENA Here, it's no' a ticket at a', it's a cheque.

MRS BRYSON A cheque! How much fur?

RENA Fifteen . . . Ah don't believe it.

MR BRYSON Well Ah telt ye no' tae look at it, didn't Ah?

MRS BRYSON How much is it fur?

RENA Well it says here . . . fifteen thousand pounds.

MRS BRYSON Eh?

JADIE Fifteen thousand pou'?

MR BRYSON Aw keep yur hair on, everybody.

MRS BRYSON Where did you get this?

MR BRYSON Ach, never mind.

MRS BRYSON Aye Ah'll mind a' right. Whit's a man like you daein wi the like o' this in his pocket – have you been up tae somethin?

JADIE Did ye do up a bank, oul-yin?

MR BRYSON If Ah do up a bank Ah'll grab somethin a helluva sight better than that.

(Pause)

COLIN Where d'ye get it, Boab?

MR BRYSON Look, Colin, it's nuthin. Ah'll likely end up lightin ma pipe wi it.

COLIN But your name's on it, Boab.

MR BRYSON Aye, an' d'ye see who else's name's on it? Signed at the bottom?

COLIN Stephen Bradley . . . Ye don't mean Big Steve the bookie?

MR BRYSON Exactly.

(COLIN hands back the cheque and smiles)

MRS BRYSON Whit does a' this mean?

JADIE Aw, Ah know whit it means now all right. This Steve's the big balloon that goes round the district bettin mugs that he can drink six pints in a row withoot stoppin, then dishin oot bum cheques when he loses. That right, Faither?

MR BRYSON You're never wrang, are ye, big mouth?

JADIE 'Sup wi ye?

MRS BRYSON Jist a minute, are you wan o' the mugs that wis bettin' wi this . . . Steve?

285

MR BRYSON Ah'm nae mug!

MRS BRYSON Ye wur bettin against him a' the same?

MR BRYSON Aw give us a chance . . . look, this thing fa's oot ma' pocket, it's ma business, in't it? Nothin desperate's gonny happen – Ah'm no in any trouble. The cheque's no' worth a curdie except whit Ah wanted it for.

RENA An' whit did ye want it fur?

MR BRYSON Have you no' done enough damage?

JADIE Ye might as well tell us, oul-yin.

MR BRYSON Ah'm tellin yese nothin! It's ma business.

MRS BRYSON It'll be everybody's business if the polis come up here wonderin how a man like you gets the haud o' a cheque for a' that money.

MR BRYSON God stiff me . . . look, as long as it's only this thing . . . this bit o' paper here that Ah've got, an' no' the money, the polis cannae dae a thing. Have ye nae sense? D'ye think Ah'm stupid enough tae imagine that Ah'll get fifteen thousand quid fur this?

MRS BRYSON Whit ye keeping it fur then?

MR BRYSON Ah only got it last night.

MRS BRYSON How d'ye get it?

MR BRYSON . . . All right . . . if ye must know . . . Ah won it.

MRS BRYSON Aye, Ah knew it. Ye wur bettin against this . . . Steve . . . or whatever ye call him.

MR BRYSON Aw right, Agnes, aw right, Ah wis bettin then.

MRS BRYSON When wis this?

MR BRYSON Last night.

MRS BRYSON An' whit did ye use fur money?

MR BRYSON The money you gave me aff ma pension. You gave me seven an' tanner, didn't ye? All right . . . Ah backed a couple o' horses an' got fifteen bob back. Big Steve makes me a bet that Ah considered tae be a good long-shot, an' that cost me nine shillins.

MRS BRYSON Ah thought ye said ye won.

MR BRYSON So Ah did but it costit me money.

RENA Some win that – how's that come aboot?

MR BRYSON Well if Ah had time Ah wid explain it tae ye, but Ah cannae be bothered.

MRS BRYSON Take some explainin . . . ye won but it cost ye nine shillins. Ah don't know much aboot bettin, but Ah know that when ye win, you're the wan that's supposed tae get peyed.

COLIN Wait a minute, Agnes, wait a minute. Look – Jadie mentioned that this big Steve character sometimes gets the boys on for a bet – well the bet goes like this: Steve bets – say – maybe five pounds against the cost of six pints o' beer that he can drink these six pints in a row without stopping – provided the man he's bettin against puts up the money for the beer, see?

MRS BRYSON That's jist aboot the daftest thing Ah ever heard o'.

COLIN Very likely, Agnes, but d'ye see whit Ah'm gettin at?

MRS BRYSON Ah'm no sure. How many pints o' beer did you have tae pey fur, mister?

MR BRYSON . . . Six . . .

MRS BRYSON And d'ye mean tae say that this man bet you fifteen thousand pounds for six pints o' beer . . . aw that's too much tae believe.

MR BRYSON Naebody's askin ye tae believe anythin, yur hellava dense so ye urr! It's easy if ye'll just listen. This bloke disnae bet fifteen thousand nicker tae six jugs o' beer – he bets me a fiver – five poun' that he can scoff the lot without breathin. Noo d'ye understaun?

MRS BRYSON Ah'm no' sure. You say you won?

MR BRYSON Yes – he could only punish off five pints.

JADIE Ah'll bet you wired intae the last yin, eh, Da?

MR BRYSON Big midden, he poured it intae the sawdust.

MRS BRYSON An' whit aboot the five pounds?

MR BRYSON Aw sufferin, savvyin Jasus . . . gie's ma coat, gie's ma jaicket, gie's ma bunnet – Ah'm awa' tae hell oot o' here.

MRS BRYSON You're sittin right there till Ah hear aboot this five pounds.

MR BRYSON Ah hey, Colin, throw us a lifebelt, wull ye?

COLIN Aye haud on, Agnes. Ye see, Big Steve's been at this gem for years. Now, he's worth a lot o' money, we know that – but he never carries any about wi him. Whenever he needs anythin he uses the chequebook, ye understand? Well he's got a funny sense o' humour, in fact he's got a bliddy cruel sense o' humour – so, when he meets a man like Boab here and loses a bet tae him, instead o' handin over a cheque for the right amount, he hands over one that's bliddy well impossible; then he lifts his hat and says goodnight and that's all there's to it.

RENA An' whit can ye dae aboot that?

COLIN Nothin a man like your faither can dae aboot that, Rena. Steve's a big man in more ways than one. Touch him and ye touch plenty.

JADIE He'd receive the severe banjo on the lug if he tried that wi me!

COLIN Aye, aye, Jadie, but your da's no' the brave man you are.

RENA Ye say he's been gettin away wi it for years, Colin.

COLIN Aye, a long time. Of course he's well known for it, but he can always dig up a mug somewhere.

MR BRYSON Except that Ah'm no mug, Colin; that's the difference.

MRS BRYSON Did you know a' aboot the man?

MR BRYSON 'Course Ah knew. Think Ah'm glaikit a' thegither?

MRS BRYSON Ye must be if ye knew aboot it yet went on wi it.

MR BRYSON Ah told ye Ah considered the bet tae be a good long shot, didn't Ah? Ah still think it wis.

MRS BRYSON Wur ye blind or drunk or whit when this happened.

MR BRYSON Dead sober. Ah peyed fur the beer, the big fulla cannae drink it. So he writes out the cheque, haunds it me an' says, 'I think that should cover it.' Then he laughs like hell an' walks oot the door. Ah look at the cheque, tell masel tae forget it, an' stick it in ma pocket.

COLIN But how did ye expect tae get anythin out o' it in the first place, Boab?

MR BRYSON That's the long shot Ah wis talkin about.

RENA Well fur God's sake tell us whit ye mean!

MR BRYSON All right, yese see this *(Holding cheque)*; this is Big Steve's idea o' a joke; but he's slipped up a couple o' times before. Wan o' the times he gave a bloke a cheque for ten poun an' forgot tae tell the bank tae stever it, so the bloke got peyed. Another time a bloke got twenty quid in the same wey. Well that's all Ah wis hopin for, but Big Steve's a fly boy. Tae cover himsell now, in case he should forget tae tell the bank, he's taken tae handin out cheques like this for impossible bliddy sums o' money. Who'd be stupit enough tae try an' collect fifteen thousand poun? The bank wid hunt ye. That's how Steve covers himsell, see.

COLIN An' you thought that Steve might've slipped up an' given you a cheque for a fiver or a tenner then forgotten all about it.

MR BRYSON Exactly, Colin. He might jist have slipped up wance more.

COLIN A long shot right enough, Boab.

MR BRYSON Aye, but the odds were good so Ah thought Ah'd have a go.

JADIE Well ye backed a deuce, oul-yin. Might as well chip that thing in the fire.

MR BRYSON So Ah will, sometime. But 'fore Ah dae Ah'll have a bit o' fun showin it round the boys.

MRS BRYSON Well Ah hope they'll staun ye drink on the strength o' it, fur ye'll get nothin merr oot o' me this week. Nine shillings fur a man that's rollin in money, huh!

MR BRYSON 'Sup wi you? It wis buckshee dough anyway.

MRS BRYSON Aye, bookie's money. Ye're a scunner right enough. Ye take it aff wan bookie an' gie it back tae another – who is he anywey, this Big Steve?

COLIN Ye're bound tae have seen him, Agnes. Big fat fella. Beery face. Always knockin about the district.

MRS BRYSON Must be daft if he knocks aboot roon here. Ye say he's got plenty o' money?

MR BRYSON Money! He's stinkin wi it. Ah'll wager he's got fifty street bookies workin fur him at least. They tell me he lives on his own in a big hotel up the town an' jist likes tae come back roon the old district fur a laugh an' a bit o' company. Big midden! By Jees, Ah mind the time his School-board combies were doon ablow his knees.

JADIE Aye, they say he wis born an' brought up jist doon the road therr. He must've been some boy for the coppers.

MR BRYSON Ah tell ye, he started makin a wee book jist after the first war. Now look at him – swankin high in a big hotel an' a bank book that'd frighten a factor. Big eediot!

MRS BRYSON Eediot or no' he took nine shillins oot o' you.

MR BRYSON All right, all right, forget it!

MRS BRYSON Galoot that ye are. Rena, hen, watch yur time for meetin Peter.

(RENA rises, sorts her hair at mirror)

COLIN Must be makin a move myself. See ye later?

MR BRYSON Ah'm no' sure, Colin.

(COLIN exits. Long pause.)

MR BRYSON Aggie, gonny gie's a couple o' bob tae go doon for a pint wi Colin?

MRS BRYSON Ha, ha!

JADIE Ha ha ha, yur a comedian right enough, oul-yin. Gaun, gie him it, Maw, he deserves it.

MRS BRYSON He can take it aff the fifteen thousand.

JADIE Ha ha, that wid kill ye, widn't it? All that dough in the bing then he puts the hammer on the ole-lady, ha ha.

MR BRYSON Yese wid all have got yur share if it had come off.

RENA Aye, pie in the sky.

MR BRYSON Oh right enough yese wid give the sick. Wherr's ma jaicket? Be better lyin-up in some model or somethin . . .

(He exits)

RENA Ah well, Ah better run or Ah'll be late.

MRS BRYSON Aye, away ye go, hen. An' look, here's hauf a croon, run efter that oul midden an' gie it tae him.

(RENA takes money and moves towards the door as the curtain falls)

CURTAIN

ACT I

Scene 2

The following day. Shortly after one o'clock. JADIE, NICOLL and COLIN sit at the table smoking. MRS BRYSON clears away the used dishes.

MRS BRYSON Noo, noo, don't move, Colin, Ah'll jist take these things away and ye can finish yer smoke in peace. C'mon you, Nicoll, sit ower fae the table an' Ah'll lay that place for Rena; she'll be in directly.

JADIE Aye and ye must be on yur toes fur the ole Setturday wages, eh, Maw?

MRS BRYSON Oh aye, aye. I like the Setturdays, Jadie; must look efter ma Rena and ma Allan the day.

NICOLL Where did Allan get tae anywey – he wis off like a shot the day.

MRS BRYSON He's away up tae some tool-shop. He's been peyin up some instryment fur months noo, and he gets it hame the day.

COLIN He couldnae sleep last night fur talkin about it. It works in decimal points and measures tae a thousandth o' a inch. Ah dozed off after a severe couple o' hours o' decimal equivalents.

JADIE Well if he's no' a first-class tradesman when his time's oot, it'll no' be fur the want o' all the Cunarders the two o' yese have built in yur beds at night.

NICOLL That's jist the same as me. See when Ah'm lyin back in the bed therr, Ah'm trouncin them all right an' left at the snooker; sinking the pots fae every angle. It's nae bother – in bed.

JADIE Aye, Ah felt ye guidin a couple home the other night, ye nearly shoved yur elbow through my jacksie . . . How'd it go last night?

NICOLL Ah wis doin' well fur a couple a hours. The boys were backin me an' Ah wis drawin the original bet on a three timer. Then Ah took Ting Cassidy on; an' he wired intae me.

JADIE Ye should lay aff Ting, he's too good fur ye.

NICOLL Don't know aboot that. Ah think Ah've got his measure now all right. He loses the head when he runs intae snookers. Ah fancy Ah'll beat him the next time we're on thegither.

JADIE Aye but watch him all the same. He disnae like gettin beat, and that mob o' the Gancher's don't like him tae get beat.

NICOLL Whit's it got tae dae wi them?

JADIE The Gancher's winchin Ting's sister – did ye nutt know? – and whenever he wants a bet in the billiard hall, he likes tae see that Ting's gettin a snuff o' it.

NICOLL An' whit am Ah supposed tae dae when Ah come up again' Ting – throw up the cue?

JADIE Naw, naw, but jist watch yursell.

MRS BRYSON Nice folk the two o' yese know; and yese talk about them as though ye a' go tae the same Bandy Hope.

JADIE Nae use gettin upset aboot people like that; ye meet them everywhere.

MRS BRYSON No in here Ah hope!

JADIE Naw, naw, naw, no' in here, Maw.

MRS BRYSON Yese should stey away fae these places.

NICOLL Where else wid we go?

MRS BRYSON Anywhere! Walk anywhere! Therr's a fine day ootside the day; away oot on the caur tae the country or somewhere.

NICOLL The country! 'Magine you an' me oot in the country, Jadie!

JADIE Aye ye ken! Ye ken! It's a gey wheen braw country yokels – up yur jumper!

(They laugh)

NICOLL Ah but hey, mate, ye should chat the oul-man about it – Ah guarantee he'd fancy it strongly.

JADIE That must be the favourite in the three-thirty yur talkin aboot, Ah heard him ravin aboot it this mornin.

(NICOLL joins the joke and COLIN can't help smiling)

MRS BRYSON God forgie ye – poor oul Boab. Ah'll be lucky if he gets oot his bed before five o'clock the day.

(RENA comes in)

RENA Whit's the joke?

MRS BRYSON Oh jist makin fun o' yur poor oul faither, hen. Sit doon, Ah'm ready fur ye.

COLIN Well, Rena, another week by, eh?

RENA Aye, that's it, Colin. Here ye are, Mammy.

(She hands over a pay packet)

MRS BRYSON Thanks, hen.

COLIN Tired?

RENA Weary. The muck ye pick up in wan day in a bag work wid keep ye stourie fur a lifetime.

JADIE Ye'd wonder how these blocks dig up the ideas for makin the dough! Canvas bags, eh – 'magine somebody sittin doon an' thinkin up an idea like that. A fortune in it.

RENA Aye, no' half. Oh but it must be swell tae have a nice clean job in a nice clean place . . .

COLIN Better no' tae think about it, Rena; better keepin the old head down an' wirin in.

(Front doorbell)

MRS BRYSON Anybody behind ye on the stair, Rena?

(Pause)

RENA Well . . . there wis a man lookin at nameplates on the first landin.
MRS BRYSON Whit kind a man?
RENA Eh . . . a kinna well-dressed man.
JADIE Oho, oho! Now then, young Nicoll, whit ye been up tae?
NICOLL How?
JADIE The CID right on yur tail.
NICOLL Whit – aye – ha ha – naw, no me! Keep the heid, you!
JADIE Ho, ho, that shook ye, eh?

(Doorbell again)

COLIN Ah'll get it.
RENA Naw, stey where ye are, Colin. Ah'll go.

(RENA goes out and returns with the LAWYER. He is a man of about sixty: kindly, quiet and shrewd.)

In here, please. *(Pause)* This is ma mother.
LAWYER How do you do? My name's Marr.
MRS BRYSON Oh – oh – how d'you do?
LAWYER I'm very well, thank you. Is Mr Bryson in, Mr Robert Bryson?
MRS BRYSON Aye, he's in right enough, but he's in his bed.
LAWYER Is he ill?
MRS BRYSON No, no . . . just . . . eh . . . tired.
LAWYER Oh, is he asleep?
MRS BRYSON Aye, very likely – d'ye want tae see him?
LAWYER Yes, I'd like to see him.
MRS BRYSON Nicoll, call yer faither.

(Pause. Wee bit embarrassment all round.)

LAWYER Nice day outside.
MRS BRYSON Aye, Ah wis jist sayin so before ye came in.
COLIN Nice fishing weather.
LAWYER Now how did you know to make a remark like that to me?
COLIN The flies in your hat.
LAWYER Aye, aye. Nice weather indeed for a bit of fishing.
MRS BRYSON D'you know Boab? Eh, Ah mean ma husband, mister?
LAWYER No, my dear, I'm afraid I've never met him.
MRS BRYSON Is somethin wrong then?
LAWYER No . . . no, I wouldn't say there was anything wrong . . .
MRS BRYSON Nae trouble, I hope.

LAWYER No, Mrs Bryson, nae trouble.

(Another pause)

Do you mind if I sit for a minute; your stairs are steep.

(COLIN gets him a chair)

I suppose you're all wondering who I am and what I'm doing here. Well I'd like to tell you but I'd rather see Mr Bryson first.

MRS BRYSON Oh yes. Eh, he'll no' be a minute.

(NICOLL re-enters; shortly followed by MR BRYSON, pulling on his braces. He is dressed in shirt, trousers, boots and bunnet.)

This is ma husband.

(LAWYER rises, offers hand)

LAWYER How d'you do, Mr Bryson, my name's Robert Marr.

MR BRYSON Aye?

LAWYER I'm a lawyer.

MR BRYSON A lawyer, whit's the matter, whit's up?

LAWYER Well . . . this may be something you'd want to discuss privately.

MR BRYSON Oh Ah see. Well Ah don't know, this is the only place Ah've got.

COLIN Ah'll away through for a bit, Boab.

MR BRYSON Naw, naw, hing on, Colin. Eh, this is no' bad news or anything like that, is it, oh . . . Mr – eh?

LAWYER No, nothing like that.

MR BRYSON In that case then ye might as well tell us all right here. This is ma two boys and the lassie an' the wife's brother.

LAWYER Very good. Eh, can I sit again; this might take a minute or two?

MR BRYSON Go ahead, welcome . . .

(LAWYER sits)

LAWYER Mr Bryson, do you hold a cheque for fifteen thousand pounds?

MR BRYSON Whit!

LAWYER A cheque for fifteen thousand pounds, signed by Stephen Bradley, bookmaker?

MR BRYSON Eh, jist a minute, Mr Marr . . .

LAWYER Well, do you or don't you?

MR BRYSON Ah said, jist a minute –

MRS BRYSON Oh, fur goodness sake, Boab –

MR BRYSON Now, Agnes, you keep out o' this. Now. Mr Marr, let me tell you somethin . . .

LAWYER Look, Mr Bryson, I haven't come here . . .

MR BRYSON Ah know, Ah know, ye said ye didna come here tae make trouble, so before ye start jist let me say this . . .

LAWYER Oh please, Mr Bryson . . .

MR BRYSON Naw, naw, please nothin. Understand whit Ah'm gonny tell ye, Ah've done nothing wrong here see . . .

LAWYER I haven't said a thing about . . .

MR BRYSON Naw, Ah know ye havnae, but all the same Ah want ye tae know this . . .

LAWYER And I want you to know this . . .

MR BRYSON Jist a minute Ah said, jist a minute. Now then, this cheque you're talkin aboot . . .

LAWYER Mrs Bryson, I appeal to you . . .

MRS BRYSON Boab, don't make a noise.

JADIE Aye, haud your tongue, oul yin! See whit the man wants tae say.

MR BRYSON An' who the hell are you talkin tae!

JADIE Ah'm talkin tae you. The man cannae eat ye.

LAWYER *(Amused)* Quite right. I'm not going to eat anybody, and I'm not going to make trouble. Let me absolutely assure you of that, Mr Bryson.

JADIE Therr ye are, see; stiff me, you're gittering away like a lassie an' the man jist wants tae talk tae ye.

MR BRYSON That'll be enough fae you. All right, Ah've got a cheque for fifteen thousand poun', signed by Big Steve. Whit aboot it?

LAWYER Can I ask how you got it?

MR BRYSON I thought ye said ye wurnae here tae make bother!

LAWYER I'm not, Mr Bryson, I promise you. I just want to ask you a few questions. Of course, you don't have to answer if you don't want to.

MR BRYSON Whit ye askin fur then?

LAWYER Because there are one or two things I need to find out that I think you can tell me. And if you tell me, there's maybe something I can tell you.

MR BRYSON Did the polis sen' ye?

LAWYER Definitely not. Can we start now?

MR BRYSON Ah well, go ahead.

LAWYER Why did Mr Bradley give you this cheque?

MR BRYSON Ach, it's too long a story – don't start that again.

LAWYER All right, where did he give it to you?

MR BRYSON *(Reluctantly)* In a pub.

LAWYER I see. Tell me, then, did he give it to you in payment of a bet?

MR BRYSON Aye.

LAWYER Mmm. You know, of course, that if this cheque should be questioned in a court of law it could become worthless.

MR BRYSON It's worthless the noo. Whit's merr, it's gaun right in the fire the minute you're out the door.

LAWYER Ach, I don't think that's necessary, Mr Bryson. In fact, as it stands I imagine it's a perfectly good cheque.

MR BRYSON Ah that's the reason you're here – I know – the big fulla sent you out to get it back, big b—

LAWYER Well I wouldn't say anything about him now, Mr Bryson. Can I see the cheque?

MR BRYSON Wherr's ma jaicket?

(NICOLL fetches jacket)

Therr it is.

LAWYER Mmm. Yes . . . that seems to be all right, thank you.

(Hands it back)

MRS BRYSON Dae ye no' want tae keep it?

LAWYER Oh no, it's your cheque, not mine.

MR BRYSON 'Snae use tae me.

LAWYER Well I don't know. It's a perfectly good cheque.

MR BRYSON Aye, but it'll be worth an onion when Big Steve pits the hammer on it.

LAWYER He won't be doing that, Mr Bryson.

MR BRYSON Why no'?

LAWYER When did Mr Bradley give you the cheque?

MR BRYSON Thursday night.

LAWYER Well he died that night in the bedroom of his hotel.

(Long pause)

MR BRYSON Oh well . . . I'm sorry tae hear that, Mr Marr. He wis no' a bad fulla, Big Steve.

LAWYER Aye, aye. He had a heart attack – didn't last long. The police called me yesterday. I looked through his papers and saw your name and address on the counterfoil of his chequebook. That's how I knew all about it, of course.

MR BRYSON Aye, of course.

LAWYER So, Mr Bryson, can I ask you now what you intend to do with the cheque?

MR BRYSON Whit can Ah dae wi it?

LAWYER Are you going to present it?

MR BRYSON At the bank? Nutt on your life – Ah'd end up in Barlinnie or somewhere.

LAWYER I don't think so.

MR BRYSON Ye mean, they'd pey it!?

LAWYER Oh I didn't say that.

MR BRYSON Whit d'ye mean then?

LAWYER Look, Mr Bryson, I can't give you any advice about this matter, it wouldn't be right for me to do that . . .

MR BRYSON Aw now, Ah'm not askin for it, am Ah?

LAWYER No you're not; but a few minutes ago I said that if you told me something, I might be able to tell you something. So I'll tell you as much as I can. I'll start at the beginning. Mr Bradley, I think, was born somewhere near here, wasn't he?

MR BRYSON That's right, Ah knew him when he wis a boy.

LAWYER Funny thing is, Bradley was his mother's name, so I think we must assume that his father was a bit of a . . . eh . . . mystery.

MR BRYSON Get away, Ah never knew that.

LAWYER So far as I'm aware he died without having a single relative in the world. Certainly none that he knew and, I think, none who knew about him. That means that there's nobody who can inherit his estate. Mr Bradley left no will – I don't think he suspected that his health wasn't too good – so his entire estate will go to the Crown. Now if you present your cheque against his estate the Crown may accept it and pay it off without question, but on the other hand, they may come back to me and ask what it's all about – and I'm afraid I would have to tell them. I'd have to say, in honesty, that this is a cheque made out in payment of a gambling debt.

MR BRYSON Ah can imagine whit wid happen efter that.

LAWYER So can I, Mr Bryson. Well I must be going.

(He rises)

MR BRYSON Is that all there's to it?

LAWYER How do you mean?

MR BRYSON Well Ah mean, is that all ye came for . . . jist tae tell us that the cheque was no use?

LAWYER Well no, I came because I'm trustee of the Bradley estate and because fifteen thousand pounds is a lot of money. If I have to answer for that amount eventually, well . . . naturally I prefer to know all about it. Although there's one thing I still don't know and that is the kind of bet that would involve so much money.

MR BRYSON Ach it wis a kinna stupit bet on my part – Ah should've known better. The bet wis actually five poun' tae the price o' six pints o' beer. Big Steve lost an' instead o' peying up he gies me this cheque. Calls it fifteen thousand and makes it impossible to cash.

LAWYER Ah yes, I see now. Rather a nasty way of doing things.

MR BRYSON Aye. Well thanks for tellin us all ye did. We might jist have done the wrong thing after we heard that Steve had snuffed it.

LAWYER That's all right, it was really in my own interest to make the position clear. Sorry I can't be more helpful. No doubt that amount of money would have been very handy, but the law's the law.

MR BRYSON Aye, you're right, mister, it wid have been very handy. Eh, Aggie, eh?

MRS BRYSON No' half – a nice new hoose fur wan thing.

LAWYER Aye . . . a pretty cruel joke on people like yourselves. Have you lived a long time in this property?

MR BRYSON Since the day we were married.

LAWYER Aye . . . I sometimes handle the sale of property quite like this. First time I've ever been inside one though.

COLIN We'll invite ye down for the weekend sometime.

LAWYER *(Laughing)* Thanks very much but I think I'll stick to the fishing at the weekends. Goodbye, Mr Bryson; if you feel you ought to have a shot at presenting that cheque, don't let anything I've said put you off. If the Crown people don't question it, it'll be no skin off my back. Goodbye, Mrs Bryson. *(To COLIN)* Goodbye to you, sir.

COLIN Good luck wi the fishin.

LAWYER Thank you. If I get a salmon I'll send you a bit. You like salmon, Mrs Bryson?

MRS BRYSON *(Smiling)* Ah forget.

LAWYER Aye . . . yes. It's not easy to come by, is it? *(He stands looking round the kitchen)* Hmm . . . You know, it's a wonderful fish the salmon. Do you know anything about salmon, Mr Bryson?

MR BRYSON Just that it's helluva dear.

LAWYER You don't know anything about its habits, though?

MR BRYSON Naw, no' me.

LAWYER Well it's a most remarkable fish. In fact in one way it's rather like that cheque you have there. Or maybe I ought to say that there's a point of law which can apply to the cheque, that's very similar to a point of natural law that applies to the salmon. *(He considers carefully what he is going to say)* You see, when the fish reaches a certain size it leaves the river where it was born and makes a journey out to sea. It stays there for a long time and then makes its way back to that original river, to spawn. No matter how far it travels it will always make its way back to its own river. But in the sea it gets a wee bittie dirty. Other creatures in the sea attach themselves to the fish and it gets . . . well . . . dirty. But as soon as that fish strikes the river, the fresh water, it becomes clean again; clean and clever and very desirable – that's why men like me spend so much time chasing after it. Now then, Mr Bryson, you have a cheque there that's not too clean, shall we say; it has a wee bit of dirt about it and, strangely enough, there's a . . . channel . . . a channel through which it can pass and become clean.

MR BRYSON Whit d'ye mean?

LAWYER All right . . . there's a point of law applying to cheques which says roughly this. If a signed cheque for a certain amount of money has been given to one person and instead of presenting that cheque at the bank in the normal way, that person negotiates it through a second person who pays either in goods or in cash an amount equal to all or part of the value of the cheque, that cheque becomes, immediately, an obligation upon the drawer, the person who signed it originally, and its value must then be paid in full to the second party. What we call Value – has been passed on the cheque, and because the second party is in no way responsible for any doubts that might

297

exist about the cheque, the second party's claim must be met in full. So there you are, the fish becomes clean in fresh water and a cheque can become clean when Value is passed on it. Odd, isn't it?

COLIN That's very interestin; but what if the man that signed the cheque is dead?

LAWYER He still has executors. They must become responsible.

MR BRYSON Jist a minute, Ah'm no' too clear aboot this.

LAWYER I'm sorry, Mr Bryson, but I must rush. Once I start talking about fish there's no telling how I might blether. Well, goodbye again, all . . . and good luck.

(Exit LAWYER)

JADIE Did you understaun a' that, Colin?

COLIN Ah think so, Ah'm jist workin it out.

MR BRYSON Whit the hell did he mean; did he mean the cheque is all right efter a'?

COLIN Haud on a minute, Boab, let me think about this.

MRS BRYSON You be careful noo, Boab. Don't try anything that might get ye intae trouble.

JADIE It's all right, Maw. Ah didnae understaun much that lawyer fulla wis sayin about first persons and second parties, but it sounded tae me as if he wis tryin tae give us the wire that there's a chance o' comin out o' this wi a few poun' yet. Eh, Da, whit dae you think?

MR BRYSON Aye, aye, keep quiet a minute wull ye.

JADIE Keep quiet when there's maybe fifteen thousand knockin at the door? Stop talkin like a lollipop. Whit d'you say, Nicoll?

NICOLL Imagine Big Steve snuffin it an' leavin all his gelt tae the government.

JADIE Ah know a few punters that'll no be sorry tae hear aboot that. An' his oul-man jumped the tote, oh hallo, hallo!

RENA If youse two wid jist keep quiet maybe Colin could tell us somethin sensible.

MR BRYSON Aye, fur God's sake shut up! Well, Colin, whit d'ye say?

COLIN It seems tae me that all you've got tae do is find somebody tae cash the cheque and everything's okay.

MR BRYSON How's that?

COLIN Whit the man meant wis this: the cheque's perfectly good but if you want tae cash it through the bank ye'd have tae wait and see whit the Crown says about it – and they might wash it out altogether. But if you know anybody that'll cash it for ye in the meantime, then the Crown cannae cancel it even if they want tae, because the bloke that cashes it for you has nothing tae do wi Big Steve or the game that he wis playin. So what happens is, you get the dough from the man that cashes it and he gets it back fae the Crown. At least, I think that's what the lawyer meant.

MR BRYSON By Jeesoh, whit? Whit ye make o' that, Aggie? We'll all be gallopin about like toffs afore we're done yet!

RENA Aye. All ye've got tae do is get wan o' yur pals tae save up his pension for aboot fifty years an' then cash it for ye.

JADIE Aw get tonsilitis, madam! Ye put the hems on every hope in the house.

MRS BRYSON Well is she no' right, Jadie – who dis yur faither know that wid cash that thing?

NICOLL Ye don't know anybody, dae ye, mister?

MR BRYSON Ah'm jist thinkin aboot it! An' who the hell ye callin mister? Yese talk tae me as if Ah wis a new-laid ludger or somethin. Sorry, Colin, Ah'm no' gettin at you.

COLIN That's a' right, Boab. Any ideas?

MR BRYSON Ah'm jist thinkin . . .

JADIE If the worst comes tae the worst ye can always get . . . eh . . . goods fur it. The lawyer boy said somethin aboot goods, didn't he?

MR BRYSON Listen tae it . . . oh you're the goods . . . fifteen thousand poun' worth o' goods . . . get yursell a new heid while yur at it.

RENA Get me a new coat, Ah'm feart tae pass the ragman.

NICOLL Put me down for a new tin flute wi the tonky stove-pipe paraffin.

MR BRYSON Aw be quiet will yese! Only wan kind o' goods Ah'd swap this fur an' it makes me thirsty thinkin aboot it.

JADIE Oh yes, Ah'm along wi ye therr, Pater.

MR BRYSON Aye . . . now I wonder, Colin, wid there be any law against me takin less dough for the cheque than whit's actually mentioned on it?

COLIN Naw. The lawyer stated that. He said somethin about all or part o' the value of it.

MR BRYSON I see . . . that means we're in the position tae bargain then, disn' it? Ah think Ah know a fulla that wouldn't mind askin a few poun' for hissell an' maybe a plenty few for us too.

MRS BRYSON Noo, Boab, Ah've warned ye, don't . . .

MR BRYSON 'Sall right, Agnes, it's all right. Jadie, get yur jaicket. Wherr's mine?

MRS BRYSON In yer lap.

MR BRYSON Oh . . . Wherr's ma bunnet?

NICOLL On yur nut.

MR BRYSON Oh aye, it wis cauld in bed last night.

JADIE Wherr we headin' fur, boss?

MR BRYSON Down tae see Lachie Mackay the publican.

MRS BRYSON Whit good will that dae ye?

MR BRYSON Ah'll tell ye when we get back. If this comes off we'll all be in Paradise. Keep the heart up, Aggie. We're gettin near the post!

(Exit)

CURTAIN

ACT I

Scene 3

The same night. Background of slight festivity. The FAMILY and PETER are present.

JADIE Aye an' this is how it should be every Setterday night; ye know, jist among wursells; quiet, but plenty. That right, Da – that right, Aggie?

MRS BRYSON Here, less o' the Aggie.

JADIE Have another jag o' this, Maw.

MRS BRYSON Naw, nae merr o' that whisky fur me.

MR BRYSON Ach go ahead, Aggie, it'll dae ye good. Ah'll have a drap tae, son.

JADIE Right, Faither, right; medals an' golden halfs fur you an' yur wee jackpot.

MR BRYSON That bottle's gettin kinna low. Ah hope ye minded tae bring that other five-jiller wi ye, Jadie.

JADIE D'ye think Jadie's a Joe Soap? Therr it's ower on the dresser therr. We'll open it in a jick when this yin's done. Feelin happy, Maw, eh?

MRS BRYSON Aye, aye, we've waited a long time fur this. Ach Ah could hug ye, ya oul rascal.

MR BRYSON Now, now, don't get too frisky!

JADIE Ye can go up next week an' pey a couple o' years' rent on the ole shack here. Gerrit off yur back fur a while.

MRS BRYSON Got it aff ma back is right. Wan o' these days Rena an' I'll be takin a wee walk tae have a look at somethin that we've talked aboot for a long time. Some o' these hooses that are up for sale wid jist suit us fine. Now's wur chance.

MR BRYSON Sure, Aggie, sure. We'll all be toffs in no time. Nicoll therr'll be takin taxis doon tae the billiards, an' Ah'll be gettin a brand new lumhat fur gaun doon tae collect ma pension.

MRS BRYSON Mebby yese will, but Rena an' I are still gaun fur that wee walk someday.

MR BRYSON Plenty o' time, Aggie, plenty o' time.

JADIE How ye doin therr, Nick; will ye no' have a go at this?

MRS BRYSON Don't you gie that lauddie that stuff – bad enough him drinkin beer.

JADIE Aw let the boy enjoy hissell. It's no' every night this kinna thing happens tae us; that right, Da?

MR BRYSON Aye, aye – gie Nicoll a half – he'll no' overdo it.

JADIE Come on, snooker-boy, get that wee gless therr – we'll give ye a wet.

(NICOLL gives JADIE's arm an encouraging tilt while he is pouring)

MRS BRYSON That's too much, Jadie – now Ah'm tellin ye . . .

MR BRYSON Ach stop worryin. Jadie, ye're no' attendin tae Peter an' Rena; gie them somethin – an' see's ower another screw-tap while yur at it.

JADIE Come on therr youse winchers; Peter, drink up, ye're sittin therr like a wally dug – wire intae this!

PETER Easy, easy, Jadie. This tack's a bit hard for me.

JADIE Well ye might as well get used tae it now. We'll kill this bottle aff atween yese; plenty merr. How ye doin, Rena, hen?

RENA Fine!

JADIE Wait tae ye see Madam here next week, Peter. Ho, ho, she'll be swankin it like a London Duchess. Ye'll have tae be keepin a sharp eye on her after this.

PETER That's right, Jadie.

JADIE Ah, don't you worry, Peter, the oul man'll no' miss you out. Nothin tae stop yese gettin tied up now, eh?

PETER Well . . . don't know about that, Jadie.

JADIE *(Confidentially)* Don't be shy – don't be shy – you think it over; the right word in the oul man's ear wid go a long wey.

PETER Well, it's no' jist as simple as that.

JADIE Nuthin easier. Rena here's always been a great pet wi her oul daddy.

PETER It sounds great, Jadie, but . . .

RENA Oh never heed him, Peter. Ye'd think ma da wis a millionnaire tae hear Jadie.

JADIE Well Ah'm only tryin tae make things a bit easier fur yese, that's all. It's no' every day ye get the promise o' plenty shoved intae yur tail. We're all right – you'll see.

PETER Sure thing, Jadie; Ah think it's the goods. But the fact that Ah happen tae be winchin Rena disnae entitle me tae a claim.

JADIE Naw . . . but all the same, a wee sub here or therr wid do no harm.

PETER *(Smiling)* Aye, sure, Jadie.

JADIE Yes, yes, Peter, you think it over . . . oh wull ye have a gander at the young yin therr. Hey, Allan, whit are you so happy aboot – whit's that yur drinkin?

ALLAN Lemonade.

JADIE Whit – nae beer in it? Hey, Nick, haun us ower a screw-tap tae we gie the boy something merr liker the occasion.

ALLAN Naw, no' fur me, Ah don't like beer.

JADIE It's a shandy ye're gettin.

ALLAN Ah don't fancy it, Jadie.

JADIE Eh . . . come on, celebration!

ALLAN Naw honest, Jadie, Ah don't like beer.

JADIE Okay, okay . . . whit's that ye're playin wi?

ALLAN A micrometer.

JADIE Whit's it fur?

ALLAN Ma work. It's an instrument fur measuring.

JADIE S'at the thing that ye peyed up at a shillin a week?

ALLAN Aye.

JADIE Hard lines ye didnae wait a while, the oul man wid've bought ye a couple.

ALLAN Wan's enough fur whit Ah'm daein meantime. Anywey Ah wanted tae buy it masel.

JADIE Let's see it. Looks merr like a clamp tae me. How the hell d'ye manage tae measure wi this thing, nae numbers on it as faur as Ah can see?

ALLAN See there's numbers on the barrel. It's fur fine work. It's graded tae a thousandth o' an inch.

JADIE S'at a fact. Be a handy thing tae have aboot the hoose, eh? Sure ye'll no' have a shandy?

ALLAN Naw right enough, Jadie.

JADIE Ah well . . . don't get too serious aboot this workin stuff, ye might be able tae chuck it soon.

ALLAN But Ah don't want tae chuck it. Ah like it.

JADIE You're aff yur nut! Never mind, ye'll get wise. Yes, Nicoll! And how's it feel now, eh?

NICOLL Champion.

(They look to see if MRS BRYSON is watching and JADIE fills up NICOLL's whisky glass again. NICOLL swigs it in a hurry and coughs violently.)

MRS BRYSON Is that you giein Nicoll merr whisky – Ah thought Ah tellt ye . . .

JADIE Naw, naw, on the level, Maw, that wis some he had left an' it went doon the wrang wey. That right, Nick? Come on, brother, cough it up! Get happy everybody – get happy! Drink up. Aw it wid make ye want tae sing. Ah think Ah'll give yese a wee song. Whit dae ye say, Maw, yur favourite, 'The Meeting of the Waters', eh?

MRS BRYSON That wid be nice, son, nice and quiet.

(JADIE starts to sing in traditional Glasgow voice. He sings one verse and COLIN comes in. JADIE stops.)

COLIN So this is where all the drinkin's bein done. Hullo, Peter, havenae seen you for a while.

(He shakes hands with PETER)

MRS BRYSON That you, Colin? Come on ower tae the fire.

MR BRYSON Aye, come on in, Colin. Jadie, gie Colin a half.

(COLIN draws in a chair and takes the large glass of whisky JADIE offers)

COLIN Well, well, very nice, eh. Looks as though Ah'm drinkin tae your good fortune. Well, Boab and Agnes, everybody, best respects. Ah, very nice.

MR BRYSON Ah meant tae see ye in the Star Bar the night, but ach, Jadie an' I thought somebody might get suspicious at the sight o' a few fivers so we dodged round the district drinkin casual.

COLIN Wise man, Boab. Ah waited in quite a while for ye the day but there was no sign o' ye.

MR BRYSON Ah well . . . Jadie an' I were, eh . . . busy this afternoon, Colin.

COLIN Aye?

MR BRYSON Aye.

JADIE Here, Colin, fill that up.

COLIN Naw that's enough for me. Ah've had a few halfs the night already.

JADIE Come on, Uncle, have a go.

COLIN Naw Ah've had enough, Jadie: but eh . . . Ah'll take a bottle o' beer if ye have wan.

JADIE Sure, certainly. Plenty beer, an' plenty merr where this comes fae.

COLIN That's a good sign . . .

MRS BRYSON Boab, stop sittin therr like an MP an' tell Colin how ye got on.

MR BRYSON *(Deflated)* The hell ye talkin aboot, MP? Ah'm gonny tell him.

MRS BRYSON On ye go then.

MR BRYSON 'Sup wi ye? Tell him yursell if it's worryin ye.

COLIN Give him time, Agnes.

MR BRYSON Ah've tellt her twice already, Colin.

JADIE Aye but ye havnae tellt Colin. Gaun, Da, you're burstin tae tell it anywey.

MR BRYSON You're burstin tae jeyn in ye mean.

JADIE Well it's a' wan – go ahead.

MR BRYSON *(Waits for silence)* It's like this, Colin: Jadie and I goes down tae see Lachie Mackay at the Kyle Arms, but Lachie's no therr, he's doin a tour o' inspection round some o' his other pubs and the barman tells us he'll no' be back till wan o'clock. So we takes a bit stagger roon aboot tae it's near time an' then we goes back. So he's in by this time an' I call him up tae the end o' the bar. Course he wunners whit it's a' aboot so I whips out the cheque an' shows it tae him. Well he jist looks at it an' laughs an' asks me whit I expect him tae dae aboot it. He knows about Big Steve and the bum cheques an' thinks this is jist another. So I gets started. First thing Ah tells

303

him is that Big Steve's dead; that he died on the night this cheque was given tae me. Right away Lachie picks up his ears, 'Oh' he says, 'Is that so?' 'Yes,' says I, 'and whit's more there's been a lawyer down tae see us an' he says the cheque stands good.' So Lachie looks at it fur a minute then he asks again whit I expect him tae do about it, an' although Ah'm managin tae keep the heid quite well, Ah'm beginnin tae feel a bit flustered if Ah've got tae tell him a' that the lawyer says.

JADIE No half, ye were sweatin like a biler.

MR BRYSON Aye, an' you wurnae helpin much. Anywey, Colin, I think hard and somehow I manage tae let Lachie see whit the position is in regards tae me tryin tae get this cheque through on ma own. Ah tell him aboot the Crown an' a' that an' he seems tae understaun whit Ah mean. Then Ah tell him aboot the other thing – that if somebody cashes it beforehand it must be peyed back at the wind-up. So then Ah say that it might be worth his while in the long run if he takes tae deal wi it. He changes like a shot. Eh, Jadie?

JADIE Right away! Glasses an' pints right away. Starts callin the oul-man Robert.

MR BRYSON Sure enough! After we have a good belt at wur pints, Lachie says, 'Now then, Robert, what's on your mind?' So Ah tells him that if he cashes the cheque it'll be worth a good thing to him. Well the bar's gettin a bit crowded by this time so Lachie then tells us tae follow him. He takes us intae his office; gets out the bottle an' again – glasses fur Jadie an' me. Lachie walks up an' doon fur aboot five minutes. Suddenly he says, 'I'll give you fourteen thousand pounds for it!' 'You're on,' Ah says. He puts out his hand an' we shake, then he tells us to wait there for a few minutes. Jadie an' I wait for about twenty minutes an' when Lachie comes back he tells us he's been on the phone tae his lawyer an' everythin's all right. Jadie an' I think he's hedgin it but he's no'; he's jist thinkin oot the best wey tae explain this tae us. He says that the most important point about this is that he must accept the cheque in good faith – in good faith min' ye – that it's a perfectly good cheque. Somehow that's very important. Ye see, until he gets it back fae the Crown we must never breathe a word aboot the deal we make. Well that's all right, Ah tell him, Ah'm no broadcastin it. Next thing is that he cannae give us the money until he actually gets it himsel. That although he's got a string o' pubs tae his name, at the same time he hasnae got fourteen thousand lyin around buckshee, so at this Jadie an' I are beginnin tae get a bit suspicious. We're wunnerin whit he's up tae.

JADIE Nutt half. In fact we refuse another glass jist in case he's at the smoodgin.

MR BRYSON But it's actually okay. Lachie must've seen we wurnae too sure because he says this, that if we'll sign the cheque over to him he'll give us a small sum on the spot an' a small sum any time up tae the time his bank tells him that everythin's okay. Then we can get the main load through. So that sounds good tae me and Jadie, especially when Lachie says that it's no possible for him tae fraud us, because a public row about this might bar the whole thing for everybody. Then he asks if fifty poun' wid do fur a start. Well that's good enough fur me, Ah . . . endorses . . . the cheque an' gives it to him. An' that's how it stands, Colin.

JADIE Fifty poun', eh. Whit ye make o' that, Nick? Hear that, Peter? Ye'd have tae graft a week or two at the trade afore ye had a gander at fifty poun', eh?

PETER True enough, Jadie.

COLIN So that's how it stands, Boab?

MR BRYSON That's it, Colin. Whit d'ye think o' it?

COLIN Sounds all right tae me. Lachie's well known as a decent man.

MR BRYSON Yur right therr. He kept us in the back shop tae three o'clock. We drunk the best part o' a bottle o' whisky. He put ten fivers right in my hand and says, 'Now remember, everything here is done in good faith.' He's a decent man all right.

JADIE Ah'll tell the town he is. So drink up in good faith everybody, drink up.

(*JADIE is about to pour more drinks when there is a loud knock at the front door, accompanied by laughter and the loud voices of a crowd of people*)

MRS BRYSON Who can that be?

MR BRYSON Sounds like big Tina tae me.

RENA Aye and the rest.

MRS BRYSON Wonder whit they want . . . they cannae have heard surely.

MR BRYSON No' unless some o' us tellt them.

MRS BRYSON Well Ah havnae said a word.

MR BRYSON Did you, Rena?

RENA Not me.

MR BRYSON Naebody saw us along at the Shandon, did they, Jadie?

JADIE Don't think so.

MR BRYSON Nicoll! Did you tell anybody?

NICOLL Eh . . . Well naw . . . no exactly.

MR BRYSON Whit d'ye mean, no exactly? Either ye did or ye didnae.

NICOLL Well, Joe Gibb saw me flashin the poun' ye gave me the night, so Ah told him . . . eh that –

JADIE Aw Nicoll, Nicoll – Ah thought ye'd have kept the heid a bit better than that.

MR BRYSON Wait a minute. Did ye tell him the lot . . . everythin?

NICOLL Aw naw, naw, Ah jist sayed that ye had come by a few poun'.

COLIN How many pounds exactly, Nicoll?

NICOLL Well anything up tae a hundred.

MR BRYSON Ye bliddy eediot! The hell d'ye want tae say that fur?

NICOLL Ach, Ah don't know. Ah wis feelin good about it, an Ah wis . . . kinna wantin tae . . . speak up. Ah said it 'fore Ah knew Ah'd said it.

MR BRYSON Ho, ye're a sharp lauddie. Ah gie ye a poun' an' ye jump down tae the street an' tell Joe Gibb your oul-man's worth a small fortune. Now Joe's oul-lady's at the door and hauf the district at her big behind.

NICOLL Ah didnae mean tae shop ye, Da, honest!

MR BRYSON Ach never mind, cannae be helped noo.

RENA Of course, ye don't have tae open the door.

JADIE Aw . . . we'll need tae open the door.

RENA Oh aye, go ahead, big man.

MR BRYSON Might as well. They've got tae hear aboot it sometime, Ah suppose; but afore ye dae open it, Jadie, plank some a' that five-jiller an' a couple a' screw-taps fur the mornin.

COLIN Ah think Ah'll away tae ma bed.

MRS BRYSON Stey fur a wee minute, Colin.

COLIN Ah well . . . okay.

(The voices outside grow louder as the crowd enter. They are almost on stage when the curtain falls.)

CURTAIN

END OF ACT I

ACT II

Scene 1

The scene opens in the middle of a crowded party; everyone is well-oiled; a few are a little further on in drink. MR BRYSON sits in an armchair next to the fire, drunk and half asleep. Downstage at the other end of the fire ALLAN sits quietly. To the left of MR BRYSON sits MRS BRYSON and TINA GIBB. A little further and back near the sink sit RENA and PETER. Further left still are NICOLL and four of his boys, and three of JADIE's handers. In the area of the dresser is congregated the GANCHER and his bunch of five hangers-on. The GANCHER is a cynical gent who stutters just a little. There is a very well-stocked table near the centre of the floor, from which a small scruffy-looking CRAITUR in a long coat, bunnet and scarf performs a stealthy appropriation of screw-tops. He starts near MR BRYSON exhorting him to drink up and not forget an old pal he ran about with fifteen years ago. Then he begins his drunken dance over to the table. Up the juke goes another screw-top, and off he rolls towards the door. (The idea is, of course, that he is forming a wee plank for the road home.) When he returns he makes for Boab again, waits a minute or two, then begins the sleekit purloin once more. JADIE stands with his back to the fireplace, with a half-empty whisky bottle in his downstage pocket. When the curtain rises he is speaking in a loud voice across to his and NICOLL's particular guests; though with the intention of impressing all present.

JADIE Eight hundret poun' it cost! Sixty mile an hour nae bother. The oul man nearly had a baby when Ah tellt him the price. But it's a brammer – worth every copper o' the cash. Ye'll all get a jaunt in it sometime.
TINA Ye'll need tae get a shaffoor fur it, Jadie.
JADIE There's only wan 'hoor' gets drivin that barra, an' that's Jadie here; except the Nicoll boy therr. He's comin oot the morra tae get learnt. Or mebbe the young yin here'll get havin a jig at it; Ah guarantee he'd pick it up like a shot. Oh this is the deep fella here all right. Daft aboot the trade. Jist like Peter therr – that right, Peter boy, eh? Ye had a look at the new car yet, Peter? *(PETER shakes his head)* She's a nice bit o' gear. Ye drive, Peter?
PETER Used tae.
JADIE That a fact? Must give ye a len o' it sometime. You and Rena can dive out the country.
1st HANDER Didnae know ye could drive, Jadie.
JADIE Aye! That's ma gem, drivin. Ah drove a breid van when Ah wis workin.
2nd HANDER So ye did work at wan time.

JADIE Yes! But never again, Santy, never again! Ye only sign on for plenty wance in a lifetime, an' that's enough.

(There is some laughter and general conversation. At this point the CRAITUR gets going.)

JADIE C'mon, Peter, slap that inside ye. You tae, Rena. Youse ought tae be . . . happy, or something. When yese gonny get married now, eh?
RENA Be quiet, Jadie.
JADIE Naw, but you be quiet. Yese should get married right away. The oul-man wid set yese up in a wanner. Don't blush, Peter, it's all right. We know you're jist a plumber, an' Rena here's the daughter of fourteen thousand nicker, but we like ye in here. You wire in, boy. Hey, whit d'ye think o' that, everybody? Ah'm tellin the winchers they ought tae get married immediately, that right? Whit d'you think, Maw?

(He puts his arm around her neck and affects a cuddle, PETER stands as if to leave but RENA pulls him back into his chair)

JADIE How wid ye like tae loss yur wee Rena, eh, Maw?
MRS BRYSON Peter's a nice fella. Be nae loss that.
TINA Better watch or mebbe she's losin her wee Jadie tae.
JADIE Don't you believe it. Aggie here's ma wan an' only. Here, have another rattle at this.

(He fills up the women's glasses then goes off-stage to the room to collect another bottle of whisky)

TINA Well here's tae you and yours again, Mrs Bryson. Ma man better watch oot fur me the night, haw, haw, eh? *(She drinks)* When ye thinkin o' shiftin fae here noo, Agnes?
MRS BRYSON Whenever Ah can get him sober long enough tae get doon tae a decent factor an' make the arrangements. Look at him, whit a picture o' energy.

(TINA winks and goes over to shake MR BRYSON)

TINA Hey, hey, poppy-nose, when are you gonny take this good wee wife o' yours tae a new hoose? Time ye wur thinking aboot it.
MR BRYSON Eh – eh – oh, aye, aye . . . ooh God Blimey whit a fright ye gied us!
TINA Whit's up, ye got the horrors?
MR BRYSON Naw . . . Ah . . . Ah wis dreamin aboot . . . aboot a racehorse an when Ah wakent up . . . Ah thought . . . Ah thought you wur it!
TINA Gaun, ye cheeky oul sod ye!
JADIE *(Returning)* 'S the matter, Tina, the oul-man makin ye a proposition?

TINA Ah'll make him a proposition – fur the undertaker. He's resemblin me tae a racehorse.

JADIE A, ha, that's flattery compared tae whit yur man calls ye sometimes.

TINA Huh, cheek!

JADIE Never mind, Tina, hen, have another wee jag tae mak it up.

TINA Aw, Jadie son, ye can cry me anythin under the sun, as long as thurr's a wee lip o' the johnnie aback o' it tae keep me fae greetin ma eyes oot. That's lovely, Jadie, that's lovely.

JADIE Go ahead, Tina, go ahead. How's the badge therr, Nick? Plenty o' this left?

NICOLL Aye, bags.

JADIE *(Passing over the remainder of the unfinished bottle)* Here, haun that ower tae the Gancher. All right, Gancher? Get mowed intae that – plenty merr. *(Turns to look at MR BRYSON)* Hey, hey! Wherr's yur manners? Ye're snortin away like a bull therr.

MR BRYSON That's a' right, that's a' right.

JADIE C'mon, oul-yin, enjoy yersulf.

MR BRYSON Ah'm doin fine, doin fine.

JADIE Ye'd be doin better wi a load o' this under yur semmit. Here!

(MR BRYSON takes it and drinks half, then leans back again)

(The CRAITUR has just returned from one of his expeditions)

CRAITUR Good oul Boab, he's a good fulla. You're his ouldest, aren't ye? Ah ran aboot wi Boab fifteen year ago. He's a good fella, a good fella.

JADIE Aye he's all right, the oul-man. Ye fur a half? Get yersell a gless. *(As JADIE turns back to MR BRYSON, the CRAITUR produces a glass from his pocket)* Hey, Da, come on, waken up. Here an oul pal o' yours ower tae see ye. *(Filling the CRAITUR's glass)* His ole nut's away the night, eh. Ye no' hear whit Ah wis sayin, Da – here an oul china o' yours here. Whit d'ye make o' that . . . *(But the CRAITUR has gone. JADIE finds himself alone. He moves to ALLAN and ruffles his hair, but his reception here is not enthusiastic, so he makes for the group of boys.)* Hullo, lads, yese doin all right; all right, Gancher?

GANCHER S-sure eh we're s-s-stickin it eh all right.

JADIE The gem, the gem! *(Addressing his own bunch again)* Whit d'ye make o' this yin, eh? Comin on in't he! Look at the cut o' him. Ye want tae see the couple o' bran' new suits he's got in that room therr. Oho he's a charmer this.

NICOLL Ye don't do so miserable yursell, brother; Ah'll gamble ye've bought half the flash coats in the country by this time; an' wi the new car there's nae telling whit ye'll get up tae.

JADIE Ah, but Ah haven't got the suede-shoe magic. Classy Nicoll Bryson, the double-breasted boy; the dead man's deed for the ladies.

NICOLL Your heid's snookered, mac, right off the table.

JADIE Oh yes, yes! Powerful patter that; billiard talk, monkey-chatter. Ye be tellin next that ye've won a gem o' snooker recently.

NICOLL Ah'll tell ye it now.

JADIE Whit! Don't tell me some gaub walked in.

NICOLL Aye, Ting Cassidy!

JADIE Oh, so ye done him at last?

NICOLL Aye, regular fur the past three weeks.

JADIE Hey, Gancher, ye hear that? The Nicoll fulla here's been takin the drawers aff Ting Cassidy!

GANCHER S-s-so Ah wis h-hearin.

JADIE He's gettin on, eh?

GANCHER Aye it's n-n-nice tae see him gettin on, but it m-might be kinna n-nice tae if he eh l-l-l-lost a table noo and then.

JADIE How?

GANCHER W-we-well he's a eh b-bit o' a t-ti-ticket, Ting.

NICOLL He's a bit o' Gilbert if ye ask me.

GANCHER Ah w-wid-widnae be eh too s-sure. Anyway e-e-everybody isnae eh G-Gilberts.

JADIE Whit's that mean?

GANCHER Aw n-nothin; but eh the b-boy Ah think sh-should s-screw the eh n-nut a wee while.

JADIE Ah don't savvy this.

GANCHER *(Slyly)* Naw, naw, it's eh j-jist that T-Ting an' eh some other people are eh k-k-kinna handy wi the eh c-cues tae ye know.

JADIE That could mean two or three things, Gancher.

GANCHER Aye it's eh a' right, b-b-but Ah w-w-widnae eh like tae see the boy eh g-gettin the wr-wr-wrang end o' the s-s-stick if ye eh s-see whit Ah m-mean.

JADIE Well we know whit tae dae aboot that!

GANCHER *(Laying down his glass)* Whit!?

JADIE *(Singing)*
> 'Oh don't stand an' look around
> When the cues are upside down.'

(The tension is relieved. The BOYS laugh and GANCHER retires.)

1st HANDER Is that the billiard song, Jadie?

JADIE Aye.

2nd HANDER Perform it, Jadie – gaun.

(CHORUS of 'Aye sure; wire in, Jadie,' 'Go ahead,' etc.)

JADIE No swankin?

(Someone calls 'Quiet therr fur a song fae Jadie!' He makes some modest preparation and is about to begin the first word when . . .)

TINA We-ell! Gaun yersell, Jadie!

(Loud derisive laughter from GANCHER's end. CHORUS of 'Quiet therr!' 'Order!' etc.)

JADIE *(Singing)*
    Now Govan is a busy place upon a Friday night,
    And the billiard halls down there are busy too,
    And there's many a strongly fancied lad
    Been rattled in a fight
    For fiddlin with the colours and the cue.

CHORUS *(Singing)*
    Oh don't stand and look around
    When the cues are upside down
    And the balls are flying fast from far and near,
    For whether you're tae blame, ye'd be better safe at hame,
    When they're handin out the stitches at yur ear.

JADIE
    Now 'twas on a certain Friday I went to a saloon
    For I'd heard some fancy things about this dive,
    So I moved up to a table where two boys were trying hard
    To win three sets of snooker out of five.

CHORUS
    Oh don't stand and look around . . . *(etc.)*

JADIE
    There were nearly three-score Govan boys
    With bunnets to the fore
    Standing round upon the benches looking grim,
    For the wire had got around that one lad was two sets down
    And his chances now were getting rather thin.

    One half of this mob had bet their dough
    Upon the losing guy
    And the rest were on the boy whose game was made,
    But the leary losing punters knew that when the game was by,
    The other mob just weren't getting payed.

    Now the cool dab-lad, the winning boy was lined up for the kill,
    He'd been stickin home the tricks in fives and threes,
    When the losing rascal calls, as he jungles up the balls,
    'That's all, the gem's a-bogey, if you please.'

CHORUS
    Oh don't stand and look around *(etc.)*

(All the BOYS join in heartily on the last chorus, with many handshakes

and lots of pantomime. The CRAITUR has taken advantage of the situation by dancing over to the table and stuffing a couple of bottles into his underwear. GANCHER'S MOB is not impressed. When the song and the excitement is over there is some natural expectation of a drink. The party is well on now, with NICOLL particularly showing his drink. The refill has just been completed when the GANCHER'S BOYS begin, slowly and deliberately, to sing. Their song is 'Come down to the Corner'.)

GANCHER'S MOB

> Come down to the corner
> Make no delay
> There you'll find the Gancher mob
> Any time of the day.
> We chased the Cheeky Forty up the Garngad
> For we are the Gancher Foley boys.
>
> Hullo! Hullo! We are the Gancher boys,
> Hullo! Hullo! You'll know us by our noise,
> We've done the Cheeky Forty, the Ricey and the Toi,
> The Milligan Boys, the Paddy and the Plum.

(NICOLL'S and JADIE'S BOYS are prepared for anything)

MRS BRYSON Here, here, that's gaun a bit too faur. My goodness whit a noise.

(She signals JADIE to stop the row. The song has made the singers very truculent.)

JADIE Aw, hey hey, Gancher! Shurrup therr! Ye'll have hauf the neds in the country at the door.
GANCHER Eh Ah wh-whit?
JADIE We don't mind yese havin a song, but stiff me there's nae need fur that.
GANCHER 'Sup – wh-whit's eh whit's wrang wi ye?
JADIE Nothin wrang wi me; jist tellin ye tae keep the heid a bit.
GANCHER Aw Ah eh see, it's your eh p-party, y-you can get eh s-s-singin but eh w-we cannae, is eh is 'at it?
JADIE Naw, naw. Jist the oul-lady disnae like it, that's a'.
GANCHER 'S 'at a eh f-fact now?
JADIE That's a fact now!
GANCHER An' eh sh-she's sent eh the eh b-big lauddie ower eh tae eh s-s-settle it eh?
JADIE Aye sure.
GANCHER Eh w-well eh h-have a b-buzz at it then.

JADIE Ah don't mind!
MRS BRYSON Here, nane o' that!

(She grabs JADIE from behind, round his neck and pulls him back where RENA and PETER hold him back)

If youse cannae behave yursells yese shouldnae hae come.
GANCHER Ah eh the eh P-Parish Brysons gettin a eh b-bit too eh goo-good fur us, eh?
MRS BRYSON We want nane o' yur kind here.
GANCHER Wh-wh-whit eh whit's up wi eh eh oor kind?
NICOLL *(Stepping in front of GANCHER and imitating the latter's impediment)* Y-y-ye're a shower o' p-p-poe-naggers, that's whit's up wi yese.
GANCHER Y-ya b-bastard!

(He dunts NICOLL in the face, sending him flying into the table, overturning the lot with a clatter; immediately there is a call of 'Handers-handers' and the pals move in for the shemozzle; and shemozzle it is. The fight lasts for some minutes, during which the CRAITUR, realising the party is over, is desperately salvaging what he can from the ruins of the bottles, and sticking them into every available corner of his clothes. At one point BOAB wakens and makes his way round to the front. When he realises what is happening he begins issuing challenges and making enormous swipes at thin air, until he is hauled back by the unceremonious hand of TINA.)

TINA Och for God's sake, Boab, sit on yur bum or ye'll gie us a' the cauld.

(The fight continues until a policeman's whistle is heard from the back court below, and a voice shouting:)

VOICE Here, what's goin on up there?
TINA *(Going to window)* Oh nuthin, nuthin, jist a wee argyment, that's a'.
VOICE Well cut it out immediately or we'll have a van at the close for the lot o' ye!

(For a moment the situation is still touch and go, but GANCHER'S MOB think again. They begin to leave. NICOLL is helped to the downstage fireside chair by ALLAN.)

GANCHER Me an' eh Ting'll s-see yese all eh kna-knackert for this eh y-y-yet.
JADIE Ach away an' peddle yur duff.

(Again things look a little dangerous, but the GANCHER'S MOB

313

eventually leave. They have just been gone for a second when one of them pokes his head round the door and spits into the face of one of the remaining scrappers, then shoots off with a slam of the door.)

MRS BRYSON *(Coming between the boys and the door)* Noo, noo, fur God's sake nae merr, nae merr. Go'n back fae the door an' let there be nae merr o' that. Ah never thought Ah'd see the day when a thing like that wid happen in ma ain hoose. Whit a disgrace, whit a disgrace!

JADIE Worse'n that; whit a dead lyin down liberty. They come up and drink' yur booze all night, then get needled up because Nicoll does hissell a bit o' good down at the billiards. It's a disgrace all right.

MRS BRYSON Whit's Nicoll got tae dae wi them anyway?

JADIE It's jist the thing that Ah wis sayin tae Nick the other day. The Gancher's on the nod wi Ting Cassidy's sister. Nicoll's been playin Ting at billiards a few times lately an' beatin him. The Gancher bets his money on Ting an' Nicoll takes it. So the stutterin beauty thinks it's up tae him tae do somethin aboot it.

MRS BRYSON Huh. How people like that can get intae decent folk's hooses Ah don't know. Yese must be blind no tae have seen they were ettlin that wey a' night.

JADIE Ach screw yur nut, Maw! They were in the pub an' they folloyed us up here. So ye haun roun' a gless here and therr – ye don't expect them tae take yur ears aff intae the bargain.

MRS BRYSON Folk like that wid take yur life – efter they've taken yur money.

JADIE Aye all right – all right, don't preach. It'll no happen again.

MRS BRYSON Well see tae it – if ye can.

JADIE Whit's that mean?

MRS BRYSON Oh never mind. Are ye a'right, youse lauddies? That's an awful face you've got, son.

(She goes to a lad with a very bruised face. She produces a handkerchief.)

Gimme ower some o' that whisky.

(She wets the hanky and holds it to the lad's face)

Tina, away through tae that room windae an' see if these hooligans are oot the street. It's a mercy some o' you boys didnae get killed.

(She spots another lad whose nose is bleeding freely)

Jadie, gie that lauddie yur hanky tae haud tae his nose at the sink. Oh boys, boys, your mothers'll no' think much o' me when yese go hame in that state the night.

(There is a pause here for the wiping of bruises, etc.)

JADIE The lads can stey here tae they get thursells straightened up.

MRS BRYSON The lads wid be better getting aff hame tae their beds efter that rammy.

TINA The street's clear except fur two polis at the corner.

MRS BRYSON Come on then, boys. Watch yursells on the road hame.

JADIE Yese off, lads? We'll nutt forget yese fur standin by the night. Mebbe yese a' better have a half before yese go.

MRS BRYSON The boys are needin nae merr halfs the night, Jadie.

JADIE Okay, okay, see yese the morra. Yese done well. Hey, Nick, the boys are off; ach he's chucked it.

(NICOLL has passed out on his chair. The BOYS clear off.)

Best crowd o' boys in the city. By jees, if the polis hadnae ha' blew that whistle, the Gancher mob wis for the burial.

RENA It's a lot tae be proud o'. Wan crowd knocks the wits oot o' another crowd an' you feel like a hallelujah band. Ye're wise right enough.

JADIE 'Sup wi you, madam?

RENA Oh nuthin up wi me. Hauf a host o' hooligans come in an' try tae massacre the other hauf – ma mammy's near demented wi the disgrace o' it – Nicoll's sittin therr like a meth-drinker on the ran-dan; whit the hell dae ye think is up wi me!

JADIE Peter, Ah think ye better take Miss Snottery here oot fur some fresh air.

PETER That's a good idea. Get your coat, Rena. Goodnight, Mrs Bryson.

RENA Ah'll no' be long, Mammy.

MRS BRYSON Right, Rena. Goodnight, Peter.

(They both leave as COLIN enters)

COLIN Ye makin off, Peter?

PETER Aye, goodnight, Colin.

COLIN 'Night.

(There is a tremendous clatter of bottles from the street. Big TINA makes a dive for the room. JADIE moves towards the door.)

MRS BRYSON Don't you go doon therr, Jadie Bryson.

JADIE That sounds like the boys in trouble.

MRS BRYSON Never you heed them. You an' your drink have done enough damage fur wan night.

JADIE Aw Ah suppose Ah'm tae blame fur it noo.

MRS BRYSON Ye certainly are – you an' Nicoll and yer faither – so ye can jist stey here an' let them fight it oot themsells.

(TINA returns)

Is that them at it again?

TINA Aw naw naw. Jist some wee man lyin doon therr among a bevy o' beer bottles.

COLIN H'm . . . been havin a party?

MRS BRYSON Aye, some party. Ye're late the night, Colin.

COLIN Yes. Ah heard the celebrations. Ye're doin well – six parties in as many weeks, Ah thought Ah'd give it a miss the night and keep ma distance till the parasites had moved off.

JADIE Aw, are you all set fur the big moan tae.

COLIN Naw naw, Jadie, it's got nothin to do wi me.

JADIE Aye all right. We'll waken ye fur the Bible Class in the mornin. Ah'll away tae ma scratcher.

MRS BRYSON (*Indicating NICOLL and MR BRYSON*) Take these two alang wi ye.

(*JADIE makes for NICOLL first, shakes his head a little and gets him on his feet. TINA prepares to leave.*)

TINA Wull Ah gie ye a wee haun tae clear this up, Aggie?

MRS BRYSON Naw, Tina, Rena an' me'll manage that. Sorry yur night wis spiled.

TINA That's a' right, Aggie. Don't be botherin aboot anythin, darlin; everybody has a good barney in their hoose wance in a lifetime. Goodnight, Colin.

COLIN Goodnight, Tina. It wisnae you Ah meant when Ah mentioned parasites.

TINA Parasites right enough, Colin – they're never done fightin. Goodnight, Aggie.

MRS BRYSON Goodnight, Tina.

JADIE (*Entering*) Come on, Da, get aff yer knees.

MRS BRYSON Is Nicoll all right?

JADIE Aye, champion. Ah bunged him intae bed as he wis.

MRS BRYSON Wi that good suit on!

JADIE Ach plenty suits. Come on, oul yin, on yur feet.

MR BRYSON Eh whit – eh whit – whose money is it anywey – who signed the ole . . . Lachie Mackay . . .

JADIE C'mon, on yur way.

(*There is a pause after they leave. While COLIN looks around, he suddenly becomes aware of ALLAN.*)

COLIN You still up, Allan?

ALLAN Aye.

MRS BRYSON Ye've some family tae be proud o' the night . . . go tae yur bed, son.

ALLAN Sure. 'Night, Ma.

COLIN Ah'll be along wi ye directly.

ALLAN Okay.

(He goes off)

COLIN Ah suppose he wis here durin the shemozzle?

MRS BRYSON Where else could he be?

COLIN Aye . . . This kinna thing's good fur him, Ah suppose?

MRS BRYSON It's no' good fur ony o' us. Ah hope you don't imagine that Ah like this hooligan rammy stuff. We'll jist need tae see there's nae merr o' it.

COLIN How can ye see tae that, Agnes? It's six weeks since yese got the money through and Jadie and Boab havenae been sober since; Nicoll's flashin aboot like a yo-yo, and the hoose is like a Parish Pey Desk. Jadie can buy a motor car but don't mention a hoose wi a bath. There's bound tae be burst-ups all the time if this goes on.

MRS BRYSON Ah know, Ah know, Colin – but it's jist that Boab and the boys are no' used tae it yet. They'll quieten doon efter a bit.

COLIN Well Ah hope so, Agnes – fur your sake, an' Allan's and Rena's.

MRS BRYSON An' whit's the matter wi the other three?

COLIN They've nae self-respect, ma dear; an' they seem tae have bloody little respect for you. They've nae sense o' money either, and whit it should mean. Money should be good tae people like us, Agnes . . . ach, Ah'll away tae ma bed. It's no ma business.

MRS BRYSON It's worryin ye plenty anywey.

COLIN Ah'm worried fur Allan and Rena and yourself – the other three'll be as they are as long as they've a tosser at all.

MRS BRYSON Aye right, Colin – Ah think ye've said enough fur wan night.

(He moves towards the door, then turns)

COLIN All right, Agnes; Ah'll not be sayin' it much longer. Ah'm leavin as soon as Ah get a place fixed up.

MRS BRYSON Ye – ye don't mean that, Colin.

COLIN Aye Ah mean it, Agnes. Ah've been hopin that this wis jist a spell when the boys were havin' a kinna long spree, but it's too much for me, hen.

MRS BRYSON Ah'm sorry tae hear ye sayin that, Colin.

COLIN Ah'm sorry tae be sayin it. Ah've been here a long time an' Ah wis content here. It wis good tae be able tae help wi the ludgin money; it meant somethin – but it means nuthin here now, Agnes. It wisnae much, but Ah think Ah'd rather take it somewhere else.

MRS BRYSON Well if that's how ye look at it, Colin, Ah suppose that's how it must be.

COLIN Aye . . . well goodnight, Agnes.

MRS BRYSON Goodnight . . . ye'll no' change yur mind, Colin?

COLIN Well – Ah might be wrong aboot all this; if Ah am Ah'll be glad tae stey . . .

MRS BRYSON Oh well . . .

(COLIN goes off as RENA enters)

MRS BRYSON Colin's leavin us, hen.

RENA Is he?

MRS BRYSON Aye, he's fed up wi yur faither and the boys cairryin on.

RENA Peter wis sayin the same thing.

MRS BRYSON Oh, and whit's it tae him? Whit's wrang wi ye?

RENA Ach, we had an argument aboot the drinkin an' the fightin. Noo he wants us tae get married as soon as we can arrange it.

MRS BRYSON That's sudden is it no'?

RENA A bit too sudden fur me; we meant tae wait at least a couple o' years.

MRS BRYSON Whit's his hurry?

RENA Ach, jist that he says that he disnae want me tae get the same kinna outlook as Jadie or Nicoll.

MRS BRYSON Huh, Ah never knew that money wis sich a scunner. Whit did ye tell him?

RENA Ah said Ah thought we should wait fur a while yet. He was annoyed earlier at Jadie hintin that ma daddy wid set us up, an' oot therr Ah wis daft enough tae say that if we waited a wee while ma da might dae that. He nearly had a fit! Ah think hauf the stairheid must've heard him tellin me that when he gets married it'll be when he chooses, an' no' when somebody else takes the notion tae clear the wey fur him.

MRS BRYSON That's a' very well, but a wee help wid go a long wey tae savin yese an awful lot o' bother.

RENA Help's the last thing he wants fae ma da or Jadie.

MRS BRYSON Oh well . . . it's between the two o' yese.

RENA Aye.

MRS BRYSON Ach don't worry, hen, it'll turn oot a' right.

RENA Well it better turn oot soon, or Ah'll he lookin for another boyfriend.

MRS BRYSON My, my, everybody's that full o' determination. Well, there's nuthin ye can dae aboot it the night. Come on, hen, an' gie me a wee haun tae clear this place up.

(As they begin to clear up the curtain falls)

CURTAIN

ACT II

Scene 2

The scene opens with JADIE dressing. ALLAN stands at table occupied by some technical drawing. NICOLL is dressed up and talking to JADIE.

NICOLL Come on, Jadie, give us the key. Ah told this bird doon here that Ah could chat the len o' a car. She's all swanked up fur the occasion.

JADIE Now now, sonny, ye might be gaun up fur yer licence in a few weeks' time, but ye cannae expect tae run the country in the meanwhile.

NICOLL Ye said yursell that Ah wis doin well at the drivi'.

JADIE Aye, that's it! Ah take ye out fur two weeks an' give ye a go at the wheel all the time, an' now ye want tae be off like a shot on yur own tile. Oho, yur a skoosher right enough.

NICOLL Well whit d'ye say, eh?

JADIE Who's the bird anywey?

NICOLL She's fae the high road town – ye don't know her.

JADIE Nice gimp?

NICOLL She's a looker an' a half. How about the car, eh, Jadie?

JADIE Ah see the gem here all right; playin the wee laddie up wi the big brother's buggy; naw naw, yur not on, Cassynova.

NICOLL Aw come on, Jadie, please – therr ye are. Please! She's doon therr waitin.

JADIE Wherr wis ye thinkin o' divin off tae anywey?

NICOLL Anywherr – oot the road somewherr.

JADIE The old Balloch road wi a bird in the hand, eh?

NICOLL Sure, anywherr wid do me – the night.

JADIE Ho-ho, ya beast ye!

NICOLL Whit d'ye say then?

JADIE Eh – well – naw, Ah don't think so – it's a bit risky; ye might get lost.

NICOLL Ach . . . Ah thought ye were all for it fur a minute.

JADIE Oh yur right enough – Ah'm all for it – but you're too young. Tell ye whit, tell her Jadie's doin nothin the night and he'll see her all right fur a small portion o' pantomime.

NICOLL Aye likely! But Ah fancy there widnae be enough room in the car for her – efter your heid got in.

JADIE Oh a comical gent, eh. Well Ah will tell ye whit – see if ye go intae the room therr an' bring through ma coat, ye can have the car.

NICOLL No swankin?

JADIE No swankin.

(NICOLL goes out)

That's how tae kid them along, eh, Allan boy?

ALLAN Ye're a fast man, Jadie.

JADIE Oh whit, whit's that Ah hear, you comin the wide patter eh? It's you that'll be after the car next.

ALLAN Aye an' yur birds too.

JADIE Ha, ha, ha, good ole Allan boy; the very goods! Aye, an' wi a poun' or two on yur tail Ah fancy the Jadie an' Nicoll fullas widnae stand a hope.

NICOLL *(Entering with coat)* Therr it is, Jadie.

JADIE Ta. Ah suppose ye want the key noo – therr ye are – Ah wis kiddin ye all along.

NICOLL Aw thanks, Jadie. This'll do me proud wi the pusher.

JADIE Go ahead, Nicoll boy.

(NICOLL goes, but is stopped and pulled round by JADIE who slaps his hand on NICOLL's back pocket)

Whit's this on the hip? Oh, a five-jiller – the best too, eh – whit's this fur?

NICOLL Ach jist a drop o' the johnnie tae help us along.

JADIE A picnic, eh. Don't give her too much.

NICOLL Be nae use, that.

JADIE Ah see whit ye mean. Whit age is she?

NICOLL Nineteen.

JADIE So long, baby-snatcher!

(NICOLL goes towards the door again)

Hey, jist a minute – give us a half oot o' that thing.

NICOLL Sure. Go ahead.

JADIE Oh nice, nice.

NICOLL The very kick, mister! Good fur the back. Well, be lookin at ye.

JADIE Keep yur mind on the road now.

(NICOLL exits)

He's a boy that, eh, Allan? If he jist keeps the eye on Jadie here he'll do all right.

(Putting on his coat. Singing –)

> 'You broke my heart a million ways,
> When you took those happy days.'

Whit's this here?

ALLAN Homework for the night-school.

JADIE Homework! You want tae live in the jungle.

ALLAN How?

JADIE Yur a beast – fur the work. Oh get wise, Allan boy.

ALLAN Whit's so unwise about this?

JADIE Yur wasting yur time. Ye'll go tae the army when yur time's oot. Whit'll ye dae then?

ALLAN Oh there might be somethin tae do then.

JADIE You're kiddin yursell, young yin.

ALLAN And whit dae you advise?

JADIE Me? Nothin! Oh get up the town, mac, an' have some fun.

ALLAN This is fun here.

JADIE Oh – whit d'ye call that therr?

ALLAN It's an auxiliary elevation on this pyramid.

JADIE You call that fun? Gartnavel fur you immediately! Ye niver think aboot anythin else?

ALLAN Aye – Ah think aboot the old lady sometimes.

JADIE Whit has she got tae dae wi it; don't tell us yur worryin aboot her auld age?

ALLAN Naw, that's no' whit Ah mean.

JADIE Well whitever ye mean ye can forget it. She's solid fur the rest o' her days.

ALLAN Aye sure.

JADIE Ach yur too serious, young yin. D'ye think Ah want tae see the young bree lookin like an onion all the time? People'll be thinkin we're haudin ye down. Ye'll need tae dae somethin about it, son.

ALLAN Aye sure, Jadie. Ah'll talk tae ma mother about it.

JADIE That's the ticket! Well Ah must buzz. Whit d'ye call this thing again?

ALLAN A cross-section of a slop-pipe that operates between distribution and scum.

JADIE 'Sat a fact! Sounds like a fulla Ah know, ha, ha, ha. Cheerio!

(*ALLAN returns to his board. In a moment MRS BRYSON and COLIN enter from the back room. He carries a suitcase.*)

MRS BRYSON Ye're sure ye've got everything noo, Colin?

COLIN Aye, everythin. If Ah've missed anythin Ah can always drap up fur it. Ah'll no' be far away.

MRS BRYSON Will ye be a' right where ye're gaun?

COLIN Ah'll be fine, Agnes. Ah'll be comin up noo an' again tae see ye.

MRS BRYSON As often as ye like, Colin. Well . . . therr's Allan. Colin's gaun noo, Allan.

ALLAN Aye so Ah see.

COLIN Hm . . . still at it yet, lad, eh?

ALLAN Just finishin up some homework.

COLIN That's the stuff. Keep yur eye on the old learnin. Did ye talk tae yer mother here about whit ye were sayin the other night?

ALLAN No' yet, Colin.

MRS BRYSON Whit have you two been discussin aboot noo? Goodness knows whit ideas ye get up tae when yese wur in therr bletherin tae each other.

COLIN Aye we've had a few notions in the old back room, Agnes. Never mind, Allan knows where Ah'm headin fur, he can have a walk up sometimes; we'll have a few chinwags yet.

MRS BRYSON Oh nae doot . . . Dae ye need tae go, Colin?

COLIN Yes, Agnes, Ah must. Ah don't want even tae be in danger o' gettin kind o' back-handed charity that exists here. Ah'll work fur whit Ah need.

MRS BRYSON Ye've had nae charity here, Colin, ye've insistit on peyin yur wey as usual.

COLIN Sure, hen, sure. But whit dae the ole three pounds a week mean now? A drop in the ocean. Add ten bob tae it, and tae Jadie an' Boab it'll mean two bottles o' whisky. Tae me it means nearly twenty hours' work. Ah like tae think that goes fur somethin.

ALLAN Colin's right, Ma.

MRS BRYSON Ah suppose he is. That disnae make it any easier tae see him gaun. If – if ever ye want anythin, Colin, ye'll come tae me, sure ye wull?

COLIN Ah'll come tae you, Agnes; or Allan here . . .

MRS BRYSON He'll miss you. We'll have tae put Nicoll in wi him tae keep him company.

COLIN Ay . . . hm . . . aye . . . Well Ah better move, Ah told this wife tae expect me the night. Stick in, Allan boy.

(*He pats ALLAN on the shoulder then turns towards MRS BRYSON but she has turned away towards the fireside, crying a little. COLIN hesitates, then exits.*)

ALLAN Don't greet, Ma. It wis the only thing for Colin.

MRS BRYSON Jist leave me for a wee minute, son.

(*ALLAN turns again to his board and waits till his mother speaks*)

There we are. That's better noo. Ah've known fur a week that Colin wis gaun, but Ah couldnae help masell when it came tae the bit.

ALLAN Ah wisnae far off it masell, Ma.

MRS BRYSON Ye liked your uncle Colin, eh, Allan?

ALLAN Aye . . . he's good, Colin.

MRS BRYSON Aye he's good a' right. Many's the odd ten-shillin he's slipped me when things wur lookin bad. An he's away noo withoot a whisper fae yur faither or the boys.

ALLAN They're too busy tae notice people like Colin these days.

MRS BRYSON Did Jadie say if he'd be meetin yur faither the night?

ALLAN He never mentioned.

MRS BRYSON Ah hope he does meet him. At least Jadie knows the wey home occasionally. Oh, Ah feel like a wee cup o' tea – will ye take some wi me, son?

ALLAN Certainly, Ma.

MRS BRYSON We'll make it in the pan; jist a wee fly cup fur you an' me.

(*She collects the pan and fills it. On her way back to the fireside she stops to look at ALLAN's work.*)

Dae ye understaun a' these lines, Allan?

ALLAN Aye, easily.

MRS BRYSON Whit is it, son?

ALLAN Jadie asked me that jist before he left, an' Ah gave him a fancy answer.

MRS BRYSON Whit did ye say tae him?

ALLAN Nothin much. He didnae notice it anywey.

MRS BRYSON Jadie's a' right. He's a good-hearted boy.

ALLAN That's why Ah'm sorry Ah said whit Ah did.

(*MRS BRYSON moves to the gas*)

MRS BRYSON Well never mind. Things are no' a' they could be, but let you an' me have a wee cup o' tea an' forget aboot it. It's no' often you an' I talk thegether, son; ye've been left a wee bit on yer own lately. Dae ye need tae go on wi that the noo?

ALLAN Well . . . naw . . . could easily finish it later.

(*MRS BRYSON sits beside the fire. ALLAN goes and sits beside her.*)

MRS BRYSON That's it. Ah need a wee bit comfort efter Colin gaun. He's ma wee brother, ye see, and it wisnae easy.

(*They sit for a little while without saying anything. Then MRS BRYSON speaks:*)

MRS BRYSON Whit wis it Colin meant when he asked ye if ye had talked tae me aboot somethin?

ALLAN Well Ah've been dodgin tellin ye about it. Ah'm no' too sure if ye'll be able tae appreciate whit Ah want tae say; an' Ah'm sure the old man an' Jadie'll howl at the idea.

MRS BRYSON Ye can tell me, Allan, surely.

ALLAN Of course, Ma. Ye see . . . Colin an' I had talked about me mebbe goin ahead, after ma time's served, an . . . well . . . mebbe becomin a kinda technical engineer.

MRS BRYSON And is that no whit ye're daein the noo?

ALLAN Aye well it is in some weys, but whit Ah mean is that mebbe later Ah could go further an' try an' get a degree.

MRS BRYSON That disnae mean much tae me, Allan.

ALLAN Sorry, Ma. Ye see, ye can either serve an apprenticeship an' leave it at that, or ye can carry on past that an' do somethin that's mebbe kinna merr worthwhile. Whit Colin an' I really meant wis that, later, if Ah worked hard enough, Ah might be able tae pass certain exams that wid allow me tae . . . well . . . go tae the Technical College.

MRS BRYSON An' whit's tae stop ye?

ALLAN I mean, go there durin the day.

MRS BRYSON Oh, Ah see . . . an' stop workin?

ALLAN That's right, Ma. Ye see, if Ah work hard at ma own night-school an' pass the necessary exams Ah'll be able tae go tae the Technical College – at night. From there Ah could work ma wey tae becoming a regular student.

MRS BRYSON Whit aboot this army thing?

ALLAN There's a chance they might delay the call-up till Ah got through studyin.

MRS BRYSON Is that so? Wid ye no' need a lot o' schoolin tae go tae a place like that?

ALLAN Plenty lads have done it before me. Night-school first, then full-time. Of course ye'd have tae keep me an' pey ma fees.

MRS BRYSON Ye have great notions, son. Ah suppose that's Colin's work.

ALLAN Aye – he helped.

MRS BRYSON Technical College, eh. Well we'll see aboot that.

(RENA enters. She is upset.)

Hullo, lassie, you're early back.

RENA Aye.

MRS BRYSON We're havin a wee cup o' tea – will ye take some?

RENA Eh – aye – ach, naw, Ah don' feel like it.

MRS BRYSON Whit's up wi ye, Rena?

(RENA is on the point of crying)

Allan, go'n oot fur a wee walk, son; come back in five minutes.

(ALLAN goes out)

Noo, whit's the trouble, hen?

RENA It's Peter, Mammy. He told me he widnae be seein me again.

MRS BRYSON Oh dear, is it as bad as that? Whit's up wi him noo?

RENA Whit's always up wi him these nights.

MRS BRYSON Rushin tae get married an' save ye fae yur family, eh?

RENA Aye. Ever since that night o' the fight here, he's been naggin at me tae make up ma mind. I didnae believe him when he said that wan o' these nights Ah wid be refusin fur the last time – we hadnae been oot ten minutes the night when he asked me point blank, 'Is it aye or naw?' – Ah'd hardly opened ma mouth tae say 'Wait a minute, Peter' . . . when he cut me off an' walked away.

MRS BRYSON Jist like that?

RENA Aye, jist like that.

MRS BRYSON He canna be serious, Rena, he's too fond o' ye, lassie.

RENA Aye but he's no' fond o' the fact that ma faither's a waster, an' ma two brothers'll soon be the fastest flymen in the district.

MRS BRYSON Is it you he wants tae marry or the hale family? Huh, Ah cannae get ower those folk that'll no' look at ye unless yer hoose is haudin wi hypocrites.

RENA Ach, Peter's no' like that, Mammy, an' ye know it.

MRS BRYSON Well can he no' go wi ye fur whit ye are yursell, and never mind the performance of yur faither and brothers?

RENA Ach he's frightened that Ah might start takin liberties as well, and get too fond of having too much tae waste.

MRS BRYSON My goodness, Rena, whit dis he expect – dis he want ye tae run aboot in rags, withoot a copper in yur pocket?

RENA Naw, Mammy, he's never been anythin else but pleased wi any benefits Ah've had fae the money.

MRS BRYSON Whit's eatin him then?

RENA If it wis jist a matter o' me havin plenty o' nice things tae wear, or havin a pound or two in ma bag, he widnae have minded. But because the whole business o' the money's makin madmen oot the other three, he feels that Ah might start gettin a bit reckless tae, and that if we wait the two years we had planned, Ah'll never be able tae come tae him on a weekly pey.

MRS BRYSON He cannae think much o' ye.

RENA Whit will Ah dae, Mammy?

MRS BRYSON Ah don't know, Rena . . . tell me this, hen, are ye fond enough o' Peter tae get married tae him?

RENA Of course.

MRS BRYSON Is it absolutely oot the question, yur faither gie'n ye a wee haun?

RENA Absolutely.

MRS BRYSON Oh he's a proud besum o' a boy – but ye'll never get a better, lassie.

RENA If he wid jist try an' see that Ah'm no ready tae get married yet. Is it so terrible tae want tae enjoy havin plenty, efter years o' havin nuthin?

MRS BRYSON Nuthin terrible aboot that, hen.

RENA Ah only meant tae pit him aff fur a while. Told him Ah couldna see the sense o' throwin up the chance o' bein decently comfortable for a wee while at least.

MRS BRYSON Aye, Ah see your point, but Ah think Ah can see Peter's point tae, the wey he looks at it.

(ALLAN enters and stands at the door. He says nothing.)

Whit's up, Allan – whit's wrang wi ye?
ALLAN There's somebody at the door tae see ye.

(MRS BRYSON looks at him for a moment, then goes out)

RENA Whit is it, Allan – who is it?
ALLAN It's – it's the polis. Nicoll's dead . . . He went out in Jadie's car – there's been a smash . . .

(They stand silently until their mother appears round the door)

CURTAIN

END OF ACT II

ACT III

A Saturday night three months later. The scene opens with MRS BRYSON holding JADIE's head under the tap. He is very drunk and has a large black eye. COLIN sits in a chair, while ALLAN stands at the fireplace. As the curtain rises, RENA enters from the room used by JADIE and MR BRYSON.

MRS BRYSON Ye get him intae bed a'right?

RENA Aye, wi a struggle; but he's in noo. Ah jist took aff his boots and jaicket.

MRS BRYSON Whit a perr o' dirty drunken scunners! Come on, you, get that midden's heid o' yours dried. That towel, Rena.

(RENA hands over a towel and MRS BRYSON begins to rub JADIE's head very hard)

JADIE Aw easy therr, easy easy!

RENA Ah wid easy him.

JADIE Whit's that? Think Ah didnae hear ye eh? Ah heard ye all right.

MRS BRYSON Ye'll hear less wan o' these days when they find ye wi nae ears on yur heid.

JADIE You wid easy us, eh. Aye, jist like all the rest o' them. Oh we got easied the night all right – aye – the ole forty poun'! Whit d'yese make o' that, eh? 'Magine daein that tae an aul man. Forty poun', wallet an' all – right up the ole Darkie Close in a wanner. But Jadie knows who it wis all right, an' the boys'll see the Gancher mob rummled up fur it too.

MRS BRYSON You'll never be sober long enough tae rummle a balloon.

JADIE Oh don't be too sure, missus, don't be too sure.

MRS BRYSON Aye, well they beat ye tae it the night an' chance it.

JADIE Plenty o' time – me an' the lads'll hand out a few red noses afore ye hear the end o' this. We'll take the forty nicker out o' them in punishment.

MRS BRYSON Ach get tae yur bed fur God's sake before ye sicken wur eyesight.

JADIE Sure Ah'll go tae ma bed – but whit d'yese make o' it – forty poun' they tuned fae the oul-man, an' a blaggin for me intae the bargain.

MRS BRYSON Ah suppose ye were flashin yur cheek an' yur money like a couple o' playboys.

JADIE Nutt at all – genuine, Maw – we never says a word – then they dived us, an done the oul-man fur his wallet an' his dough.

(MRS BRYSON looks at COLIN but he shakes his head)

RENA Ach people don't interfere wi ye unless ye gie them some reason.

JADIE Reason enough in the oul-man's pocket.

MRS BRYSON Aye an' if I know that Gancher, he'll have a reason or two besides that.

ALLAN Ach serves them right – they deserved it. Arrivin here blotto every night – treatin the place like a second-hand doss house. It's time somebody had a rattle at their rascal faces.

COLIN Easy, Allan.

JADIE Oh whit whit whit – hullo, scholar! Whit now eh? D'yese hear that eh? Your tongue's gettin a wee bit too big fur yur gub, sonny. Mebbe we should remove wan or two o' the teeth tae make room fur it.

ALLAN Ye'd be good at that, Jadie.

JADIE Ah'm good at a lot o' things. Don't be too clever, Allan – we a' know yur gonny be wan o' these – these student jokers – mebbe the ole 'universitee'. But don't forget, cheeky boys are entitled tae a belt on the lug noo and again.

(He pats ALLAN lightly on the cheek. COLIN looks as though he might interfere, but he is beaten to it by MRS BRYSON who whirls JADIE round and slaps him hard two or three times.)

MRS BRYSON Take yur hauns aff that boy. Don't ever touch him wi yur stupid useless paws, ya drunken rotten waster that ye are.

JADIE Aw Maw, Maw, edge up – edge up! Aw hey hey – yese are all up against poor Jadie – everybody wires intae me. Whit've Ah done, eh? Yese don't think Ah wid hit the boy, dae yese?

MRS BRYSON Naw, by God, an' ye'll never dae that!

JADIE Naw but you hutt me so ye did – you hutt me. 'Magine, 'magine you daein that tae me. God stiff me – Ah – Ah – Ah – widnae hit the boy, eh?

MRS BRYSON Naw but ye might jist poisen him wi yur sleekit corner-boy dirt!

JADIE Oh aye, all right – yes – this is ma mother talkin, ye all know.

MRS BRYSON Ach away an' get intae that bed therr beside yur senseless sot o' a faither.

JADIE All right, all right. Ye've all got the needle up at Jadie. Ah'll go tae ma bed.

MRS BRYSON Well go!

JADIE Ah'll go, Ah'll go. Naebody here gives a tosser anywey. It could be all wan if we were lyin up somewherr wi wur chanters kicked in – aye – forty poun's nothin tae youse – nothin tae me either – but ye must defen' the ole body – aye, Ah'm no trumpet! Ah'll give the lads a yodel an we'll give it to them.

RENA That must be the free wine ye're talkin aboot. Away inside therr an' stop haverin.

JADIE Aye sure, sure – Lady Bryson – sure.

(He goes off muttering 'Forty poun', eh', 'the lads', etc.)

MRS BRYSON Are ye all right, Allan?

ALLAN Ah'm fine, Ma.

MRS BRYSON Oh will this place never be anything else but a menagerie; it gets worse and worse. Where did you find them, Colin?

COLIN At the Cross. Ah wis on the other side o' the street when Ah saw the crowd. Boab wis scatterin haunfuls o' silver up in the air – Ah think the entire district must've been tappin him the night – then Ah saw the Gancher Mob breakin through an' rushin them up the Darkie Close. By the time Ah got therr they had shot the craw wi Boab's wallet, an left the pair o' them lyin.

RENA It's a pity ye picked them up, Colin.

COLIN Well if Ah hadnae lifted them, the polis wid. Nae sense in lettin that happen.

MRS BRYSON That'll happen sooner or later. Ach whit kind o' family are we at a' – we're sinkin lower intae the slabber instead o' liftin wursells clear o' it.

RENA Aye, the Boozy Brysons fae number seventy-wan.

MRS BRYSON Oh roast and perish the day we ever saw a penny ootside o' whit we ever managed on . . . ach, Ah've chinged ma Nicoll-boy fur a curse, an the other two fur madmen. God knows how it'll finish up.

COLIN It'll finish when the money finishes, Agnes.

MRS BRYSON There's a long wey tae go yet then.

COLIN Ah widnae be too sure aboot that. These two cannae move along the road but it costs them a young fortune.

MRS BRYSON Aye, the pigs – they'll squander pounds fur a pat on the back, but niver a hint aboot a decent hoose tae live in.

COLIN Did ye ever expect anythin different, Agnes?

MRS BRYSON Aye, Colin, of course. We had a wee plan or two that wid've made a difference.

COLIN Whit good are plans in the hauns o' a couple o' men like that?

MRS BRYSON It wisnae sich a lot that we wanted, Colin; jist tae move tae a better hoose some day. Ah thought that efter Nicoll was buried Boab and Jadie might settle doon, but they're worse noo than ever they were.

COLIN Aye, so Ah've been hearin; an' they'll be like that as long as there's a brass tosser o' the money left.

MRS BRYSON Surely they'll stop this carry-on sometime.

COLIN Yes, Agnes, when the money's done! Aw d'ye not see, lassie, d'ye not see? Men like Boab and Jadie cannae come intae a gold mine and handle it wi tact. The head for it's not there. Money tae them is a matter o' fiddlin, signin on, an' all kinds o' wanglin fur the sake o' a copper or two. Slidin alang, hopin for the best, an' never a move tae makin somethin half decent for themsells. Ah don't know how it is but when men start tae shuffle through an' forget whit it means tae have a well-earned copper in their pockets, they become numskulls, steambags. Whit dae ye think has kept Allan clear o' this hooligan stuff? The fact that he works and has some pride in doin it. The same goes for Peter that he hedged the whole affair. Boab's no a skelf o' the man he wis twenty year ago, an' he won't improve now. Jadie's a good enough boy but he's lost the head. Ah don't think he'll improve much either. His whole ambition wis jist tae be a fancy man. The money showed him the way. His values were wrong fae the start, Agnes, and when that's the wey of it, ye cannae do much tae change it.

MRS BRYSON Boab wis wance a treat o' a man, an' Jadie jist a lauddie wi merr cheek than he had wits.

COLIN True enough; but ye can hardly say that for them right now.

MRS BRYSON Aye, aye. They're a mess right enough . . .

COLIN So whit are ye gonny do about it?

MRS BRYSON Whit can Ah dae, Colin?

COLIN Aye, ye'll have tae stick it here Ah suppose. But how about Allan? Whit's gaun tae happen tae him?

MRS BRYSON Whit dae ye mean? Ye know he's got ideas aboot studyin an' mebbe gaun tae this college if he can.

COLIN Well that's a point I'm glad ye've come tae. D'ye suppose he could carry on an' study in here? How about Jadie and his 'universitee'? How about all the times he'll be told tae get wise tae himsell, an' all the 'Pansy-Joe-the-Toff' stuff? Ah'd give Allan a couple o' months wi that kind o' encouragement an' he'd be dodgin Jadie and the ole-man at every run.

MRS BRYSON Whit else can he dae then?

COLIN Well . . . if he wisnae here he widnae hae tae stick the needlin wid he?

MRS BRYSON (*Looking from COLIN to ALLAN*) Wait . . . ye . . . ye don't mean that Allan should leave us, Colin?

COLIN Dae ye think he could stey here, Agnes?

MRS BRYSON Of course. Whit else wid he dae? It's oot o' the question him leavin. Allan's sensible enough tae get ower a' this.

COLIN Oh is he? Allan, how long is it since ye did a bit o' studyin in the hoose here?

ALLAN Well . . . Ah don't know exactly.

COLIN Allan, how long is it?

ALLAN At least two months.

MRS BRYSON But that's no' true, son, Ah saw ye at yur books the other night.

COLIN Aye ye might've right enough; but because a bloke's lookin at a book it disnae mean tae say he's readin it. Look, son, tell yur mother how ye got on at yur night-school exams recently.

(*ALLAN doesn't answer*)

MRS BRYSON Tell me, son.

ALLAN . . . Ah failed in two subjects. Ah wis well behind in drawin an' Ah ploughed in rough at science.

MRS BRYSON Ye didnae tell me, Allan.

ALLAN You've got enough tae worry ye.

MRS BRYSON Whit wis the matter ye didnae manage, son?

ALLAN Jist didnae know the stuff. Nae concentration – the hale thing seems hopeless anyway.

COLIN There ye are – a boy o' eighteen – hopeless he says. Agnes, ma dear, you don't seem tae understand – livin in this kinna atmosphere wid make anybody throw up the sponge. Look at yursell, ye'd think ye had the worries o' the country on yur back – an' Rena here – she's lookin well, eh?

RENA It's no' the hoose that gets me down, Colin.

COLIN Ah know whit gets you down, Rena. Noo the boy's beginning tae think that everything's hopeless whit are ye gonny dae about that, Agnes?

MRS BRYSON How wid things be better fur him if he wis away fae here?

COLIN Well fur a start it wid allow him tae take himself seriously again. It wid allow him tae work at his books – all the time! Fur the first time he'd get a feelin o' responsibility towards hiself, get crackin an' waste no time. That's very important, Agnes. Up tae now this . . . ambition o' his . . . has been nae merr than a hauf notion that comes an' goes as the chances look good or bad; an' by the look o' his chances when he's livin here, he can chuck it right now. But give him a decent chance an' Ah guarantee Allan'll do the rest on his own.

(Long pause)

RENA Where could he go, Colin?

COLIN He could come tae my digs fur a kick-off. He earns enough tae pey his wey there.

RENA Ye've got it all cut an' dried, eh?

COLIN Well Ah should have, Rena, Ah've been thinkin aboot it long enough!

MRS BRYSON An' you're no' sparin us much either, are ye, Colin?

COLIN Sorry, Agnes, hen, but the boy's the merr important than a battalion o' these lay-abouts.

MRS BRYSON Mebbe so . . . How will he manage later if he goes tae this Technical College?

COLIN He'll manage all right. He widnae be the first good man tae have wired in against the odds. Anywey you could show him the bright side of a poun' note occasionally. An' even if he disnae manage it at a', at least he'll know he's made an honest stab at it. He'll no' be wan o' these queeries that go aboot a' their days greetin for whit they should've been . . . Whit d'ye say, Agnes?

MRS BRYSON Well if Allan wants tae go, Ah'll no staun in his wey.

ALLAN Don't say it that wey, Ma; that makes it too hard.

MRS BRYSON D'ye want tae go, Allan? Don't be feart tae say.

ALLAN Aye, Ma – Ah want tae go.

MRS BRYSON . . . Ah see.

(She reaches out and takes his hand)

Well there's nothing merr tae be said, is there?

(RENA comes and stands near her mother)

COLIN When, Agnes! When does he move?

MRS BRYSON When it can be arranged Ah suppose.

COLIN That means right now!

MRS BRYSON Ach, Colin, Colin, surely no' the night?

COLIN Yes, tonight, Agnes! This is the end o' a week. He'll start afresh the morra. Nothin like a good silent Sunday fur eggin ye on tae better things. Let him come now – Ah'll look after him fur ye.

MRS BRYSON This is all very sudden . . .

ALLAN Understand this, Ma, Ah don' want tae leave you an' Rena; wan word fae you an' Ah'll stey here.

MRS BRYSON Ah would never say that word, Allan son – ye're sure ye want tae go?

ALLAN Ah'm sure, Ma.

MRS BRYSON Then ye'd better go, hadn't ye? Seein how it is; there wid be nae point in pittin aff time, eh?

ALLAN Ah'll get a case.

(He goes to room)

COLIN Ye're doin well, Agnes.

MRS BRYSON Ah don't know how Ah'm doin . . . where'll he sleep, Colin?

COLIN The room next tae mine.

MRS BRYSON Is it clean?

COLIN Clean as yur ole conscience, hen.

MRS BRYSON Ye've sprung this on me that quick, Ah don't know whether Ah'm comin or goin.

RENA Whit aboot money? How much will he need?

COLIN No' a great deal – has he any at all dae ye think?

MRS BRYSON He'll no' have much; he gies me his wages every week.

COLIN He could dae wi a shillin or two.

MRS BRYSON Ah'll get him somethin.

(She goes to the bottom drawer of a chest and returns with an old handbag)

See, Ah'll gie him a poun' in his haun, but you take this, an' look efter it fur him. There's nearly a hundred poun's therr. Don't tell him aboot it yet, but keep it safe fur him.

COLIN Well . . . is it no' a wee bit soon fur this yet? He's no oot the door yet.

MRS BRYSON Ah know, an' he might be oot the door a long time before he needs it, but take it a' the same.

RENA Mammy, how did you manage tae get a haud o' a' that money?

MRS BRYSON How did that crowd o' hooligans get yur faither's money the night?

RENA They took it oot o' his pocket.

MRS BRYSON Aye well, hen, they havenae been the only wans that did that. Except that Ah didnae need tae knock him doon, he wis all out as it was. Ye see Ah wis savin it tae try an' dae somethin wi it. Ah wis lookin ahead tae a time when it might be needed.

COLIN Ye no' think ye better keep it then?

MRS BRYSON Don't you worry – Boab'll be drunk a few times yet – that'll be ma chance. He's never missed his money yet; Ah'll be quite safe.

RENA Let me know the next time ye're thinkin aboot it – four hauns are better than two.

COLIN D'ye think the boy'll want tae take it?

MRS BRYSON Look, Colin, you said yoursel that this money could be good tae us; right, let it be some good tae us. Take it an' put it away fur Allan; an' later on, if he needs any merr, mebbe Rena an' I'll have that fixed tae.

COLIN Right, Agnes; an' don't worry aboot him, he'll get along famously.

MRS BRYSON Keep an eye on him an' don't let him read too late.

COLIN Ah'll do that fur ye, Agnes.

(ALLAN enters with a suitcase)

MRS BRYSON That you ready, Allan?

ALLAN That's me.

MRS BRYSON Aye right ye are, son – oh here's this pound.

ALLAN Naw, Ah'm all right, Ma, Ah've got a few shillings here.

MRS BRYSON Ye better take this jist the same. Mrs Whit's-her-name might want a wee bit in advance. That right, Colin?

COLIN Eh . . . oh aye sure – sure – ye never know.

ALLAN Thanks, Ma.

MRS BRYSON Gimme a wee kiss noo.

(They kiss)

ALLAN Well . . .

MRS BRYSON Whit aboot Rena?

(RENA comes forward and kisses ALLAN)

COLIN Ready? Ah've got a call tae make before we reach the digs.

(They move towards the door)

MRS BRYSON Ta ta then, son; ye'll come and see us often, sure ye wull?

ALLAN Aye of course, Ma . . . the morra . . . cheerio, Rena.

(General farewell and exit)

MRS BRYSON That's two o' ma boys away noo, Rena.

(She sits down)

RENA Don't be upset, Mammy, Allan's no' that faur away, an' Ah think the change'll be best fur him.

MRS BRYSON Ah hope so, lassie. Life's aye cheyngin an' ye cannae stop it . . . although ye can gie it a wee help noo an' again . . . Sometimes Ah think that Ah could've done merr tae help the cheynge that happened when we got the money. If Ah had, mebbe Allan – and Nicoll – would've been here yet.

RENA Don't go thinkin aboot Nicoll, Mammy; that wis somethin that could've happened tae anybody.

MRS BRYSON Mebbe – but if things had been watched, it neednae have happened at all. Ah blame masell partly fur that.

RENA Nicoll wis drunk, Mammy, drivin Jadie's car withoot a licence – ye cannae blame yersell fur that.

MRS BRYSON Ah don't mean that I blame masell a'thegither fur it. But people turn oot as they've been brought up, and as the world uses them. Mebbe if Nicoll had had a wee bit mair attention in his time, things might have been different. Ye see, hen, Jadie came first – the first-born; we made a lot o' him. You came next – you were a lassie. Nicoll wis efter that – and as long as he wis the youngest he got lots o' attention; but efter Allan wis born, Nicoll got lost somewherr between the first-born, the youngest, and the only lassie. Efter a while he did the only thing he could, and that wis tae try tae copy Jadie; but poor Jadie's no wise enough tae be an example fur anybody. So Nicoll got on the wrang road – in Jadie's motor caur – and he had nae right tae be therr. Wur a' a wee bit tae blame fur Nicoll.

RENA Don't think aboot it, Mammy. It's by an' it canny be helped.

MRS BRYSON Yur right, Rena; but mebbe efter this we'll be able tae see things clearer an' no make the same kind o' mistakes again . . . as a matter o' fact we can start noo and see tae it. Fur wan thing, you and I are gaun tae see aboot some decent furniture fur this place, first thing on Monday morning, an' if Ah don't make that ole midden in therr pey fur it on the dot Ah'm no yur mammy. Ah'll be the businessman o' the hoose fae noo on.

(Enter JADIE)

RENA Where are you gaun?

JADIE Ah'm . . . gaun oot.

MRS BRYSON Jadie son, Ah'm no able tae argy wi ye, but fur ma sake away tae yur bed.

JADIE Ah'll be all right, Maw. Maybe, maybe you think that Ah'm gaun outside tae look fur trouble . . . but Ah'm nutt . . . jist needing a small stagger.

RENA Well fur heaven's sake go . . . ya . . .

MRS BRYSON Don't, Rena, hen.

JADIE You an' I, Rena . . . it seems . . . strangers, eh? Well Ah'm off.

(Goes to the door)

Who wis that that wis in here?

MRS BRYSON Colin.

JADIE Oh yes, yes . . . he brung us home the night . . . aye . . . an he's away?

RENA Aye, an' Allan along wi him.

JADIE Eh . . . how's that?

RENA Can ye wonder? Whit decent boy wid want tae live wi the likes of you?

JADIE Aw hey hey . . . ye don't mean tae say the boy's shot the craw 'cause o' me, eh? Well Ah tell ye, Ah'll jist take a walk up an' see him and Colin . . . tell them everything's solid . . . bring the boy back.

MRS BRYSON Jadie, jist you leave the boy alane; he'll dae fine fur himsell.

JADIE Ah well . . . if you say so, Maw, if you say so . . . I widnae go again' you . . .

RENA Ach away oot fur God's sake an' stop gabbin.

JADIE Very good, sister . . . very good . . .

(He goes out)

MRS BRYSON Where will he get tae noo?

RENA He'll no go faur, it's pourin rain ootside.

MRS BRYSON Aye. Ah'm feelin wearied, hen. Look, go intae the press an' ye'll find a bottle o' brandy planked behind the tins. You an' me'll have a wee sip.

RENA Brandy! you're doing well.

MRS BRYSON Ah bought that bottle aboot a month ago but Ah wis too shy tae open it. Ah'm ready fur it noo.

(RENA brings bottle and glasses from press. Ring at front doorbell.)

MRS BRYSON Answer that will ye, Rena?

(RENA goes to the door and returns with PETER)

RENA It's Peter, Mammy.

PETER How ye, Mrs Bryson?

MRS BRYSON Hullo, Peter . . . did ye see Jadie doon therr?

PETER Aye . . .

MRS BRYSON Whit's he daein?

PETER Nothin; jist standin in the rain. Anythin wrang?

MRS BRYSON No really. Sit doon, laddie – don't worry aboot the bottle, we're no on the ran-dan yet. It's jist a wee drap brandy tae cheer us up. Will ye tak a wee drap?

PETER Well – okay. Ah'll have a half.

MRS BRYSON We havenae been feelin too good, Peter – Allan's left us tae go and stey wi Colin.

PETER Aye, Colin wis tellin me.

MRS BRYSON Did ye meet him?

PETER Naw, he came up tae the hoose an' told me. He mentioned too that if Ah hurried round an' saw you, Rena, Ah might be able tae strike while the iron's hot; maybe settle something you an' I never managed tae agree about.

RENA It's good tae see ye.

PETER Well here's your health, Mrs Bryson. Sorry all this is happening tae you.

MRS BRYSON Rena's twice the lassie she wis an hour ago.

PETER How about a walk, Rena?

RENA Ah'll get ma coat.

(RENA goes to the lobby for coat and umbrella)

MRS BRYSON Be good tae her, Peter.

PETER Sure, Mrs Bryson.

MRS BRYSON We've seen a few changes here the night.

PETER Aye . . . things mount up an' up. They're bound tae change sometime.

MRS BRYSON Aye true enough. Ye're a sensible lad, Peter. See an' stey that way.

PETER Don't see why no'.

RENA Ready, Peter.

(She signals to him to wait outside)

Whit if Peter asks me again the night?

MRS BRYSON Ah hope ye know how ye'll answer him.

RENA Sure, Ah know. Ah'll be back soon.

(Off-stage JADIE can be heard mumbling to PETER)

(JADIE enters)

JADIE Whit's gaun on . . . wherr . . . wherr they off tae?

MRS BRYSON Jist for a walk.

JADIE That's nice eh . . . very nice. He's a . . . a brammer o' a fulla . . . Peter . . . a champion smashin boy . . . good eh . . . everybody's takin a powder . . . Rena . . . Allan . . . he's took a dive wi Colin . . . the lovely . . . well Ah'm sorry he maybe thinks that Ah've got the spur at him . . . not me . . . Ah liked him clever . . . told the boys all about it . . . proud o' the young yin . . . that's how it goes . . . Yes!

MRS BRYSON Go tae yur bed, Jadie son.

JADIE Certainly, Mother . . . Mother . . . yes, Mother . . . took a short powder masulf – ye know . . . jist tae get alongside masulf . . . went as far as the corner jist walkin . . . 'Oh poor little Robin walkin walkin' . . . nothin anywherr . . . nothin in the world but cats an' polis . . . rain . . . an' me . . . all of a sudden everythin wis me . . . everythin . . . put the wind up me . . . that funny . . . wisn't it, Mother?

MRS BRYSON Aye.

JADIE Ye always hope . . . ye know, ye hope that . . . eh, somehow ye'll be standin out therr like . . . a centre forward . . . Whit d'ye do . . . who's in charge . . . well we'll batter on anyway. Hullo, hullo . . . whit's in the bottle . . . Brandy eh . . . get away . . . brandy . . . funny thing . . . out all the bottles we've buyed . . . we've never yet buyed brandy . . . whose . . . ?

MRS BRYSON Mine, Jadie. It's yours if ye want it.

JADIE Well . . . Ah won't mind . . . don't mind at all . . . wherr's the . . . ach whit's the use . . . comes a point when all the drink in the world's no use tae ye . . . it's jist like wakenin in the morning . . . an' feelin it's no use anyhow. Maw . . . Mother . . . ye know whit Ah'd fancy right now, eh?

MRS BRYSON Whit . . .

JADIE Cup o' tea . . . good old cup o' char . . . whit d'ye say eh? Will ye do that for us . . . eh?

MRS BRYSON Aye, Ah'll dae that, Jadie.

JADIE That's the job, Maw, that's the job . . . you get the kettle on, Ah'll . . . Ah'll set the table . . . eh?

MRS BRYSON Naw, sit wherr ye are, Jadie, Ah'll do it.

JADIE Good for you . . . honey . . . good for . . . you. Must be a long time since Ah had a cup o' tea . . . couple o' days anyway. Nothin Ah'd fancy better than a good ole . . . cup o' tea.

(*MRS BRYSON puts kettle on and sits quietly. JADIE mumbles on.*)

FINAL CURTAIN

GLOSSARY AND NOTES

The glossary below is not exhaustive, but aims to cover all the Scots words as well as those non-Scots items which might not be available in smaller English dictionaries, either because of their colloquial nature, or because of restriction in use to the period or to particular cultural references. There is considerable variation in the spelling and, as spellings are often phonetic, it is often easy to work out what a word means simply by saying aloud what the spelling implies. There are some simple grammatical rules: the present participles and verbal nouns usually appear with *–in* endings, rather than the English *–ing*, and past tenses and past participles have *–it* where *–ed* would be expected in English; negatives are marked by *–na* or *–nae* in contrast to English *–n't*.

a, a': *see* o
a', aw: all
a-bogey: *see* bogey
aback: behind
Abernethy: a kind of plain sweet biscuit
Abigail: a personal maid
ablow: below
aboot: about
ach, auch, awch: interjection expressing impatience, disappointment, contempt, remonstrance etc
adae: ado
Adam, old Adam: *(fig.)* old (sexual) sinner
aff: off
afore: before
afterither: furthermore
again': against
Ah: I
ain: own
airm: arm
airt: direction
alane: alone
alang: along
Alowishyus College: St Aloysius College, a prestigious Roman Catholic school in Glasgow
Americky: America
Annie Laurie: romantic heroine of popular Scottish songs
an, an': and
ane: one
anither: another
antrin: strange
anywey: anyway
anywherr: anywhere

arena, arnae, areny: aren't
argy: argue
argy-bargyin': arguing
Argyle Street: one of the main shopping streets in Glasgow
argyment: argument
a'right, awright: all right
army time: two years of military service remained compulsory, with some exemptions, for all young men in Britain, until the end of the 1950s
ashet: a large dish
atween: between
auch: *see* ach
aul(d), oul(d): old
aw: oh
aw: *see* a'
awa: away
awch: *see* Ach!
awright: *see* a'right
ay(e): yes
aye: always

ba': ball
back-court: ground at the back of tenement buildings
back-end: *(of year)* autumn
back o' my hand: rejection
bag o' yeast: priest *(rhyming slang)*
bairn, bairnie: child
baith: both
balloon: boastful idiot
Bandy Hope: Band of Hope, a temperance organisation for working-class children
banjo: hit, blow

339

barley-bree: whisky
Barlinnie: a prison in Glasgow
barra: barrow; *(joc.)* a car
Barras, the Barras: a Glasgow street
    market
Barrowland: a Glasgow ballroom
bastid: bastard
Bastin: Cliff Bastin (1912–91), an English
    internationalist who starred in
    Arsenal's forward line in the 1930s
    alongside Alex James (1901–53), who
    played for Scotland
bate: beat
batter: struggle; on the batter: on a
    drinking bout
baur: joke
beat to the wide: worn out
bee-baw-babbity: a child's singing game
beefin out: complaining loudly
bekon: beckon
belang: belong
Bellahouston: a park in Glasgow; by
    Bellahouston!: *(joc.)* interjection
    expressing surprise
beltin the grape: drinking excessively
ben: through, further into the house
berries, the Berries: picking raspberries
    was a welcome source of income
    during the summer months
besom, besum: rascal
bevy: *(colloq.)* quantity of alcohol
bide: stay, live, wait
big man: a form of address, usually
    implying respect but may be used with
    irony
bile: boil
biler: boiler
billy: fellow
Billy: King Billy, King William III
Billy: a protestant, by association with
    William III
binder: bundle; earning a binder: earning
    a lot of money
bing: heap, pile
bit: bit, used idiomatically to express
    small size or insignificance as in
    'booting a bit ball'
bittie: a little bit
black-lyin: slandering
blaggin': beating up
blatter: beat
blaw: blow
bleezes: blazes, Hell

blether: talk foolishly, loquaciously or
    idly
bletherskite: someone who talks foolishly,
    loquaciously or idly
bliddy: bloody
blocks: blokes, fellows
bluid: blood
Boab: Bob
bob: shilling; = 5p
body, *see* buddy
bogey: a figure of evil; the gem's a-bogey:
    the game has to be abandoned; lay your
    bogey: exorcise your evil spirit, dispel
    your fears
bonnie, bonny: pretty, beautiful
bookit: *see* sma'-bookit
bool: bowl
borry: borrow
bowly: bowed, bandy
boys-fur-rags: rag and bone men
brae: hill
brammer: something very good of its kind
bran' new: brand new
braw: fine, good
bree: liquid in which something has
    been boiled or steeped, *see also*
    barley-bree
breeks: trousers, knickers
breid: bread
Brethern: the Plymouth Brethren, a strict
    Christian sect, committed to the literal
    truth of the Bible, baptism, and the
    Second Coming
Brigton: Bridgetown, an area of
    Glasgow
brocht: brought
brogue: accent
Broomielaw: upriver from Govan, the
    starting-point in Glasgow for pleasure
    cruises down the River Clyde
brung: brought
bubbly-jock: turkey
buddy: person
buckshee: spare
bughouse: mad
bugle, take it out o your bugle: destroy
    your reputation
bully: excellent
bummer, heid bummer: person in charge
bummin: buzzing, speaking
bumped: tricked, swindled
bunged: threw
bunnet: cap, hat

Bunyan: John Bunyan (1628–88), author of *Pilgrim's Progress* (1678–84), a popular allegory of the Christian life

Burke and Hare: William Burke and William Hare, who robbed graves, or murdered, to supply corpses for anatomy classes in Edinburgh in 1828

bur(r)oo: labour exchange

but-an'-ben, but-an-ben: two-roomed house

butties: friends

by-blow: illegitimate child

by, bye: past, over

bye byes: sleep

byornar, byordinary: unusual, extraordinary

ca', caw: call

cairry on: carry on, behave foolishly

cairt: carry

cairt: cart

cairter: carter

call-up: *see* army time

cam': came

Cameron: Richard Cameron (1648?–80), a martyr of the early Presbyterian Church in Scotland and friend of Alexander Peden (q.v.)

canna(e): can't

canny: moderate, careful

cannily: cautiously

Carnegie: Andrew Carnegie (1835–1919), a successful Scottish businessman and philanthropist

cast-affs: cast-off, second-hand clothing

cauld: cold (infection)

cauld: cold

caur: car

caw: call

cest up: cast up

chair gangs: *(joc.)* chain gangs

chairge: charge

champin: trudging

chanter, wi wur chanters kicked in: with our windpipes kicked in

chantyrassler: shifty, unscrupulous character

chap: knock

chat: get by verbal persuasion, speak to (used transitively)

Cheeky Forty: one of the Glasgow gangs

cheerybye: goodbye

cheynge, chinge: change

chib: stab

china: mate (rhyming slang from 'china plate')

chinge: *see* cheynge

chip: throw

chow: chew; chow the fat: have a discussion

chuckin: giving up

claes: clothes

clapped: put suddenly

clap: pat

clip-clash: slander, slanderous

clishmaclash: loudly nonsensical

cloot: cloth, garment

close: entry to a tenement, common passageway

clout: blow, hit

coamic: comic

coanscience: conscience

coggle: go awry

coiner: maker of coins; counterfeiter

combies: combination underwear

coo: cow; like the coo's tail: always hanging behind

coof: fool

cotter: farm labourer who lives in a tied cottage

Cottar's Saturday night: 'The Cotter's Saturday Night', poem by Robert Burns (1759–96). 'From scenes like these auld Scotia's grandeur springs' is one of its lines.

coupla: couple of

coupon: football pools form

crabbed, crabbit: bad tempered

crack: conversation; cut the cracks: get to the point

Crainer: *obscure*

craitur: creature

craw: crow

crep': crept

cripes: interjection expressing surprise

croon: crown; hauf a croon: half a crown, two shillings and sixpence; = 12.5p

cry: call, name

cuddy: horse

Cumberland; a second Cumberland: William Augustus, Duke of Cumberland (1721–65) inflicted a terrible defeat on Scottish forces at the Battle of Culloden in 1746

Cunarders: ocean liners

curdie: a very small coin

da: affectionate way of addressing or referring to one's father
dab-lad: skilful boy
dae: do
daicently: decently
Dail: the Irish Parliament
Dan: a nickname for a Roman Catholic
darg: a day's work
daun(d)er, dawner: stroll, walk slowly
daw: dawn
dawner: *see* daun(d)er
dead: utterly
dead-head: a person who gets in without paying
dee: die
defen': defend
deid: dead
deleerium: delirium, fancy
dial: face
didna, didna', didnae, didny: didn't
dight: wipe
dilutee: unqualified worker
din: done
dinger, gaun his dinger: going on with great enthusiasm
dis: does
disnae: doesn't
Dod: a mild oath, euphemism for God
don': don't
doobt: *see* doot
dook: dip, immerse
doon: down
doot, doobt; doubt, expect
dottled: mentally confused through age
dour: sullen
dram: a measure of whisky
drap: drop
drouth: thirst
duff: coal dust, inferior stuff, nonsense
dug: dog, *see also* wally dug
dugs, the dugs: greyhound racing
dumplin': a savoury fruit cake which, for special occasions, often contains small novelty gifts or coins
dunny: back passage to the rear exit of a tenement
dunt: strike, knock
dyke: wall

Earl o' Hell: the Devil
edge up: calm down
ee: eye
eediot, eejit: idiot

efter: after
efternoon: afternoon
eisen: sexual desire
Erchie: Archie
ett: ate
ettle: aim, long for, strive after
eye, did your eye in: got the better of you

fa': fall
factor: property manager
fae, frae: from
fair: extremely
faither, feyther: father
farin, faring: amount owed
fash: bother, worry
faurdin': farthing (quarter of an old penny)
feart; feared: afraid
fearty: coward
fell: very
fella, fulla, felly: fellow; fellas: *(pl)* fellies
feyther: *see* faither
fillum: film
fir, fur: for
fit, fut: foot
fitba': football
five-jiller: bottle containing five gills
flair, flerr: floor
flier, take a flier: jump
flit: move(d) house
flooer: flower
flute, tin flute: suit *(rhyming slang)*
fly: cunning, street-wise, surreptitious; fly cup: a quick cup of tea
flymen: wide-boys, street-wise wasters
folley: follow
footering: fiddling pointlessly, trifling
forbye: as well, furthermore
fore, to the fore: at the front
forenoon: morning
forgie: forgive
fotie: photograph
fou, fu': drunk
fower: four
frae: *see* fae
frien': friend
Freud: *see* psycho-paralyse
fu': *see* fou
fulla: *see* fella
fur: *see* fir
fushionless: dispirited, lacking in motivation
fut: *see* fit

ga'n, g'wan: *see* gaun
gab: talk
gae: go
gae: *see* gey
gait: road; go your own gait: go your own way
Gallacher: Hughie Gallacher (1903–57), Scottish international forward, who played for Queen of the South, Airdrieonians, Newcastle United and Chelsea
gallus: bold
galluses: *(pl)* braces, suspenders
galoot: an awkward or foolish person
gander: look
gang: go
Gartnavel: Gartnavel Royal Asylum, a psychiatric hospital in the west of Glasgow
gatchens: *(pl)* underpants
gaub: idiot, useless person
gaun: going, gone
gaun, ga'n, g'wan: go on; gaun yersel: get away
gelt: money
gem: game
gerrit: get it
gey, gae: very
gie, gi'e: give; gied: gave, given
gie's: give us, give me
Gilbert, Gilbert the Filbert: from a music hall song, 'Gilbert the Filbert, the colonel of the knuts', a vain, idle fellow
gimp: young lady
ginger-breid, gingerbreid: gingerbread
gittering: chattering, talking nonsense
glaikit: stupid
Glasga: *see* Glesca
glaumrie: glamour, magic
gled: glad
Glesca, Glesga: Glasgow
gless: glass
Goatfell: the highest mountain on the island of Arran
gomeril: oaf
gonny: going to
good-brother: brother-in-law
gosson: boy
Govan: a Glasgow district
gowk: fool
greet: weep
grosset: gooseberry; like a cock at a grosset: without hesitation

grun: ground
gub: mouth
gudeman: the head man of a household
gudewife: the householder's wife
guid: good
guidness: goodness
Guy Fawksin: talking of political revolution
gyp: mislead

ha', hae: have
haddie: haddock
hale: whole
half, hauf: half; half a gill of whisky; half a pint of beer
half a dollar: half a crown; two shillings and sixpence; = 12.5p
ham-and-haddie: a slice of ham and haddock, once a favourite breakfast in parts of Scotland, later meaning a state of confusion after a music hall song
hame: home
han': *see* haun'
handers, handers-handers: call to indicate a free-for-all; associates who get involved in the fight
hantle: a considerable quantity
ha'penny: half an old penny
happed: wrapped
haud: hold; her hoose is haudin' wi' hypocrites: her house is full of hypocrites
hauf: *see* half
hauf-deid: half dead
hauf-drooned: half drowned
haun', haun(d), han': hand
havena(e): haven't
haverin: talking nonsense
haw: interjection to attract attention, hey
haw haw: ha ha
Hawkie, Auld Hawkie: a Glasgow character
he'rt: *see* hert
hechin: wheezing, coughing
heid: head; keep the heid: keep calm
heid bummer: *see* bummer
heilan': *see* hielan'
hems: *(pl)* horse collar; put the hems on: keep under control, restrain
hen: informal address to a female
herm: harm
hersel, hersel': herself
hert, he'rt: heart

hev: have
hielan', heilan: highland
Hielans: Highlands
highfalutin': pretentious
himsel, himsel', hisel, hissell: himself
hing: hang
hisel, hissell: *see* himsel
Hogmanay, Hogmany: New Year's Eve
hole in the wa' bed: a recessed bed
hoo: how
hooh: interjection expressing surprise
hoolet: owl
hoor: whore
hoose: house
how: *(interrog.)* why
howff: meeting place, place to hang out
hundret, hunner: hundred
hurdy-gurty: hurdy-gurdy; a stringed
    musical instrument played with a wheel
    instead of a bow
hutt: hit
Huxley: Aldous Huxley (1894–1963),
    English novelist, from a scientifically
    inclined family
hydropathic: spa hotel where people went
    to drink the waters or take baths to
    improve their health

Ibrox: Glasgow Rangers football ground
    is in Ibrox, a district of Glasgow
ile: oil
ill: evil, unwell
inbye, in by: inside
ingineerin: engineering
insin-y-atin': insinuating
instryment: instrument
intae: into
Irisher: Irishman
Iron-Brew: fizzy soft drink
Ishmaelites: *see* Joseph's brethren
ither: other
itsel: itself

jacksie: *(anat.)* bottom
jag: stab
jag: swig
jaiket: jacket
jalouse: guess, surmise
Jamaica Bridge: bridge over the Clyde, in
    central Glasgow
James: *see* Bastin
Jasus: Jesus
jaw: pour

jaw: speak, nag
jeely: jelly, jam
Jees: Jesus
Jevons: William Stanley Jevons (1835–82),
    a celebrated nineteenth-century
    economist and logician
jeyn in: join in
jibin: hesitating
jick: jiffy, tick
jig: go, turn
jiggin': dancing
jiller: *see* five-jiller
jing-bang, hale jing-bang: the whole lot
jings: interjection expressing surprise or
    alarm
jist: just
Jock Tamson, we're aw Jock Tamson's
    bairns: we are all brothers and sisters
jocoes: *(pl) (informal)* Scots people
jocose: cheerful
Joe Soap: dope *(rhyming slang)*
John Splendid: a popular novel by Neil
    Munro (1863–1930), first published in
    1898
johnnie, the johnnie: Johnnie Walker
    whisky
jooler: jeweller
jools: *(pl)* jewels
Jordan: in the biblical story, the river on
    whose other side lay the Promised
    Land, and in *Pilgrim's Progress*,
    heaven, with trumpets sounding
Joseph's brethren: in the biblical story,
    Joseph's brothers sold him as a slave to
    members of the Ishmaelite tribe
juke: fist

Keating's powder: proprietary brand of
    insecticide
keek: look
keeker: black eye
keep the heid: *see* heid
Kelvinside: an affluent Glasgow district
ken: know
kill, get yer kill: die laughing
kilted: tucked up
kin: can
kinna: kind of
kirk: church; the Kirk: the Church of
    Scotland
kisser: face
kitchen: tasty food
knackert: tired out

kuss: kiss

lad, laddie, lauddie: boy, young man
laird: lord, the title given to a
  landowner
lang: long
languidge: language
lassie: girl
lauddie: *see* lad
lave: rest, remainder
lavvy: lavatory
lawin: debt, payment
lay: see lea'
'Lay of the Last Minstrel': poem by Sir
  Walter Scott (1771–1832), famous for
  the lines 'Breathes there the man, with
  soul so dead, / Who never to himself
  hath said, / This is my own, my native
  land!'
lea', lay: leave
lea rig: a length of arable land lying
  fallow
learnt: taught
leary: nervously alert
leddy: lady
leevin': leaving
len, len': loan
length, gettin' the length o': getting as far
  as
lick: a small quantity
licky: lucky
liker, merr liker: *see* merr
limmer: rascal, rogue
lings: lungs
linkit: arm in arm
lintie: linnet
lip: drink, sip
lip: dent, chip
lip: impertinence
lippen: depend
Liptons: a well-known grocery chain
Littlewoods: a football pools company
Livingstone: David Livingstone (1813–74),
  Scottish missionary and explorer,
  famously encountered in Africa
  by Henry Morton Stanley
  (1841–1904)
lobby: entrance passage
loch: lake
lods: lads
lollipop: idiot
loses the head: loses his reason
loss: lose

Low: David Low (1891–1963), a self-
  taught political cartoonist, famous
  for his work for the London *Evening
  Standard*, particularly during the
  late 1930s and the Second World
  War
ludger: lodger
ludgin: lodging; ludgin' money: money for
  board and lodging
lug: ear
luk: look
lum: chimney
lum-hat: top hat

ma: my
mac: familiar term of address to a man
Macdonald: Flora MacDonald (1725–90)
  helped Bonnie Prince Charlie to escape
  from Scotland in 1746
Machiavelli: Niccolò Machiavelli (1469–
  1527), political philosopher, often
  thought cynical or amoral in his
  recommendations about government
maggot: unfounded notion
mainners: manners
mair, merr: more
mairry: marry
maist: most
maitter: matter
mak: make
man: man, husband, male partner
Man to Man the world o'er: 'It's
  coming yet, for a' that / That man to
  man the warld o'er / Shall brothers be
  for a' that'; lines from 'For a' that
  and a' that' by Robert Burns
  (1759–96)
marrer: matter, *see also* wazza marrer
Maryhill: district of Glasgow
masel(l), masel' masulf, mesel: myself
masked: (of tea) infused
masulf: *see* masel(l)
maw: affectionate way of addressing
  one's mother
mebbe, mebby: maybe
medals: award winning brands of
  alcoholic drink
meenit: minute
menage: saving scheme
merr: more; merr liker: more suitable for
merriet: married
Merryflatts: a poorhouse in Glasgow
mesel': see masel(l)

Micawber: character in Charles Dickens's
    David Copperfield (1849–50),
    renowned for his conviction that
    'something will turn up' to rescue his
    finances
micht: might
mickey: toilet
midden: muck heap, *(fig.)* an untidy
    person
Milligan Boys: a Glasgow gang
mind: mind, remember
mines: mine
misca: slander
mither: mother
model: model lodging house,
    accommodation for the very poor or
    destitute
monkey gland: supposedly able to
    postpone ageing
mony: many
mooching: scrounging
moose: mouse
mooth: mouth
morn, the morn: tomorrow
morra, morrow, the morra, the morrow:
    tomorrow
mowed, get mowed intae that: attack that
    with vigour
mulk: milk

na, naw: no
nae: no
naebody: nobody
naethin', naething: nothing
nane: none
naphtha: *(joc.)* that which lights up,
    hence liquor
nappy beer: strong beer
naw: *see* na
near: nearly
neb: nose, low-class person
ned: ruffian
neeborly: neighbourly
newfangled: novel, innovative
never, niver: never; *also used as one-
    occasion negative, as* Ah never:
    I didn't
nicht: night
Nick: (Old) Nick, the Devil
nick: catch; g'an nick yourself: go and
    chase yourself
nicker: pounds
nippy: critical, sharp

nissen hut: a prefabricated, semi-
    cylindrical shelter of corrugated iron
    developed by the British during the
    First World War
nithin': nothing
niver: *see* never
no, no', nutt: not
noo: now
nor: than
nutt: *see* no
nyaff: puny insignificant person

o, o', a, a': of
och: oh, a dismissive exclamation
ody-colong: eau de Cologne
o'er: *see* ower
ole: *see* oul(d)
ole-lady: *see* oul-lady
ole-man: *see* oul-man
onion, lookin like an onion: looking
    miserable
ontae: onto
ony: any
onybody: anybody
onyone: anyone
oor, oors: our, ours
oorsels: ourselves
oot: out, out of
ootside: outside
Orangeman: follower of William of
    Orange; a Protestant
oul(d), owl(d), ole: old
oul-lady, old-lady, ole-lady: mother
oul-man, ole-man: father
oul-yin: mother, father
ower, owre, o'er: over
owl(d): see oul(d)
owre: *see* ower

pa: affectionate way of addressing one's
    father
Paddy, the Paddy: a Glasgow gang
pair: poor
pairris muddle: *humorous play on* Paris
    model
pairt: part
pairty: party
palings: railings
Pally: the Palace Ballroom
pan: cranium; knockin our pan out:
    working extremely hard

Panel, on the Panel: signed off work through sickness and in receipt of benefit

Pape: a Roman Catholic

paraffin, paraffin ile: style *(rhyming slang from 'paraffin oil')*

paralysed: drunk

parish, on the Parish: in receipt of unemployment benefit; Parish pey desk: pay desk at the unemployment office; parish inspector: an officer who attempts to prevent fraudulent claims for unemployment benefit

patter: banter, esp. in Glasgow dialect

pay-poke: pay packet

Peden: Alexander Peden (1626–86), one of the most well-known Covenanters and friend of Richard Cameron (q.v.)

peety: pity

per(r): pair

petted lip: protruding or quivering lower lip, expressing sulkiness

pewmony: pneumonia

pey: pay

pianny: piano

pickcher: picture

picter: picture; the picters: the cinema

piece: sandwich; piece on jelly: jelly or jam sandwich

pied: paid *(past part. of pey)*

pipeclay, a ower ma pipeclay: all over my pipeclay (pipeclay was used to clean and brighten doorsteps)

pit: put

pitmirk: darkness of Hell

plank: hoard

plank: place down in a decisive way, hoard

plates o' meat: feet *(rhyming slang)*

plots: allotments

plucking berries harsh and crude: allusion to 'Lyicdas', by John Milton (1608–74); *joc.*, going for a drink

Plum, the Plum: a Glasgow gang

plunker: a large marble, a big lump in the throat

poe-naggers: an insulting expression

poke: bag; pay poke: pay packet

polis: police; polisman: policeman

pools, the pools: weekly bet on the outcome of football results

Poorshoose: poorhouse

pou', poun('): pound

Portia: character in William Shakespeare's *The Merchant of Venice*, whose plot partly hinges on an exchange of rings

powder, take a powder: go away quickly

press: cupboard

proamise: promise

provost: Scottish equivalent of mayor

psycho-paralyse *(joc.)*: psychoanalyse, according to theories Sigmund Freud (1856–1939) developed in late nineteenth- and early twentieth-century Vienna

puddin', pudding: white pudding, a mixture of oatmeal, dripping and spices in a sausage-skin

puir: poor

Queen's, the Queen's: Queen's Park, a Glasgow football team

queer, a queer fortune: a large fortune

quiet-gaun: of habitually quiet demeanour

quietsome: quiet

Rab Ha the Glasga' glutton: Robert Hall, famous in Glasgow for his appetite

raffle hersel: get knotted (see raivelled)

raither: rather

raivelled: confused

rammy: commotion

ran-dan, on the ran-dan: on a spree, a drinking bout

randy: fuss

rare: lovely

raw: row (of houses)

Raw, the Raw: a Glasgow gang

real: really

Red Clydeside: a period of socialist radicalism, rent strikes and labour agitation in the Glasgow area, under leaders including John MacLean and Willie Gallacher, lasting from the time of the First World War until the 1930s

redd: tidy

reddin up: tidying up

reekin': smelling powerfully

reformatory: young offenders' institution

rether: rather

Ricey, the Ricey: a Glasgow gang

rid: red

rin: run

rip, the very devil o a rip for it: keen for it

347

rise, take a rise oot o': make fun of
rize: rise
road: road, way
Rob Roy: Rob Roy MacGregor (1671–
 1734), immortalised in Sir Walter
 Scott's novel *Rob Roy* (1818)
Rodine: proprietory brand of rat poison
room: the best room
roon: round
routh: a large quantity
rowed: rolled
rummle: shake

sa: *see* sae
sae: so
saft: soft
saftie: weak-minded person
sair: sore, sorely
sais: says
sang: song
Sanitary, the Sanitary: Sanitary inspectors
saps: soft food such as bread steeped in
 milk
Sassenach: Southerner *(used
 contemptuously)*
Sauchiehall Street: one of the main
 shopping streets in Glasgow
sayed: said
scart: scratch, scrape
schnorrer: beggar
schule: school
scoor: scour, scrub
scoot: squirt
Scotia; from scenes like these auld
 Scotia's grandeur springs: *see* Cottar's
 Saturday night
Scotstoun: an area of Glasgow
scratcher: bed
screed: long piece of writing
screw-tap: bottle with a top that screws
 off
screw the (yer) nut: calm down
scrunnin': scouring
scunner: nuisance
scunnered: fed up
see's: pass me
Second City: Glasgow, once referred to as
 the Second City of the (British) Empire
semmit: vest, T-shirt
sen': send
Setterday, Setturday: Saturday
seven-an'-a-tanner: seven shillings and
 sixpence; = 37.5p

sez: says
shaffoor: chauffeur
shairly: surely
Shamrock: an Irish person
Shandon: the name of a public house
shillin('): shilling, twelve old pence; = 5p
shilpit: puny
shime: shame
shot the craw: went away *(rhyming slang
 partially from 'gaed awa' following
 translation of English rhyming slang,
 'shoot the crow', 'go')*
shoulda: should have
Shylock: the miserly moneylender in
 William Shakespeare's *The Merchant
 of Venice*
sib: closely akin to
sich: such
sidey-weys: sideways
siller: silver, money
sine: rinse
sine die: without a specified limit of time
skelf: splinter *(here used fig.)*
skellington: skeleton
skelp: smack, hit, beat
skirl: make a high-pitched noise
skite: slip; *(fig.)* go away quickly
skivvy: lowly female worker
skoosher: go-ahead person
slabber: mire
sleekit: underhand, stealthy
slop-pipe: pipe for waste water
sma': small
sma'-bookit: small in size
smalls: small bread, rolls
smoogin': trickery
smoor: smother
snap-brim: hat brim of which the angle
 can be adjusted
snidy: underhand and spiteful
snottery: covered with nasal mucus
snuff: sniff *(here used figuratively)*
snuff it: die
sodger: soldier
sofie: sofa
somewherr: somewhere
sook: suck
sook an' blaw: windbag
sooker, ha'penny sooker: a hard sweet
 containing a novelty
soor: sour
sowl: soul
spaewife: fortune-teller

spiled: spoiled
Springburn: district of Glasgow
spud: potato
spunk: courage, initiative
spur, got the spur at: taken a dislike to
stairhead, stairheid: the landing on a
    tenement stair and, by extension, the
    people who live there
stan, staun: stand
Stanley: *see* Livingstone
starey-like: staring
stay: *see* stey
steambag: empty-headed person
steamie: public wash house
steerin: restless
stert: start
stever: stop, cancel
stey, stay: stay, dwell,
stick in: persevere
stickit: failed partway through
    something
stiff, (God) stiff me: God strike me down
stoat, stott: bullock
stourie: dusty
stove-pipe: used attributively, referring to
    narrow straight-legged trousers
strippit: striped; black strippit ba': mint
    boiled sweet
stumer: useless
stummick: stomach
stupit: stupid
sub: loan or donation of money
Swan, Annie: Annie S. Swan (1859–
    1943), Scottish popular novelist,
    renowned for happily romantic
    endings
swank: affectation, ostentation
swank: swagger, behave in an affected
    manner, pretend
swanked up: dressed up
sweerin': swearing
sweetie-folk: gossips
swell-head: swollen headed
swithering: vacillating
syreen: siren

tae: to
tae: too
tae: toe
ta'en: taken
tak, tak': take
Tally: an Italian
Tamson: *see* Jock

tank belly: fat belly
tanked: drunk, inebriated
tanner: six old pence
tap: top
tappin': borrowing money from
tate: small amount
taury: tarry
tellin-of: telling off
tel(l)t, tell't: told
tenement: an apartment block with a
    common entry and a common stair
terr: spree
thae, they: those
thegethir, thegither: together; a' thegither:
    altogether
theirselves, themsells, thursells:
    themselves
therr, thurr: there
they: *see* thae
thives: thieves
thole: endure
thrapple: throat
three-timer: three-way accumulator, a
    kind of bet
thurrs: there is
thursells: *see* themsells
ticket: ticket; strange-looking character;
    that's the ticket: that is just the very
    thing
tick-man: money lender
tightner: *(joc.)* a large meal
tike: scruffy dog; a rough, unkempt but
    often tenacious person
tile, on yur own tile: on your own
    account
tin flute: suit *(rhyming slang)*
Toi: the San Toy, a Glasgow gang
tomaties: tomatoes
tonky: fashionable
toon: town
toothin: teething
toots: affectionate and familiar form of
    address to a female
toots: interjection expressing
    encouragement
tosser: a small value coin; give a tosser:
    care a damn
tottie, totty: potato; a rotten totty: a bad
    person
tottie-hawker: potato harvester
tousy, towsy: rough, boisterous
towl: told
traipsin, trapesin: gadding about

Trenchard; Lord Trenchard: Viscount
   Trenchard (1873–1956), Commissioner
   of the London police force in the 1930s;
   joc. a policeman
trickly: tricky
trig: trim
tripes: *(pl)* intestines
Tron, Trongate: the street where the
   public weighbridge or 'tron' once stood
troosers: *(pl)* trousers
trumpet: *(possibly)* one who utters empty
   threats
trunks: long distance telephone calls
tumphy: a dull stupid person
T.T.: teetotal
twa: two
twal': twelve
twelve-and-six: twelve shillings and
   sixpence; = 62.5p
twinkell: twinkle (a dance step)
twust: twist

udder: other
ulsters: ulcers
understaun, underston: understand
un'er: under
universitee: university
unlegal: illegal
urr: are
us: us, me

valoory, veloory: velour
vennel: narrow alley
volcany: volcano

wa: wall
wa': *see* wae
wab-footed: web-footed, daft *(figurative)*
wad: would
wae, wa': with
wae: woeful
wain, wean: small child
wake: weak
wally: china, earthenware; wally dug:
   china ornament of a stylised King
   Charles spaniel dog
wan: one
wance: once
wanchance: misfortune
wanner, in a wanner: at one go
wash-hoose: wash house
wash-oot: dead loss
wasna(e): wasn't

wastin': spoiling
watter: water
wazza marrer?: what is the matter?
wean, wain: child
wearyin to see me: pining for me
wee: small; haud on a wee: wait a little
   moment
weel: well
weemen: *(pl)* women
weesh: wish
weesht, wheesh, wheesht: hush
well-doin: prosperous
well-oiled: showing the effects of alcohol
wey: way
wha: who
what way: why
whaur: where
wheen: lot
wheesh, wheesht: *see* weesht!
wherr: where
whiles: sometimes, occasionally
whit: what
whit wey: how
wi, wi': with
wi'oot: without
wid: would
widden: wooden; widen overcoat: coffin
wide: street wise
wife: woman
winchers: courting couple
winchin': courting
windae, windy: window
wink: wink, bit of gossip
wire in(to): get stuck in, attack
wire, ti give us the wire: to inform us
wis: was, were
wise: wise, sane
withoot: without
wrang: wrong
wulk: whelk; fu' as a wulk: extremely
   drunk
wull: will
wumman, wummin: woman
wunk: wink
wunner: wonder
wur: were
wur: our
wurrsells: ourselves

ya, yae, ye, yew: you
yella: yellow
yer, yur: your
yersel(l), yerself, yursell: yourself

yersels, yursells: yourselves
yese, youse: *(pl)* you
yew: *see* ya
yin: one
yon: that

yous(e): *see* yese
yur: *see* yer
yurrsell: *see* yersel(l)
yursells: *see* yersels

FURTHER READING

Anderson, Freddy. 'Early Days at Glasgow Unity Theatre'. *Cencrastus*, no. 46 (Autumn 1993), pp. 17–18.

Boyd, Edward. 'A Word on a Blackboard'. *New Edinburgh Review*, no. 40 (Feb. 1978), pp. 32–34.

Craig, Cairns, ed. *A History of Scottish Literature*, vol. 4, *Twentieth Century*. Aberdeen: Aberdeen University Press, 1987.

Findlay, Bill, ed. *A History of Scottish Theatre*. Edinburgh: Polygon, 1998.

—— 'By Policy a Native Theatre: Glasgow Unity Theatre and the Significance of Robert Mitchell's Scottish Adaptation of *The Lower Depths*'. *International Journal of Scottish Theatre*, vol. 2, no. 1 (June 2001). **http://art.qmuc.ac.uk/ijost/Volume2_no1/B_findlay.htm**

Flynn, Vincent. 'Looking Back . . .' *New Edinburgh Review*, no. 40 (Feb. 1978), pp. 18–20.

Hill, John. 'Towards a Scottish People's Theatre: the Rise and Fall of Glasgow Unity'. *Theatre Quarterly*, vol. 7, no. 27 (Autumn 1977), pp. 61–70.

—— 'Glasgow Unity Theatre: The Search for a "Scottish People's Theatre"'. *New Edinburgh Review*, no. 40 (Feb. 1978), pp. 27–31.

Hutchison, David. *The Modern Scottish Theatre*. Glasgow: The Molendinar Press, 1977.

Mackenney, Linda. *The Activities of Popular Dramatists and Drama Groups in Scotland, 1900–1952*. Lewiston, NY; Queenstown, Ontario; Lampeter, UK: The Edwin Mellen Press, 2000.

—— 'Glasgow Unity Theatre: The War Years'. *Scottish Theatre News*, no. 28 (June 1983), pp. 2–4.

—— 'Glasgow Unity Theatre: The Post-War Years'. *Scottish Theatre News*, no. 29 (July 1983), pp. 2–6.

McLeish, Robert. *The Gorbals Story*, ed. and intro. Linda Mackenney. Edinburgh: 7:84 Publications, 1985.

Scullion, Adrienne. 'Glasgow Unity Theatre: The Necessary Contradictions of Scottish Political Theatre'. *Twentieth Century British History*, vol. 13, no. 3, 2002, pp. 215–252.

Stewart, Ena Lamont. *Men Should Weep*, ed. and intro. Linda Mackenney. Edinburgh: 7:84 Publications, 1983.

THE ASSOCIATION FOR SCOTTISH LITERARY STUDIES

ANNUAL VOLUMES

Volumes marked * are, at the time of publication, still available from booksellers or from the address given opposite the title page of this book.

1996*   *The Christis Kirk Tradition: Scots Poems of Folk Festivity*, ed. Allan H. MacLaine
1997–8* *The Poems of William Dunbar* (two vols), ed. Priscilla Bawcutt
1999*   *The Scotswoman at Home and Abroad*, ed. Dorothy McMillan
2000*   Sir David Lyndsay, *Selected Poems*, ed. Janet Hadley Williams
2001   Sorley MacLean, *Dàin do Eimhir*, ed. Christopher Whyte
2002*   Christian Isobel Johnstone, *Clan-Albin*, ed. Andrew Monnickendam
2003*   *Modernism and Nationalism: Literature and Society in Scotland 1918–1939*, ed. Margery Palmer McCulloch
2004*   *Serving Twa Maisters: five classic plays in Scots translation*, ed. John Corbett and Bill Findlay
2005*   *The Devil to Stage: five plays by James Bridie*, ed. Gerard Carruthers
2006*   *Voices From Their Ain Countrie: the poems of Marion Angus and Violet Jacob*, ed. Katherine Gordon